# The Life and Writings of Julio C. Tello

# *The Life and Writings of Julio C. Tello*

## America's First Indigenous Archaeologist

EDITED BY RICHARD L. BURGER

*University of Iowa Press, Iowa City*

University of Iowa Press, Iowa City 52242

www.uiowapress.org
Printed in the United States of America

Design by Teresa W. Wingfield



Frontispiece and cover art courtesy El Archivo Tello,
Museo de Arqueología y Antropología, Universidad Nacional Mayor de San Marcos.

The University of Iowa Press is a member of Green Press Initiative
and is committed to preserving natural resources.

Printed on acid-free paper

LIBRARY OF CONGRESS CATALOGING-IN-PUBLICATION DATA
The life and writings of Julio C. Tello: America's first indigenous archaeologist /
edited by Richard L. Burger.
p. cm.
Includes bibliographical references and index.
ISBN-13: 978-1-58729-783-0 (pbk.)
ISBN-10: 1-58729-783-3 (pbk.)
1. Peru—Antiquities. 2. Indians of South America—Peru—Antiquities.
3. Tello, Julio C. (Julio César), 1880–1947. 4. Archaeologists—Peru—Biography.
I. Burger, Richard L.
F3429.L73 2009 2008043531
985'.0107202—dc22

*A project of the Institute of Andean Research in commemoration of its fiftieth anniversary*

# Contents

# The Life and Writings of Julio C. Tello

# Introduction

RICHARD L. BURGER

**IN 1985 THE EXECUTIVE COMMITTEE** of the Institute of Andean Research (IAR) met at the American Museum of Natural History. One of the items under discussion was how best to commemorate its fiftieth anniversary. The group, consisting of John Murra, Craig Morris, Heather Lechtman, and the author, considered what project might best reflect both the mission of the IAR and its unique history. Begun in 1936 at the initiative of Julio C. Tello, Alfred Kroeber, Samuel Lothrop, Wendell Bennett, and other distinguished scholars, the IAR has played a role in supporting numerous investigations and publications in the Andes and beyond. It has been particularly concerned with fomenting scholarly collaboration among the Andean nations as well as between Andean scholars and those outside this region. In our discussion, we noted the crucial role of Julio C. Tello in the IAR's history and explored the possibility of a commemorative project related to Tello.

Although Tello's fame in Peru has grown almost to legendary proportions since his death in 1947, few outside Peru have read his work. Many view his contribution to Andean archaeology and world prehistory on the basis of secondhand accounts or a few easily accessible articles. The reason that many of Tello's writings have been marginalized is not difficult to understand. Many of his publications appeared in newspapers or short-lived journals such as *Chaski*, *Wira-Kocha*, and *Inca*. The number of libraries outside Peru where these are available are few indeed. In addition, the Spanish favored by Tello, with its long and elaborate sentences, is not easily comprehended by a nonnative speaker.

As Murra discusses in his contribution to this volume, the tie between Tello and the IAR was particularly close. Not only was Tello a founding member of the IAR and carried out investigations with financial support from it, but, following his death, the Institute played a crucial role in the posthumous publication of two volumes on Tello's research in Paracas. Based on these considerations, the IAR Executive Committee decided to initiate a volume in English dedicated to the work of Tello in order to foment a better appreciation of his life and work by the community of scholars and students outside Peru. To accomplish this, the IAR offered to subsidize the translation of selection of his articles into English, and, as the member of the Executive Committee most closely associated with Tello's work, I accepted the responsibility of organizing and editing it.

It was a task that I accepted with pleasure. Since my first visit to Peru in 1965, I have been fascinated with Tello and his work. During my research, I had come into contact with many of Tello's students and collaborators, most notably Toribio Mejía Xesspe, Pedro Rojas Ponce, Julio Espejo, Manuel Chavez Ballón, Cirilio Huapaya, and Marino Gonzales. Each of them spoke vividly of their mentor. Although he had been dead for decades, it was clear that his spirit and memory were very much alive. While it is not uncommon for students to admire their teachers, these accomplished men continued to stand in awe of Tello and treated his memory with a deep respect that bordered on hero worship. What was it about Tello and his work that was capable of generating such devotion? Moreover, given the history of racial and cultural discrimination against indigenous highland peoples in Peru, how was Tello able to achieve such unqualified success? These questions had long intrigued me, and the preparation of this volume gave me the opportunity to explore the answers to these queries in greater depth.

In recent years, there has been a renewed interest in the history of archaeology and an increasingly inward-looking focus on the practice of archaeology. In the United States, some of these concerns have stemmed from the impact of the Native American Graves and Repatriation Act (NAGPRA). Archaeologists in the United States and elsewhere have been forced to recognize the unpleasant truth that in North America, indigenous peoples generally have been excluded or marginalized from the practice of archaeology and the shaping of its research agenda. Some scholars have argued that archaeology, as it is currently constructed, is merely an expression of mainstream Western values and political interests and, as such, constitutes but one story about the past, one that cannot be privileged over alternative stories created by indigenous groups with other intellectual orientations or evidential bases, such as oral traditions. In these discussions, the interests of native peoples and archaeologists are frequently painted in stark contrast to each other, and their adversarial character is treated as inevitable and natural.

In reading these accounts, I have frequently wondered how different things might have been if individuals of indigenous background had been brought in at the inception of archaeology to help direct its trajectory. Remarkably, this actually occurred in Peru, where Julio C. Tello, the individual viewed as the "Father of Peruvian Archaeology" by almost all Peruvians, was a native Quechua speaker raised in an indigenous community high in the mountains of Peru's central highlands.

In order to explore this remarkable phenomenon, I decided to devote the first section of the volume to three chapters that place Tello's career within the broader social and intellectual context of his day and offer an initial evaluation of how his body of work has influenced subsequent generations of scholars in Peru and abroad. Fortunately, Richard Daggett has carried out historic and archival research on Tello for two decades, and his description of Tello's life draws upon these original investigations. A second chapter, by John Murra, former IAR president and distinguished expert on *lo andino*, addresses the relationship of Tello to scholars outside Peru, a crucial element in Tello's work that is frequently overlooked. In the third chapter, I consider Tello's intellectual legacy in Peru and abroad more than half a century after his death.

These three essays set the stage for a sampling of Tello's own writings. In making the selection, I chose articles to illustrate the breadth of his interests and research. The eleven examples of his work included in this volume range from art historical analysis to physical anthropology. Tello was a great synthesizer and was rarely content to provide a simple description of a discovery, no matter how important that find might be. Consequently, I also picked examples of his pioneering synthetic efforts. Much of Tello's work was explicitly political in content, both from the perspective of using the past to shape a new sense of Peruvian nationality and in creating policies and institutions to protect Peru's archaeological heritage and foment its investigation. Several of the contributions published here, including a speech made at the opening of the Museo de Arqueología, vividly capture this aspect of Tello's vision.

Inevitably, many of Tello's writings included conclusions or speculations that have been superseded or disproved by subsequent research. Given his commitment to scientific progress, this probably would have pleased him. But many more of his insights now appear, at least to this editor, as remarkably prescient, even prophetic. Particularly germane to contemporary debate is Tello's argument that objective scientific archaeology is the natural ally of indigenous Peruvians because it serves to revindicate the historic accomplishments and talents of native peoples. In his view, establishment of the true history of native Peruvian peoples through archaeology undermines the pejorative view of indigenous peoples promoted by those nonindigenous intellectuals controlling the construction of national identity and, by extension, the shape of Peru's future.

Some of the writings of Tello republished here originally appeared in English, but many more were translated into English especially for this volume by Freda Wolf de Romero, Peruvianist and psychotherapist. As editor, I used my prerogative in modifying and giving final form to these translations, with a special effort to make them easily comprehensible without sacrificing the special flavor of Tello's style of writing.

Following Tello's writings is an annotated bibliography of Julio C. Tello's work. This is the product of Richard Daggett's long-term research as well as the much more modest efforts of the editor in this area. While a fine bibliography was published by Tello's student and colleague Julio Espejo Nuñez, the one that appears here is more detailed and complete. It also is able to incorporate posthumous publications, many of which have appeared since Espejo's bibliography. The volumes that have been published since Tello's death, thanks to the efforts of Toribio Mejía Xesspe, Ruth Shady Solís, and others, constitute some of Tello's most enduring contributions. In recognition of this, the modest royalties from this volume are being donated to the Museo de Arqueología at the Universidad Nacional Mayor de San Marcos to help support the ongoing maintenance of the Tello Archives and the continuing publication of the remaining portion of Tello's unedited work.

Finally, I want to thank the many people who have assisted me with the preparation of this volume, including Holly Carver, Victor Falcón, Kira Gallick, George Lau, Robinson Lozada, Jason Nesbitt, Sharon J. M. Rodriguez, Lucy Salazar, and Nicholas Saunders.

# *Biographical Essays*

CHAPTER ONE

# Julio C. Tello

## *An Account of His Rise to Prominence in Peruvian Archaeology*

RICHARD E. DAGGETT

**JULIO C. TELLO** was a world authority on Peruvian archaeology (Stewart and Peterson 1942:271). He has been described as an "Indian from the ranks and human dynamo, founder of three important museums and discoverer of culture after culture . . . [who] knows as much Peruvian archeology as the rest of us put together" (Kroeber 1944:5–6). He was committed to the improvement of his race, and, in part, he chose to accomplish this through politics and archaeology (Daggett 1992a:193 n.2). Toward the end of his life, he was promoted as the New World's greatest archaeologist, a national institution virtually unto himself (West 1982:87). Even his detractors were forced to admit his archaeological preeminence (e.g., Beals 1934:105–106), while their criticisms often provided Tello with the motivation he needed to succeed (Tealdo 1942:8).

This chapter chronicles Tello's rise to prominence in the sphere of Peruvian archaeology. His encyclopedic knowledge reflected a life rich in archaeological experiences. The sites he investigated as well as the lives he touched upon probably each number in the thousands. It would be futile to try to recount them all; hence, only a few of each will be identified. Controversy played an important part in Tello's career, and, as such, its discussion merits inclusion here. In addition, because Tello's career was punctuated by two periods of upheaval that followed rifts in the nation's political fabric, some details of a political nature will be provided. Finally, in this same vein, because Tello used his position in the national legislature to promote, in part, his archaeological agenda, a brief review of this aspect of his political career will be presented.

## The Preparatory Years: 1880–1912

Julio César Tello Rojas was born on April 11, 1880, in the central highland community of Huarochirí (fig. 1.1). By the age of twelve, he had distinguished himself from his siblings by his keen inquisitiveness and unusually high level of energy. At that time, his aunt María, who worked as a chambermaid in the presidential palace, urged that he be sent to Lima to continue his education. The family agreed, and father and son left on horseback early on the morning of March 29, 1893, arriving in Lima late in the afternoon of April 1. His father arranged a pensión for him and enrolled him in the Colegio de Lima on the advice of María (Mejía 1948:3–7, 1964:53–64).

At this time, Lima was still recovering from an occupation by Chilean forces during the years 1881 to 1884. The disastrous war with Chile had caused many of Peru's elite to conclude native Peruvians needed to be more fully integrated into the national framework if a recurrence of this military debacle was to be avoided. In July 1895 Nicolás de Piérola was elected president, and this initiated nearly two decades of unusually stable government in Peru (Werlich 1978:112–141). Hence, it was a most propitious time for native Peruvians like Tello to be in Lima. Unfortunately, his father's untimely death around this time left him financially bereft, and, save his aunt María's commitment to pay his school fees, he became responsible for all his expenses. He survived by selling newspapers on the street and by carrying luggage at the train station (Niles 1937:75–76). Too, he found work in a surgeon's office, and this experience so impressed him that he decided that he wanted to become a surgeon himself (Mejía 1964:66–67).

Tello excelled in school, despite his economic hardship, and he became friendly with one classmate in particular, Ricardo Palma (hereafter, Ricardo). Ricardo was the son of *the* Ricardo Palma, traditionalist and director of the Biblioteca Nacional. Through his son, he came to appreciate Tello's intellect as well as his plight, and he endeavored to help. The elder Palma hired Tello to deliver his mail to him daily, insisting that this be done during the noon hour, ensuring, thereby, that Tello had at least one meal a day (Niles 1937:76).

In March 1900 Tello and his friend Ricardo entered the Facultad de Ciencias of the Universidad Nacional Mayor de San Marcos in Lima (Mejía 1964:69). Sometime later, however, Tello received a letter from

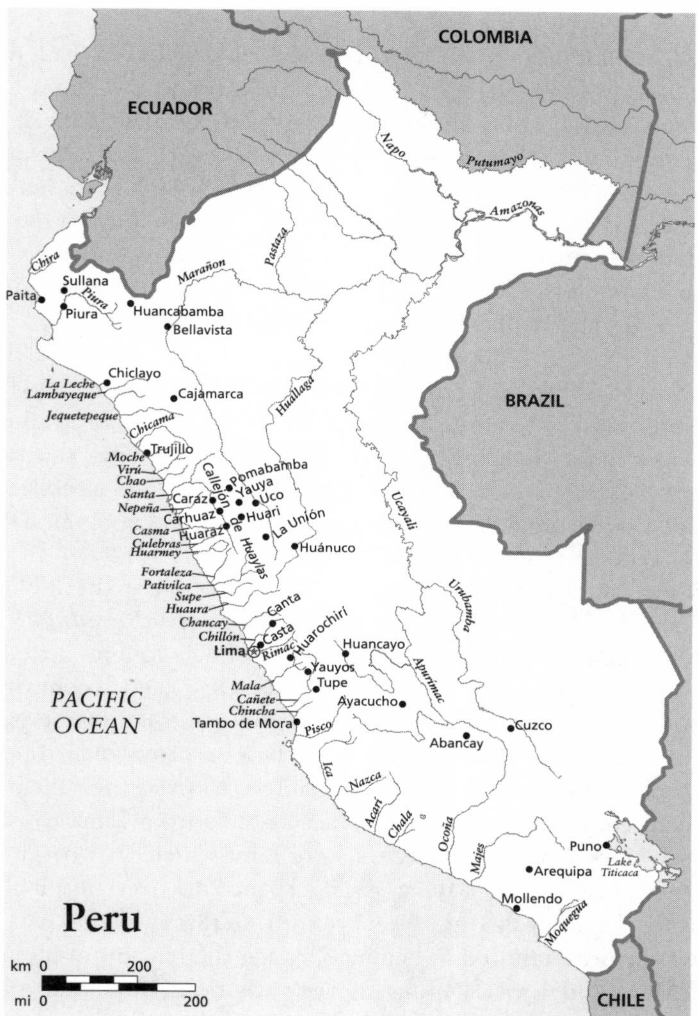


1.1. *Geographical locations mentioned in the text.*

home in which he was told that money was no longer available to help him with his schooling and that he must return to Huarochirí. This crisis was averted through an "amazing coincidence." According to the story, a position unexpectedly became available at the Biblioteca Nacional, and Tello was hired by the elder Palma to work at the library beginning July 7, 1900 (Anonymous 1958). Whether true or not, certainly the elder Palma had indicated a strong inclination to help Tello and was in a position to do so.

During 1901 Tello took a course in natural science with José

Sebastián Barranca. Then seventy years old, Barranca had developed a strong interest in linguistics, and he found in Tello a native Quechua speaker who could assist him with his research. At Barranca's request, Tello conducted his first fieldwork that year during a vacation period (Mejía 1948:8). During February 1902 he made his first trip to Tupe in Yauyos Province to begin his study of the Kauqui dialect, returning in 1905 and later in 1926 to complete his work (Espejo 1959:24). On March 29, 1902, he and Ricardo entered their first year in the Facultad de Medicina at San Marcos (Mejía 1964:73). On April 7, 1902, Tello was made an official conservator at the Biblioteca Nacional (Espejo 1959:22), and in 1903 he was given a position to last through 1904 at the Museo de Raimondi located in an annex of the Facultad de Medicina (Mejía 1948:8–9). At this time, this facility was the closest thing to a national museum in Peru, and its collections included archaeological, ethnological, botanical, and zoological specimens (Tello and Mejía 1967:44, 52).

While cataloging the anthropological collection at the Biblioteca Nacional during 1904, Tello came upon the *Sixteenth Annual Report of the Bureau of American Ethnology.* This thick volume included a report on trephination (Muñiz and McGee 1897) and accompanying photos of trephinated skulls. Tello was stunned. One of the photos was of a skull that had been collected by one of his older brothers (Lothrop 1948:51) on behalf of his father, who was then the mayor of Huarochirí and had received official orders from Lima to collect skulls. This skull and others were sent to Lima, where they became the property of Manuel A. Muñiz. Tello's chance discovery inspired him to study the English language (Lothrop 1948:51; Tealdo 1942:8). He was likewise inspired to begin collecting the remains of his ancestors (Mejía 1967b:vii). During his 1905 vacations, Tello began a systematic exploration of the provinces of Huarochirí and Yauyos (Mejía 1948:9). At times alone, at times with Ricardo, he visited numerous archaeological sites (Mejía 1964:73). Members of the Tello family and local laborers were used when needed (Palma 1957). Tello and his classmate returned to Lima with an especially rich collection of pathological skulls in March 1906. After consulting with his faculty advisers, Tello shifted the emphasis of his research from linguistics to the study of these skulls (Espejo 1959:63).

On Friday evening, May 4, 1906, in the salon of Lima's Sociedad Geográfica, Tello made his public debut. He presented a detailed discussion on trephination that was illustrated by thirty trephinated skulls, a number of mummies, and various accompanying artifacts that he and

Ricardo had recently found at sites in the vicinity of Huarochirí (Espejo 1959:62–65). Among those in attendance was the German archaeologist Max Uhle (Anonymous 1906), who had recently been contracted by the Peruvian government to create and direct a national museum of archaeology.

At the turn of the century, there had developed an enthusiasm for Peru's ancient past previously unknown in Lima's intellectual circles (Rowe 1954:11). Tapping into this enthusiasm, the enlightened government of José Pardo created, in February 1905, the Instituto Histórico del Perú. In part, it was charged with the protection of the nation's archaeological heritage. Then, in May, the government founded the Museo de Historia Nacional, which was to operate under the institute (Tello 1959:36). What was needed was someone with expertise to run the museum, and Uhle was an obvious choice. He had conducted extensive fieldwork in Peru during 1896–1897, 1899–1901, and 1903–1905; had been the first to conduct stratigraphic excavations in Peru (Rowe 1959:5–6); and, during this period, had effectively laid the framework for Andean archaeology (Rowe 1954:1). Late in 1905, upon his return to Lima from an extensive expedition sponsored by the University of California, Uhle agreed to accept the challenge of establishing a national museum of archaeology (Rowe 1954:11).

The Museo de Historia Nacional officially opened on July 29, 1906 (Tello 1959:36), and Uhle immediately began work at various sites in the Rimac Valley. In effect, Lima bore witness to the birth of a national program of archaeological investigation, and the museum, which served to showcase the collected artifacts, became a new resource for students like Tello and his friend Ricardo. Modeled pottery at this museum, which exemplified specific pathologies pertinent to his research, became an integral part of Ricardo's thesis on the suggestion of Tello, who first saw the pieces on display (Palma 1908:56).

On May 15, 1907, Tello began work as an intern at the university's hospital, and on November 16, 1908, he successfully defended his thesis on the antiquity of syphilis in Peru (Mejía 1948:9). His thesis was accepted by acclamation, a first for the university. He had amassed an incredible collection of some 15,000 skulls and mummies. More than 1,000 of these skulls evidenced pathologies, while more than 500 showed evidence of trephination. His thesis committee recommended that the nation purchase Tello's collection for the purpose of establishing a Museum of Pathological Anatomy at San Marcos (Espejo 1959:28–29).

Tello was subsequently advised by the elder Palma to attend a dinner being held to honor a recent graduate of San Marcos. Palma, as one of the featured speakers, used this occasion to extol the achievements of Tello and, in effect, to introduce Tello to the intellectual elite of Lima (Tealdo 1942:9). Palma continued to advance Tello's cause at every opportunity. The university had published a special edition of Tello's thesis, and a copy was read at the First Pan American Congress, which was being held in Santiago, Chile (Espejo 1959:29). Two Americans who attended this congress later visited the Biblioteca Nacional. Antonio Miró Quesada accompanied them, and he introduced them to the elder Palma. Palma, in turn, introduced them to Tello. As they were leaving, Miró Quesada said to Tello that he was going to see to it that these Americans helped him with his career. Miró Quesada, a lawyer, journalist, politician, and member of the family that owned and operated the Lima daily *El Comercio*, made good on his promise. Tello later received by mail a Harvard catalog and grant application (Tealdo 1942:9).

On April 30, 1909, after completing his internship and passing his final exams, Tello was made doctor and surgeon by San Marcos (Mejía 1948:9). A month later, on May 29, a brother and two sons of the late president Nicolás de Piérola led an attack on the presidential palace. Loyal soldiers quickly put down this attempted coup, and Augusto B. Leguía, who had been elected president the previous year, took this opportunity to arrest not only the participants but other critics of his as well. Students from the Universidad Nacional Mayor de San Marcos demonstrated for their release, and mounted soldiers and police attacked the students, killing one and wounding six others (Werlich 1978:133). In this suddenly unstable political atmosphere, Tello contemplated his future. The city of Lima, in its municipal session of July 28, 1909, awarded Tello a gold medal. This may have inspired the Leguía government to act because on August 21 Tello was awarded a two-year scholarship to study abroad (Mejía 1948:9). Though he had been leaning toward continuing his studies in France, he decided to go to the United States when Harvard University offered him free tuition (Lothrop 1948:51). After paying respects to his family in Huarochirí and to the Palma family in Lima, Tello left for the United States aboard the steamship *Loa* (Mejía 1967b:viii), arriving in New York City on September 30, 1909 (Mejía 1964:80).

At Harvard, Tello studied under such notable anthropologists as Frederic W. Putnam, Franz Boas, Pliny E. Goddard, and Roland B. Dixon (Mejía 1948:51), the last of whom helped Tello adjust to his new surroundings by tutoring him in English (Lothrop 1948:51). Tello took courses in archaeology, sociology, ethnology, and linguistics (Mejía 1967b:ix) and, with Dixon's help (Tello 1914b), produced a study on the South American Arawak language (Tello 1913a). He had numerous opportunities to interact with American scholars, the Northeast then being the nation's center for anthropological studies. The annual meeting of the American Anthropological Association was held late in December in Boston (MacCurdy 1910) and in Providence (MacCurdy 1911) in 1909 and 1910, respectively, and Tello was listed as a new member at the 1910 meeting (MacCurdy 1911:100).

In a letter to the elder Palma dated June 24, 1910, Tello mentions a forthcoming trip to Arizona with a Dr. "Ferokes" of the Smithsonian Institution (Palma 1949, 2:425). This would have been Jesse W. Fewkes, and the trip would have entailed an exploration of Pueblo ruins in northern Arizona (Editor 1910:348). In the same letter, Tello indicated that he hoped to meet with Ales Hrdlicka (Palma 1949, 2:425). Hrdlicka, then curator of the Division of Physical Anthropology at the Smithsonian Institution, was scheduled to return from a trip to South America. In September of that year, he presented, at the Seventeenth International Congress of Americanists held in Mexico City, a preliminary report that included a discussion of the human remains that he had collected at archaeological sites in Peru. Subsequently, on May 3, 1911, he spoke in Washington, D.C., on the same subject at a special joint meeting of the Anthropological Society of Washington, D.C., and the Medical Society of the District of Columbia (Michelson 1911:318–319). It is unknown whether Tello attended either or both of these talks. It is known, however, that he was named to represent Peru at the 1911 meeting of the Association of U.S. Army Surgeons held in Richmond, Virginia (Mejía 1964:81). Tello (1915) later reported that one of the nineteen trephinated skulls comprising the Muñiz collection was stored at the U.S. Military Medical Museum, while the remaining eighteen were to be found at the Bureau of Ethnology in Washington, D.C. This suggests that Tello traveled at the expense of the Peruvian government to study the collection of skulls that had inspired him to become an archaeologist.

During June 1911 Tello received a master's degree in anthropology from Harvard University (Mejía 1948:10). With the active assistance of the elder Palma (Miró Quesada 1966:418–420; Palma 1949, 2:433), Tello was allowed to continue his education abroad in a government resolution dated September 2 of that year (Mejía 1964:81). He left for England at the end of October (Mejía 1967b:ix), accompanied by his friend Ricardo, who had also been granted a scholarship to study abroad (Mejía 1948:10). A later government decree, dated December 16, 1911, obliged Tello to present a paper at the upcoming Eighteenth International Congress of Americanists to be held in London. In January 1912 he received official notification that he had been named to represent his country as an honorary delegate at this meeting (Mejía 1964:81–82). During the ensuing period, Tello assisted in special anthropological courses at London University before giving his talk on May 28 (Mejía 1967b:ix). In his paper, which dealt with the trephinated skulls he had found in the highlands east of Lima, he reported that part of his skeletal collection was housed at Harvard University's Warren Museum (Tello 1912:76). He had offered his collection to the Leguía government in 1909, but this offer had been rejected for financial reasons, which prompted the elder Palma to advise him to offer it elsewhere (Miró Quesada 1966:418). Hrdlicka attended Tello's talk, and he publicly praised Tello for his work (Editor 1912:xxxix).

During late June 1912 Tello traveled to Germany, where he assisted Felix von Luschan in courses being taught at the University of Berlin. Later he went to the University of Paris, where he studied ethnology and American sociology. As he had done in America, he used these opportunities to visit the principal libraries and museums of each nation (Mejía 1967b:ix). He returned to England and on September 29, 1912, wrote a letter to Alfred M. Tozzer of the Harvard University Peabody Museum of Archaeology and Ethnology. While at the London congress, Tozzer and Tello had spoken. Tozzer had suggested that Tello seek a formal arrangement with the museum at Harvard prior to returning to Peru. With this in mind, Tello wrote to Tozzer. In response, he received a letter from Frederic Putnam, Honorary Curator at the Peabody Museum since his retirement from Harvard in 1909 (Kroeber 1915). In this letter, dated November 13, Tello was informed that he had been appointed an associate in anthropological research in Peru for 1912–1913 and that, for a stipend, he would be expected to "do a little exploring and collecting of specimens for the Museum" (Daggett 1997:2). On November 20, 1912, Tello married Olive Mabel Cheesman (Mejía 1948:10), who had been a student at London University. The couple left England in mid December 1912 (Mejía 1964:83).

## The Contentious Years: 1913–1918

Tello and his wife arrived in Lima during the second half of January 1913 accompanied by Hrdlicka, who had come to expand his collection

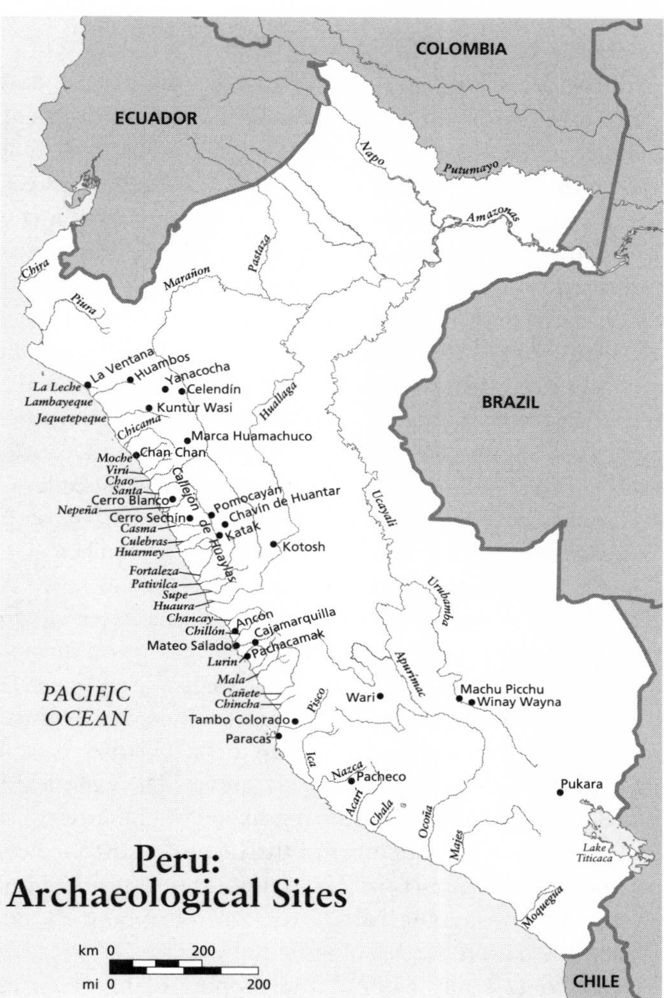


*1.2. Archaeological sites mentioned in the text.*

of prehistoric Peruvian skeletal remains. On January 30 Tello received official permission to join Hrdlicka's expedition, which was already in progress. Together they explored the Huarochirí area before returning to the coast, likely by way of the Mala Valley. After visiting the site of Ancón (fig. 1.2), they explored sites in the Chancay and Huaura valleys before turning southward. They visited the ruins of Pachacamac in Lurín and then moved to the Chilca Valley, where they ended their joint explorations (Hrdlicka 1914; Tello 1913b).

Tello's official report (1913b), dated March 19, 1913, was published in the Lima press. It consisted of an introductory section that provided some specifics on the expedition. The body of the report, however, provided a long and detailed justification for the use of the science of anthropology in the investigation of Peru's archaeological record, in general, and for Tello's unique qualifications to assume such an investigation, in particular. Barranca had urged Tello to break away from the classical school of thought then prevalent in Lima (Mejía 1948:8), so, in a way, Tello was paying homage to his mentor with this public affirmation of the value of science as opposed to history. By the same token, Tello may have been inspired by recent events.

On September 23, 1911, Uhle's contract was canceled, and the government authorized that a search be started to replace him with a new foreign specialist. Inexplicably, no action was taken, and this forced the government to close the Museo de Historia Nacional on December 31. On March 14, 1912, Emilio Gutiérrez de Quintanilla (hereafter Gutiérrez) was hired as interim director of the museum (Tello 1959:40). His position was then made permanent the following September (Tello and Mejía 1967:81). While a student at Harvard, Tello had heard rumors about Uhle (Anonymous 1918:682–683), and in a letter he wrote to Putnam in April 1914, he stated that upon his return to Lima in 1913, he had become aware of a distinctly "anti-Yankee" sentiment. In this charged atmosphere, Uhle's opponents had falsely accused him of clandestinely sending artifacts from the Museo de Historia Nacional to museums outside the country (Daggett 1997:3). The net effect was to replace the archaeologist Uhle with the historian Gutiérrez. That the latter had been a founding member of the Instituto Histórico del Perú (Tauro 1966, 2:65) suggests that Tello, upon his return to Lima, had willingly entered an ongoing battle over control of both the national museum and the nation's archaeological resources.

Tello entered this fray without the support of his mentors Barranca and Palma. Barranca had passed away in December 1909 (Milla 1986:380), ending a close relationship that had existed throughout Tello's days as a student at San Marcos (Vara 1953). As for Palma, he had resigned as director of the Biblioteca Nacional in March 1912 (Miró Quesada 1966:414–416). The period 1911–1912 was politically volatile in Peru, and President Leguía's increasingly dictatorial rule had led to near anarchy. In 1912 Guillermo Billinghurst, a compromise candidate, became president, and Leguía was sent into exile (Werlich 1978:135–137).

On March 30, 1913, Tello petitioned the Billinghurst government to create within the Museo de Historia Nacional an anthropological section. He asked, too, that he be made chief of this new section. On June 12 Tello's requests were granted (Tello and Mejía 1967:82–85).

During his brief tenure as director of the museum, the hispanophile Gutiérrez had set into motion the process of changing the emphasis of the facility from archaeology to history. Uhle's collections were reduced to the status of miscellanea and were treated with such indifference that many were lost or irreparably damaged (Tello 1959:40). In an attempt to reverse this process, Tello proposed, in July 1913, a plan to re-create the institution as an archaeological entity (Tello and Mejía 1967:85–95). This infuriated Gutiérrez, who thereupon initiated a campaign of total opposition to the idea (Tello 1959:40). The two men feuded for months, and the government was forced to close the museum in November. The following month, the government created the Museo de Arqueología y Antropología, with Tello named as director. The absence of an alternative facility meant that Tello and Gutiérrez were forced to operate their respective museums in the same building (Tello and Mejía 1967:95).

There were complications beyond those created by the two antagonists, however. President Billinghurst's position was tenuous, and on February 4, 1914, he was ousted from office in a coup headed by Colonel Oscar R. Benavides (Matos et al. 1981:179). On April 28 the new dual museum was opened, but in the months that followed cold indifference within the Benavides government made Tello's position increasingly untenable (Tello and Mejía 1967:96–98). Then Tello made the mistake of becoming embroiled in a public debate.

The historian Horacio H. Urteaga had published an article (1914b) in the Lima press in which he discussed archaeological sites on the Central Coast of Peru. This was a selection from a series of such articles he had recently published in book form (1914a), and Tello may have viewed this as an attempt by Urteaga to establish himself as an expert in the field of archaeology. In any case, Tello (1914a) attempted to engage Urteaga in an intellectual debate on the comparative merits of science (anthropology) and history in the study of archaeological remains. In his sarcastic reply to Tello, Urteaga (1914c) suggested that Tello had belittled the efforts of many Peruvian scholars. This served to put Tello on the defensive, and he answered (Tello 1914b) by touting his past relationship with Barranca and his educational experiences at Harvard and at other major institutions of learning in Europe. This led Urteaga (1915a) to criticize Tello's foreign associations and to cast doubt on his contributions to science as well as his intellectual integrity. Tello (1915) was forced to provide a detailed refutation of the accusations, accusations that he said echoed the anonymous rumors that had dogged him for months. Urteaga, clearly more skilled than

Tello in this form of debate, had the final say in the matter (1915b) and used the occasion to reiterate points made earlier.

The debate with Urteaga did nothing to enhance Tello's standing, and his not-so-public feud with Gutiérrez continued unabated. Finding his position hopeless, Tello finally tendered his resignation on March 20, 1915 (Tello and Mejía 1967:96–100). A commission was then appointed to oversee the museum inventory, which became requisite upon the acceptance of Tello's resignation. Reports dated April 10 and 14 were prepared and submitted to the government by this commission (Tello and Mejía 1967:101–104).

Earlier, in a letter he wrote to Putnam dated January 11, 1915, Tello had noted that he planned to make a trip as far south as the Nazca Valley to collect artifacts for the Peabody Museum. He made no mention of his ill-fated debate with Urteaga. In his reply to Tello, Putnam offered to send more money given the need to expand the museum's very limited collection of artifacts belonging to the Nazca culture. Tello responded on April 9, saying that the trip had been postponed because of the difficulties he had faced at the national museum and which had ultimately led to his resignation there. He went on to say that he hoped to leave for Nazca in a week's time and that despite the fact that he had received some money from Victoria Aguirre of Argentina to help defray the expenses of his expedition, he needed further sponsorship. He requested more help from Putnam and said that he planned to write to Hrdlicka for help as well. He finally left Lima on or about April 24, 1915 (Daggett 1997:4).

Traveling by way of the port of Mollendo, his highland itinerary included Arequipa, Puno, Lake Titicaca, and Cuzco. He backtracked, and, upon his arrival at the port of Chala, he began an investigation of sites on the South Coast (Mejía 1964:87–91). Moving northward, he worked in the Chala, Yauca, Acarí, Nazca, Ica, and Pisco valleys (Tello 1959:44–47). Tello's excavations in Acarí and Nazca were monitored by members of an antiquarian society, who questioned the legality of his actions, and their report that Tello was excavating without a permit was published in the Lima press (Gutiérrez 1922:57). This forced Tello to return to Lima on or about July 22, 1915 (Daggett 1997:8).

Actions taken by the Pardo government in 1905, previously discussed, were intended, in part, to strictly control excavations in Peru as well as the exportation of artifacts (e.g., Rowe 1954:11). Problems persisted, however, and in 1911 the Leguía government was forced to publicly state its position on these matters (Tello and Mejía 1967:76–77). Yet the absence of a consistent policy of enforcement created a situation in which investigators, especially foreigners, felt comfortable working outside bureaucratic controls (e.g., Bingham 1989:304–305). By 1915, however, such individuals were increasingly being subjected to public scrutiny (Bingham 1989:305–310; López and García-Miró 1992:233–236), and having been, until just recently, part of this bureaucracy, Tello would have been very conscious of this climate of tighter enforcement. Yet he chose to ignore the law. When he decided to excavate without a permit, Tello may have had in mind the fact that as head of the Museo de Historia Nacional, Gutiérrez was authorized to require that all artifacts obtained through licensed excavations be housed at the national museum (Daggett 1997:10).

In any case, Tello succeeded in retaining control of the artifacts he had obtained on his expedition. Government decrees issued in August and in October 1915 allowed him to bring the material to Lima. The October decree stipulated that he was to exhibit the artifacts in Lima and that none of the artifacts were to leave the country (Gutiérrez 1922:55–57). Regarding the latter stipulation, it is worth noting that Tello wrote on July 22 to Putnam that he had already made arrangements to have some specimens sent to the Peabody Museum and that he planned to send some of the best specimens collected to Aguirre in Argentina (Daggett 1997:9). Tello never did receive a reply from Putnam. The latter died on August 14, 1915 (Kroeber 1915:712), and his death effectively ended the sponsorship of Tello's fieldwork by the Peabody Museum (Daggett 1997:9).

During October 1915 Tello resumed his excavations in the Nazca Valley. He traveled south by way of Chincha, Tambo de Mora, and Pisco, in each of which he explored many ruins and ancient cemeteries (Tello 1918:504). In Pisco, he purchased a unique collection of ancient textiles, which had been offered for sale to him in July prior to his return to Lima. Initially he was forced to decline for lack of sufficient funds, but in the capital city he had enlisted the aid of two friends, who agreed to help with the purchase price. Upon consummation of the transaction, the collection was equally divided among them (Daggett 1991:36–38). Though Tello certainly retained the enmity of some in high circles subsequent to his demise at the national museum, it appears that others still advanced his cause. Not only was Tello allowed to continue his work in Nazca, he was appointed to represent his nation at an international meeting for the purpose of presenting a report on his recently concluded expedition.

As a delegate of Peru, Tello attended the Nineteenth International Congress of Americanists and the Second Pan American Congress, each of which was being held in Washington, D.C., late in December 1915. His report provided the first detailed information about burial practices of the Nazca culture in the Nazca Valley (Daggett 1997:12). Hrdlicka was in attendance. He commented on the veracity of Tello's findings and applauded Tello for the success of his work in the face of challenges that would have daunted many individuals (Tello 1917:291). Tello then used this travel opportunity to arrange for the sale, in Boston, of some of the textiles purchased in Pisco. He had exhibited them in Washington, D.C., and they were part of the share owned by one of his copurchasers. He visited Harvard, where he was tendered an invitation to join an expedition to northern Peru to be sponsored jointly by the Museum of Comparative Zoology and the School of Tropical Medicine (Brues 1917:383). Meanwhile, during the January 5, 1916, session of the Cámara de Diputados in Lima, debate on the budget for the Museo Nacional de Historia provided an opportunity for members to show their support for Gutiérrez. At this time, Tello was attacked by Deputy Jorge M. Corbacho (Gutiérrez 1922:58–74), a well-known collector of antiquities (Daggett 1991:37).

At some point during 1916, Tello conducted research in the Chincha Valley (Tello 1942b:687), perhaps before his trip north to join up with the Harvard team. In any case, prior to getting together with the Harvard expeditionary team at Paita toward the end of July 1916, Tello explored ruins in the Santa, Virú, Moche, Chicama, Jequetepeque, and Lambayeque valleys (Mejía 1964:93). Passing through portions of the La Chira and Piura drainages, the Harvard team moved into the highlands. They explored Sullana, Huancabamba, Tutumberos, Bellavista, and Huambos before arriving, in mid October, at the coastal city of Chiclayo (Daggett 1992b:8–10).

After returning to Lima, Tello learned that the incumbent holding the Huarochirí seat in the Cámara de Diputados had decided not to run for reelection. Tello initiated his campaign for that seat on January 6, 1917, and he was elected on June 19. There was an attempt made to nullify his election, but, after a demonstration on his behalf by some 2,000 Huarochireños, he was allowed to take his place in this legislative body on July 28 (Mejía 1964:94–96). He wasted little time. On November 4, 1917, he proposed a law that would reorganize the Museo de Historia Nacional and give him effective control by placing this institution under the aegis of the Universidad Nacional Mayor de San Marcos (Tello and Mejía 1967:106). Tello reintroduced this plan in the session held on September 17, 1918, and it ignited a fierce debate between Tello and a number of supporters of

Gutiérrez, including Corbacho. The following day, Tello prevented a letter addressed to his three opponents from being read on the floor of the assembly (Anonymous 1918:502–516). Written that day by Gutiérrez, the letter consisted of a brief accounting of discrepancies found by the 1915 commission overseeing Tello's resignation from the national museum (Gutiérrez 1922:80–81). On September 26 Gutiérrez prepared a much more detailed summation for an official report. This summation he later submitted for publication in the Lima press on October 1 (Gutiérrez 1922:81–89). Tello was outraged, and he responded with an impassioned speech the following day on the floor of the Cámara de Diputados (Anonymous 1918:680–689).

The debate between Tello and the congressional proxies of Gutiérrez again flared during the October 31, 1918, session of the Cámara de Diputados. At that time Tello called for an official investigation of a proposed shipment of artifacts to Buenos Aires (Anonymous 1918:49–53). A commission of two, which included Urteaga, looked into the matter and concluded that there was no reason to deny the shipment. Subsequently, Tello was said to have admitted that he had complained about the shipment because of the charges that had been made against him by Gutiérrez (Gutiérrez 1922:112–118). Tello continued to press his attack against Gutiérrez on the floor of the Cámara de Diputados during the session of November 4, 1918. At that time he informed this body that the university's rector, Javier Prado Ugarteche, had himself argued for the incorporation of the national museum by the university in his inaugural address of 1916 (Anonymous 1918:62). Tello's motion regarding the Museo de Historia Nacional was then read into the record the following day (Anonymous 1918:76–77). Tello then shifted his attention to other plans he had set into motion regarding the establishment of another museum of archaeology.

During June 1918 Tello had discovered a number of wooden objects on sale in Lima said to have come from the Huarmey Valley. With these artifacts in mind, he spoke to Prado and suggested that the university fund an archaeological expedition for the purpose of establishing a museum. Prado agreed, but there was a problem. Tello's affiliation was with the Facultad de Medicina, and he needed affiliation in either the Facultad de Letras or the Facultad de Ciencias at San Marcos. This problem was resolved when, on August 6, Tello presented to the Facultad de Ciencias his doctoral thesis (1918) on the use of artificially mummified heads in ancient Peruvian art (Mejía 1967a:4). Subsequently, he began giving a series of lectures at the university (Santisteban 1956:20). Then, on November 25, he presented an expeditionary plan for approval to the university (Mejía 1967a:4). This plan was accepted unanimously (Mejía 1964:97).

## The Establishment Years: 1919–1930

On January 8, 1919, Tello left Lima on what was to be a nearly five-month expedition. He was accompanied by a number of students from the Universidad Nacional Mayor de San Marcos. Moving northward, they worked in the Huarmey and Culebras valleys before traveling to the Callejón de Huaylas by way of the Huarmey drainage. They made major discoveries at the sites of Pomakayán and Katak. They then made important discoveries at Chavín de Huantar, Yauya, Pomabamba, Huari, and other highland locations (Mejía 1947). The materials they brought back to Lima from this expedition formed the basis for the university's Museo de Arqueología, which was founded on October 21, 1919 (Mejía 1964:98).

In February 1919 Leguía returned from exile. Then, in May, he won the popular vote in the presidential election but was initially prevented from taking office. A popular uprising followed, and on July 4 he was installed as president (Werlich 1978:150–151). As for Tello, he won reelection that year, but the results were contested. Beginning September 30 and extending into October, Tello and his opponent engaged in a fierce debate on the floor of the Cámara de Diputados. Legislators were reminded of the charges made against Tello by Gutiérrez. Nonetheless, on November 17 certification of Tello's reelection was approved (Anonymous 1919:171–199, 600–606). This was to be the last time he would face such opposition, and he won subsequent reelections with ease.

During September 1919 Tello received a visit from a friend while organizing the exhibition of artifacts for what was to become the university's new museum of archaeology. His friend communicated the desire of Victor Larco Herrera to establish a permanent archaeological exposition in Lima to coincide with the first centennial celebration of Peru's independence. Tello suggested the founding of an archaeological museum based on the purchase of private collections of artifacts presently held in Peru, and his idea was accepted. Tello and Larco traveled up the North Coast and initiated the process of purchasing collections held in Trujillo, Chicama, Chiclayo, Jequetepeque, and Lambayeque. Subsequently, collections held in Huaura, Lima, Ica, and Cuzco were purchased. In less than five months, a collection of more than 20,000 artifacts was amassed for the Museo Arqueológico Victor

Larco Herrera, which was officially founded on November 3, 1919 (Mejía 1948:20–21).

As the director of this fledgling museum, Tello spent much of 1920 classifying and cataloging the artifacts purchased by Larco. On May 10, 1921, however, during a fit of rage Larco destroyed a collection of tracings of archaeological designs. Tello resigned, but not before securing a letter of recommendation. Tello was followed at the museum by a succession of four directors, the last being Urteaga, who served in this capacity from 1922 to 1924. Larco had a new facility built for his collection, yet as early as September 21, 1921, he wrote to Tello regarding the sale of the collection to the government (Tello and Mejía 1967:120–122).

Upon leaving Larco's employ, Tello redirected his attention to his various capacities at San Marcos University. However, events were set into motion that would influence his work there as well. In May 1921 President Leguía responded to political disruption on the campus by firing Prado and a large number of the faculty. Prado protested and later died when the government sought to reorganize the university. A commission was established to try to resolve the dispute, and Tello was one of two members selected to represent the Cámara de Diputados. In the end, however, continuing protests led Leguía to discard the recommendations of the commission and to reopen the university in April 1922 without any changes in its constitution. Problems persisted off and on between the university and the Leguía government into 1925 (Basadre 1964, 9:4333–4336).

Tello stayed active with the publication of a major theoretical work (Tello 1921) in which he argued that prehistoric Peruvian civilization was indigenous in nature and in which he first noted the presence of a Chavín culture in Central Peru. This placed Tello at odds with Uhle, who conceptualized Peruvian civilization as an offshoot of Central American civilization (Rowe 1954:21). Then, in December 1921, Tello again argued on the floor of the Cámara de Diputados for the takeover of the national museum by the university (Tello and Mejía 1967:108–109). This was to presage the final confrontation between Tello and Gutiérrez, a confrontation that occurred at a most propitious time for Tello.

During 1920 Tello had initiated a series of discussions that led to the formation of the Asociación Peruana para el Progreso de la Ciencia the following year (Editor 1921a:5–6). At the meeting of this association held on June 13, 1921, he spoke about his 1919 expedition (Editor 1921b:149), while during the session held on October 26 of that year he spoke about university reform legislation in the Cámara de Diputados (Editor 1921b:151).

A special public session of the association was held on July 30, 1922, attended by numerous officials, including President Leguía. Tello was the principal speaker, and he used the occasion to repeat arguments that he had been making for a decade. He argued that while science was the wave of the future, formal education in Peru remained stuck in the past. In Peru, universities remained committed to producing scholars, while the nation desperately needed trained specialists. He cited Barranca as one of three who merited praise for having promoted science. He argued against the existing system of intellectual elitism and for the need to open up higher education to all. Finally, he called for the establishment of university seminars to focus on specific problems and for the need to better organize and utilize university libraries and museums (Editor 1922:155–167).

A few days later, a new book by Gutiérrez circulated in Lima. In this book Gutiérrez defended his own actions during his struggle with Tello for control of the national museum while laying a series of charges against his foe. Most of these charges had been presented earlier, but a few new ones were added. Gutiérrez now gave voice to the suspicion that Tello had illegally sent artifacts to Aguirre in Argentina (Gutiérrez 1922:141). In addition, he provided evidence to support the accusations that Tello had sold a collection of skulls to Harvard and that he had sold to various North American institutions some of the textiles he had purchased in Pisco in 1915. Information on these sales was derived from Deputy Corbacho, who had traveled to North America late in 1919 on behalf of the Sociedad de Anticuarios Peruanos to investigate Tello's dealings (Gutiérrez 1922:131–138).

An outraged Tello brought the matter of Gutiérrez's book to the floor of the Cámara de Diputados on August 3, 1922. He characterized the book as libelous, and his anger extended to the fact that Gutiérrez had published his book with government money specifically designated for a history of the Museo de Historia Nacional. Tello demanded official action (Anonymous 1922a). During the days that followed, Tello and Corbacho participated in an acrimonious debate (Anonymous 1922b–d). This time Tello won, and the chamber approved his resolution during the session held on August 11 (Anonymous 1922e). Despite the best efforts of Gutiérrez, Corbacho, and others, Tello's career continued to flourish.

At some point during 1922, Tello conducted an archaeological exploration of the Casta region in the upper Rimac drainage. He published the results of this fieldwork (Tello and Miranda 1923) in a new journal, *Inca*, which he edited for the university's museum of archaeology. Four issues comprising the first volume of this journal were published in 1923 (Espejo 1948:21–22). It was during 1923, too, that he began the process of training Peru's first generation of archaeologists. When Uhle had been contracted to establish a national museum of archaeology, there were no trained professionals in Peru from which he could draw to staff his facility and to help with fieldwork. He was forced to deal with an existing subculture of collectors, dealers, and grave robbers (*huaqueros*) (e.g., Tello 1959:37). When he had conducted his fieldwork on the South Coast in 1915, Tello likewise was forced to associate with people of this ilk. However, unlike Uhle, Tello took advantage of this unique collaboration and was able to trace the site provenience of artifacts and collections obtained by individuals and institutions both inside and outside the country prior to 1915 (Daggett 1997:13).

In 1923 (Gonzáles 1936), Tello met the first of what were to prove to be his two most important disciples. Rebeca Carrión Cachot was then but seventeen years old and completely unaware of Peru's rich prehistoric heritage. Though her naïveté angered Tello during their first encounter at the university's museum of archaeology, she persisted and was later given an opportunity to work at this facility. During a difficult two-week period, Tello sorely tested Carrión, but she passed this trial, and he hired her to work at the museum (Seegers 1950:10, 40).

Around this time, negotiations were being conducted between Larco and representatives of the Leguía government over the purchase of Larco's museum of archaeology. For reasons both political and economic, Larco was unable to sustain his museum and was forced to sell it. On December 13, 1924, Larco's museum became the Museo de Arqueología Peruana, with Tello as its director (Mejía 1964:99). At Tello's request, on January 25, 1925, all archaeological material held at the Museo de Historia Nacional was transferred to this new museum. Though legal issues were to remain unresolved in the courts for years to come (Tello 1930c), the dispute between Tello and Gutiérrez had essentially ended in a draw. Tello had his national museum of archaeology and was in control of all the nation's archaeological resources, while Gutiérrez retained directorship of the nation's museum of history.

Tello was named professor of general anthropology in San Marcos University's Facultad de Ciencias in 1923 (Santisteban 1956:20), and the following year he advertised his first seminar in archaeology. Toribio

Mejía Xesspe enrolled, and at the end of the course Tello brought his students to the site of Cajamarquilla to introduce them to field archaeology. Mejía made his interest known to Tello. Tello then hired Mejía to administer *Inca* (Buse 1974). In this way, Tello became involved with his other principal disciple and the man who, in later years, would become his chief field companion.

On December 31, 1924, and again on January 2, 1925, Tello chaired archaeology sessions of the Third Pan American Scientific Congress, which were being held at the Biblioteca Nacional (Anonymous 1925a). Later in January the American anthropologist Alfred L. Kroeber made his first visit to Peru. Sponsored by Chicago's Field Museum of Natural History, he intended to conduct archaeological explorations for the purpose of expanding on the work done years earlier by Uhle. Many of Uhle's Peruvian collections were stored at the University of California at Berkeley, where Kroeber taught. After ascertaining that Uhle had no intention of doing so himself, Kroeber had begun a program there in 1922 to study these collections. Kroeber met Tello soon after his arrival in Lima, and the two became good friends (Rowe 1962:400–403).

Heavy rains fell on the North Coast of Peru during the early months of 1925, so Kroeber concentrated on sites in the Rimac and Chillón valleys before shifting, in April, to the Cañete Valley. His work in Cañete lasted into May, and most of it was done in collaboration with staff of the national Museo de Arqueología Peruana (Rowe 1962:403). Between April and June, Tello conducted work on the South Central Coast with the aid of Mejía and Antonio Hurtado. Artifacts that were discovered during these excavations in the Asia and Cañete valleys were added to the collections in the university and national museums that Tello headed (Mejía 1948:13–14). Tello assigned Hurtado to work with Kroeber (Kroeber 1926a:348). Later in May and during June, Kroeber made reconnaissance trips to Trujillo and to the Paracas-Nazca areas. A misunderstanding between Kroeber and his guide prevented Kroeber from making a major discovery on the Paracas Peninsula at that time, but he did decide to work there on his return the following year, while keeping this fact from Tello (Rowe 1962:403–404).

Toward the end of June 1925, the press in Trujillo reported concerns about a rise in illegal excavations at sites in the Moche Valley. According to these reports, Tello had not yet responded to this situation, and the site of Chan Chan was especially affected (Anonymous 1925b). During the interim between his initial layover in Trujillo in January 1925 and his subsequent trip there that year, Kroeber (1926b:12) had noted that the heavy rains had done serious damage to Chan Chan. Apparently authorities in Trujillo were awaiting Tello's arrival so that an assessment of the damage caused by flooding and looting could be made, but the arrival of another American anthropologist during the second half of July drew Tello's attention away from the North Coast.

Samuel K. Lothrop had both time and money to spend when he introduced himself to Tello. This was a golden opportunity for Tello, who was still trying to discover the origin of the textiles that he had purchased in Pisco in 1915. After visiting sites in the Chincha Valley, they went to the port of Pisco, where Tello made inquiries. On July 26 they were guided to the site of Paracas on the peninsula of that name. This was the same site that Kroeber had nearly discovered a few weeks earlier. During the ensuing months, excavations were conducted at Paracas, directed at various times by Tello, Hurtado, or Mejía. Though Tello was careful not to advertise this work, the American William M. McGovern made an announcement to the press. He had been invited to accompany a group from the university to see the site in January 1926. Especially galling to Tello was the fact that McGovern implied an active role for himself in the discovery of Paracas (Daggett 1991:40–45, 2007:58–59).

During August 1926 Tello explored the Santa, Virú, Moche, and Chicama valleys. In Moche, he studied Chan Chan and worked on a plan of the site. Then, during September, he worked with Kroeber in the Nazca Valley (Mejía 1948:14). Tello later accompanied Kroeber on a tour of North Coast valleys from Trujillo to Chiclayo (Kroeber 1930:53). On September 18, 1926, the Sociedad de Arqueología y Artes Peruanas held its first meeting in Lima. Tello was in attendance, as were Carrión and Mejía. As cofounder of this society, Tello agreed to codify the society's by-laws with the aid of Carrión (Anonymous 1926).

In anticipation of an upcoming Spanish-American Exposition to be held in Seville, Spain, Tello organized a new expedition to the South Coast at the start of 1927 under the auspices of Peru's Seville Commission and the Museo de Arqueología Peruana. He wanted to continue his explorations of this part of the coast, and the commission wanted artifacts to display at its exhibit in Seville. Mejía was placed in charge of a small team that left Lima on January 27 headed for the Nazca Valley (Daggett 1991:45–46). At some point, Tello joined the team in this valley, and on July 31, 1927, Tello and Mejía made what was to prove to be an important discovery at Pacheco. A major excavation was begun at this site on August 2 (Tello 1959:49–50), and it resulted in the discovery of the shattered remains of a number of huge ceremonial vessels.

Under orders from Tello, Mejía then moved the team from the Nazca Valley northward to the site of Paracas on September 27. Nearly a month later, on October 25, they discovered the first of what was to prove to be hundreds of mummy bundles there. This find brought Tello to the site, and he directed the recovery efforts. On December 23 a special Paracas exhibit was opened at the Museo de Arqueología Peruana to coincide with the Congreso Latino Americano de Medicina then being held in Lima. Then, on January 6, 1928, Tello sent a small team back to Paracas. Headed by Hurtado, this team concluded the process of removing the mummy bundles by June (Daggett 1991:46–47, 2007:59–60).

During 1928 Tello began offering a course on American and Peruvian archaeology in the university's Facultad de Letras (Mejía 1948:28). In his report to the rector regarding the activities of the university's Museo de Arqueología for the year 1928, Tello (1929) indicated that no explorations or excavations had been conducted and that the journal *Inca* was in recess. Instead, the staff had concentrated their efforts on conducting a general inventory, with the aim of preparing an illustrated catalog. He indicated his desire to establish an anthropological institute within the museum and the need for uniformed guards, given the increased usage of the museum by the public. Finally, he requested funds to publish a great backlog of unedited manuscripts in *Inca* as well as money to augment funds already included in the government's budget for excavations at Chavín de Huantar.

Throughout 1928 Tello and his staff at the Museo de Arqueología Peruana were kept busy with the now famous Paracas mummy bundles. In June of that year Tello presented an official report on the 1927 expedition, and the following month he reported on the status of his work on the Seville exhibit (Daggett 1991:47). Not mentioned in this report were related difficulties created by Tello's ex-employer, Larco.

Rumors had circulated in Lima in May 1928 that Larco and Tello had a violent altercation recently at the Museo de Arqueología Peruana. Larco was interviewed regarding this matter (Anonymous 1928), and he explained that an incident, nonviolent in nature, had indeed taken place, but not at the museum. Rather, it had taken place at a building on property owned by him that abutted the museum's land. Larco explained that he had wanted to raze this building so that he could develop his property but that Tello had prevented him from doing so. Artifacts from the museum were being stored in the building, and though Larco had been informed by one authority that this was to be temporary, Tello's insistence that the land and building belonged to the museum suggested otherwise. The confrontation had occurred, according to Larco, when museum staff refused him passage through this disputed area to the museum, where he wanted to speak directly with Tello.

Tello presented his version of events the following day in a letter to the editor (Tello 1928a). He noted that on May 8, at 3:30 in the afternoon, Larco had attacked a museum guard with an iron staff, which he used as a club. Larco then proceeded to use a stone to smash two large ritual urns that museum staff had patiently taken six months to reassemble from the pottery sherds discovered at the site of Pacheco in the Nazca Valley. Museum staff and others who had accompanied Larco witnessed these attacks. The attacks had taken place in a workshop that had been set up in a building situated adjacent to the museum and belonging to the museum.

Larco (1928) then accused Tello of misusing money designated by the government for the purchase of display cases to be installed in the Museo de Arqueología Peruana. Furthermore, he claimed that he had fired Tello in 1921 because of his crass ignorance of archaeological matters. This dispute concluded, at least in the press, when Tello (1928b) published copies of an official letter pertinent to the display cases in question and the letter of recommendation he had received from Larco in 1921.

Tello then traveled to New York City, where he participated in the Twenty-third International Congress of Americanists held during the week of September 17–22. He presented a paper (1930b) that drew upon data recovered during his 1919 expedition to the North Central Coast and highlands and in which he expanded his thoughts on the development of civilization in Peru. Under the aegis of the Carnegie Institution, he then gave a series of lectures at the universities of Cornell, Pittsburgh, Western Reserve, Indiana, Pennsylvania, and Rutgers. During the first week of December, after returning to Lima, he honored the touring American president-elect Herbert Hoover with the gift of a Paracas textile (Daggett 1991:47).

In his report to the Rector of San Marcos for the year 1929, Tello (1930a) presented the results of the inventory at the university's Museo de Arqueología. He noted, too, that museum staff had focused much of their attention on a study of Inca quipus housed at this and other museums in Lima. As for the national Museo de Arqueología Peruana, staff there had continued working with the Paracas mummy bundles in 1929. The Seville Commission sought control of all of the artifacts discovered by museum staff in Nazca and at Paracas during 1927 and 1928, but, after a long fight, it was decided that, rather than all, only six of the mummy bundles would be sent to Spain (Daggett 1991:58–59, n.27). Tello selected these six bundles in January 1929, and by July he and his staff had assembled 1,380 artifacts for shipment to Seville. In anticipation of a major new exhibit to open in conjunction with the upcoming Segundo Congreso Sudamericano de Turismo, Tello and his staff began the process of unwrapping individual mummy bundles. At the opening of this exhibit on October 16, President Leguía spoke at the museum. Tello spoke as well, indicating the increased needs of the museum given the discovery of the mummy bundles. In response, a decree was issued authorizing the enlargement of the facility (Daggett 1991:47, 1994:56–57).

Three other actions involving Tello should be mentioned for 1929. On September 26 Tello lodged a complaint against Hurtado for his theft of a large Paracas textile. Hurtado made a countercharge against Tello after being caught in the act of having the textile appraised for sale (Daggett 1991:48–49). This affair ended their association. Later, on October 5, Tello, as a charter member, attended the opening session of the Patronato Nacional de Arqueología. The stated purpose of this body was to provide government and professional oversight of the nation's prehistoric heritage (Anonymous 1929). In the Cámara de Diputados, Tello had previously spoken on behalf of proposed legislation regarding the conservation of archaeological monuments (Mejía 1948:12), legislation that led to the formation of this overseeing body. Tello would remain active in the Patronato Nacional de Arqueología throughout the remainder of his life. Finally, Tello did not run for reelection in 1929, preferring instead to concentrate on archaeological pursuits. Despite political differences, he had allied himself with Leguía in 1919 because they had shared an interest in the advancement of indigenous rights. By 1929, however, Tello no longer felt comfortable with Leguía's policies (Weiss et al. 1977:8).

During February 1930 Tello occupied himself with an archaeological exploration of the Chilca Valley (Mejía 1948:14). At the same time, discoveries were being made on his behalf at the site of Paracas by staff of the Museo de Arqueología Peruana. Additional discoveries were made at Paracas by staff of this museum in May and in June. In July Peru's Seville exhibit was shut down, a victim of the political and economic instability wrought by the Great Depression. A coup led by

Colonel Luís M. Sánchez Cerro brought down the government of Leguía the following month (Matos et al. 1981:259). On September 26, 1930, an interim government headed by Sánchez Cerro authorized a new exposition at the Museo de Arqueología Peruana, and Tello's position seemed secure. However, on October 9 Tello received official word that Luís E. Valcárcel had replaced him as director of this museum. At first Tello refused to leave the museum, but he finally had to concede (Matos et al. 1981:262). In support of their fallen leader, the staff of the museum, including Carrión and Mejía, resigned en masse (Daggett 1991:49, 1994a:57–58). During the balance of 1930, Tello, Carrión, and Mejía were kept busy conducting the inventory of the museum, which was required before Valcárcel could assume control (Tello and Mejía 1967:176–177).

Tello's demise was brought about by a series of articles that appeared in *Libertad*, one of a number of anti-Leguía publications given birth by the coup. The attack against Tello began in the second edition published on August 31, 1930. In this unsigned article (Anonymous 1930c), readers were promised proof that Tello had committed theft while director of the national museum. On September 2 two more articles attacking Tello were printed, both bearing a signature. In one (Degorce 1930), Tello was accused of having helped Leguía amass a huge fortune, which was held in foreign banks, and he was accused of having sold museum artifacts. In the other (R. Hurtado 1930), Tello was said to be a wealthy man, with an incredible array of assets being attributed to him, and he is said to have helped the American merchant A. Hyatt Verrill export seventeen crates of artifacts taken from the Museo de Arqueología Peruana.

On September 7 (Anonymous 1930b), and then again on September 9 (Anonymous 1930c), readers were reminded of charges made against Tello in years past by Gutiérrez and Larco. On September 10 Tello was accused (Rodríguez 1930) of misappropriating a valuable collection of gold idols, of general malfeasance, and of overcharging the Seville Commission for excavations conducted on the South Coast, this latter charge coming from Antonio Hurtado, who had worked for Tello on these excavations. Carrión Cachot was implicated in Tello's theft of artifacts from the national museum, and Tello and his entire museum staff were said to have plotted with the Leguía government to defeat Sánchez Cerro.

Tello finally responded to the attack with a letter (1930c) to one of Lima's long-standing newspapers in which he identified the editor of *Libertad*, an "old mud-slinging pamphleteer," as the person responsible. Tello offered notarized evidence that Francisco A. Loayza had used fictitious names and addresses for the supposed authors of the articles in question. In this way, he exposed Loayza, who, he said, had been abetted by Hurtado, the ex-employee of the national museum. This forced both of these men to come out and to defend themselves.

Writing as a collaborator of *Libertad*, Hurtado (1930a, b) attempted to shift the blame to Tello. As he had done in 1929 when he had been caught red-handed by the police, he claimed that it was Tello who was guilty of theft. The complete absence of any supporting evidence, however, greatly weakened his argument (Daggett 1996:7–8). As for Loayza, he admitted (1930b) that he had written the articles against Tello but left the reader, and Tello (1930c), to wonder why.

A few years earlier, Loayza had published a book (Loayza 1926) in which he speculated about Asiatic influences in the development of prehispanic civilization in the Americas. Mejía Xesspe (1928) gave it a bad review, and Loayza (1928a) took immediate exception, indirectly accusing Tello of being behind the review. Subsequently, Loayza (1928c) began publishing a series of articles in the Lima press in which he argued Chinese colonists had settled in the Americas in prehistoric times. A. Hyatt Verrill, an American explorer who was then in Lima on behalf of the American Heye Foundation in New York City, completely debunked this idea in his review (1929) published in the Lima press. This would explain Verrill's inclusion in the *Libertad* attack against Tello. Loayza had a long history of taking up the pen to attack his enemies (Farrar 1930). In his attack against Tello, he employed all of the tricks of the trade. He mixed truth with half-truths and out-and-out lies, wrapped them in patriotic rhetoric, and served them up without a hint of supporting documentation. It was mudslinging pure and simple, and Loayza had his revenge (Daggett 1996:9).

## The Dark Years: 1931–1936

A series of proclamations issued by the Sánchez government during the first half of 1931 served to create the Museo Nacional. The nation's museums of archaeology and history—the Museo de Arqueología Peruana, the Museo Nacional de Historia, and the Museo Bolivariano—were merged to form this new entity. Headed by Valcárcel, it consisted of distinct sections of archaeology and history, with dynamic organs being created for each. In this way, the Instituto de Investigaciones Antropológicas was created for the archaeology section. Through an agreement reached between the Museo Nacional and the Universidad Nacional Mayor de San Marcos, the role of this new institute was assumed by the university's Instituto Nacional de Antropología. As director of the university's institute, Tello became director of the Instituto de Investigaciones Antropológicas. The Museo Bolivariano became the headquarters of this new institute, and, during September, the transfer of the Paracas mummy bundles to this location was begun (Daggett 1994:58).

Tello was involved in a number of disparate activities during 1931. At the start of that year, he began publishing *Wira-Kocha*. He was the editor of this new anthropological journal, and, among others, Carrión and Mejía assisted him in this endeavor. Unknown difficulties inhibited the publication of a second issue, which was to have been published in November of that year (Espejo 1948:23). *Huaqueros* were active on the Paracas Peninsula in February and in July as well. Valcárcel responded by going to the site of Paracas in July at the head of a museum team that did not include Tello (Daggett 1991:51–52). Later in July Tello undertook a university-sponsored archaeological expedition (Mejía 1969:118). He led a small team to Ayacucho by way of Huancayo. The team visited a number of sites in and around each of these highland cities, and it was at this time that Tello first explored the ruins of Wari (Mejía 1948:14; see Daggett 2007).

During May 1932 *huaqueros* looted Paracas, and this so infuriated Tello that he publicly denounced Valcárcel and his staff at the Museo Nacional (Daggett 1991:54, 2007:87–88). That same month, civil unrest caused the Sánchez government to close the Universidad Nacional Mayor de San Marcos for what would prove to be a period of three years (Valcárcel 1981:269). During this time, Tello was denied access to the university's library and its archaeology museum, where his manuscripts, notes, and the like were stored (Tello 1975–1976:3). Fortunately, Tello was able to secure a teaching position at Lima's Pontificia Universidad Católica, a post he held until 1936 (Mejía 1948:28).

Tello and Carrión reinitiated the process of unwrapping individual Paracas mummy bundles during the second week of January 1933 (Daggett 1994:58). Shortly thereafter, thieves stole a collection of gold artifacts from the Museo Nacional. Tello and Valcárcel presented a report on this theft at the May 22 meeting of the Patronato Nacional de Arqueología (Tello and Mejía 1967:197). This meeting would have occurred in an atmosphere of political uncertainty. President Sánchez had been assassinated on April 30, and General Oscar Benavides had been selected by Congress to complete the presidential term (Keen and Wasserman 1988:414–415). This was the same officer who had led the coup of 1914 that had ousted President Billinghurst.

During February 1933 Tello accompanied the wife of the English ambassador to Peru on a trip of the North Central Coast. They explored sites in the Nepeña, Casma, and Huaura valleys, and Tello was so inspired by what he saw in Nepeña that he made a return trip. He left Lima in July 1933 to begin an archaeological exploration of the northern coast. He headed a team that included Mejía. After exploring sites in the Chicama, Moche, Virú, Chao, and Santa valleys, Tello returned to Nepeña with Mejía, and there they initiated excavations. In August Tello made public in the press his notification to officials in Lima of the early success of his work at the Chavín-related site of Cerro Blanco and his request for government funding to continue this work. This created an uproar, and a team of two, including Valcárcel, was dispatched to Nepeña to investigate the matter. Tello was removed as head of the excavations but was reinstated when the investigation was resolved in his favor (Daggett 1987:112–114, 2007:88–89).

The timing of the Nepeña crisis could not have been worse for Valcárcel. At that time, after months of planning, he had announced (Valcárcel 1933a) that the Museo Nacional had been authorized by the government to conduct cleaning, repair, and restoration at principal archaeological sites in and around Cuzco in preparation for the fourth centennial celebration of that southern highland city. This led to the suggestion in the Lima press (Editor 1933) that some of the Cuzco money be used to help Tello with his research in Nepeña. Valcárcel (1933b) was forced to state that the money had been specifically appropriated for work in Cuzco and that it could not by law be diverted elsewhere. This public discussion served to focus attention on the fact that a serious effort was under way to have Cuzco replace Lima as the nation's center for archaeological research. The idea of a national museum of archaeology being created in Cuzco had only just been proposed by one of its citizens, Atilio Sivirichi (1933a; see Daggett 2007:90–92).

The historian Sivirichi had taken part years earlier in an archaeological expedition headed by Loayza (1928b). Then, in 1930, he had published a book on Peruvian prehistory in which he sided with Uhle on the question of the development of civilization (Sivirichi 1930:82–86). Not surprisingly, his book received praise from Loayza (1930a), and his career took off at the same time that Tello's was about to receive a terrible blow with his removal from the national museum. By the end of 1933, Sivirichi (1933b) was confident enough of his standing to state that the work done in Nepeña had validated Uhle's position and not Tello's. Interestingly, Valcárcel (Anonymous 1933a) came to Tello's defense in this matter.

Though Loayza (1933a, b) used the Nepeña crisis to again attack him, Tello was beginning to reemerge as his nation's foremost archaeologist. A dinner held in his honor on October 26, 1933, was attended by many of the nation's elite, including Valcárcel (Anonymous 1933b). Not in attendance, however, was another individual who may have been galled by the lavish praise heaped on Tello at this function.

Eugenio Yacovleff was a Russian whose strong interest in history and geography had brought him to Lima in 1923 (Anonymous 1934e). He was among the staff of the Museo de Arqueología Peruana who had resigned when Tello had been fired as director (Tello and Mejía 1967:179). He later decided to work for Valcárcel at the Museo Nacional, however, and became one of his brightest collaborators (Matos et al. 1981:284). Tello would have been deeply offended by Yacovleff's disloyalty and angered by his participation in fieldwork that excluded Tello (Daggett 1991:52, 2007:88). Jealousy and animosity marked their relationship (Matos et al. 1981:282). Yacovleff had accompanied Valcárcel to the site of Paracas in 1932, and in the subsequent report published by the Museo Nacional, he (Yacovleff and Muelle 1932:48) disputed claims made earlier by Tello (1929:131, 134) regarding the process of mummification. Yacovleff (1933) expanded this criticism immediately after Tello's honorary dinner, and the tone of this attack was such that Valcárcel (1933c) felt obliged to disassociate the Museo Nacional from it. Yacovleff's premature death in December 1934, after months of illness (Anonymous 1934e), probably cut short what certainly promised to be a long and very bitter rivalry between he and Tello (Daggett 1991:55).

In December *huaqueros* were again active on the Paracas Peninsula, and Tello was included in a two-man investigative team sent by the Patronato Nacional de Arqueología (Tello and Mejía 1967:196). Tello created a local uproar when he denounced the illegal excavations (Anonymous 1934b). In January 1934 Tello (1934a) subtly criticized Valcárcel and the staff of the Museo Nacional for the theft the year earlier of the museum's collection of gold artifacts. Two months later, Tello (1934b) not so subtly criticized Valcárcel and his museum staff for the excavations they were conducting in and around Cuzco. His criticism came on the heels of reports coming out of Cuzco that had called for an investigation into purported financial mismanagement of the excavations (e.g., Anonymous 1934c). Sivirichi (1934) had his say in the matter, chiding Tello for his remarks and disdainfully reviewing what he argued was Tello's less-than-sterling record of excavation. Despite Sivirichi's attack, Tello's situation continued to improve. In May he was offered a teaching position at Colegio Antonio Raimondi in Lima. He accepted this offer, and the money that he earned over the next two years for teaching classes at this secondary school supplemented the meager stipend he earned at the Pontificia Universidad Católica (Santisteban 1956:20, 25).

In January 1934 Tello had been granted official permission to conduct archaeological research in North Central Peru and specifically at Chavín de Huantar (Anonymous 1934a). He began this field trip on July 24 accompanied by two American students. After stopping to study ruins in the Huaura, Fortaleza, Huarmey, and Casma valleys, they focused their attention on investigating the Great Wall of the Santa Valley. They then explored sites in the Callejón de Huaylas, especially near Caraz and Huaraz, before heading to Chavín de Huantar (Roosevelt 1935). Subsequently, Tello traveled to Uco, where he explored a number of ruins (Tello 1960:5) before returning in late August to conduct further research, first at Chavín de Huantar (Anonymous 1934d) and then, during September, at sites in the Carhuaz area (Tello 1942b:664–668; see Daggett 2007:92–94).

Tello resumed fieldwork in February 1935, focusing his attention on sites in the Rimac, Chillón, and Chancay valleys (Mejía 1948:15). From May 15 through July 24, 1935, he gave a series of six archaeology lectures in English at the British embassy in Lima (Mejía 1948:28–29). It was during this period that the Universidad Nacional Mayor de San Marcos was reopened, and Tello (1935) was forced to respond to the false charge that part of the university's archaeological collection was missing. In late July Tello led a small team on an expedition that included exploration of sites in and around the communities of Canta (Anonymous 1935a), Huánuco, and La Unión (Mejía 1967b:xvi), as well as in the Callejón de Huaylas (Mejía 1956:320). At the site of Kotosh, near Huánuco, Tello discovered artifacts similar to those that he had found at Chavín de Huantar (Tello 1942b:635; see Daggett 2007:94–95).

Finally, beginning in October, Tello concluded a very busy year in the field by accompanying Valcárcel on an exploration of sites in southern Peru (Anonymous 1935b). Valcárcel had asked Tello to come because of his expertise. Together they explored sites in and around Arequipa and Cuzco (Matos et al. 1981:298) before moving to Pukara, where artifacts were found that reminded Tello of the ones that he had found recently in Huánuco and at Chavín de Huantar (Tello 1942a:240–241). Tello and Valcárcel later presented a detailed report of their discoveries to the Patronato Nacional de Arqueología (Anonymous 1935c; see Daggett 2007:95–96). Tello concluded his field activities in 1935 with excavations at the site of Mateo Salado in Lima (Anonymous 1941d).

In July 1936 Tello traveled to the United States by way of Chile and Panama. In August he presented a series of twenty-four lectures on Peruvian archaeology at the summer field session of the University of New Mexico. This session was being held at Chaco Canyon under the joint auspices of the School of American Research, the University of New Mexico, and Southwestern University. Tello was made a member of the School of American Research on August 29. Subsequently, he presented a series of lectures in California, Minnesota, and Mexico City. The purpose of his trip was to visit museums and to secure support for his research. The latter goal was accomplished on September 23 with the founding, in New York City, of the Institute of Andean Research (Daggett 1994:58–60).

By any measure, Tello's trip was highly successful. While traveling, he received many honors, visited numerous museums, and had ample opportunity to speak on matters of importance to him (Mejía 1948:29–30). Throughout his trip, Tello stressed to colleagues the need for coordinated research in the Andes, and his persistence was rewarded when he and a select group of American scholars founded the Institute of Andean Research (Strong 1943:2–4).

## The Golden Years: 1937–1947

Not long after his return to Peru, Tello was sent on an official mission to investigate illegal excavations that had been conducted in the Lambayeque region beginning in December 1936 (Tello and Mejía 1967:193–194). The discovery of prehistoric gold and silver artifacts had caught the attention of officials there, and these artifacts were confiscated and shipped to the Banco Central de Reserva in Lima the following month. As head of the Instituto de Investigaciones Antropológicas, Tello was sent to investigate the matter (Anonymous 1937). Under this authority, Tello and Mejía conducted excavations near the end of January at the site of La Ventana in the La Leche Valley (Tello 1937).

On May 15, 1937, Tello received a visit from the American philanthropist Nelson Rockefeller, who was in the midst of a business tour of

South America. The visit occurred at the Instituto de Investigaciones, which had been poorly funded by the government since its inception. Rockefeller was so shocked by what he saw that he offered financial support to help defray the cost of preserving the Paracas mummy bundles. The government accepted this aid, and, in the hope of generating further support, it agreed to ship five of the Paracas mummy bundles to the New York Metropolitan Museum of Art (Daggett 1994:58, 60–61).

During May 1937 Tello and his staff at the Museo de Arqueología of the Universidad Nacional Mayor de San Marcos made plans to equip an expedition financed, in part, by Nelson Rockefeller (Mejía 1948:15). Funds were also provided by the Institute of Andean Research, and on June 16 Tello left Lima at the head of a team that included, among others, Mejía and three North American students (Tello 1942a:236). The team explored sites in the Chancay, Huaura, Supe, Pativilca, and Fortaleza valleys before reaching the Casma Valley on June 28. Though initial explorations suggested that this would not be a promising place in which to work, the discovery of the Chavín-related site of Cerro Sechín on July 1 kept them in Casma investigating this and dozens of other sites until September 28. On that day they headed northward, stopping to investigate ruins in the Nepeña, Lacramarca, Santa, Moche, and Jequetepeque valleys before reaching Cajamarca on October 5. This began the highland phase of their exploration, and important sites were investigated in and around the cities of Cajamarca, Yanacancha, Celendín, and Huamachuco. On December 15, while in Huamachuco, Tello was informed of the death of his eldest daughter, and he immediately ended the expedition, arriving back in Lima three days later (Mejía 1956:337).

Tello did not make any field trips in 1938; instead, he concentrated on other activities. The second and final volume of *Inca* was published that year (Espejo 1948:22). He also gave considerable attention to museum work. During the first six months of the year, he and his staff at the Instituto de Investigaciones Antropológicas worked to preserve the Paracas collection, and in July Tello gave Rockefeller a complete accounting of the money that Rockefeller had given to the institute for this purpose. A total of 346 Paracas textiles had been saved, and 181 had been placed on exhibit. Then, on August 15, President Benavides made an unexpected visit to the institute to view this exhibit. Due to Rockefeller's interest and because Lima would be hosting the Eighth Pan American Congress in December, Benavides authorized Tello to build a new museum in which to house the Paracas collection (Daggett 1994:61).

Though Valcárcel had great plans for the Museo Nacional in 1938, its functions began to be reduced that year (Daggett 1988:17). At Tello's insistence, most of the Paracas material still held by Valcárcel in the Museo Nacional was transferred to the new museum. A law reorganizing the nation's museums was enacted on September 22, 1938, and on October 8 the Museo de Antropología was created by presidential decree. On December 25, at an enlarged and modernized locale, the Instituto de Investigaciones Antropológicas opened its doors as the Museo de Antropología. Tello was officially made its director on January 3, 1939 (Daggett 1994:62).

On May 16, 1939, the Patronato Nacional de Arqueología met in extraordinary session. Archaeological sites were being threatened in a number of Peru's departments, and Tello, Valcárcel, and their colleagues met to resolve this problem (Anonymous 1939a). Reform measures were decided upon, and these measures were incorporated in a presidential decree published in early July (Benavides 1939).

Toward the end of August 1939, Tello returned by steamship from Mexico City, where he had attended the first session of the Twenty-seventh International Congress of Americanists (Anonymous 1939b). There he had presented a paper (Tello 1942a) in which he first announced his discovery that the Chavín culture was the earliest culture in Peru. He supported this contention with a chronicle of the discoveries that he had made at Chavín de Huantar as well as at sites such as La Ventana, Cerro Blanco, Cerro Sechín, Paracas, Kotosh, and Pukara.

The second session of the Twenty-seventh International Congress of Americanists was held in Lima, and at this meeting Tello presented a paper (Tello 1942b) that represented his defining work on the prehistory of Peru. He hosted a reception for the delegates of the congress at the Museo de Antropología, and he led excursions taken by delegates to the sites of Cajamarquilla and Pachacamac (Basadre 1942:lv–lvi). After the conclusion of the congress, Tello and Mejía led a group of delegates, in late September, on a visit to archaeological sites in northern Peru. After stops in the Chancay, Supe, Fortaleza, and Casma valleys, visits were made to the Callejón de Huaylas and Chavín de Huantar. In the Callejón, the ruins of Pomakayán and Katak, among others, were explored. While Tello led the group back to Lima, Mejía remained at Katak with an artist from the Museo de Antropología (Anonymous 1939c). This began for Mejía a period of exploration and excavation in the Callejón and in the upper reaches of the Casma Valley (Mejía 1940).

Stimulated perhaps by the recent congress, Carrión, Mejía, Valcárcel, and others gathered at Tello's home on September 21, 1939, to discuss the formation of a new national association of archaeology. The Asociación Peruana de Arqueología was created to coordinate, direct, and oversee archaeological research done in Peru by its members. Included among the honorary members of the association were the president of the Patronato Nacional de Arqueología and the rector of the Universidad Nacional Mayor de San Marcos. A consulting board, headed by Tello and with Valcárcel as its general secretary, was established for a two-year period to end September 21, 1941. Meetings of the Asociación Peruana de Arqueología were held generally at the university's Museo de Arqueología (Editor 1940:78–84).

Tello and Carrión were appointed to the editorial board of the association's publication, *Chaski*, and three issues of this journal were published during 1940–1941 (Espejo 1948:22). The last known meeting of this association was held at the Museo de Antropología on June 30, 1941. Among those in attendance were Tello, Valcárcel, Carrión, Mejía, and Uhle (Anonymous 1941h). Uhle had come to Peru in September 1939 as a member of the German delegation to the International Congress of Americanists (Basadre 1942:xv). On January 2, 1940, he was made an honorary member of the Asociación Peruana de Arqueología (Editor 1940:84–85).

On May 13, 1940, Tello and his staff at the Museo de Antropología began excavations at Pachacamac. Carrión and Mejía, among others, were involved, and work was to continue at this site through 1946. Tello had been asked by agents of the Junta Departmental Pro-Desocupados of Lima in January 1940 to conduct work at one or more sites of national importance, and Pachacamac was agreed upon. In September 1938 Tello had publicized his concerns about work then being done at this site on behalf of the Museo Nacional, and this had created an uproar. Though Pachacamac was only a short ride by car from Lima, the work done there in 1940 was accomplished without distraction. This changed when two reporters visited the site in July. They learned of the major discoveries that had been made there, and this information was immediately made public (Daggett 1988:14, 17–20). This news generated keen interest at all levels of Peruvian society, and during August Tello led the president of Peru and other dignitaries on a tour of the site (Anonymous 1940c). Tello remained in the Lima area during this period, in part because he was involved in teaching evening archaeology classes to North American students. These classes were held at the university's Museo de Arqueología (Anonymous 1940b).

The Patronato Nacional de Arqueología had begun to expand its activities in June 1940 with the formation of inspection commissions. Valcárcel and Tello were appointed to the archaeological commissions responsible for museums and monuments, respectively (Anonymous 1940a). During December 1939 Tello, as an associate member, had agreed to the request of the Sociedad Geográfica of Lima that he create an archaeological map of Peru (Anonymous 1939d). A year or so later, the Oficina de Inspección de Monumentos was established in an annex of the Museo de Antropología. This was done at the request of the Patronato Nacional de Arqueología. In addition to overseeing sites in the Lima region, the two inspectors assigned to this office devoted time to the preparation of an archaeological map of Peru (Tello 1941:75).

Tello made a trip down the coast to conduct archaeological explorations in the Nazca region during September 1940. Mejía, Valcárcel, and the American archaeologist William Duncan Strong accompanied Tello on this trip (Strong 1948:55–56). As a student at Berkeley in the 1920s, Strong had worked with Kroeber on the study of Uhle's collections, and this was Strong's first trip to Peru (Rowe 1962:401, 405). He had come to conduct a preliminary survey in anticipation of archaeological work to be done under the auspices of the Institute of Andean Research (Strong 1943:3).

During October 1940 Tello attended a meeting of the Patronato Nacional de Arqueología, at which time he was requested to formulate a definitive plan of organization for the Inspección General de Monumentos Antiguos (Anonymous 1940d). Then, on November 16, Tello and Mejía, accompanied by an engineer, arrived at Chavín de Huantar for what was announced to be a two-week stay (Anonymous 1940e). Concern about possible damage to these ruins by rising floodwaters had caused the president of Peru to issue a decree on September 14 authorizing Tello to go to this site and to initiate preventive measures. A subsequent ministerial resolution dated October 24 authorized Tello and a team from the Museo de Antropología to go to Chavín de Huantar for this very purpose. While at the site, excavations were conducted during the period November 16–25. The 119 principal artifacts discovered during these excavations were installed in a site museum that was inaugurated on December 11 (Tello 1960:135; 361). This was the nation's first such museum.

During January 1941 the site of Chavín de Huantar was declared the property of the state because of its inherent historic and touristic value (Anonymous 1941a). This act initiated a public debate, and

Tello argued for the creation of a series of national historic parks modeled after the national parks that he had seen on his 1936 trip to the United States. Among others, he argued that the sites of Chavín de Huantar, Pomakayán, Katak, Chan Chan, Cerro Sechín, Pachacamac, and Tambo Colorado and the more important ruins in the Cuzco area should be converted into national parks (Anonymous 1941b). Tello was then commissioned to study the ruins of Pomakayán and others in the Huaraz area for the purpose of including them in just such a park (Anonymous 1941c).

At a meeting of the Patronato Nacional de Arqueología held the beginning of February 1941, Tello spoke against work being conducted by a private firm at the site of Mateo Salado. He had visited the site on January 28 of that year, and he wanted the excavations that he had just witnessed there stopped. He was supported in this demand. At this same meeting, it was noted that fieldwork, including excavations, was being conducted at Cajamarquilla (Anonymous 1941d). At a meeting months earlier, members had authorized the drawing up of plans of these ruins (Anonymous 1940d).

In late March 1941 Tello was appointed to Peru's delegation to the Third Asamblea General del Instituto Panamericano de Geografía e Historia, soon to be hosted in Lima (Anonymous 1941e). This gave Tello yet another opportunity to exchange ideas about Peru's prehistory in an international forum, and, not surprisingly, he took the opportunity to lead a tour of delegates to Pachacamac (Anonymous 1941f). In June the Patronato Nacional de Arqueología passed a request for the restoration of the ruins of Tambo Colorado to the Comisión de Inspección de Monumentos (Anonymous 1941g). At a meeting of the Asociación Peruana de Arqueología held later that month, Tello reported on work that had been done at this site situated in the middle Pisco Valley (Anonymous 1941h). During 1940–1941 staff at the Museo de Antropología worked on preparing a plan and a model of the ruins of Tambo Colorado (Tello and Mejía 1967:230–231, 234).

Beginning in 1941, the Institute of Andean Research sent several teams of researchers to different parts of Peru. Lothrop, for example, was sent to Lima to work with Tello as codirector with him on a project dealing with the Paracas mummy bundles (Strong 1943:7; Willey 1988:90, 206). Tello spent time visiting archaeological sites with some of the researchers sent by the institute. Strong was the director of the Central Coast team that excavated at a number of locations, including the site of Ancón. In 1941 Tello invited its members to conduct excavations at Pachacamac (Willey 1988:87–90). Strong directed these excavations from July 23 to September 10 (Daggett 1988:19).

Tello returned to Chavín de Huantar toward the end of 1941 (Anonymous 1941i). He left a team from the Museo de Antropología there with instructions to conduct a thorough archaeological reconnaissance of the region from Chavín de Huantar to Uco (Mejía 1948:15). In December Tello traveled to Huarochirí, where he was honored by induction into the Academia de Ciencias Físicas (Anonymous 1941j).

Tello did not return to the field for several months, though he did make a short trip with an old friend. Alfred Kroeber returned to Peru in March 1942 to begin two months of research on behalf of the Committee on Inter-American Artistic and Intellectual Relations. He spent three weeks in Lima and the remaining five weeks on the road. Tello accompanied Kroeber on the first day of his trip up to the North Coast (Kroeber 1944:5, 43). During Kroeber's visit, a number of researchers affiliated with the Institute of Andean Research were still in Peru, including Lothrop (Willey 1988:183). The Asociación Peruana de Arqueología held a reception in honor of Kroeber in late April. Tello hosted this reception at the Museo de Antropología (Anonymous 1942).

On June 21, 1942, Tello left Lima at the head of an archaeological expedition sponsored by the Viking Fund of New York. The team, which included Mejía, arrived in Cuzco on July 23 after first visiting sites in the vicinity of Huancayo and Ayacucho. This part of the trip essentially mirrored the trip Tello made in 1931. Excavations were conducted at a number of sites, including Wari. Upon their arrival at Cuzco, the team immediately moved to an area south of the ruins of Machu Picchu, where sites had recently been discovered. A period of exploration followed and culminated, on August 25, with the discovery of the ruins of Wiñay Wayna. The members of the team worked at this site until October 14, at which time they headed back to Cuzco. There they visited many sites, and Tello gave a talk during ceremonies honoring him at the Universidad de Cuzco. In November they went to Machu Picchu before shifting their attention to the coast. Arriving in Nazca, they began the final phase of their exploration, which included stops in the Acarí, Ocoña, Majes, and Moquegua valleys (Mejía 1967a:7).

In 1941 a retired Peruvian senator, Germán Luna Iglesias, offered to donate land adjacent to the Museo de Antropología so that this facility could be expanded. Lack of funds prevented the government from acting upon this generous offer. Money was found, however, when Luna offered to donate an even larger parcel of land. On August 23, 1943, a decree was issued to this effect, and on December 2 an agreement to construct a new facility for the Museo de Antropología was formalized. In this way, the Museo Nacional de Antropología y Arqueología was created on January 29, 1945, with Tello as its director. Subsequently, on April 24, 1946, an agreement of federation was formalized between this new national museum and the Museo de Arqueología of the Universidad Nacional Mayor de San Marcos (Daggett 1994:63). The result of all these actions was to place Tello in complete charge of his nation's archaeological collections. The Museo Nacional was closed, and Valcárcel was made director of Peru's museums of history (Matos et al. 1981:359). Finally, during June 1946 Tello was named honorary Inspector General de Monumentos Arqueológicos (Anonymous 1946a).

Tello remained very active during the early to middle 1940s. In 1941 he initiated a program of exploration to be conducted by staff of the Museo de Antropología. That same year he sent Mejía to explore the south-central highlands by way of the upper Cañete Valley. Later that year he sent Mejía to the Ica Valley. In June 1943 he commissioned Mejía to lead an expedition to the as yet unknown region of the South Coast situated between the Ocoña and Majes valleys. The headwaters of the Rimac Valley were explored on Tello's behalf in 1944. In 1945 he sent a team to explore the Abancay and the Urubamba regions, and in 1946 a team he had sent to the Cajamarca area discovered the Chavín-related site of Kuntur Wasi (Mejía 1948:15–17).

During this period, Tello began to concentrate on sites in and around the Rimac Valley (Mejía 1948:16–17). For example, in 1944 he conducted excavations at Cajamarquilla (Anonymous 1946b), and in 1945 he began work at Ancón. The excavations at Ancón were begun at the request of the Patronato Nacional de Arqueología, which was concerned about recent work done at the site by a local construction firm (Tello 1946).

Late in July 1946, Tello became ill, and in September he traveled to the United States for treatment. He did not return to Lima until November 28 (Daggett 1994:63). Prior to his return, Tello was named by executive order to a commission responsible for detailing and studying the many artifacts recovered by Strong during recent excavations on the North Coast. In this work, Tello was to be aided by Carrión (Anonymous 1946c). Tello was treated periodically for his illness during the ensuing months, but his condition eventually worsened, and, following emergency surgery, he died on June 3, 1947 (Daggett 1994:63).

The entire country grieved Tello's passing, and he was buried with full national honors (Daggett 1992a:191). A year later, his remains were brought to the Museo Nacional de Antropología y Arqueología, where they were interred in a mausoleum that Luna had donated (Daggett 1994:63). In his will, Tello generously bequeathed his books and his unedited papers to the Universidad Nacional de San Marcos, and there an archive was established in his name. Posthumous publications based on this rich archive have served to expand knowledge of Tello's extraordinary accomplishments (Daggett 1992a:194).

Assistance provided me by the respective staffs of the Archive Office of Harvard University's Peabody Museum of American Archaeology and Ethnology; the Interlibrary Loan Office at the University of Massachusetts, Amherst; and the Biblioteca Nacional de Lima all greatly facilitated research on this essay. I would like to take this opportunity to express my appreciation.

## REFERENCES CITED

Anonymous

1906 La craniectomía en el Perú prehistórico: Conferencia dada a noche en la Sociedad Geográfica. *El Comercio*, May 5, p. 2. Lima.

1918 *Diario de los Debates, Cámara de Diputados.* Lima.

1919 *Diario de los Debates, Cámara de Diputados.* Lima.

1922a Cámara de Diputados. La sesión de ayer. La Cámara acuerda a pedido del Sr. Tello, oficiar al Ministro de Instrucción, para que separe de su puesto, al Director del Museo Nacional. *La Crónica*, August 4, p. 3. Lima.

1922b Cámara de Diputados. La sesión de ayer. El Señor Corbacho reconsideración del acuerdo para destitutir al Director del Museo Nacional; intervienen en este incidente los señores Corbacho y Tello. *La Crónica*, August 6, p. 6. Lima.

1922c Cámara de Diputados. La sesión de ayer. Continúa el debate sobre el asunto Tello-Quintanilla; nueva intervención del Señor Tello. *La Crónica*, August 8, p. 2. Lima.

1922d Cámara de Diputados. La sesión de ayer. Nuevo aspecto en el ruidoso asunto Tello-Quintanilla; intervención del Señor Corbacho. *La Crónica*, August 9, p. 2. Lima.

1922e Cámara de Diputados. La sesión de ayer. El asunto Tello-Quintanilla. *La Crónica*, August 12, p. 3. Lima.

1925a Tercer Congreso Científico Panamericano. *El Comercio*, January 7, p. 11. Lima.

1925b Las ruinas de Chan Chán. *El Comercio*, July 4, p. 8. Lima.

1926 Sociedad de Arqueología y Artes Peruanas. *El Comercio*, September 21, p. 2. Lima.

1928 La verdad de lo ocurrido en el Museo de Arqueología: El Señor Víctor Larco Herrera nos explica el origen del incidente que tuvo con el

Director Julio Tello y la exactitud de sus proporciones. Los terrenos colindantes con el Museo. *El Tiempo*, May 13, p. 13. Lima.
1929 Instalación del Patronato Nacional de Arqueología. *El Comercio*, October 6, p. 2. Lima.
1930a El Museo de Arqueología. *Libertad*, August 31, p. 4. Lima.
1930b En el Museo Nacional de Arqueología no se trata de entrega de listas y libros, sino de cuantiosos robos y grandes negociados con lo más sagrado que tiene un pueblo: Lo tradicional. *Libertad*, September 7, p. 2. Lima.
1930c Las depredaciones en el Museo Arqueológico de Lima. *Libertad*, September 9, p. 2. Lima.
1933a Las ruinas del Valle de Nepeña: Lo que refieren los doctores Tello, Valcárcel y Antúnez de Mayolo. *El Comercio*, October 5, p. 7. Lima.
1933b Agasajo al Doctor Julio C. Tello. *El Comercio*, October 27, p. 5. Lima.
1934a Exploraciones arqueológicas en Chavín. *El Comercio*, January 12, p. 10. Lima.
1934b Causan sensación en Ica las declaraciones hechas por el catedrático Doctor J. Tello: Dice que se han llevado a cabo excavaciones sin el respectivo permiso. *El Comercio*, January 20, p. 11. Lima.
1934c Lanza una denuncia grave el periódico "El Sol" del Cuzco: Asegura que se malgastan los dineros dedicados a restaurar los monumentos. *El Comercio*, March 4, p. 13. Lima.
1934d El Doctor Tello regresó a Chavín, de su viaje a las ruinas del Marañón. *El Comercio*, August 25, p. 14. Lima.
1934e Eugenio Yacovleff. *Revista del Museo Nacional* 3(3): 323–326. Lima.
1935a Visitó a las ruinas de Kantamarca el Dr. Julio C. Tello. *El Comercio*, afternoon edition, July 27, p. 6. Lima.
1935b Realizan trabajos arqueológicas en Arequipa y Cuzco. *El Comercio*, October 25, p. 13. Lima.
1935c Patronato Nacional de Arqueología. *El Comercio*, December 6, p. 12. Lima.
1937 Los hallazgos de Lambayeque. *El Comercio*, January 12, p. 2. Lima.
1939a Patronato Nacional de Arqueología. *El Comercio*, May 18, p. 1. Lima.
1939b XXVII Congreso Internacional de Americanistas: Sesión de Lima, Boletín No. 6. *El Comercio*, August 23, p. 2. Lima.
1939c Regreso de la excursión a Ancash organizada por el Congreso de Americanistas. *El Comercio*, September 30, p. 3. Lima.
1939d Sociedad Geográfica de Lima. *El Comercio*, December 15, p. 5. Lima.
1940a Constituir las Comisiones de Inspección de Museos y Registro de Especies Arqueológicas y de Inspección de Monumentos Arqueológicas, Conservación y Registro. *El Comercio*, June 24, p. 3. Lima.
1940b Las actividades de ayer en la "Escuela de Verano." *El Comercio*, July 18, p. 4. Lima.
1940c El Jefe del Estado visitó las ruinas descubiertas en Pachacamac. *El Comercio*, August 26, p. 3. Lima.

1940d Patronato Nacional de Arqueología. *El Comercio*, afternoon edition, October 8, p. 2. Lima.
1940e Chavín. *El Comercio*, November 18, p. 13. Lima.
1941a El Castillo de Chavín: Ley No. 9298. *El Comercio*, January 24, p. 2. Lima.
1941b La creación de Parques Históricos Nacionales: Conversando con el Doctor Julio C. Tello. *El Comercio*, January 29, pp. 3, 5. Lima.
1941c La conservación de las ruinas históricas de Ancash. *El Comercio*, January 31, p. 2. Lima.
1941d Patronato Nacional de Arqueología. *El Comercio*, February 2, p. 7. Lima.
1941e La delegación del Perú a la III Asamblea General del Instituto Panamericano de Geografía e Historia. *El Comercio*, March 28, p. 2. Lima.
1941f Excursión a las ruinas de Pachacamac y almuerzos ofrecidos a los delegados. *El Comercio*, April 4, p. 3. Lima.
1941g Patronato Nacional de Arqueología. *El Comercio*, June 23, p. 2. Lima.
1941h Asociación Peruana de Arqueología. *El Comercio*, July 2, p. 2. Lima.
1941i Huaraz. *El Comercio*, November 13, p. 15. Lima.
1941j Huarochirí. *El Comercio*, December 15, p. 17. Lima.
1942 Museo de Antropología. *El Comercio*, April 25, p. 3. Lima.
1946a Resoluciones Supremas. *El Comercio*, June 26, p. 2. Lima.
1946b La conferencia de anoche en el Museo de Antropología. *El Comercio*, November 1, p. 3. Lima.
1946c Patronato Nacional de Arqueología. *El Comercio*, November 6, p. 2. Lima.
1958 El Dr. Ricardo Palma, Prof. de Anatomía de 35 generaciones de galenos. *El Comercio*, afternoon edition, March 15, p. 3. Lima.

Basadre, Jorge, ed.
1942 *Actas del XXVII Congreso Internacional de Americanistas.* 2 vols. Lima, 1939.
1964 Historia de la República del Perú. 10 vols., 5th ed. Ediciones "Historia." Lima.

Beals, Carlton
1934 *Fire on the Andes.* Philadelphia: J. B. Lipponcott.

Benavides, Oscar R.
1939 Reforma de los Patronatos Arqueológicos. *El Comercio*, July 5, p. 2. Lima.

Bingham, Alfred M.
1989 *Portrait of an Explorer: Hiram Bingham, Discoverer of Machu Picchu.* Ames: Iowa State University Press.

Brues, Charles T.
1917 A New Species of Peripatius from the Mountains of Northern Peru. *Bulletin of the Museum of Comparative Zoology* 61(10): 381–387.

Buse, Herman
1974 Mejía Xesspe, 50 años en la arqueología. *El Comercio*, April 12, p. 2. Lima.

Daggett, Richard E.
1987 Reconstructing the Evidence for Cerro Blanco and Punkuri. *Andean Past* 1:111–163.
1988 The Pachacamac Studies: 1938–1941. *Michigan Studies in Anthropology* 8:13–22.
1991 Paracas: Discovery and Controversy. In *Paracas Art and Architecture: Object and Context in South Coastal Peru*, edited by Anne Paul, pp. 35–60. Iowa City: University of Iowa Press.
1992a Tello, the Press and Peruvian Archaeology. In *Rediscovering Our Past: Essays on the History of American Archaeology*, edited by Jonathan E. Reyman, pp. 191–202. Hampshire, England: Avebury.
1992b The Incidental Archaeologist: Tello and the Peruvian Expeditions of 1913 and 1916. Paper presented at the Eleventh Annual Northeast Conference on Andean Archaeology and Ethnohistory, Colgate University, Hamilton, New York, November 22.
1994 The Paracas Mummy Bundles of the Great Necropolis of Wari Kayan: A History. *Andean Past* 4:53–75.
1996 The *Libertad* Campaign against Tello: Setting the Record Straight. Paper presented at the Fifteenth Annual Northeast Conference on Andean Archaeology and Ethnohistory, Rainey Auditorium, University of Pennsylvania Museum of Archaeology and Anthropology, Philadelphia, October 19.
1997 Tello's 1915 Trip to Southern Peru and Bolivia: A First Look. Paper presented at the Sixteenth Annual Northeast Conference on Andean Archaeology and Ethnohistory, University of Maine, Orono, October 4.
2005 Introducción a las investigaciones de Julio C. Tello en la peninsula de Paracas. In *Paracas Primera Parte*, by Julio C. Tello. *Obras Completas*, vol. 2, pp. 53–66. Lima: Fondo Editorial Universidad Nacional Mayor de San Marcos.
2007 Tello's "Lost Years": 1931–1935. *Andean Past* 8:81–108.
Degorce, E.
1930 El origen de la deuda pública. *Libertad*, September 2, p. 4. Lima.
Editor
1910 Anthropologic Miscellanea. *American Anthropologist* 12:337–348.
1912 *Proceedings of the XVIII International Congress of Americanists.* London.
1921a La Asociación para el Progreso de la Ciencia. *Archivos de la Asociación Peruana para el Progreso de la Ciencia* 1:5–6. Impresa Americana, Lima.
1921b Extractos de las actas de las sesiones celebrados para la asociacíon. *Archivos de la Asociación Peruana para el Progreso de la Ciencia* 1:149–153. Impresa Americana, Lima.
1922 Extractos de las actas de las sesiones celebradas por la Asociación. *Archivos de la Asociación Peruana para el Progreso de la Ciencia* 2:145–171. Impresa Americana, Lima.
1933 La restauración de los monumentos arqueológicos. *El Comercio*, September 15, p. 1. Lima.

1940 Noticias y estatuto de la Asociación Peruana de Arqueología. *Chaski* 1(1): 78–86. Lima.

Espejo Núñez, Teófilo

1948 3 Revistas de Antropología Peruana: Inca, Wira Kocha y Chaski. *Boletín Bibliográfico* 18(1–2): 21–38. Lima.

1959 *Formación Universitaria de Julio C. Tello (1900–1912)*. Lima.

Farrar, F. P.

1930 Loayza of *Libertad*: Litterateur, Archaeologist and Fighting Man. *West Coast Leader*, November 18, pp. 13, 15.

González de Vallier, N.

1936 Rebeca Carrión Cachot. *El Comercio*, June 14, p. 8. Lima.

Gutiérrez de Quintanilla, Emilio

1922 *El Manco Capac de la Arqueología Peruana Julio C. Tello (Señor de Huarochirí)*. Lima.

Hrdlicka, Ales

1914 Anthropological Work in Peru in 1913, with Notes on the Pathology of the Ancient Peruvians. *Smithsonian Miscellaneous Collections* 61(18).

Hurtado, Antonio

1930a !Pruebas y más pruebas: Julio C. Tello no solo ha robado al Museo de Arqueología Nacional, sino que lanza asesinos contra un colaborador de *Libertad*! *Libertad*, September 15, p. 4. Lima.

1930b !La víctima de Julio Tello! !Pruebas, no palabras! *Libertad*, September 18, p. 4. Lima.

Hurtado, Ricardo M.

1930 Descubrimiento a un canalla y vil ratero. *Libertad*, September 2, p. 4. Lima.

Keen, Benjamin, and Mark Wasserman

1988 *A History of Latin America*, 3rd ed. Boston: Houghton Mifflin.

Kroeber, Alfred L.

1915 Frederic Ward Putnam. *American Anthropologist* 17:712–718.

1926a Culture Stratifications in Peru. *American Anthropologist* 28:331–351.

1926b Archaeological Explorations in Peru, Part I: Ancient Pottery from Trujillo. *Anthropology Memoirs Field Museum of Natural History* 2(1). Chicago.

1930 Archaeological Explorations in Peru, Part II: The Northern Coast. Anthropology Memoirs Field Museum of Natural History 2(2). Chicago.

1944 *Peruvian Archeology in 1942*. New York: Viking Fund.

Larco Herrera, Victor

1928 Las acusaciones de Don Victor Larco Herrera a Don Julio C. Tello. *El Tiempo*, May 17. Lima.

Loayza, Francisco A.

1926 *Manko-Kapa*. Brazil.

1928a Elogio crítico al libro "Manko Kapa" del conservador del Museo de Antropología Peruana. *El Tiempo*, May 17, p. 5. Lima.

1928b La expedición arqueológico de "El Tiempo." *El Tiempo*, May 30, pp. 1, 9. Lima.
1928c Chinos vinieron a la América antes que Colon. *El Comercio*, November 4, p. 9. Lima.
1930a "Prehistoria Peruana." *El Comercio*, February 26, p. 7. Lima.
1930b Al Señor Julio Tello. *Libertad*, September 18, p. 1. Lima.
1933a Por la historia y por la ley. *El Comercio*, afternoon edition, October 4, p. 1. Lima.
1933b El asunto de Nepeña. *El Comercio*, October 7, p. 3. Lima.

López Martínez, Héctor, and Luís García-Miró Peschiera
1992 *El Siglo XX en el Perú a Través de "El Comercio": Tomo II, 1911/1921.* Edición de "El Comercio." Lima.

Lothrop, Samuel K.
1948 Julio C. Tello, 1880–1947. *American Antiquity* 14:49–56.

MacCurdy, George G.
1910 Anthropology at the Boston Meeting with Proceedings of the American Anthropological Association for 1909. *American Anthropologist* 12:61–71.
1911 Anthropology at the Providence Meeting with Proceedings of the American Anthropological Association for 1910. *American Anthropologist* 13:99–120.

Matos Mar, José, José C. Deustua, and José Luis Rénique, eds.
1981 *Luís E. Valcárcel, Memorias.* Instituto Estudios Peruanos, Lima.

Mejía Xesspe, Toribio
1928 El origen nipon de los antiguos peruanos. *El Tiempo*, May 15, p. 2. Lima.
1940 Walun y Chichawas: Dos nuevas sitios arqueológicas de la Cordillera Negra. *Chaski* 1(1): 18–24. Lima.
1947 Algunos descubrimientos arqueológicos del sabio peruano Doctor Julio C. Tello en el país de los inkas. *El Comercio*, July 28, p. 14. Lima.
1948 Apuntes biográficos sobre el Doctor Julio C. Tello. Reprint of *Revista del Museo Nacional de Antropología y Arqueologóa* 2(1–2). Lima.
1956 Historia de la Expedición Arqueológica al Marañónde 1937. In *Arqueología del Valle de Casma. Culturas: Chavín, Santa o Huaylas Yunga y Sub-Chimú*, by Julio C. Tello, pp. 319–337. Lima: Universidad Nacional Mayor de San Marcos.
1964 Julio C. Tello. *Biblioteca Hombres del Perú*, 3rd series, vol. 28, edited by Hernán Alva Orlandini, pp. 51–111. Lima: Editorial Universitaria.
1967a Expediciones arqueológicas dirigidas por Julio C. Tello. *Cultura y Pueblo* 4(11–12): 4–7. Lima.
1967b Prólogo. In *Páginas Escogidas*, by Julio C. Tello, selection by Toribio Mejía Xesspe, pp. v–xxiii. Lima: Universidad Nacional Mayor de San Marcos.
1969 El antiguo Perú a través de la arqueología. In *Mesa Redonda de Ciencias Prehistóricas y Antropológicas*, vol. 2, pp. 108–124. Lima: Pontifica Universidad Católica.

Michelson, Truman
1911 Proceedings of the Anthropological Society of Washington. *American Anthropologist* 13:313–319.
Milla Batres, Carlos, ed.
1986 *Diccionario Histórico y Bibliográfico del Perú: Siglos XV–XX.* 9 vols. Lima: Editorial Milla Batres, S. A.
Miró Quesada S., Aurelio
1966 *20 Temas Peruanos.* Lima: Talleres Gráficos P. L. Villanueva, S. A.
Muñiz, Manuel A., and W. J. McGee
1897 Primitive Trephining in Peru. *Sixteenth Annual Report, Bureau of American Ethnology.* Washington, D.C.: Smithsonian Institution.
Niles, Blair
1937 *A Journey in Time.* New York: Bobbs-Merrill.
Palma, Ricardo
1949 *Epistolario.* Vols. 1–2. Lima: Editorial Cultura Antartica, S. A. Palma, Ricardo (son)
1908 *La Uta del Perú.* Lima: Imprenta Liberal.
1957 Cirugía, ortopedia y cerámica pre-colombina. *El Comercio*, supplement, May 26, p. 2. Lima.
Rodríguez S., Fidel
1930 Siguen contra Tello. *Libertad*, September 10, p. 4. Lima.
Roosevelt, Cornelius Van S.
1935 Ancient Civilizations of the Santa Valley and Chavin. *Geographical Review* 25:21–42.
Rowe, John H.
1954 Max Uhle: 1856–1944: A Memoir of the Father of Peruvian Archaeology. *University of California Publications in American Archaeology and Ethnology* 46. Berkeley: University of California Press.
1959 Cuadro cronológico de exploraciones y descubrimientos en la arqueología peruana, 1863–1955. *Arqueológicas* 4:1–17. Lima.
1962 Alfred Louis Kroeber, 1876–1960. *American Antiquity* 27:397–515.
Santisteban Tello, Oscar
1956 *La Obra Docente y Doctrinaria de Julio C. Tello.* Lima.
Seegers, Scott
1950 Rebeca and the Mummy. *Americas* 2:6–10, 40–41.
Sivirichi, Atilio
1930 *Prehistoria Peruana.* Editorial "La Revista" de Carlos Vasquez Lapere. Lima.
1933a El Museo Arqueológico Americano del Cuzco. *El Comercio*, August 15, p. 2. Lima.
1933b Los descubrimientos arqueológicos de Nepeña. *El Comercio*, afternoon edition, October 4, p. 1. Lima.
1934 Las excavaciones arqueológicas en el Perú. *El Comercio*, April 6, p. 10. Lima.
Stewart, Watt, and Harold F. Peterson
1942 *Builders of Latin America.* New York: Harper and Brothers.

Strong, William Duncan
1943 Cross Sections of New World Prehistory: A Brief Report on the Work of the Institute of Andean Research, 1941–1942. *Smithsonian Miscellaneous Collections* 104(2): 1–46.
1948 Julio C. Tello, compañero y guía. *Revista del Museo Nacional de Antropología y Arqueología* 2(1): 55–57. Lima.
Tauro, Alberto
1966 *Diccionario Enciclopédico del Perú*. Editorial Juan Mejía Baca. Lima.
Tealdo, Alfonso
1942 Julio C. Tello. *Turismo*, May, pp. 8–9. Lima.
Tello, Julio C.
1912 Prehistoric Trephining among the Yauyos of Peru. *Proceedings of the XVIII International Congress of Americanists*, pp. 75–83. London.
1913a *Arawak: Fragmento de linguístca indígena sud americana*. Lima.
1913b La ciencia antropológica en el Perú. *La Prensa*, March 23, pp. 1–2. Lima.
1914a Las supuestas maravillas del Valle de Rimac. *La Crónica*, December 19, pp. 12–13. Lima.
1914b Las antiguas riquezas del Valle de Lima. *La Crónica*, December 30, p. 5. Lima.
1915 El curioso final de una polémica arqueológica. *La Crónica*, January 15, p. 13. Lima.
1917 Los antiguos cementerios del Valle de Nasca. *Proceedings of the Second Pan American Scientific Congress*, sec. 1, vol. 1, pp. 283–291. Washington, D.C.
1918 El uso de las cabezas humanas artificialmente mumificadas y su representación en el antiguo arte peruano. *Revista Universitaria*, vol. 1, part 2, pp. 478–533. Lima.
1921 *Introducción a la Historia Antigua del Perú*. Editorial Euforión, Lima.
1928a La verdad de lo ocurrido en el Museo de Arqueología Peruana: Una carta del director Dr. Julio C. Tello. *El Tiempo*, May 14, p. 2. Lima.
1928b Campo neutral: Las acusaciones de don Victor Larco Herrera a don Julio C. Tello. *La Prensa*, May 18, p. 9. Lima.
1929 Memoria del Director del Museo de Arqueología. *Revista Universitaria* 23(1): 319–322. Lima.
1930a Memoria del Director del Museo de Arqueología. *Revista Universitaria* 24(2): 357–360. Lima.
1930b Andean civilization: Some problems of Peruvian archaeology. *Proceedings of the XXIII International Congress of Americanists*, pp. 259–290. New York.
1930c Intereses Generales: Una carta del Director del Museo de Arqueología Peruana. *El Comercio*, September 16, p. 15. Lima.
1934a El oro en el antiguo Perú. *El Comercio*, January 1, p. 9. Lima.
1934b Las excavaciones arqueológicas en el Departamento del Cuzco. *El Comercio*, March 12, p. 10, and March 13, pp. 2–3. Lima.
1935 Sobre la desaparación de objetos arqueológicos. *El Comercio*, September 1, p. 16. Lima.

1937 Los trabajos arqueológicos en el Departamento de Lambayeque. *El Comercio*, January 29, p. 5, January 30, p. 10, and January 31, p. 7. Lima.

1941 El Museo de Antropología e Instituto de Investigaciones Antropológicas. *Chaski* 1(3): 72–78. Lima.

1942a Sobre el descubrimiento de la cultura Chavín del Perú. *Actas del XXVII Congreso Internacional de Americanistas*, first session, vol. 1, pp. 231–252. Mexico City.

1942b Origen y desarrollo de las civilizaciones prehistóricas andinas. *Actas del XXVII Congreso Internacional de Americanistas*, second session, vol. 1, pp. 589–720. Lima.

1946 Los tesoros arqueológicos de Ancón. *El Comercio*, March 17, p. 3. Lima.

1959 *Paracas: Primera parte*. Empresa Gráfica T. Scheuch, S.A. Lima.

1960 *Chavín. Cultura matriz de la civilización andina: Primera parte*. Lima: Universidad Nacional Mayor de San Marcos.

1975–1976 Del epistolario de Riva-Agüero. *Arqueología PUC* 17–18:3–6. Lima.

Tello, Julio C., and Toribio Mejía Xesspe

1967 Historia de los museos nacionales del Perú, 1822–1946. *Arqueológicas* 10. Lima.

Tello, Julio C., and Próspero Miranda

1923 Wallallo: Ceremonias gentílicas realizadas en la región cis andina del Perú central (Distrito arqueológico de Casta). *Inca* 1(2): 475–549. Lima.

Urteaga, Horacio H.

1914a *El Perú: Bocetos Históricos. Estudios arqueológicos, tradicionales e histórico-críticos*. Lima: Casa Editora E. Rosay.

1914b Las antiguas riquezas del Valle del Rimac. *La Crónica*, December 14. Lima.

1914c Las antiguas riquezas del Valle del Rimac: Contestación al Doctor Tello. *La Crónica*, December 20, pp. 13–14. Lima.

1915a Las antiguas riquezas del Valle del Rimac: Contestando al Dr. Tello. *La Crónica*, January 7, pp. 12–13. Lima.

1915b Una réplica necesaria. *La Crónica*, January 20, p. 11. Lima.

Valcárcel, Luís E.

1933a En el IV Centenario del Cuzco. *El Comercio*, September 14, p. 2. Lima.

1933b La restauración de los monumentos arqueológicos. *El Comercio*, September 16, p. 3. Lima.

1933c Sobre cuestiones arqueológicas. *El Comercio*, October 29, p. 2. Lima.

1981 *Memorias*. Lima: Instituto de Estudios Peruanos.

Vara Cadillo, N. Saturino

1953 Indios Eminentes del Perú. Barranca y Tello: Como y donde los conocimos. *Folklore* 1:1024. Lima.

Verrill, A. Hyatt

1929 La cuestión de los primeros chinos llegados al Perú. *El Comercio*, May 23, pp. 6, 8. Lima.

Weiss, Pedro, Jorge Basadre, and Toribio Mejía Xesspe

1977 Testimonios. *Runa* 3:6–9. Lima.

Werlich, David P.

1978 *Peru: A Short History*. Carbondale: Southern Illinois University Press.

West, Robert C., ed.

1982 *Andean Reflections: Letters from Carl O. Sauer While on a South American Trip under a Grant from the Rockefeller Foundation, 1942*. Boulder, Colo.: Westview Press.

Willey, Gordon R.

1988 *Portraits in American Archaeology: Remembrances of Some Distinguished Americanists*. Albuquerque: University of New Mexico Press.

Yacovleff, Eugenio

1933 Sobre cuestiones arqueológicas. *El Comercio*, October 28, p. 6. Lima.

Yacovleff, Eugenio, and Jorge C. Muelle

1932 Una exploración en Cerro Colorado: Informe y observaciones. *Revista del Museo Nacional* 1(2): 31–59. Lima.

CHAPTER TWO

# The International Relevance of Julio C. Tello

JOHN V. MURRA

**IN 1982 OUR PERUVIAN COLLEAGUES** celebrated the centennial of Julio C. Tello's birth. Even during his lifetime, his contributions were widely appreciated both in his native country and abroad. If we check the two biographical notes published soon after his death (Mejía 1948; Lothrop 1948), we find that Tello's ideas about the cultural development of Andean societies received early professional attention as well as popular acclaim. Few prophets have enjoyed such echo in their own land.

The Peabody Museum of Archaeology and Anthropology at Harvard University, where the recently graduated Tello traveled to study in 1909, was, in those days, a research rather than a teaching institution, and a rather autonomous part of Harvard University. Directed by Frederic Ward Putnam, the Peabody Museum was then and, in some ways, still is a neighbor and ally of disciplines like botany and geology. Such courses as were offered took place in the laboratory and were attended by young men initially trained in biology with clinical experience, maybe even fieldwork. The importance highlander Julio C. Tello attributed to the geographic dimension in explaining the achievements of Andean people was thus confirmed in Cambridge.

There was another influence that affected the new graduate student. Putnam taught anthropology, but he was also a great organizer of institutions. Putnam not only encouraged anthropology at his own institution but also helped organize museums with a natural history emphasis at Chicago, New York, and Berkeley, and he always made place for anthropology. In 1909 there were only three postgraduate departments and around ten professionals in the field. To train researchers in the new discipline, he imported specialists from abroad. In his youth, Putnam had collaborated with Lewis Henry Morgan; now he sponsored the immigration to the United States of researchers like Franz Boas and Ales Hrdlicka, whom he protected and advised during the difficult decades when there was no tradition of graduate work.

The organization of natural history that Tello found at Harvard when he arrived strengthened and validated the one he already shared from his medical training at San Marcos University in Lima. There, he had not only helped José Sebastián Barranca collect archaeological materials but also sought out wild and cultivated plants, and vocabularies of Kauki, a language then still spoken in the village of Tupe. In Europe, archaeology, linguistics, and ethnology had each developed as separate inquiries, each part of a different faculty. In contrast, at the Harvard Peabody Museum, Tello saw firsthand a natural history endeavor that considered these different inquiries as facets of a single strategy for better understanding ancient American civilization. The anthropological tasks, apparently so different one from the other, owed their convergence in the Harvard Peabody Museum and in Peru to the fact that they were part of a single strategy for better understanding the pre-Columbian world. In the ceremonies organized on the occasion of the Tello centenary, archaeology received the lion's share of the participants' attention. However, we should recall that all of the many journals Tello edited during his lifetime (*Inca*, *Chaski*, *Wira-Kocha*, and so forth) also published articles on folklore, linguistics, and history, and they were written not only by Tello but also by his collaborators.

The thesis that Tello defended at Harvard to obtain his master's in anthropology dealt with the trephination of the skulls from Huarochirí, a topic that connected his medical thesis at Lima with museum experience (fig. 2.1). Tello was made an honorary conservator at the Harvard Peabody Museum, a position he enjoyed for the rest of his life. In his last will and testament, Tello recalled the foreign universities that had welcomed him, and in the Harvard Peabody Museum collections, we still find the skulls that Tello donated.

While in Cambridge, Tello met a whole generation of scholars, primarily archaeologists, who would later undertake the study of various regions of the New World, and especially Mesoamericanists. Here I will mention only Samuel K. Lothrop, who accompanied Tello in some of his excavations at Paracas and who, after Tello's

*2.1. Tello receiving his master's degree in anthropology from Harvard University in 1911. Courtesy of the Museo Nacional de Antropología, Arqueología e Historia.*

death in 1947, searched for ways of financing the publication of his unpublished work (Lothrop 1953).

Those of us who, in recent years, have attended the meetings of the International Congress of Americanists (ICA) have frequently been left with the impression that we were taking part in a giant fair. With many of those present attending as observers (or tourists), it is often difficult to follow an argument as it is debated. Moreover, the papers read at these meetings are affected. This situation contrasts with the Americanist meetings a century ago. These were only attended by a few dozen scholars, arriving at Bilbao or New Orleans after weeks at sea and years of saving to finance the trip. Such gatherings involved leaves of absence, expenditure of personal savings, and months of preparation. Beginning at London in 1912 (where he met his wife, Olive Mabel Cheesman) and later at Buenos Aires and Rome, Tello prepared carefully for his participation in the ICA. At these meetings, he kept colleagues on other continents informed of his ideas on the formative role of Chavín civilization, the mantles from Paracas, or the new sequence of Andean cultures that emerged from his research (see chapters 7, 8, 10, 13 this volume).

Tello's international participation culminated at the Twenty-seventh ICA, which convened in 1939 at Lima just as the Second World War was looming. Among the participants were Jacinto Jijón y Caamaño and Max Uhle. The report that Tello presented to this gathering was a lengthy account summarizing all the author had learned in the thirty years since Harvard. It deserves a new, annotated edition.

I can still recall how we missed Tello at the Twenty-eighth ICA when it gathered at New York in 1947. For those trying to understand the Andean world, Tello's absence meant that the only Andean voice heard at the Museum of Natural History was that of Jacinto Jijón y Caamaño, who bemoaned the inability to debate his ideas with the "*sabio de Huarochirí*."

Tello's insistence on the role of Chavín as the Andean *cultura matriz* (cultural matrix) is familiar to many scholars. Less well known is Tello's insistence on attributing such generative roles to cultures in Mesoamerica as well. At a round table on Mesoamerica gathered at Tuxtla Gutierrez, one no longer talked of the Olmec as merely a notable achievement, but now a fundamental manifestation that linked the torrid zones of Veracruz and Tabasco with Toltec highlands. The early enthusiasts of things Olmec and Toltec, people like Miguel Covarrubias and Piña Chan, were familiar with and influenced by Tello's hypotheses.

The role of a *cultura matriz* and the possible contacts between the Olmec and Chavín were already debated in Tello's lifetime and continue to be debated (Henderson 1979). For example, during the symposium on Andean Mesoamerican contacts gathered at Salinas (Ecuador) in 1971, as at the comparative seminar organized by Angel Palerm in Mexico City in 1972, the participants from the Andean republics were able to evaluate new formulations of such comparative hypotheses.

During the years of the Great Depression of the 1930s, when research grants were difficult to obtain, Tello returned to the United States. In addition to visiting his alma mater, the Harvard Peabody Museum, he traveled throughout much of the country. There were now more museums and anthropology departments in the United

States than earlier; in fact, they were three times as common as in 1909. Beyond announcing his new discoveries, Tello argued for the coordination of several approaches employed in Americanist research.

When he returned to Lima, Tello wrote in his report to Solf y Muro, the director of San Marcos University:

> The archaeology chair in our universities includes few students. Those who study this career do it for mere ornament or supplement of their humanist culture and not for practical application. . . . They do not acquire the indispensable practical preliminary training which would allow them to follow a professional archaeological career. . . . All this adds to the prevailing empiricism in both study and research and leads to indifference about the protection and conservation of archaeological remains. . . .
>
> The experience I have accumulated in thirty years of archaeological work in Peru and abroad leads me to the conviction that if they do not count with scientifically trained personnel and the economic support they require . . . the Museum and the teaching opportunities . . . cannot fulfill efficiently their high duty to *preserve*, *research* and *teach* the facts and the events of antiquity, which form the intellectual heirloom of the Nation.

Further in the same memorandum, Tello states:

> In my recent trip to the United States and in fulfillment of the mission with which I was entrusted by the University to acquaint myself with the prevailing organization of archaeological knowledge and teaching in that country, I solicited the collaboration and advice of people in charge of archaeological and anthropological institutions. . . .
>
> After visiting the main universities and museums and after exchanging ideas with their staffs about the desirability of joining our efforts to advance americanist studies. . . . [I called on them] to attend a meeting. This took place on the 13th of October of last year [1936] at the American Museum of Natural History in New York. To those gathered there I suggested a plan to create an *Institute of Andean Research* whose aim would be to encourage, direct and coordinate research about the Andean region through archaeology, ethnology, physical anthropology and other related matters. By "Andean region" we understood the vast area of Tawantinsuyu.

Among the organizers with Andean experience were Alfred L. Kroeber, who had collaborated with Tello in 1926 on the coastal cultures of Peru; Tello's old friend Samuel K. Lothrop; and young Wendell C. Bennett, the secretary of the newly organized institute, whose research in Cañari territory, at Chavín, and at Tiahuanaco is still widely cited today.

One of the earliest activities of the recently created institute was to grant a subsidy to Tello of $2,000 for an expedition that, according to Tello, was "designed to explore the eastern slopes of the Andes, the valleys of the upper Marañon and the Huallaga, of the Mantaro and the Apurimac, regions with high archaeological possibilities where I have located important traces of very old cultures that according to my impressions are the original stalks from which later cultures on both highland and the coast grew."

In 1941 the opportunity arose to expand the activities of the Institute of Andean Research (IAR) as a result of new subsidies coming from funds devoted to the struggle against nazism; their administrator was Nelson Rockefeller. The institute recruited new members: Duncan Strong, a student of Alfred Kroeber, who taught at Columbia; Junius Bird, a curator at the American Museum of Natural History; and Alfred Kidder II, a professor at Harvard who did research at Pukara. The organizers formulated twelve projects, not all of them in the Andes. Some were meant for Mesoamerica and parts of the Caribbean. Project 8, jointly directed by Tello and Lothrop, differed from all others. Rather than proposing new excavations, it aimed to consolidate work done some fifteen years earlier at Paracas. Both Tello and his collaborators were aware that Tello's involvement in the editing of many journals and the creation of museums had interfered with the publication of archaeological monographs describing these excavations at Paracas and the subsequent laboratory analyses of the recovered materials.

In that wartime context, a contract for publications describing the excavations at Paracas was signed by Tello and Lothrop in the name of the IAR. The first volume was meant to illustrate the archaeological materials from Paracas, while the second was to detail the archaeological findings at Cavernas and Necropolis. A third volume was supposed to analyze the cultural relations between the materials at Paracas and later civilizations of the coast and highlands. But at the time of Tello's death in 1947, the printers had received only seventeen pages of text to go with the plates for volume 1. It was not until 1959 that it became possible to publish the first volume, edited by the subdirector of the National Museum of Anthropology and Archeology, Toribio

Mejía Xesspe. Eventually, volume 2, some 500 pages in length, was published jointly by the San Marcos University and the IAR.

It seems worthwhile to mention here that barely four days before his death in 1947, Tello included the following in his last will and testament:

> It is in the public domain that I have devoted most of my life to the study of the native cultures of Peru. . . . I have contributed, using all my faculties to the clarification and the dating of the antiquity and content of our autochthonous civilizations. I am aware that I have achieved only a minimal part of my aspirations. I hope that others will complete them. Meanwhile . . . I believe that I have rendered well-deserved credit to the creative genius of the Peruvian native, the basis of our nationality. Despite my efforts, it has not been possible to analyze and study in a definitive way the immense quantities of materials discovered and accumulated during many years of efforts. The public is aware of only a small part of these.
>
> Fortunately, my closest collaborators, particularly Dr. Rebeca Carrión Cachot and Mr. Toribio Mejía Xesspe, are familiar with them in all of their fullness and content, with their respective inventories, notes, drawings and explanatory reports in whose preparation they have lent their services with disinterest, ability and loyalty.

The fact that Tello insisted on the autochthonous character of Andean civilization does not mean that he rejected contacts and influences from other parts of the American continent. Tello believed the Pan-American distribution of cotton, maize, and other cultivars indicate that such contacts took place throughout history. However, the Andean complex of crops developed in the crucible of thousands of years of Andean cultural history, a fact that now seems obvious, but grows directly from insights we owe to Tello.

There is a notable absence of chauvinism in the writings that Tello left us and in the journals that he edited for decades. When Max Uhle returned to Peru to attend the 1939 Congress of Americanists, Tello received him like a colleague with whom he differed on professional matters, but whose achievements in the Andean field were beyond doubt. Alberto Tauro of the San Marcos University left us a profile of the German octogenarian who was held in Peru because of the Second World War: "The respectful sympathy with which his works were received and the familiarity with his advances . . . must have seemed a prologue to what his works would achieve. And as he seemed likely to hold on to the outline of his work we noted that he retained his conceptions even if obsolete. Perhaps, he thus forged a splendid isolation" (Tauro 1969:7).

While awaiting his repatriation to Berlin, Uhle took part in the symposia of the Peruvian Society of Archaeology, presided over by Tello and with Luís E. Valcárcel as secretary. In the proceedings published in Tello's journal *Chaski*, we hear the voice of the aged researcher commenting on the papers read.

The tie that bound Tello to Alfred Kroeber was more delicate and subtle than his link to Uhle. Kroeber was one of the very few of Tello's associates who was older. Early in the century, Kroeber had been a protégé of Putnam, who had backed Kroeber's moving to the University of California at Berkeley. There, Kroeber had inherited the Peruvian coastal collections assembled early in the century by Uhle, and he came to know this material well. In 1926 Kroeber joined Tello in Peru and had become familiar with Tello's notions about the archaeology of the Peruvian coast. Ten years later, Kroeber supported Tello's plans for the creation of the IAR, and he accepted the position as the IAR's first president. In 1942 Kroeber traveled to Peru, and on this occasion he spent much of his time in Tello's company. His report, *Peruvian Archaeology in 1942*, published two years later, still deserves translation into Spanish. At the time, monographic materials dealing with the Andes were few, and Kroeber found himself in a situation where he was attracted by the solutions that Tello offered, while remaining skeptical since, in 1942, it was still impossible to verify many of the solutions offered.

Kroeber says:

> The real developer of the concept of a Chavín culture, stratum, or influence is Tello, who visited the site on his first major expedition and revisited it several times, as well as exploring to the north, west and south. It is due to his energy that practically all the discovered major Chavín sculptures have been made accessible in Lima either in the original or in casts. Tello has long proclaimed the primordiality of Chavín or as he sometimes called it, Andean Archaic. . . .
>
> In the main, he has proved his point: there was an early culture which we can legitimately call Chavín because its highest aesthetic—and possibly religious—expression is represented at Chavín. Irrespective of where and how this culture originated, its influence was widespread, at any rate in northern and central Peru. While its precise place in time is not quite assured, all indications are that it was

early: pre-Tihuanaco, almost certainly before Mochica and Nazca, which were formerly reckoned as the first known cultures. All this is due to Tello: the concept is his, and most of the actual discoveries.

> His position is in some ways like that of Schliemann in Near Eastern archaeology. Like Schliemann, Tello is endowed with extraordinary energy, with intuitional insight, with the gift of making startling finds and weaving them into constructive syntheses. Like Schliemann, he uses the evidence which seems significant to him; and the basis of choice is by standards which he does not define, and which sometimes remain baffling to others. In a large sense, his results are both novel and right. In detail, his constructs fail to convince at some points, because he is impatient with detailed presentation. The rest of us will apparently have to do the analysis ourselves, and remarshal his evidence as we get hold of it. Here is the point at which greater rapport is possible. If he would make more of his data accessible in print, in scientific publication with proper illustrations, that large portion of his views which will receive ultimate acceptance would undoubtedly be accepted at once, instead of the whole fused mass of his interpretations continuing to be received with hesitation. Similarly, the Marañón culture now forms part of the Tello system. But how can the corps of archaeology, with the best will in the world, accept this system and operate with it, as long as it does not know what the Marañón culture is?
>
> In short, if Tello could temporarily forego insistence on his system and present his primary data more fully, he probably would be surprised at the alacrity with which much of his system would be generally adopted. (Kroeber 1944:82, 92–93)

Fortunately, the "primary materials" Kroeber requested gradually have been published after 1947. The Publishing Commission, presided over by Luís E. Valcárcel, benefited from the devoted work of the San Marcos professor Toribio Mejía Xesspe. Over a period of twenty-five years, this intimate collaborator of Tello contributed four monographs on Tello's research for publication. First came *Arqueología del Valle de Casma* (1956) while Kroeber was still alive. We have not had access to the personal archives of the great Berkeley Americanist, and we don't know if the materials selected for publication by Mejía satisfied Kroeber. In 1959 a second Tello monograph was printed: the second volume of *Paracas* already mentioned. In 1960 the publishing committee of the IAR sponsored the publication of the Chavín materials, a much-awaited work both within and outside of Peru that brings together materials from several campaigns in the field. Together with an article published in *American Antiquity* in 1943 (Tello 1943), and reprinted in this volume, it is likely to be the last word on Tello's interpretations on Chavín. Finally, in 1979 Mejía concluded the preparation of the second volume of *Paracas*, a detailed study utilizing Tello's notebooks of the burials, which had been found in Cavernas and Necropolis (1925–1931). Its publication was planned for 1980, the date of Tello's centenary. For various reasons, the publication was delayed and the work appeared only on April 15, 1982, sponsored by San Marcos University and the IAR. This was a final collaboration between the scholar from Huarochirí and the IAR.

In recent years, thanks to the efforts of Ruth Shady Solís, director of the Museo Arqueológico at San Marcos University and others, the voluminous and largely unpublished Tello Archive has been reorganized and inventoried. A project to publish this vast corpus of material has already resulted in the appearance of two volumes, *Arqueología del Valle de Lima* (1999) and *Arqueología del Valle de Asia: Huaca Malena* (2001). Thus, in the six decades since his death, Tello's wish to make the full range of his pioneering research available to the world is well along the way to becoming a reality.

Revised version of "La dimensión internacional de la obra de Julio C. Tello," *Histórica* 6(1) (1982): 53–63, Lima.

## REFERENCES CITED

Henderson, John S.

1979 *Atopulo, Guerrero, and the Olmec Horizons in MesoAmerica*. Yale University Publications in Anthropology, Vol. 77. New Haven, Conn.

Kroeber, Alfred L.

1944 *Peruvian Archaeology in 1942*. New York: Viking Fund.

Lothrop, Samuel K.

1948 Julio C. Tello, 1880–1947. *American Antiquity* 14:50–56.

1953 Un recuerdo del Dr. Julio C. Tello y Paracas. *Revista del Museo de Arqueología* 2. Lima.

Mejía Xesspe, Toribio

1948 Apuntes biográficos sobre el Dr. Julio C. Tello. *Revista del Museo de Arqueología* 1(2). Lima.

Tauro, Alberto

1969 Nota preliminaria. In *Estudios sobre historia incaica*, by Max Uhle, pp. 29–69. Lima: Universidad Nacional Mayor de San Marcos.

Tello, Julio C.

1943 Discovery of the Chavín Culture in Peru. *American Antiquity* 9:135–166.

CHAPTER THREE

# The Intellectual Legacy of Julio C. Tello

RICHARD L. BURGER

**JOHN MURRA** (chapter 2, this volume) has observed that few prophets have found so much acclaim in their own lands as Julio Cesar Tello. While this statement smacks of hyperbole, it is, in truth, an understatement. Virtually no person in Peru who has attended school, even at an elementary level, is unaware of Tello or his contributions to the nation (fig. 3.1). Throughout Peru, hundreds, perhaps even thousands, of places are named for him, and these include streets, squatter settlements (*pueblos jóvenes*), day-care centers, technical institutes, site museums, agricultural cooperatives, and towns. In a recent updating of Guaman Poma's 1614 Nueva Crónica del Perú, historian Pablo Macera profiled the fourteen crucial individuals of the Peruvian world (*personajes del mundo Peruano*) who shaped Peru during the twentieth century. Not surprisingly, Tello was featured among them, along with Abimael Guzmán, leader of the Sendero Luminoso revolutionary movement, and Sarita Colonia, a mystical figure worshipped by Peru's poor for the miracles she is said to work (Macera and Forns 2000).

What other archaeologist besides Julio C. Tello has ever achieved such prominence in his or her homeland? Not even historic figures such as Heinrich Schliemann, Arthur Evans, or Hiram Bingham III achieved comparable renown, despite their spectacular and well-publicized discoveries. In spite of his special place in Peruvian culture, Tello has never received the kind of international recognition accorded to many other influential archaeologists. One looks for Tello's name in vain, for example, in Bruce Trigger's *A History of Archaeological*

*3.1. Tello standing in front of the New Temple of Chavín de Huantar in 1940. Courtesy of the Museo Nacional de Antropología, Arqueología e Historia.*

*Thought* (1989), even though the author is explicitly committed to considering archaeological traditions outside the United States. Even during Tello's lifetime, his influence on archaeological thought within the borders of Peru was quite different than outside of it, and this continues to be the case. I will explore the reasons for this pattern, and consider the enduring impact of Tello's work and thought in modern archaeology, both within and beyond Peru.

## Tello as Symbol and Paradigm

Tello's archaeological contributions and his personal life were inseparable, and much of his impact stemmed from the way he embodied those traits in ancient Peru, which he sought to vindicate through his research. In this sense, he became both a symbol of Peru's glorious past and a paradigm of the exemplary and enduring indigenous qualities that produced those achievements. The powerful melding of personal life and professional accomplishment achieved by Julio Tello, Mohandas Gandhi, Albert Einstein, or Bob Marley resulted in these individuals becoming the embodiment of something that transcends the specifics of a particular discovery, political victory, new concept, or musical composition.

For most Peruvians, Tello's principal achievement was demonstrating that ancient Peruvian civilization was the product of local or autochthonous development rather than the result of influence from Central America or Asia, as earlier scholars such as Max Uhle had sustained (Moore 1977). The latter position consciously or unconsciously devalued the artistic and technological accomplishments of Peru's prehispanic cultures, reducing them to mere reflections or byproducts of foreign cultures. For Tello, the prehispanic ruins and associated objects were eloquent testimony to the genius of the indigenous Peruvian people.

The magnificence of these constructions and artifacts was as relevant to understanding the potential for the future as it was for appreciating the glories of the past. Tello's championing of the autochthonous position was linked to his critique of Peru's modern problems, which he believed began with the Spanish Conquest and deepened with the continuing oppression of indigenous peoples during the ensuing four centuries. Thus, for Tello, the prehispanic past offered practical solutions as well as academic insights. As he wrote in "Collisions of Two Civilizations" (chapter 6, this volume), "Our present Hispanic-Peruvian civilization cannot stand except on an indigenous pedestal. . . . The present generation is obligated to revive the past and retrieve everything that can be glorified." The fact that Tello was himself a native Quechua speaker, a self-identified "indio" from Huarochirí, gave his findings a salience they would have otherwise lacked. That Tello was disproving the prevailing views of foreigners such as Max Uhle or members of the Hispanicized coastal elites such as Emilio Gutiérrez de Quintanilla (Valcárcel 1981) only added to the heroic character of his academic struggle.

It should be emphasized that it was Tello who identified the issue of autochthonism as the central issue that Peruvian archaeology should be addressing (see chapter 13, this volume), and that he explicitly made the link between this vision of the past and the present situation in Peru. This framing of the archaeological enterprise went directly against the currents of his day, which focused on chronological sequences and maintained that archaeology belonged to a world of neutral scholarship distinct from contemporary issues. The political agenda of Tello's work must be placed within the context of Peru during the early twentieth century, a time when the Peruvian Congress debated the "Indian problem," and solutions such as the prohibition of reproduction by Indians and the importation of superior races from western Europe were seriously discussed as possible solutions (Lumbreras 1977). Archaeologist Rogger Ravines (1977:16) has written: "In Peru it would be difficult to find a man like Tello who transmits to us more directly a sentiment of nationalism and country. His voice, with its mixture of Indian pride, nationalist passion and scientific knowledge, speaks with an austere depth."

Tello, unwilling to limit his efforts for social change to the world of academia, was elected to Peru's Congress from his highland community and served there for eleven years. During his election campaign, he stated, "Today we begin a campaign against the tyranny of humiliation, of hypocrisy, of distrust and enslavement." Tello often spoke of how the character of indigenous people had degenerated under the heavy weight of Spanish tyranny and ignorance. He worked in the Congress for improved elementary education in rural areas, the elimination of alcoholism and addiction to coca, and the improvement of the highway system in order to reduce the economic and cultural isolation of indigenous communities. Tello even founded the Peruvian Society for the Progress of Society.

These formal political activities were dwarfed, however, by his organizational efforts within the field of archaeology (Mejía 1967; Tello and Mejía 1967). During his career, he founded three different museums

(Museo de Arqueología en la Universidad Nacional Mayor de San Marcos, Museo de Arqueología Peruana, and Museo de Antropología de Pueblo Libre), initiated the publication of three different journals (*Inca*, *Wira-Kocha*, and *Chaski*), and created the legal basis for the protection of archaeological academic monuments (Law No. 6634, June 13, 1929).

In all of these activities, Tello's intended audience extended well beyond that of his academic colleagues, and he sought to reach the broader Peruvian public. In order to do this, he gave countless public lectures and published widely in the daily newspapers in the capital and the provinces. In fact, several of his most important discoveries only appeared in newspapers, and this led to frequent criticism in academic circles outside Latin America. Tello's report on the ruins of Wari (chapter 12, this volume), which appeared in the daily morning newspaper *El Perú*, is an example of these publications.

In Tello's efforts to disseminate his vision of the Peruvian past, he explicitly emphasized his personal motivation for studying his nation's past. For example, he attributed his decision to enter anthropology to a skull collected in his ancestral home of Huarochirí. According to Mejía (1967:viii), Tello declared: "The first time I had in my hands the skull of an Inca mummy to study, I felt a profound emotion. That skull, honored by the centuries, connected with my heart and made me feel the message of the race whose blood ran through my veins. From that moment I became an anthropologist." By insisting on this personal link, and on the relevance of archaeology to individual and national identity, Tello reconceptualized the role of archaeology in Peru, and placed it at the core of nation building.

Part of Tello's mystique was his conviction that archaeology was an almost sacred vocation rather than a simple career or a profession. This was reflected in all aspects of Tello's daily life. For example, it was his custom to schedule his university classes at 7:00 A.M. His extensive explorations on horseback through poorly known highland areas, sometimes during torrential rains, began each day at 4:00 A.M. and continued seven days a week (Mejía 1977; Weiss 1977). Tello's modest, almost monastic, lifestyle and his commitment to hard work echoed the Spartan ethos of the Incas (fig. 3.2). His reputation for uncompromising resistance to his opponents likewise resonated with the ethnic stereotype of the stubborn Indian. Tello played upon these impressions, describing himself as "El Indio Tello" (the Indian Tello), and, despite his advanced training at San Marcos, Harvard, Berlin, London, and Paris, he sometimes joked, "I am not a professor nor writer, I

*3.2. Tello in Wiñay Wayna with Genaro Farfan, Julio Espejo, Manuel Chavez Ballon, Luis Ccosi Salas, and Pedro Rojas Ponce, Cuzco, in 1942. Courtesy of the Museo Nacional de Antropología, Arqueología e Historia.*

am only a man of the fields, a *huaquero* (a grave robber)" (Valcárcel 1981:282). Despite these poses, Tello is probably best described as a public intellectual who carefully shaped his personal image to reinforce the message of his research and political agenda.

While Tello must be considered the most successful indigenous archaeologist to have emerged in the Americas, his intellectual basis and personal convictions differ from those common today among the Native American community. Trained first in medicine, Tello was first and foremost a scientist, and he saw the scientific method as a tool to reveal the truth about Peru's past (fig. 3.3). The truth, he was convinced, would revindicate and revalorize the genius of his ancestors. Only science would permit him to overturn the inaccurate and prejudicial preconceptions about antiquity that had been disseminated by Peru's nonindigenous dominant class. Thus Tello viewed science and indigenous peoples as natural allies rather than as being incompatible or at odds with each other (fig. 3.4).

*3.3. Tello unwrapping a mummy bundle.*
*Courtesy of the Museo Nacional de Antropología, Arqueología e Historia.*

*3.4. Tello in the field accompanied by American archaeologist William Duncan Strong.*
*Courtesy of the Museo Nacional de Antropología, Arqueología e Historia.*

Tello, although a nationalist, lacked the often associated trait of xenophobia. The reason why can probably be traced to his formative years. While at Harvard, he mastered English thanks to being tutored in the evenings by Roland Dixon (Lothrop 1948:51). In England at the Congress of Americanists in 1912, Tello met and married Olive Mabel Cheesman, an English woman attending London University. He was deeply grateful for the support and education he received from abroad, especially the United States, and Harvard was even mentioned in his last will and testament (Lothrop 1948:51). Given this personal history, it is not surprising that Tello had great respect for and worked closely with foreign scholars.

Tello traveled abroad throughout his career, and for decades he was one of the most prominent figures at the International Congress of Americanists (see chapter 2, this volume). Despite a busy schedule, he took time out from his own research to help foreign scholars such as Alfred Kroeber and Ales Hrdlicka conduct research in Peru. He brought American students such as Donald Collier and Cornelius Roosevelt along with him on his expeditions, and published his work in English in the United States and Europe. Thus Tello, the rural Indian, coexisted in harmony with Tello, the international scientist.

In Peru, where prejudice against indigenous highlanders remains a potent force, even in the twenty-first century, Tello's personal success and nationalist vision remain an inspiration for Peruvians who recognize that social and cultural transformation is as essential as economic change if Peru's future is to be as impressive as its prehispanic past. It is within this specific historic and cultural context that Tello's life and work have served as a symbol and paradigm. Unfortunately, the relevance of this aspect of Tello's legacy becomes increasingly incomprehensible, perhaps even irrelevant, as one moves beyond the Andes.

## Tello's Intellectual Contributions

During his lifetime, Tello scoured the country in search of unknown or poorly understood archaeological sites. Despite the enormous logistical challenges that existed, his explorations covered most of highland and coastal Peru, and even his most severe critics recognized that Tello's knowledge of Peruvian antiquities was unparalleled (Rowe 1947). Nonetheless, many archaeologists, particularly those outside Peru, remained frustrated that Tello tended to focus on the broad issues and general conclusions that were suggested by his work rather than on detailed accounts of the discoveries themselves. His style of presentation, as well as the popular venues he often chose for publication, did not conform to the genre of archaeological scholarship favored by his colleagues in the United States. In one memorable passage, published only four years before his death, Alfred Kroeber (1944:93) stated:

> [Tello's] position is in some ways like that of Schliemann in Near Eastern archaeology. Like Schliemann, Tello is endowed with extraordinary energy, with intuitional insight, with the gift of making startling finds and weaving them into constructive syntheses. Like Schliemann, he uses the evidence which seems significant to him; and the basis of the choice is by standards which he does not define, and which sometimes remain baffling to others. In a large sense, his results are both novel and right. In detail, his constructs fail to convince at some points, because he is impatient with detailed presentation. . . . If he would make more of his data accessible in print, in scientific publication with proper illustrations, that large portion of his views which will receive ultimate acceptance would undoubtedly be accepted at once, instead of the whole fused mass of interpretations continuing to be received with hesitation.

For most archaeologists outside of Peru, including Kroeber, Tello's intellectual legacy was and continues to be viewed through the lens of his field investigations and the resulting discoveries. Several of his findings revolutionized the way in which Andean archaeology was conceptualized, and they are so widely accepted today as to seem almost commonplace.

Notable among these was Tello's insistence on the centrality of the highlands in the development of Peruvian civilization. For complex historical reasons, prior to Tello, research by foreign and national investigators had focused almost exclusively along the narrow Pacific coast, despite the fact that the demographic and economic center of gravity had been, until recent times, in the high intermontane valleys to the east. Tello's investigations convincingly demonstrated the cultural richness of highland archaeology, and, drawing upon his investigations at Chavín de Huantar and Wari (Ayacucho), he was able to argue convincingly that the highlands had repeatedly influenced and dominated the cultures of the coast (see chapters 8, 9, and 12, this volume). Tello's substantive research and general vision highlighted the serious problem of coastal bias, and he took steps to rectify it. Nonetheless, it is telling that many of the most important highland sites identified by Tello, such as the major Recuay center of Yayno near Pomabamba (chapter 13, this volume), have only recently begun to be investigated six decades since his death. Despite Tello's efforts, an unjustified emphasis on the coastal cultures remains a weakness in Central Andean archaeology.

Another of the broad insights that pervades Tello's writings was his conviction of the intimate developmental links in prehistory between the tropical forest, the highlands, and the coast. In colonial times following the Spanish Conquest, these interzonal interactions became increasingly attenuated as populations declined, rural zones were abandoned, and focus shifted toward maritime trade with and tribute to the Iberian Peninsula. Tello's work demonstrated that beginning in very early times, there were important linkages across these radically different environments. Moreover, Tello prophetically signaled the crucial role of these ties in the origins of agriculture and in the emergence of Peru's earliest civilization. His explorations and excavations led him to emphasize the importance of the steep eastern slopes of the Andes, largely covered with cloud forests, which provided a bridge between the resources of the Amazonian drainage and the high Andean pasturelands and valleys. Tello's 1919 explorations along the Marañon and his later excavations at the site of Kotosh in the Huallaga Valley dispelled initial skepticism about what was, at the time, a very radical reformulation of these interzonal relationships (see chapter 8, this volume). Similarly, in his writings, Tello was comfortable drawing upon tropical forest ethnography and mythology in order to help explicate cultural patterns found at archaeological sites in the Peruvian highlands and coast (chapters 9 and 11, this volume). He did this consciously out of a conviction that the cultures of these very different macrogeographic zones shared a common past.

A third major conclusion stemming from Tello's fieldwork, now widely accepted, is that civilization in the Central Andes is much older than was believed by Tello's contemporaries, scholars such as Uhle, Muelle, Bennett, and Kroeber. Before Tello, scholars considered that Peruvian civilization began with what is now called the Early Intermediate Period or the Regional Developmental Period (ca. 100 B.C.–A.D. 600) with cultures such as Moche (or proto-Chimú). Tello argued that a civilization existed before these, and that it could be traced back to perhaps 1,000 B.C. Tello hypothesized that this early civilization crystallized at Chavín de Huantar in the mountains of northern Peru, as a result of cultural stimuli from the eastern lowlands (see chapter 8, this volume). Once fully developed in the Mosna drainage, the influence

*3.5. Tello at the excavation of a stone mortar at Punkurí, Nepeña Valley, in 1933. Courtesy of the Museo Nacional de Antropología, Arqueología e Historia.*

of the highland Chavín civilization subsequently spread north and south to other parts of the highlands and west to the coastal valleys (fig. 3.5). With astounding intuition, Tello correctly suggested that the early remains at Kotosh, located in a cloud shadow on the eastern Andean slopes, might provide insight into the origins of Chavín. In 1960 archaeologists from the University of Tokyo confirmed Tello's hypothesis.

In addition to these general conclusions, Tello made a host of specific discoveries and, in the process, drew attention to many of the most important archaeological sites in the Central Andes (fig. 3.6). Famous sites such as Sechín Alto, Moxeke-Pampa de las Llamas, Cerro Sechín, Cerro Colorado, Kuntur Wasi, Cumbemayo, Kotosh, and Wari were first studied by Tello and his students. Later studies building upon Tello's work at these sites have shaped our current understanding of early Central Andean prehistory. In fact, it is difficult to imagine a synthesis of Peruvian archaeology without a consideration of the sites first popularized by Tello.

As one reviews Tello's writings, including those reprinted in this volume, it is hard not to be impressed by his intuition, not only about the significance of specific sites but also about the outlines of Peru's cultural chronology. Two examples may suffice to convey some idea of

*3.6. Tello during the unearthing of the stone sculptures at Cerro Sechín, Casma Valley, in 1937. Courtesy of the Museo Nacional de Antropología, Arqueología e Historia.*

this. Tello was writing before the introduction of radiocarbon measurements. It was a time when eminent scholars could claim that Chavín was derived from the late Nasca style (Muelle 1937). Tello was not only able to infer that Chavín preceded both Paracas and Nasca but was also able to give an approximate date for it, which was later shown by C14 analyses to be remarkably close to the true age (Burger 1981). Similarly, Tello's estimate for the population of the Inca empire at ten million inhabitants was much closer to modern approximations (Cook 1981) than Kroeber's estimate of three million (Kroeber 1934:Table 6).

Despite Tello's remarkable prescience, he was not infallible. As would be expected, his publications include their share of flawed judgments. For example, in his essay "Wira Kocha" (see excerpt in chapter 9, this volume), Tello relies on archaistic specimens of the Moche culture (figs. 9.8, 9.9), which he presumes to be Chavín (Rowe 1971). Similarly in error, Tello considers the Wari "turquoise" figurines from Pikillaqta as typically Inca, and he argues that the megalithic walls in Cuzco, like those at Sacsahuaman, predate the Incas (chapter 14, this volume).

While Tello occasionally made mistakes, he was willing to correct them when evidence to the contrary became available. This was the case for blackware pottery from the North Coast, which he originally considered as reflecting Chimú influence, but which he later realized was related to influences of the much earlier Chavín cultural tradition (chapter 4, this volume). Similarly, late in his career Tello realized his error in considering the Recuay culture as preceding Chavín within his Andean Archaic stage.

For some scholars, such as Kauffmann Doig (1997) and Ravines (1977), Tello's commitment to viewing archaeology as an objective science rather than a subjective humanistic endeavor is, in itself, an important part of his intellectual legacy. To make this point, Ravines (1977) quotes Tello's 1914 statement in the newspaper *La Crónica*: "The great error of our predecessors has been principally based on the false conception that scientific problems can be resolved by way of philosophical speculations."

Tello attempted to introduce anthropology into Peru, and he believed that the future of archaeology should be in the hands of specialists from this international science. He argued that just as illness required intervention of specialized surgeons, so the problems raised in archaeology required intervention by professionally trained archaeologists. This position would seem self-evident, but considering the well-known investigations carried out by nonprofessisonals such as historians Hiram Bingham III and Luis Valcárcel and, more recently, by explorers such as Gene Savoy and Thor Hyerdahl, Tello's point remains worthy of reiteration.

Nevertheless, the image of Tello as a source of political rather than scientific inspiration dominates many of the posthumous testimonials offered by contemporary scholars. Carlos Williams (1977:13), for example, stated:

> Tello has helped me understand that the study of the past, when executed with the intention that Tello had, can serve to revindicate Andean Man in order to increase his ability to defend himself against the economic oppression and deprecation with which Western culture has treated him. With Tello I have learned to see the contemporary relevance of studies of the Peruvian past as a means to relate the nation to its history, to reaffirm its personality, and to accelerate the processes of economic and cultural independence.

The position that an archaeology inspired by Tello's work can have an impact on contemporary social change is common among Peruvian scholars. In this spirit, Ruth Shady (1997) credits Tello with being the pioneer of "social archaeology," a distinctively Latin American approach that views the main goal of archaeology as enabling us to "better understand and modify reality at the present time in order to take desirable social action in the future." This interpretation of Tello's work, while widespread, is not shared by all Peruvian investigators. Kauffmann Doig (1997), for example, argues that Tello's work placed objectivity and scientific truth above ideology and politics, and he consequently concludes that the politicized "social archaeology," which used archaeology in the name of the class struggle, was, in reality, a betrayal of Tello's legacy.

As in most emotional debates, there is some truth to both sides. However, a close reading of Tello's writings reinforces the image of Tello first and foremost as a man of science. This point is nicely illustrated by an anecdote related by one of Peru's most famous historians, Jorge Basadre (1997:7). In his memoirs, he describes how he, in 1931, asked Tello whether he should devote himself to the political struggle between the APRA Party and the supporters of Sanchez Cerro or, alternatively, go to the United States on a grant from Cornell University to study the organization of libraries there. Despite Tello's involvement in Congress and other political activities, he advised his young friend Basadre to accept the grant because, in the long run, the knowledge he acquired in the United States would be more important for Peru than his activism.

## The "Tello School," Academic Traditions, and Intellectual Continuity

As the first Peruvian to receive formal graduate training in archaeology and as the dominant figure in the teaching of archaeology at the Universidad Nacional Mayor de San Marcos (UNMSM), it is surprising that Tello's intellectual legacy was not passed on primarily through the professionals he trained. During his lifetime, Tello developed a distinctive school of archaeology. It combined active fieldwork (both explorations and excavations); a deep knowledge of contemporary Andean and Amazonian ethnology; a special interest in iconography, mythology, and geography; expertise in physical anthropology; concern for linguistic evidence; and a critically informed interest in historical records. As can be seen from this list, Tello's approach to archaeology was consistent with the four-field concept of anthropology as advocated by Boas and other founders of the discipline in the United States. Its breadth and richness seemed particularly appropriate to Peru, where so much biological, linguistic, and cultural continuity seemed to exist between contemporary indigenous peoples and the nation's prehistoric cultures. Tello's mastery of Quechua, as a result of his childhood in Huarochirí, and his special facility in physical anthropology, as a consequence of his medical training, made this approach particularly compatible with his own talents and inclinations.

In his essay "The Empire of the Incas" (chapter 14, this volume), Tello argues that Peru's prehispanic past can be understood from three sources of evidence: eyewitness accounts from the fall of the Inca empire (Tawantinsuyu); archaeological evidence; and the tradition of living Indians. Perhaps most noteworthy is the prominence in this list not only of archaeology but also of "the tradition of living Indians." In virtually all of Tello's writings, ethnographic observations are prominently featured. His discussion of ancient social organization, for example, drew upon his understanding of *ayllu* organization in the modern Rimac Valley (chapter 14, this volume), while his discussions of prehispanic clothing and ceramics took into account Quechua terminologies and patterns of craft production. Tello's intimate understanding of highland herding, irrigation, and other farming practices led him to emphasize the crucial link between the environment, cultural knowledge, and the success of early Peruvian cultures. In many respects, his focus on environment and subsistence strategies as structuring culture anticipates later archaeological work on the cultural ecology of Andean civilization. At the same time, Tello's ethnographic experiences led him to highlight the profoundly religious nature of Andean culture and the way that these specific beliefs likewise were reflected in the archaeological record. Much of Tello's work is concerned with sacrifice, initiation, the propitiation of nature, shamanism, and other religious activities, and these themes likewise pervade the writings of his students, such as Carrión Cachot.

While Tello mentioned historical research as one of the three sources of information on the prehispanic past, he was far more skeptical about the value of this evidence than many of his contemporaries (chapter 4, this volume). His specification of "eyewitness accounts" rather than the broader category of Spanish chronicles or historical records is significant since many of Tello's colleagues relied heavily on the writings of Garcilaso de la Vega and Bernabé Cobo and other secondhand accounts of the Incas. Tello repeatedly questioned the reliability of Spanish accounts because of their biased perspective and lack of cultural sensitivity. He likewise downplayed the importance of the Incas in the development of Andean civilization and, by extension, diminished the potential importance of a historic record that is unable to shed

*3.7. Tello dressed in a poncho during his travels in the highlands.*
*Courtesy of the Museo Nacional de Antropología, Arqueología e Historia.*

light on those cultures preceding these late interlopers. For Tello, the limited value of the written record left by the Spaniards reinforced the central importance of archaeology and ethnography for understanding Andean civilization. While Tello's competitor, the historian Luis Valcárcel (1981:283), saw his "little confidence in written sources" as one of Tello's most serious limitations, it presaged an approach adopted by many modern anthropological archaeologists, including those working on the Incas (e.g., Morris 1988).

Tello's selection of collaborators put a premium on their loyalty and their willingness to fulfill specific tasks in the field, rather than on their intellectual potential, university training, or independence (fig. 3.7) (Weiss 1977). As a consequence, Tello's students were often drawn from rural areas rather than metropolitan Lima. Many had special talents as artists, photographers, or draftsmen. Eventually, Tello's protégés, such as Toribio Mejía Xesspe, Felix Caycho, Pedro Rojas Ponce, Julio Espejo, Cirilio Huaypaya, and Rebeca Carrión Cachot, found positions in museums rather than universities, and, after Tello's death, they dedicated themselves to maintaining the institutions he had founded. Mejía, in particular, devoted decades to publishing Tello's unedited manuscripts. Others, like Marino Gonzales, spent their lives protecting and investigating archaeological sites on which Tello had focused. Carrión Cachot (1955, 1959) was unusual in publishing numerous original works after Tello's demise. These developed themes that had concerned Tello and employed an approach similar to the one in his 1923 article, "Wira Kocha."

Nonetheless, as Pablo Macera (1977:xlii) noted, during the ten years following Tello's death in 1947, none of these disciples had the power or charisma sufficient to replace him, and, as a consequence, his distinctive school of Peruvian archaeology was dismantled by historians such as Luis Valcárcel. The theoretical vacuum created by this collapse was partially filled by archaeologists from the United States, first brought by the Viru Valley Project in the late 1940s and later by the Fulbright-Hayes Commission in the late 1950s. Indeed, most of the senior Peruvian archaeologists today, such as Luis Lumbreras, Rogger Ravines, Rosa Fung, Ramiro Matos, and Duccio Bonavia, had formative training in American or European projects and were not linked directly to Tello or his students. In the writings of Lumbreras, Fung, and Bonavia, one looks in vain for the kinds of insights drawn from modern ethnography and Quechua terminology that characterized Tello's writings. Also absent from their work is Tello's focus on Andean religion as a central focus of archaeological concern.

At the same time, it would be a mistake to assume that a complete break exists between Tello's school of archaeology and contemporary Peruvian archaeology. One of Tello's students, Manuel Chavez Ballón, did become a professor at the Universidad Nacional San Antonio de Abad in Cuzco. In that capacity, he trained generations of archaeologists from Cuzco, Puno, and Arequipa using an approach similar to the one he had learned from Tello. Moreover, as the preeminent archaeologist working in Cuzco, Chavez Ballón had considerable contact with foreign scholars, such as John Rowe, Richard Schaedel, and Tom Zuidema, who were carrying out research in this zone. Chavez Ballón influenced some of these scholars with the distinctive approach he learned from Tello, and they subsequently passed it on to their own students in the United States.

In some cases, Tello's writings had a powerful impact on scholars who did not work directly with him. Perhaps the best example of this is Donald Lathrap, whose admiration for Tello and his ideas resulted in a research program designed to demonstrate the Amazonian origins of Chavín civilization, an idea that Tello had never fully explored in the field (Lathrap 1971). Lathrap likewise took up Tello's iconographic and cosmological research and elevated it to a new level of analysis (Lathrap 1973, 1985). Although Lathrap had not known Tello, he had studied at the University of California, Berkeley, with Kroeber and the cultural geographer Carl Sauer. Kroeber, of course, was a close friend of Tello, and Sauer had been deeply impressed by Tello during a 1942 visit to Peru. In fact, Sauer (1982:87) wrote: "Tello is a national institution all by himself, and there is more work going on in his museum with a higher class of personnel than I have seen anywhere else. This old Indian is really as good as the tales that are told about him, and if he falls short by some academic standards, I'll still maintain that he is the greatest archaeologist in the New World, and I'll argue the point in detail if someone wishes me to." It is likely that Sauer or Kroeber (or both) exposed Lathrap, still an impressionable undergraduate, to Tello's writings and that this profoundly influenced him the rest of his career.

Lathrap's fascination with Tello's approach to art and cosmology was eventually passed on to his students, most notably Peter Roe (1982). Other American scholars, such as the author, have likewise been influenced by Tello's writings. For example, in my writings I have explored Tello's idea that the Chavín culture provided a civilizational matrix that unified the cultures of the Early Horizon and provided the common basis for later developments (Burger 1988, 1992).

## Tello and Peru's National Patrimony

One of Tello's most significant contributions was his focus on Peru's archaeological heritage as a fragile and nonrenewable resource that required care and protection. In contrast to most foreign scholars, Tello worked long and hard to limit the destruction of archaeological sites by grave robbers and other harmful forces unleashed by modern society. In 1913, two months after his return from postgraduate work in Europe, Tello proposed the creation of the position of the head of the section of anthropology of the National History Museum with the explicit purpose of fighting against the vandalism affecting Peru's archaeological sites. This position was established, and Tello was named as its first leader. Concern with the archaeological patrimony characterized Tello's entire career, and his passion for these issues is expressed in his essay "The Defense of the Archaeological Heritage" (chapter 4). Significantly, his concerns were not limited to the abuses of *huaqueros*, but also extended to those archaeologists whose excavations were more concerned with the search for objects than the contexts in which they were buried.

Tello's preoccupation with issues of national patrimony led him to formulate and promote Law No. 6634, a crucial piece of legislation that declares ruins to be the property of the state and thereby lays the basis for their protection (Fung 1977). By making archaeological sites the property of the state, the law shifted the burden for their protection and conservation from the private sector to governmental authorities. This institutional arrangement, although far from perfect, has had an important role in preventing the destruction of the archaeological record, though recently it has been undermined by new laws with their increased emphasis on the role of property rights and the negative effects of government regulation.

As might be expected, Tello's concern with issues of national patrimony were personal and deeply felt. Jorge Basadre tells an anecdote that well illustrates this point. In 1929 the government of Peru joined in an international exposition in Seville, Spain, sponsored by King Alfonso XIII, and the Peruvian government offered to loan four mummies recovered by Tello from his Paracas excavations. When a request for them was made to the Museo de Arqueología Peruana, Tello refused to turn them over, and they were only made available when an explicit order came from the president of Peru. When Tello related this incident to Basadre, he became so upset that he began to cry (Basadre 1997:2). Whether his tears were out of frustration for the way in which national treasures were manipulated for political gestures, or whether he feared for their loss, or both, cannot be determined with certainty. However, years later, when Basadre visited Spain, he was unable to locate two of the mummies that had been sent against Tello's wishes.

Late in Tello's career (1940–1947), he initiated the excavation, clearing, and restoration of the Mamacona complex at the archaeological site of Pachacamac in the Lurín Valley. This was the first prehispanic building complex in Peru to be reconstructed on a large scale. Tello's plans, tragically interrupted by his death, included the creation of an adjacent site museum (Rowe 1947:292). Tello's activities at Pachacamac reflected his conviction that investigation and conservation must go hand in hand (figs. 3.8, 3.9).

For many years, Peruvian and foreign archaeologists ridiculed restoration projects like that attempted by Tello in the Mamacona complex in favor of less problematic projects of pure research. Some investigators, most notably Arturo Jiménez Borja, in the spirit of Tello's

*3.8. The Mamacona complex at Pachacamac, Lurín Valley, excavated and restored by Tello. Photo: Richard Burger.*

*3.9. Bronze bust honoring Tello on display at the archaeological site of Pachacamac. Photo: Richard Burger.*

initiative, continued insisting that without the restoration of major monuments, the sites could not be preserved against the onslaught of urbanization and other powerful economic interests. Over the last two decades, there has been a gradual realization in Peru that there is truth in this proposition, and numerous projects of large-scale restoration at sites on the coast (Cajamarquilla, Huaca El Brujo, Huaca de la Luna) and the highlands (Cuelap, Tipón, Choqquequirau) have been initiated with funding from the government and from Peruvian corporations, international agencies, and foundations. Tello can be seen as the pioneer of these efforts.

In Peru, Tello's writings remain influential, as evidenced by the outpouring of dedicatory essays that appeared in 1977 and 1997 to commemorate the thirtieth and fiftieth anniversaries, respectively, of his death. Yet in reading these testimonials, it becomes clear that there is little consensus about what is valuable in Tello's work, above and beyond the nationalist message of autochthonism discussed earlier. Some Peruvian archaeologists, most notably Daniel Morales, are trying to rejuvenate Tello's research program through new investigations of Formative sites in the tropical forest and adjacent highlands (Morales 1993). Others, such as Ruth Shady Solís and Rafael Vega-Centeno, continue the task of publishing Tello's unedited manuscripts at UNMSM.

It is significant that Tello's efforts to promote archaeology as part of a larger anthropological enterprise failed in most of Peru. At Tello's alma mater, UNMSM, archaeology separated from anthropology and became a freestanding major, although it remains within the faculty of social sciences. At Peru's leading private university, Pontificia Universidad Católica, where Tello also taught, archaeology is a humanities program closely linked to the university's history department. These institutional changes have resulted in a narrowing of archaeology in a way that is inconsistent with Tello's vision (Bonavia and Matos 1992).

Other institutional efforts by Tello, such as the creation of a dynamic university archaeology museum at UNMSM and the establishment of a major national museum of archaeology and anthropology (Museo Nacional de Antropología y Arqueología), have fared better over the last half-century. Tello's recognition of the value of Harvard Peabody Museum and his insistence on the centrality of investigation at national museums reflected his early training in the United States and Europe. The importance of these museums in Peru and their involvement in active research programs are easy to take for granted unless one compares the situation in Peru with that in the neighboring countries of Ecuador and Bolivia, where comparable institutions are still absent. Nonetheless, the inadequate funding for investigation at most Peruvian museums has undermined the implementation of Tello's vision.

## Conclusion

Tello's intellectual legacy was complex and profound. It was not limited to a particular idea or discovery. He created a style of archaeology that continues to influence both Peruvian and foreign scholars. Particular concepts and discoveries first disseminated by Tello gave Peruvian archaeology much of its current form and content. Tello's perspective extended well beyond the narrow world of academia and helped to shape the very notion of the Peruvian nation and the recognition of its indigenous foundations. By insisting on the link between conservation and investigation, Tello led the way to a modern perspective on archaeological resources and cultural policy.

During his lifetime and in subsequent years, Tello was often criticized and sometimes even accused of dishonesty; in some attacks, he was reduced to a caricature or a cliché. The distinguished physician and physical anthropologist Pedro Weiss wanted to defend Tello against these unjust attacks, but Tello told him: "Don't get involved in these matters Weiss. These are entirely transitory. What I have done for my land, no one can erase . . . no one can erase it" (Weiss 1977:7). As in so many cases, Tello's words have proven to be prophetic.

While Tello has often been ignored outside of Peru despite being the most successful indigenous archaeologist to have emerged in the Americas, his career and contributions remain widely appreciated in his homeland. It is my hope that this volume will stimulate greater interest in his life and work among those living outside of the Andes.

### REFERENCES CITED

Basadre, Jorge

1997 Tello: Testimonio de Jorge Basadre. *Gaceta Sanmarquina* 7(30): 2.

Bonavia, Duccio, and Ramiro Matos

1992 *Enseñanza de la Arqueología en el Perú.* Lima: FOMCIENCIAS.

Burger, Richard L.

1981 The Radiocarbon Evidence for the Temporal Priority of Chavín de Huantar. *American Antiquity* 46:592–602.

1988 Unity and Heterogeneity within the Chavin Horizon. In *Peruvian Prehistory*, edited by Richard Keatinge, pp. 99–144. London: Cambridge University Press.

1992 *Chavin and the Origins of Andean Civilization*. London: Thames and Hudson.

Carrión Cachot, Rebeca

1955 El Culto al Agua en el Antiguo Perú. *Revista del Museo Nacional de Antropología* 2(2): 50–140.

1959 *La Religión en el Antiguo Perú*. Lima: Tipografia Peruana.

Cook, David Noble

1981 *Demographic Collapse: Indian Peru, 1520–1620*. Cambridge: Cambridge University Press.

Fung, Rosa

1977 Opiniones. Homenaje a Tello. *Runa* 7(30): 14.

Kauffmann Doig, Federico

1997 Tello: Hizo ciencia como los Incas. *Gaceta Sanmarquina* 7(30): 3.

Kroeber, Alfred L.

1934 Native American Population. *American Anthropologist* 36(1): 1–25.

1944 *Peruvian Archaeology in 1942*. New York: Viking Fund.

Lathrap, Donald

1971 The Tropical Forest and the Cultural Context of Chavin. In *Dumbarton Oaks Conference on Chavin*, edited by Elizabeth Benson, pp. 73–100. Washington, D.C.: Dumbarton Oaks.

1973 Gifts of the Cayman: Some Thoughts on the Subsistence Basis of Chavin. In *Variation in Anthropology: Essays in Honor of John McGregor*, edited by Donald Lathrap and Jody Douglas, pp. 91–105. Urbana: Illinois Archaeological Survey.

1985 Jaws: The Control of Power in the Early Nuclear American Ceremonial Center. In *Early Ceremonial Architecture in the Andes*, edited by Christopher Donnan, pp. 241–267. Washington, D.C.: Dumbarton Oaks.

Lothrop, Samuel K.

1948 Julio C. Tello, 1880–1947. *American Antiquity* 13:50–56.

Lumbreras, Luis

1977 Tello y su tiempo. *Runa* 3:4–5.

Macera, Pablo

1977 *Trabajos de Historia Tomo I*. Lima: Instituto Nacional de Cultura.

Macera, Pablo, and Santiago Forns

2000 *Nueva Crónica del Perú Siglo XX*. Lima: Fondo Editorial del Congreso del Perú.

Mejía Xesspe, Toribio

1967 Prólogo. In *Páginas Escogidas*, by Julio C. Tello, pp. v–xxiii. Lima: Universidad Nacional Mayor de San Marcos.

1977 Testimonios. Homenaje a Tello. *Runa* 3:8–9.

Moore, Ernesto

1977 Tello y la Estatura Peruana. *Runa* 3:10–11.

Morales, Daniel

1993 Historia arqueológica del Perú. In *Compendio Histórico del Peru*, Vol. 1. Lima: Milla Batres.

Morris, Craig
1988 Progress and Prospect in the Archaeology of the Inca. In *Peruvian Prehistory*, edited by Richard Keatinge, pp. 233–256. Cambridge: Cambridge University Press.
Muelle, Jorge
1937 Filogenia de la Estela Raimondi. *Revista del Museo Nacional* 6(1): 135–150.
Ravines, Rogger
1977 Opiniones. Homenaje a Tello. *Runa* 3:16–17.
Roe, Peter
1982 *The Cosmic Zygote: Cosmology in the Amazon Basin*. New Brunswick, N.J.: Rutgers University Press.
Rowe, John H.
1947 Julio C. Tello. *Boletín de Arqueología* 2(3): 291–292. Bogotá.
1971 The Influence of Chavín Art on Later Styles. In *Dumbarton Oaks Conference on Chavín*, edited by Elizabeth P. Benson, pp. 101–124. Washington, D.C.: Dumbarton Oaks.
Sauer, Carl
1982 Andean Reflections. *Dellplain Latin American Studies*, No. 11. Boulder, Colo.: Westview Press.
Shady, Ruth
1997 Tello y la Situación de la Arqueología Peruana. *Gaceta Sanmarquina* 7(30): 4–5.
Tello, Julio C., and Toribio Mejía Xesspe
1967 Historia de los Museos Nacionales del Perú 1822–1946. *Arqueológicas* 10:1–268. Lima.
Trigger, Bruce
1989 *A History of Archaeological Thought*. Cambridge: Cambridge University Press.
Valcárcel, Luís E.
1981 *Memorias*. Lima: Instituto de Estudios Peruanos.
Weiss, Pedro.
1977 Testimonios. Homenaje a Tello. *Runa* 3:6–7.
Williams, Carlos
1977 Opiniones. Homenaje a Tello. *Runa* 3:13.

# *Selected Writings by Julio C. Tello*

# CHAPTER FOUR

# The Defense of the Archaeological Heritage

## The Meaning of Excavations

The excavations which have been carried out in Peru for some time in an eager rush to discover new evidences of vanished aboriginal civilizations deserve being taken under serious consideration by the government and by the well-informed public opinion of the country. In the interests of history, it is advisable to look at this subject not just in terms of the enthusiasm triggered by finds of relics of the past, but as the real and permanent contribution of such work to historical knowledge.

In my opinion, the excavations executed up until now by persons not versed in the practice of archaeology are going to produce enormous and irreparable damage to the national historical heritage. Archaeology is a specialized science as is medicine or engineering, the professional exercise of which necessarily requires proper, prior technical training.

To excavate archaeologically, simple common sense does not suffice nor does unspecialized intelligence, no matter how brilliant; nor does professional competence in other scientific or literary disciplines, just as it is not enough to be graced with these excellent attributes in order to cure medically or surgically.

The archaeologist, like the doctor, cannot improvise. He must possess experience and archaeological knowledge in order to observe, examine, and appraise with efficiency the multiple facts and phenomena which present themselves in the process of excavation and in order to grasp the no less multiple and complex problems raised by that process.

The archaeologist is, strictly speaking, the receiver of the teachings which the excavation offers, the intelligent keeper of all that which, in a given moment, reveals its secrets to be heard, just once, by whomever has ears sufficiently educated to hear them, since the soil, which contains the historical proof and facts worth being remembered, does not return to its original state after being disturbed. In this lies the importance of the archaeological excavation, and this demands special preparation by the person who carries it out.

Peru possesses, in its thousand-year-old monuments, which rival the best of America, and in its cemeteries and middens, the richest archive of the race to which we belong—whose history is ours and whose civilization is intimately linked to ours. For that very reason, it is the duty of every Peruvian to keep watch over the integrity of these monuments and of this archive. They constitute the most valuable heritage of the nation.

The importance of these monuments is the light they throw on the history of the peoples who preceded us in the possession of our country's soil and in the teachings which we can get out of the experiences accumulated by people morally conditioned like us. Therefore, to make an attempt to harm the integrity of these monuments is to make an attempt against the very foundations of the history of Peru.

In order to be able to calculate the value of this kind of excavation from a correct and comprehensive perspective, I am going to briefly review, in a general way, the nature of the excavations carried out up to now in Peru relative to the motives and causes determining their execution. At the same time, I will call attention to the necessity of carrying out these labors in accordance with the new basic principles of modern archaeology.

Needless to say, previous to the Conquest of Peru, the monuments and cemeteries were, for the Indians, *wakas*, or sacred relics, the places where their gods or the spirit of their ancestors dwelled. *Waka* until today signifies, for the Indian, all the marvelous works of his gods and of his legendary ancestors. *Waka* is, therefore, for him, an intangible and invulnerable place, a taboo. No conscientious native dares, even today, to profane his *wakas*. *Wakas* are all the ancient monuments of Peru.

In the long process of the exploitation of antiquities, almost uninterrupted for four centuries, different phases can be distinguished and characterized according to the incentives or motives which led to the plundering. Such phases correspond to two clearly defined ways of approaching antiquity. In one, importance is given solely to the treasure hidden in the ground according to its intrinsic value, as in the case of the precious metals and stones, or according to its purely historical or artistic value, as in the case of monuments or objects of exceptional importance because of their mode of manufacture, decoration, or form. In the other, the principal importance is given to the ground where the monument or object is found, based on the theory that the value depends not so much on the value of the object or monument itself as much as on its associations, which only scientific excavation can discover.

## The First Approach to Antiquity

The plundering of antiquities begins with the Conquest. Thirst for gold and religious fanaticism are the most important factors of destruction in this epoch. The ambition of the adventurer to improve his fortune by means of chance, the booty of war, and illicit appropriation of the treasures of the Incas leads to the sacking of the temples and royal tombs. Even the most excellent products of indigenous gold work are broken or melted down, because what is of interest is the metal for the value it has in and of itself, for its monetary value, and for its value as an official standard.

Since the monuments of Peru contained enormous riches, the search for treasure becomes a lucrative industry and a rich vein of exploitation for the Crown and the colonists. The "*mita* of the *wakas*" is established, and special dispositions are pronounced for the exercise of the new industry.

The exploitation of the gold contained in the *wakas* becomes equal to that of the exploitation of gold contained in the mines; the first, at the expense of history and art, and the second, at the expense of the sweat and blood of the Indians. In the year 1572, an able examiner of treasure converted himself into the defender of the Indians in order to pry from them the secret of their burials, and snatch from their dwellings the mummies of the Incas Huayna Capac, Amaru Tupac Inca, Pachacutec Inca, Yupanqui Inca, and Mama Ocllo, the mother of Huayna Capac, which "were found as fresh as if they were alive and locked up in copper cages."

As with everything else in antiquity, monument or object of art, even the bodies of the ancestors were sacred things for the Indians and diabolic ones for the Spaniards. A campaign for the destruction of it all is begun. In this zealous rush, the monuments are torn down, the tombs are sacked, and the mummies are burned, together with the most valuable textiles and adornments. This vandalism achieves maximum intensity at the beginning of the seventeenth century. An example will suffice to illustrate the disasters of this fateful period. In just four years, from 1615 to 1619, in which Francisco de Borja governed Peru, 10,422 idols were seized from the Indians, among them 1,365 mummies of their ancestors, and some who corresponded to the heads of their primitive lineages and the founders of their people. The destruction of the monuments and the looting of the tombs during the Conquest and the colonial period are real historical facts.

In this period, crucial history is not yet known; what is asserted is blindly believed. The history written by the chroniclers of the Indies is based principally on narrations of events and incidents considered important by those in control, under the influence of the prejudices and prevailing ideas of the epoch. This history, written by rude adventurers, soldiers, religious and learned men, or by mestizos or Indians with a Spanish soul on the basis of such evidence, is a tangle of fragments of indigenous legends and fables. Almost all of this history is of an emotional and romantic character, partial, and governed by self-interest. These narratives principally refer to the diabolical beliefs of the Indians, and the government, social organization, and other sociological themes. Only through analysis, dissection, and severe criticism can one today get to the bottom of the reliable historical datum, which appears disfigured and hidden by a great number of erroneous concepts.

In short, the history of this period is real in respect to the feats of destruction and the looting of the monuments, to the extirpation of idolatry, and the extermination of the population; but it is fantastic and muddled with respect to the manners, customs, arts, industries, and life of the people in general and the Inca sovereigns. Beyond the Inca traditions, which go back less than four centuries, there are only tales of giants and confusion.

The treasure hunter type, which prevailed during the Conquest and the first century of the colonial period, has his counterpart today, who, in a different sphere, continues this work of destruction. He sacrifices any monument, no matter how valuable, often just to satisfy his curiosity. He carries out his work sometimes blindly risking large amounts of capital. His labor is ill fated, like that of the treasure hunter of times past. To achieve his end, he makes an opening or perforates the monuments and, in some way, determines whether or not there is any treasure, guiding himself by the information and indications contributed by legends, superstitious and spiritistic practices, and contrived means.

The present-day search for treasure, mostly in certain coastal valleys, is a pastime or sport comparable to hunting. The nature of this work requires no special conditions in terms of training or experience in order to excavate, nothing but capital and the decision to risk it. The treasure hunter is usually devoid of any artistic or historical interest.

A new approach to the study of antiquity begins with the conviction that the monuments and objects are curiosities worth preserving as historical and artistic evidence. Admiration for the gigantic works of Indians and for their wonderful objects of art was felt even by some Spaniards. Thus, in the year 1572, Francisco de Toledo suggested to Philip II the advantage of exhibiting some valuable examples of indigenous art in the armories and wardrobes of the king for the entertainment and admiration of any prince who might visit the court. Some chroniclers, among them Cieza, marveled at the monumental works of the Incas.

The regard for monuments and antiquities as mere curiosities slowly grows during the eighteenth century and reaches greater intensity at the beginning of the nineteenth century, when the European intellectual world recognizes that the works of classical antiquity are the valuable exponents of civilizations that have disappeared. Actually, since the middle of the eighteenth century, a new spirit dominates Europe in the study of classical antiquity, an imaginative and versatile spirit of the Latin race. Principal importance is given to objective and tangible evidence and facts. The objective datum is superimposed on the merely traditional, speculative datum, which leads the historical investigation in the direction of privileging the study of art objects and monuments which, defying the action of time, are still preserved in centers of old civilizations.

The interest in buying up ancient objects, prompted by this realist-materialist spirit predominant in research, is not generally limited to antiquities. This new way of thinking is reflected in Peru in the last century of the colonial period and at the beginning of the Republic, and it is shown at this time in an increasing demand for ancient objects and by the increasingly felt necessity to explore the territory in order to get to know its monuments.

This is the way the search for curiosities starts, and, with it, the art of pothunting, which consists of discovering and excavating graves in order to take out of them the offerings, mostly the ceramic pieces, or *wakos*, which accompanied the body.

The pothunter, in the exercise of this destructive activity, becomes, by and by, an experienced craftsman. He is no longer a vulgar day laborer. He is an expert in the art of locating graves and, at times, a virtuoso, a true master and a very able assistant to the archaeologist. He points out, without much work, the site which has to be excavated drawing on the information provided from his own experience. He works without any tools except for a steel rod with which he tests the earth, whose condition indicates whether it has ever been disturbed. It is not he, but his laborers or apprentices who carry out the excavation. He directs the work, taking the contents out of the burial, choosing the best specimens, and even skillfully repairing the broken ones. He trades them in the nearest market, or he sells them to a middleman who is almost always the agent of an antiquities business or of some collector. Like the treasure hunter of yesteryear who preferred precious stones and metals, he prefers the fine, marketable pots.

As a consequence of this new approach to antiquity and as a product of the plundering of archaeological deposits, the first collections of pottery are formed in Peru and are exported to Europe, where they are avidly acquired by museums and collectors. The major museums of the world, especially the German ones, acquire Peruvian antiquities through agents in Peru who buy them by proxy from the looters and traffickers.

To impede this exportation of antiquities, the government of Torre Tagle responded with Decree 2 of April 1822, in which, for the first time, it is recognized "that the monuments and treasures which are left from the antiquity of Peru are property of the Nation because they belong to the glory which derives from them." An additional response was the diverse attempts on behalf of the government to found the National Museum of Natural History and Antiquities, which culminated with the Decree of Orbegoso, on June 3, 1836, by which the museum was established in a locale on Espiritu Santo Street, and the regulations for its functioning were established by law.

The Peruvian collections of antiquities in this epoch were studied as works of art, in some cases treated as a miscellaneous whole as revelations of indigenous art and, in others, classified typologically even though all are included under the common label of "antiquities of the Incas." In certain cases, thanks to the abundant material to be made use of, a study of decorative art of a genetic or evolutionary character was begun, such as certain works of Arthur Baessler on pottery and of Max Schmidt on textiles, without taking into account the exact provenience of the various types studied, or their cultural or chronological position.

Furthermore, some travelers and scientists explored Peru, describing, although imperfectly, its principal ruins and monuments. The work of E. George Squier, *Incidents of Travel and Exploration in the Land of the Incas*, is, in this respect, one of the most important of these for the exactitude of his observations and for the maps and descriptions of the monuments he visited.

On the other hand, and almost parallel to the development of this new spirit of archaeological research, there began a labor of compilation and criticism of the historical sources, and the cleaning up of the data contained in them, trying to coordinate and illustrate them with data of archaeological origin. Prescott is, in this sense, the true pioneer of this type of work. Historical criticism has its best exponents in the work of Markham, Bandelier, Jiménez de la Espada, Pietschmann, and Means.

Strictly speaking, archaeology in this phase is only an art or a pseudo-science of merely descriptive character, a simple auxiliary of history, to which archaeology, with its objective evidence, contributes to illustrate it. The domain and field of operations is the material products of human activity. It has principally to do with the tangible facts stripped of the forms of expression, of romanticism, and of the prejudices of the epoch.

For the ends which the antiquarian pursues as a simple collector or hoarder of antiquities, like the historian who buys up books or any other written evidence, it is not indispensable that he look for them in their own soil or deposit. With sufficient funds, he can acquire the material in his own study or museum. Almost all of the collections of Peruvian antiquities existing in the European and American museums have been acquired through buying by proxy from the looters, such as the notable collections of Macedo, Ferreyros, Sáenz, Montes, Gaffron, Graetzer, Mazzei, Centeno, the Larco Herrera brothers, Caparó Muñiz, Bruning, etc.

Until this point, there has been no importance given to the earth which covered or hid the monuments or to the conditions in which the objects were discovered. But the new methods of anthropological investigation applied to archaeology oblige the student to study in an integrated manner not only all the materials found in the graves but also those selected according to the criteria of the looter, and to guarantee the integrity and conservation of the material acquired.

Since it is thought that this is the only possible way to obtain concrete data on the arts, industries, manners, and customs of the ancients, the excavator tries to guarantee the integrity of the find, to reproduce the objects with the greatest exactitude and thus form an archive of trustworthy evidence. With it, an unswerving step toward the true science of archaeology is made. The study of Reiss and Stübel, *The Necropolis of Ancón*, can be considered a model of this kind of study. In this study, one obtains a clear concept of the extent of material culture attained by the primitive settlers of this region of the coast, but it teaches nothing about the cultural and chronological position of this culture.

Likewise, in respect to the study of monuments in this phase of archaeology, the main thing was to uncover the monument with the greatest care so that its preservation is guaranteed: clean it, photograph it, measure it, and, if possible, repair it. The earth, which covers said monument or which covers the ruins of a settlement, is not given the least importance in Peru.

When the excavations were begun in Pompeii, the volcanic ash which covered the city was eliminated by an army of laborers. For the desired purpose, the best and the only possible thing to do with the earth was to throw it away as fast and as far as possible. For this kind of work, nothing is needed but the cooperation of capable laborers, overseers, and, perhaps, engineers who could attend to the preservation of the monuments and watchmen who prevent the theft of the objects found.

The success of an excavation carried out in this way depends, in short, only on the greater number of workers; on the hardness or softness of the soil depending on the season of the year in which it is removed (hard in the summer, soft in the winter); on the efficiency of the machines and the tools used to eliminate the earth; and on a larger quantity of watchmen so that the machines and the workers do not hurt the objects. Only two questions concern the person who directs or has the responsibility of this kind of work: to know where the monument, tomb, or burial of ancient objects is to be found, and to take all manner of precautions so that the objects found do not suffer any damage or are liable to get lost. In order to succeed in these two aims, of course, no specialized technical preparation is required. A contingent of active and honorable workers and watchmen, something like a tournament of competence which establishes prizes for the one who finds or uncovers a monument or an archaeological object, would be sufficient requirements in order to ensure the desired result. This procedure today, archaeologically speaking, is a monstrosity.

The attitude of the archaeologist of today is different, gained only after the experience acquired through time and through progress in the methods of anthropological research. Barely three months ago, Rhys Carpenter, one of the most exalted modern archaeologists, revealed in this respect what I transcribe as follows. Let us hope that this authorized opinion will be meditated upon by the archaeologists who have entered into open competition to discover archaeological treasures, not only in the Department of Cuzco but in those of La Libertad and Ancash.

> Unfortunately, the modern excavator is possessed by a social conscience and the fear of his colleagues. He is no longer digging for his own amusement or his own edification; he is an emissary of science representing all the members of his profession, now alive or to live in future days.
>
> *To excavate a site is to destroy it.* The moment of excavation is unique: it represents for most objects a translation from an undisturbed (but hitherto invisible) historical setting to a visible (but historically irrelevant) environment. The potsherd on the museum shelf still has its artistic value; but it has probably lost its historical importance. It now dates nothing but itself.
>
> The excavator wishes to know not only what he has found, but everything that has been going on in the spot where he found it. The minutest information from stratification and surrounding soil may at times be crucial for an archaeological find. I say, *may at times*; and herein lies the misfortune. The excavator himself cannot tell how much of his data will be valuable. If he is not an incurable romanticist or too busy with what he is doing to stop to think at all, he must be aware, even while he is compiling it, that between 90 and 100 percent of the information with which he has loaded his daybook is utterly valueless. But since he cannot know what fact, what aspect, somewhere, some day, will be important or interesting to someone, he must go on with his routine, deliberately making himself as uncritically methodical as possible. For the excavator who insists on being intelligent and, like Adam, distinguishes good from evil, is a dangerous nuisance around an excavation. In his arrogance he has dared to judge what no man at the moment can possibly decide. And so, with nose to the meter-stick and eyes glued to the breaking sod, the excavator must carry out his infinitely tedious routine. For he is in the front line, and behind him waits the vast rank and file of scholars born and unborn. To encourage him he has self-confidence of an aspiring science; to keep him at his post he has the knowledge that he must not betray his trust.[1]

## The Scientific Approach to Antiquity

In the preceding section, I have dealt with the empirical approach to antiquity by which the importance given an archaeological monument or object is in terms of its intrinsic value, monumental or artistic, leaving aside the information which the study of the earth in which it is found might offer. Now I am going to deal with the scientific approach to antiquity by which, aside from the importance given to the monument or object for the value which it has in and of itself, preferential importance is given to the earth which hides it or inside which it is found, and for the information which the study of the soil contributes to the knowledge of the history of the object or monument.

In the first case, archaeological evidence is appreciated for its specific, individual value: gold because it is gold, and the artistic object because of its manufacture, its character, and its symbolism. In the second case, it is appreciated for the value it has in relation to other objects or in association with the stratigraphic information brought to light in the process of the excavation.

During the last years, thanks to the application of the scientific method in historical research, the procedures followed in the study of material culture of the peoples of the ancient past have been perfected. The careful description of archaeological information has been succeeded by its classification into types or styles and its being put in order, in a series or within a system.

The architecture, sculpture, painting, etc., of antiquity have been recently studied with biological or evolutionary criteria, considering that any species is a simple constituent element in the series of technological or artistic manifestations of a historical process. This procedure has its most solid foundation in the correlation which is discovered between different cultural types and the different chronological stages.

For historical reconstruction, the study of the object or the monument independent of the soil is not enough, as the study of the soil independent of the monument or object is not enough. Both factors complement each other. Historical knowledge is the result of the information which these two factors contribute.

The soil is like the patina of the monument, patina formed sometimes over many centuries and by many generations who have left their traces impressed in it as plants and animals which have lived in other geological ages have left their imprint on rocks. Similarly, as it is not possible to know the history of the plants and animals by studying only their fossils without taking into consideration the different strata in which they are found, neither is it possible to get to know the history of the monuments and objects without taking into consideration the careful study of the soil and of the accumulations of the garbage left by the different generations which followed one another through the passing of the centuries.

The archaeology of today is field archaeology. It is based in this kind of archaeological aphorism: "The process of excavation is like the reading of a book, the pages of which begin to burn up, one by one, as they are read." This demands the presence of the archaeologist in situ as the only one responsible for registering of the memories of the excavation which, without his cooperation, would be lost forever.

In the archaeological centers of Peru, the earth is sometimes formed by the wastes of human activity, accumulated for many generations, which frequently hide the ruins and cemeteries corresponding to people of different epochs and cultures; at other times, by landslides or deliberately executed destructions, as in the case of wars or of conquests, and by earthquakes, volcanic eruptions, floods, and many other phenomena. Although in the case in which the earth covering a monument might not offer any remains of human origin, as in the case of the earth formed by volcanic ash or by alluvial soil, the teachings which are obtained from the study of the soil are always important.

The volcanic ash covering Pompeii, which, in the beginning, was eliminated in large masses in the eager rush to uncover the buried city, has been protected today by archaeology, because, thanks to the examination of this ash, very interesting information has been obtained about things which, although they have not left remains, have left clear traces of their existence. Thanks to these, the reconstruction and identification of plants cultivated 2,000 years ago in the gardens of Pompeii have been achieved in the present.

In the lower layers of the volcanic ash which cover the ruins of Wari, in Ayacucho, exposed by the currents of water which had cut them almost vertically and to a considerable depth, I found remains of stone tools which make us suspect that inside the deep layers of this ash will be found very valuable information about the antiquity of human culture in this region of Peru.

In 1919, when I examined for the first time the Temple of Chavín de Huantar, from the first moment what induced me to think of its great antiquity was the fact of finding the temple under the ground covered, in part, by garbage, and, in part, by a thick layer of cultivated alluvial soil, and the fact that the superb interior galleries were found filled to a certain height with earth and stones, the presence of which was not easy for me to comprehend. In this layer of earth that covers Chavín and that which covers part of its galleries, the archaeologist of tomorrow will surely find important information about the history and antiquity of Chavín.

It is Uhle who, for the first time, gave importance to the earth in the study of Peruvian antiquity. The excavations scientifically carried out by him have made the first valuable and effective contribution on the chronology of the primitive civilizations, and his chronological and cultural system has served as a basis and a guide for the later research on the soil.

The work carried out subsequently has widened the archaeological horizon of Peru, based on the scientific study of the materials from the museums and of the results of explorations and excavations carried out in the new archaeological centers discovered. Thanks to this work, the establishment of a chronological succession of the different cultures of Peru has been achieved. The excavations carried out in the most important archaeological centers, such as Paracas, have led to the conviction that the deposits are true deposits of facts and proof—true archives of indispensable documents in order to acquire an exact knowledge of the history of Peru and in order to determine the antiquity of its different civilizations.

Moreover, today it is finally acknowledged that the intrinsic value of an archaeological object is not what is important for the historical reconstruction. A bead from a necklace or a *chaquira* found in a determined place in a clearly defined stratum is of greater value than a gold nugget or a work of art without the history of its discovery. Because that very *chaquira* could prove, for example, that glass was already made in any period of ancient Peru. Perhaps a find like this could be related to the glass *chaquiras* of very primitive manufacture, which were found a short time ago in abundance inside one of the looted tombs of the Waka "La Misa" in Chan Chan and whose presence in that place remains a mystery. In contrast, the gold nugget or the object of art, exhibited in a showcase and obtained from the hands of a laborer, does not prove anything.

1. Rhys Carpenter, *The Humanistic Value of Archaeology.* Martin Classics Lectures Vol. 4 (Cambridge, Mass.: Harvard University Press, 1933).

*El Comercio*, March 12 and 13, 1934, Lima. Translated by Freda Wolf de Romero.

CHAPTER FIVE

# The Museum of Peruvian Anthropology

## Aims and Objectives

This ceremony is of great significance in our national life. A scientific institution is being hereby inaugurated for the purpose of conserving the relics of the antiquity of Peru, of studying and using them as they should be used in public education to strengthen national awareness, maintaining alive in the present generation the feeling of ethnic dignity based on the idea of great works accomplished in the past, in order to intensify our faith and confidence in the even greater works which we are bound to carry out in the future.

## The Museum as Custodian of the Historical Relics of the Nation

This museum is created with the objective of preserving the products of man's manifold activities in Peru, those which illustrate his biological history as well as that of his arts, industries, practices, customs, and all the historical evidence which allows us to know about his civilization, investigate his origins, and trace his ethnic relationships. An effort will be made to exhibit properly classified objects extracted from the great archive of the pre-Columbian cemeteries, replicas of monuments, reconstructions of principal cities, temples, obelisks, statues, and reliefs which still remain within Peruvian territory.

Furthermore, the museum will try to serve as a center of information for everything related to the study of our aboriginal race. It will compile the works of writers and analysts who were concerned about the Indians as a result of the Conquest, the works of modern investigators who study our past, and, finally, it will preserve the traditions, myths, and narratives of non-Christian ceremonies and all that inheritance of ideas and precepts which still control the physical, intellectual, and emotional life of our people.

For the first time, a scientific institution has been created in Peru designated for the study of the civilization of our forebears, to satisfy not only a national but a universal need. The study of ancient Peru is not only of interest to Peruvians whose obligation it is to know the history of their own country, but to all those who believe that history is an active force, which not only illuminates the future but which inexorably marks the destiny of humanity. It is for this reason that the most cultured nations on the globe avidly hoard our archaeological relics in their museums, and those who dedicate themselves to indigenous history bitterly censure our indifference and carelessness in the conservation and study of the antiquities of Peru.

In 1885, Tschudi wrote:

> It could perhaps be supposed that in Lima, the capital of Peru, at a distance of just a few miles from one of the most important necropolises of the country, some of the antiquities would have been kept. But that did not happen, since the National Museum has always been the poorest museum in the capital, so that many of the private collections of Europe possess an isolated number of Peruvian antiquities which are immensely superior to any which were ever possible to assemble in the public collections of Lima. The public collections of Lima have several times been the object of plunder and theft; recently, they were roundly sacked by the conquering Chileans. In this case, the ruling circles were also to blame for their indolence and ignorance, especially the governments which incurred in irreparable negligence, committing a true crime against their own country. Nevertheless, right now much good could be done with a noble government and a Ministry of Education which in their enlightenment would bring together the love for science with that for their own country.

And, in 1915, Uhle, at the Second Panamerican Scientific Congress, expressed himself with these moving sentences, which should be meditated upon by every Peruvian:

The American states are young in the most diverse spheres of life; they have not yet awakened to the realization of their duty. They dissipate the strength of their youth without thinking of the needs they will have in the time of their maturity. Now history seems of little importance to them. They enjoy life as though the time never had to come in which they will need the strength taken from the teachings of the past in order to keep themselves upright. Nevertheless, this time must come to them as it has come to every other modern State in the world. For that reason the time will come in which they will by necessity have to remember the sources of the pre-Columbian history of the land they occupy in order to maybe find themselves afterwards, exhausted by the punishing indifference of the past centuries. Then they will lack roots thrust deeply into the soil by means of history, and, like aquatic plants, without roots, they will perish when exposed on being dislodged by the wind in the ocean of the continent which they never made theirs by penetrating its past. That which has been lost in the years gone by cannot be gotten back in the years to come. But a necessity for existing states would be to protect, preserve and insure what is still left of the heritage of antiquity in the form of remains, be they in ancient cemeteries which are still undiscovered, but at any moment discoverable, or in isolated burials which have escaped the rapacity of the plunderers, or in monuments that are not yet destroyed or decayed, but whose disappearance is at every moment threatened. At the same time, those which have not yet begun to undertake the task of reconstructing the pre-Columbian history of their land through archaeology and anthropology should begin with the organization of those studies directed toward a better understanding of their own foundations. Because the degree of maturity of the type of civilization to which they belong demands it. Furthermore, there is no better way to react against common lethargy and the complete devastation of the documents of antiquity which weaken a civilization's future than carrying out the positive work of well directed historical studies.

Today, the institution insistently seeks to open its doors. An exposition of curiosities to serve as recreation for the people or as distraction for tourists is not being inaugurated, but rather, what is going to be a center of scientific investigations and a school where the future ideals of our country will be forged—an institution bent upon extending the present limits of our historical knowledge which strengthens our spirit and ensures our faith in the progress of the country.

We are obligated to know the history of the soil which holds the sacred ashes of our fathers, the territory they defended with their blood, which they worked with their sweat and utilized to benefit themselves and posterity.

## The Museum as a Center of Scientific Research

This labor cannot be carried out except by a museum which keeps itself constantly active, which explores the national territory, which carries out excavations in non-Christian cemeteries, and which inevitably makes known the results of its work by way of suitable publications for specialists as well as for the general public.

The archaeological objects accumulated up until now in foreign and national museums, despite their artistic or illustrative value, do not have all their historical value. Since the majority of them were snatched out of graves by inexpert persons and traffickers in antiquities, they lack certain essential conditions such as an accurate knowledge of the place where they were discovered. Moreover, up to now, they have not been methodically classified because certain types of objects taken from a determined site in Peru have been disseminated all over the world and others have not been collected, which, even though they do not have artistic or representative value, do have historical and scientific value.

Given the number and variety of objects the museum being inaugurated has which are derived almost entirely from just two regions of the Peruvian coast, it will be possible to undertake a systematic trial classification, and to form a series of similar types of objects which illustrate an ethnological theme or clearly defined historical event. The evolutionary history of the decorative art can likewise be studied while gaining a knowledge, in some cases almost complete, of certain fashions, customs, practices, and religious rites. In this way, many pages and perhaps entire chapters of the great book of the history of our country will be reconstructed.

In an institution like this, which begins life with the largest collection of Peruvian antiquities in the world, it is possible to initiate work which opens new horizons, not only in the knowledge of ancient Peru but also in the methods and procedures of archaeological research.

Simultaneously making use of all the historical sources; surveying ruins; reconstructing ancient towns; transferring gigantic roads and irrigation canals onto maps; reproducing characteristic models of temples, forts, and tombs; and accumulating originals and replicas of all kinds which might have historical significance will permit us to obtain a set of pure facts and certainty in the interpretation of the plastic and graphic representations in the ancient art of Peru. The role played by ancient Peru in the history of civilization will be appreciated on its own merits.

## The Museum as an Educational Center

Furthermore, this institution will be an educational center. Here the researcher will find original historical sources. The university professor will be able to illustrate his lessons with the most genuine historical evidence. Schoolteachers and students will be able to become familiar with the characteristics of art and knowledge of the most outstanding events of the past. The Museum is the democratic educational institution par excellence. It is the most effective medium to popularize the teachings of history.

If we are conscientious in our duties toward the destiny of our country, we are obligated to work persistently in the great labor of educating the people, awakening the spirit of group solidarity and thus forging national consciousness. We well know how the unexpected cataclysm of the Conquest inopportunely paralyzed the creative activities of indigenous peoples. Along with their civilization, it destroyed the foundations of nationality.

The political theme of the Incas was specialized, cooperatively organized work, the basis of all physical, intellectual, and social progress. In the heroic times of the Empire, everything was directed from childhood toward converting man into a dynamic factor oriented toward the domination of nature and the exploitation of the riches of the soil by means of cooperative, intense, and tenacious work. Work was pleasure, not pain.

Those who work under the rod and the mortal threat of a master with divine and absolute power are not those who specialize in arts and industries which demand exercising the higher mental and emotional faculties. Under such conditions, they would never have been able to produce those works which reveal patient, delicate, and spiritual work. Work so specialized it turns into a pleasant occupation, organized cooperative labor is what produced yesterday's amazing civilization. If the biological laws are to be fulfilled once again in Peruvian society, that is what will produce future greatness.

The Conquest caused disequilibrium in the society. On one hand, the Indian, faced with the painful spectacle of Spanish domination, remained apathetic. In his disillusion, he lost the notion of progress. On the other hand, the conqueror strove to replace in the vanquished class the positive and worldly ideals of looking for happiness in this life through work and control of natural powers and resources by that in which life is considered the place of expiation and pain for the sake of happiness beyond this earth. Awareness of nationality, the group spirit, the powerful tie which unites men by the feeling, intimate and intense, of dignity for their natal land, enlivened by the memory of great deeds carried out in the past, becomes weak and almost disappears.

Abandoned are the great indigenous cities built amid extensive artificial gardens. The palaces built on ample platforms and majestic pyramidal temples are converted into masses of rubble. Abandoned are the roads and irrigation canals crossing enormous distances, and the extensive fields irrigated by works which endure until today to the astonishment of modern engineering. The huge population is enslaved and destroyed. Its works of art are destroyed and burned as a means of extirpating every objective revelation of indigenous religious feeling.

The history of these events comes to us by way of reports, chronicles, and annals written with criteria and moral standards completely different from those of the indigenous people. Thus, we have never managed to know, when there are no other sources to investigate besides the written documents, the truth about aboriginal history. Only when one studies man scientifically, when the truth is sought leaving partial and impassioned criteria aside, does one acquire a clear notion of the importance and the degree of culture reached by our predecessors, and the dignity of the patrimony is restored.

As children of indigenous mothers, of the autochthonous mother homeland, the great and unique mother, it falls to us by right of inheritance to imitate her example, to follow her teachings and glorify her memory. If we are worthy of belonging to the human species, our first duty is to ourselves, to faithfully and religiously preserve our traditions, in order to work for the life and happiness of that portion of the Peruvian family that one finds in our care and free ourselves of our responsibilities to posterity.

To convert a man semi-enslaved by the weight of the ignorance and injustices of four centuries into a man worthy and proud of his ancestry through accurate knowledge of his glorious past, is the best, if not the only, way of asserting the foundations of future ethnic prosperity and to definitively reconsecrate our nationality.

Our genealogical tree has profound and vigorous roots which, in other times, extracted from this land the sap which nourished a race of giants. Then, the stalk was cut by the European Conquest, but new and vigorous shoots of the gigantic trunk of nationality—new sprouts—begin to appear. They grow and they will grow, nourished by the indigenous sap itself at the urging of new ideas from the century in which we are living.

This Museum is due to the spirit, idealistic and practical, at the same time, of the philanthropist Victor Larco Herrera, who spared neither energy nor money in order to carry out his patriotic obligation of gathering together this great treasure of Peruvian antiquities, this collection, without rival in the world, which was found disseminated in private hands, and thus always in danger of leaving the country.

Mister President, in my opinion, their acquisition by the state signifies one of the most important and transcendental acts of your government. With it, you eloquently reveal your philosophy of life—your optimistic philosophy—which shows us the luminous lighthouse of future glory on the penumbra of the national horizon. Patriot of courage, invoke the gigantic soul of our race to the fate which guides our nation's fortunes, vibrating the most sensitive fibers of the heart of the homeland, strengthening the faith and the hope of its grandiose future, and very deeply engaging our national gratitude.

Speech given at the inauguration ceremony of the Museum of Peruvian Anthropology, December 13, 1924, and published in *El Comercio*, December 14, 1924, Lima. Republished in *Páginas Escogidas*, by Julio C. Tello, pp. 105–110 (Lima: UNMSM, 1967). Translated by Freda Wolf de Romero.

CHAPTER SIX

# Collision of Two Civilizations

**THE SPANISH BROUGHT** completely different manners, customs, habits, illnesses, religion, language, ideals, and, in general, civilization, from that of the indigenous Peruvian peoples. The Conquest produced something like a great cataclysm which demolished, almost from its foundations, the national structure shaped by the indigenous spirit during many centuries. The great irrigation canals and dams were abandoned, the roads destroyed, the temples were plundered and fell, the religion persecuted, the arts forgotten, and the population humiliated and enslaved.

The resulting miscegenation of Indian and Spanish created two classes. One, holding out in Andean redoubts and supporting themselves poorly, begins to degenerate under the action of alcohol, coca, illness, and religious fanaticism, living sluggishly and ignorant of its past, traversing the same dark road year after year, century after century, without a light strong enough to awaken it and guide it to civilization. The other class, adapting itself to the ideas, feelings, aspirations, manners, customs, etc., of European civilization, makes an effort to shape a nationality on the Spanish or Latin base, putting aside the bases left by the aboriginal civilization. They imitate the characteristics of other lands and other nationalities, without using the knowledge and methods of science as they should be used, which would permit us to know our soil and our history, to subjugate the egotism of men, to establish the economic equilibrium of the social classes and thus secure our nationality.

Our present Hispanic-Peruvian civilization cannot stand except on an indigenous pedestal. It cannot stand firm and last for a long time if it does not completely adapt itself to its surroundings, if men do not try to use our own resources to discover the secrets and wonders of our own nature, admire the labor of our ancestors, glorify the generations which lived on our own soil which holds their ashes and from which they took their sustenance, and which they defended and used for many centuries.

The present generation is obligated to revive the past and retrieve everything that can be glorified.

Excerpt from *Introducción a la Historia Antigua del Perú* (Lima: Editorial Euforión, 1921). Translated by Freda Wolf de Romero.

CHAPTER SEVEN

# Prehistoric Trephining among the Yauyos of Peru

**TOWARD THE EAST OF THE PROVINCE** of Lima extends a zone of intricate deep valleys and gullies, extensive tablelands, inaccessible summits and *puna*, bounded by the western branch of the Cordilleras of the Andes. This region was the habitat of the Yauyos and the Huarochiris who had been incorporated with the Chinchaysuyu by the Inca Pachacutec, and whose territory, in conformity with the Inca administration, had been divided into Anan-Yauyos and Lorin-Yauyos, at the present time the provinces of Yauyos and Huarochiri, respectively.

The ruins existing to this day in that territory are still unexplored. Nature has contributed to the preservation of the testimony of life and culture among these people, for the material isolation of the land due to its abrupt and rugged form has prevented the arrival there of the conqueror, the tourist, or the dealer in antiquities, who would have removed forever some of the most important sources of archaeological and ethnological information. It is for this reason that the Aymara language which was formerly spoken has survived until the present time in that zone, preserving archaic characters that have resisted the influence of the Quechua language by which it is surrounded, and which the Incas made every effort to spread. In the same way have been preserved, almost unscathed until now, the ruins where methodical exploration will certainly clear up problems of the utmost importance in the anthropology of Peru.

Inspection of the ruins shows at first glance the existence of three principal groups: (1) Caverns or natural caves, undoubtedly tribal dwellings, on the floors of which are found more or less superficial remains of kitchen refuse, stone objects, and, above all, human bones. (2) *Chaukallas*, dwellings which scarcely rose more than a meter above the level of the ground, of a quadrilateral form, built of stone and mud, either single or with various divisions, which constitute the most common type in the mountain regions of Peru. Under the floors are found objects of stone, rough pottery, copper utensils, and numerous remains of skeletons. (3) *Llactas*, which were buildings with walls of stone and roofs probably of straw, grouped together to form villages of varying extent. Everything leads us to believe that the first two types correspond to the most ancient dwellers of the region, while the third appears to be of genuine Inca construction, for these buildings undoubtedly belonged to the people subjugated in the period of the viceroyalty of Don Francisco de Toledo. From the caverns and *chaukallas* we extracted about 10,000 crania and mummies, some of which form the collection now at the Warren Museum of Harvard University; and from the same region also came the eleven crania which were presented to Dr. Muñiz at Lima. These eleven crania, together with eight others of different origin, were studied by Dr. MacGee.

The writer's collection provides abundant material, and opens up a wide field for the better knowledge:

1. Of the operating motives
2. Of the processes or methods employed.
3. For the appreciation of the results obtained in the practice of trephining.

The accompanying plates show a few examples. This paper will deal only with some of the most interesting aspects as preliminary to a more detailed study on which the writer has been engaged for a considerable time.

## I

In Dr. MacGee's work on the Muñiz Collection, the question of the motives which led the ancient Peruvians to practice trephining was left, in my opinion, quite undecided on the point whether it was due to religious or thaumaturgic reasons as Dr. MacGee thought, or whether it was essentially therapeutic.

Examination of the majority of the trephined skulls in our collection shows that four fundamental motives led the operator to adopt therapeutic measures:

1. An antecedent fracture.
2. A simple traumatism of the cranium which denuded the periosteum and was followed, or not, by an inflammatory process.
3. A circumscribed periostitis or osteoperiostitis, perhaps also of traumatic origin.
4. Lesions—probably of a syphilitic nature.

1. Fractures of the dome of the skull generally assume two principal forms: (a) fractures that collapse, i.e., depressed fractures, and (b) radiating fractures.

Let us consider some examples of the first form. Specimen L1-5 (fig. 7.1a) shows in the occipital a depressive fracture, and above and below the sunken segment the traces left by two rectilinear incisions made without doubt with the intention of removing it. The cause or traumatic motive of the operation can be clearly seen.

In specimen K-8 (fig. 7.1b), as in the above case, there has evidently been a depressive fracture of the posterior portion of the left parietal, and the sunken segment has been dealt with or removed by means of a laborious operation.

In not a few cases the removal of the depressed fragment has been carried out with greater minuteness; the fracture can be seen surrounded in the periphery by small rectilinear incisions, the ends of which cross each other, thus forming a polygon, which shows the intention of the operator in the most evident fashion.

The mummy L1-a (fig. 7.1c) shows on the right side of the frontal bone an incomplete operation which has also been attempted for the purpose of removing the fragments produced by a depressed fracture. The curvilinear incisions seem almost parallel to the upper edge of the opening. All these cases corroborate the preexistence of a depressed fracture as the cause or motive of the operation, and this is as fully justifiable as it would be at the present time in similar cases.

The second form, i.e., the radiated fractures, may now be examined.

The cranium Kun-1 (fig. 7.1d) presents in the upper portion of the frontal bone and toward the middle line the rectilinear traces of an operation carried out for the purpose of removing the sequestrums produced by a traumatic agent which has at the same time caused the radiation on the frontal bone.

In the center of the frontal bone of the cranium Pak-11 (fig. 7.1e),

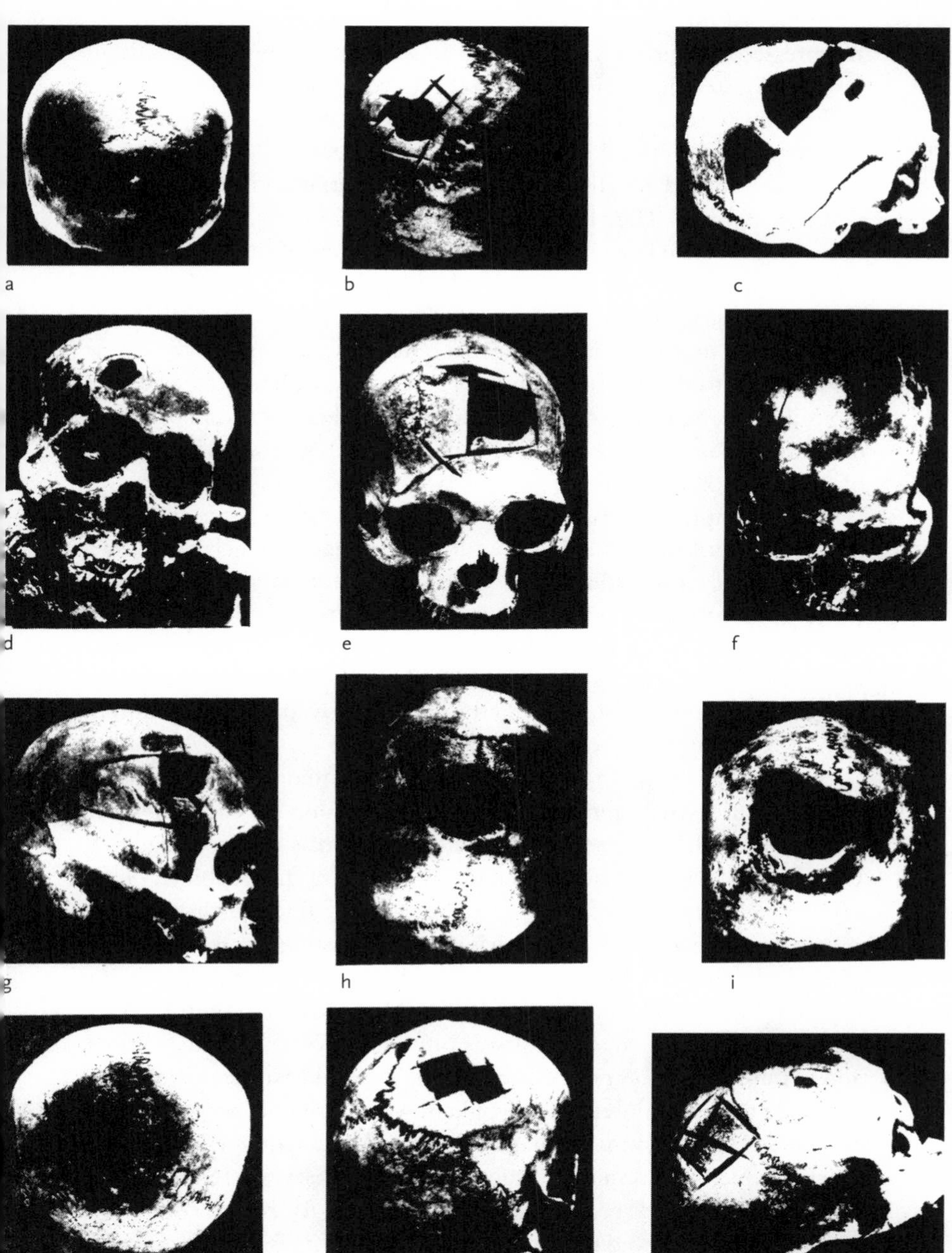


*7.1. Trephined skulls from Yauyos, Peru.*

a depressed fracture is visible which in its turn has produced a long fissure. The rectilinear incisions which border the opening probably facilitated the removal of some sequestrums. The rectilinear incisions appear to have been guided by the line of fracture.

The cranium H-33 (fig. 7.1f) has had three operations on the right side of the dome. The absolute absence of operating scratches on the lower edges of the large openings and the fracture of the bridge which separates them on a level with this edge should be noticed. These two facts give a clear explanation both as to the direction of the openings and as to the motive. It is evident that a radiating fracture of the dome existed prior to the operation, and the fracture must have had its center around the bregma from which it radiated, following the middle line of the right parietal until it reached and became lost toward the middle of the lambdoidal suture.

The incomplete operation which is seen in specimen A-17 (fig. 7.1g) was on account of a radiating fracture, the traces of which are shown by two fissures, one radiating over the frontal bone and the other following the fronto-temporal crest and radiating toward the apex of the outer projection of the orbit. It is possible that the quadrilateral operation may have removed splinters, and perhaps the operator mistook the temporal parietal suture for a fracture, and followed it with the intention of removing the supposed bony splinters.

Specimen S-6 (fig. 7.1h) presents toward the interior half of the interparietal suture a trephining of circular form, the rounded edges of which are beveled at the expense of the outer layer. The reason here is manifest, because a fissure radiates from the external edge of the trephined opening, which is undoubtedly the remainder of the fracture that was the reason for the operation. By following the said fissure, traces can be seen of a roughening, and this proves here, as in many cases, that the fissure suggested to the operator the way he should follow, although the procedure of making a cut along it was often unnecessary and dangerous, and in numerous cases even caused death. The fact that the operator did not cease this procedure, which would now appear improper, was due to an inherited empiricism, to the rational knowledge acquired by previous practice which had resulted in success, in those cases where the following of the fissure was really logical because it led to the removal of the splinters, and produced relief or cured the patient.

2. Let us now examine a few examples in which the motive for the operation is a simple traumatism of the cranium which had laid bare the periosteum, and has been followed by an inflammatory process.

In specimen A-1 (fig. 7.1i) the operation is complete, though recent, for, on the edges, grooves are still noticeable, and there is no regenerative work whatever. Surrounding the opening is a zone of a dark color, bordered toward the periphery by the traces of an inflammatory process of exfoliated rarefying osteitis. In this case we have to decide whether the lesion which is here visible was subsequent to the operation or whether, on the contrary, it was the actual motive for it. The form, more or less quadrilateral, of the trephining in this example is worthy of notice, being similar in the zone of dark coloring which surrounds it, and in the zone of rarefying osteitis which, in turn, surrounds the latter. It would appear therefore that as regards form, there is a subordination of the two zones referred to, with regard to the zone of the trephining, and this is apparently an argument in favor of the fact that the pathological lesion was subsequent to the operation.

In the cranium Sak-8 (fig. 7.1j) the operation has been carried out with the object of dealing with a lambdoidal Wormian bone, probably of the same size, as it is a symmetrical one. This case confirms what was said before, i.e., that the linear suture was mistaken for a traumatic fissure. This fact confirms the assumption of the existence of a prior traumatism. Along the sagittal suture numerous grooves are seen which were undoubtedly due to the same cause. As in the previous example, the operation is in a field of dark coloration, surrounded peripherally by a zone of periostitis or osteoperiostitis, but in this case the operation is not concentric with the said zones, as in the previous one, but is situated in the extreme posterior portion of the field. Here also there would appear to be a doubt as to whether the operation was the reason for the pathological lesion or vice versa. Cranium L1-9 (fig. 7.1k) shows a recent operation, probably incomplete, and the zone bordering on the trephined opening is discolored over a very considerable extent, and, as in figure 7.1j, toward its periphery it is limited by a zone of periostitis.

In my opinion the lesions which are observed in these cases are those which proceed from a denudation of the periosteum and from the subsequent infectious phlegmatic phenomena which preceded the operation and were undoubtedly the reason for it. If the contrary is assumed it is not easy to explain the following facts: Why was the operation in many cases left uncompleted? Why is the operation in other cases not in harmony with the lesion, because it very frequently presents itself eccentrically to the denudation in its borders or even outside, and why in small circumscribed operations was there extensive denudation of the periosteum, which it is necessary to assume in order to explain the cases in which a discolored zone appears, bordered by exfoliated osteitis embracing almost a third of the dome? All this would be explained if we consider that the lesion preceded the operation, and that it was the lesion itself which caused a sufficiently intense traumatism to denude the periosteum and subsequently to become the site of common suppurative processes. Should this be so, in the cases in which a discolored zone appears around a recent trephining, as, among other typical examples, in the Inca skull of Squier (which led Broca to imagine that the patient had survived the operation seven days, and Nott and Nelaton to suppose the interval fifteen days), the said zone may have been due to the traumatism which led to the operation, and not subsequent to it.

3. In the examples of this group the localization of the operation required in consequence of a previous pathological lesion is still more manifest. Cranium Puk-5 (fig. 7.1l) has an abandoned operation in which the bony fragments intended to be removed clearly show the traces of a circumscribed osteoperiostitis. This specimen affords the most convincing evidence of the therapeutic nature of the motive. Whatever might be the nature of the pathological lesion, perhaps a simple subsequent periostitis following a traumatic cause, or specific lesion of another kind, there is no doubt that it was the reason for the operation which was attempted with a view to the elimination of the affected part.

The cranium Lu-1 (fig. 7.2a) shows in the same way the motive for the operation. In a mortified zone of the bone, the site of rarefied osteitis, are seen the traces of a fresh incision which could have no other object than the elimination of this part of the mortified bone.

4. In the collection there are some examples in which the lesions observable are undoubtedly of a syphilitic nature. The cranium Kal-2 (fig. 7.2b) presents in the middle of the frontal bone a peculiar lesion, the nature of which has led many to consider it the trace left on the bone by a circumscribed gumma. This class of lesion is in every respect similar to that described by Virchow as stellar gumma cicatrices. The center is found to be rarefied as though it had been the seat of a gumma tumor which only involved the external layer and the diploe, and in the periphery there is a clearly manifested ring of condensing osteitis. This species of lesion, undoubtedly pathological, can only be attributed to syphilis, and our opinion is confirmed by various authorities in this matter, and among them by Dr. Hrdlicka, who has examined the cranium.

In view of the existence of this species of lesion and the undeniable fact that the operation was carried out in the presence of lesions, it is

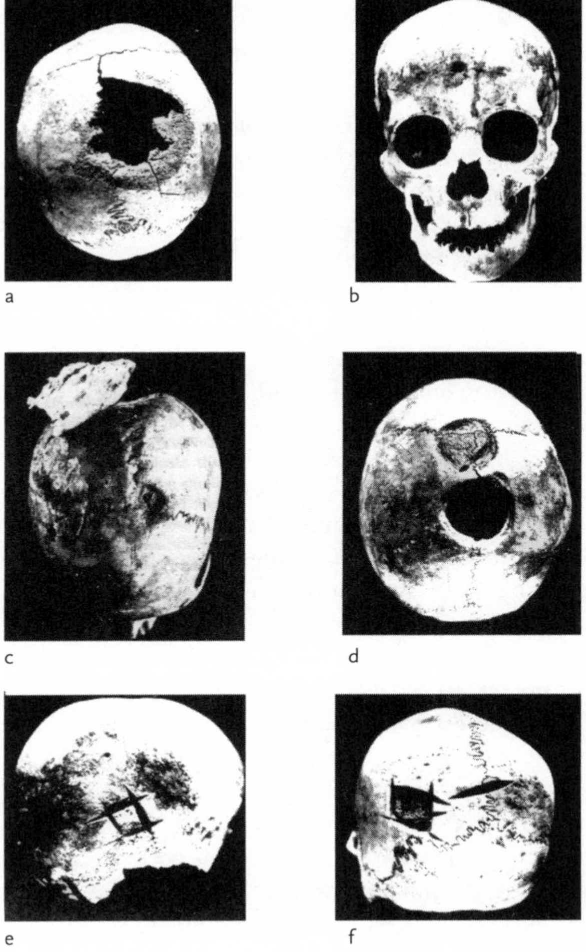


*7.2. Trephined skulls from Yauyos, Peru.*

logical to assume that in specimen K-2 (fig. 7.2c), where a trephining operation is circumscribed by abrasion, as in many others of the kind, the operation was carried out with a view to dealing with similar lesions.

## II

The examination of a considerable number of examples with perfectly defined operations (that is to say, in which there are no concomitant cicatrized or other processes which might injure the clearness of the traces of the operation) enables us to say what has been the evolution of the different operating stages and to determine the nature of the instrument employed.

If it is borne in mind that a more or less sharp, cutting instrument of stone was used in these operations, we may see now it has been possible for a single instrument to leave traces morphologically different, owing to the fact that the operator had handled it in a different manner in each case. It may have been used by working with the point, edge, or face. In working with the point it has been used perpendicularly to the bony surface, and it has left traces which vary from the small rectilinear incision, a simple superficial groove, to large incisions of some centimeters in length and of sufficient depth to involve the whole thickness of bone in the central parts.

It is natural to suppose that, considering the nature of the bony surface, there must have been deviations or slips of the instrument in commencing one of these incisions. To these are due the little scratches or marginal grooves made before the instrument began to bite into the outer layer and, by a to-and-fro movement, formed a channel and slowly and carefully perforated the vitreous lamina. This constitutes the fundamental element of all the operations and, in many cases, is in itself the entire operation. The groove thus left is not in reality an incision, as it is called for convenience of speech; it is an abrasion caused by the to-and-fro motion of an instrument which rubs away the bone. The incision or elementary operation is fusiform, and, as Dr. MacGee points out, in a vertical section it has the form of a V, and in the horizontal section the form of a canoe. This perforation of the vitreous lamina toward its central portion may constitute the whole operation, or may be one of the stages of a more complete operation (fig. 7.3a). It is not surprising therefore to find the fusiform incision, either isolated or accompanied by one or more similarly arranged, with such a divergence (fig. 7.3b) of direction as to remove any suspicion that they could have been made with the object of forming the polygons, to which we shall refer later, employed for craniectomia.

In other cases two fusiform parallel incisions (fig. 7.3c) appear so close to one another that the bony space which separates them is smaller than the actual width of each of the incisions. It cannot, therefore, be suspected that they have been traced with the object of eliminating the intervening segment; they really constitute the complete operation, since both perforate the cranium to a considerable extent.

Everything leads us to believe that these parallel incisions suggested to the operator the idea of crossing them by others in such a way as to form a rectangle to serve for the common form of craniectomia,

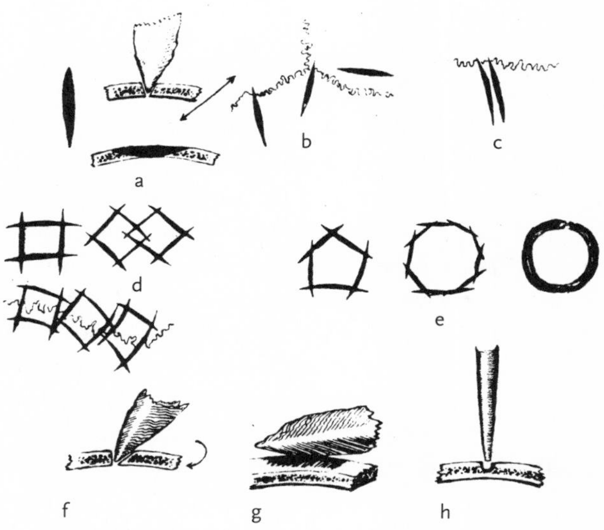


*7.3. Techniques of trephination from Yauyos, Peru.*

first known from the examples which Squier took from the museum of Señora Centeño of Cuzco. According to the intention of the operator, he made only a quadrilateral, or various quadrilaterals, joined in a more or less arbitrary fashion (fig. 7.3d). Finally, the fusiform incisions worked in pairs, originate a series of figures which run from the simple pentagon to a polygon, the sides of which grow indefinitely until they approach a circular form (fig. 7.3e). On reaching this stage of the evolutionary process of incision, the instrument had to adapt itself to the new circumstances. As it became mechanically impossible to follow them by working perpendicularly to the surface, the instrument was inclined, and by working obliquely it was possible to carry out these môre or less circular operations.

When the point of the instrument acts obliquely (fig. 7.3f) it leaves a curvilinear trace of greater or less length, the form of which is due in some cases to the convexity of the cranial dome, in others to the natural obstacles which come in the way of the instrument and prevent it sliding rectilinearly. Sometimes it has been the intention of the operator to limit himself to discoidal form.

Of course, the same types are not presented in the rectilinear incisions as in the curvilinear incisions, but as a rule the latter are combined with the former. In this species of incision the inclination of the instrument has caused a wearing away of the posterior edge of the incision, that is to say, it has made a bevel at the expense of the outer layer of the bone, and hence the tendency to leave the vitreous lamina untouched over a more or less extensive area. See example P-7 (fig. 7.2d).

Three processes have been employed to remove the fragment bounded by the incisions. The rectilinear incisions forming a polygon in the cranium Sak-24 (fig. 7.2e) have been sufficiently deep, particularly in their central part, to penetrate the vitreous lamina, the fragment thus remaining attached by its angles in such a way that a slight effort with the end of the instrument would suffice to pry it up. When the fragment which it is proposed to lift is too large and requires a powerful effort with the lever, a more rational method has been employed. The bony segments previously marked out by the deep incisions are crossed by a series of incisions. The field being now divided into small quadrangular zones, these partial sections are eliminated by the process already mentioned. The roughening is the second process made use of by the operator to eliminate the sections previously marked out. In specimen L-10 (fig. 7.2f) we see that a segment marked out by an incomplete operation has been roughened with the idea of eliminating it, and the cranium P-6 (fig. 7.4a) has even clearer traces of an extensive roughening made for the purpose of removing the segments formed by previous incisions.

In tracing the incisions, the instrument described a to-and-fro movement, either perpendicularly or obliquely to the surface. This was, so to say, a longitudinal rubbing away. In the group which we are now about to consider, the instrument acting with the point, or sides, or edges (fig. 7.3g) has been worked with a rotating movement which wore away or rubbed the bone, thus engendering the various forms of rubbing, from the very circumscribed ones, as in cranium Q-3 (fig. 7.4b), to the extensive rubbings which take in a considerable extent of the cranial dome.

The rubbing does not always involve the whole thickness of the bone. In some cases operations were confined to the external layer and diploe, the vitreous lamina having been left untouched, either because there was an intention to adapt a lamina or obduratic disk to the trephined opening, as in cranium Q-4 (fig. 7.4c), or because the assistance which the vitreous lamina renders in the regeneration of the bone has been recognized. The rubbing sometimes assumes a lenticular form, at others it is almost circular or oval, or it may have a lengthened form which is adapted to, or follows the direction of, a line of fracture.

It only remains to refer to one of the most interesting groups of the collection of trephined crania, typically represented by example L1-35 (fig. 7.4d). This is the cranium of an adult male, which presents an operation situated toward the center of the frontal bone, 55 mm above the nasion and 38 mm below the bregma. The metopic line passes

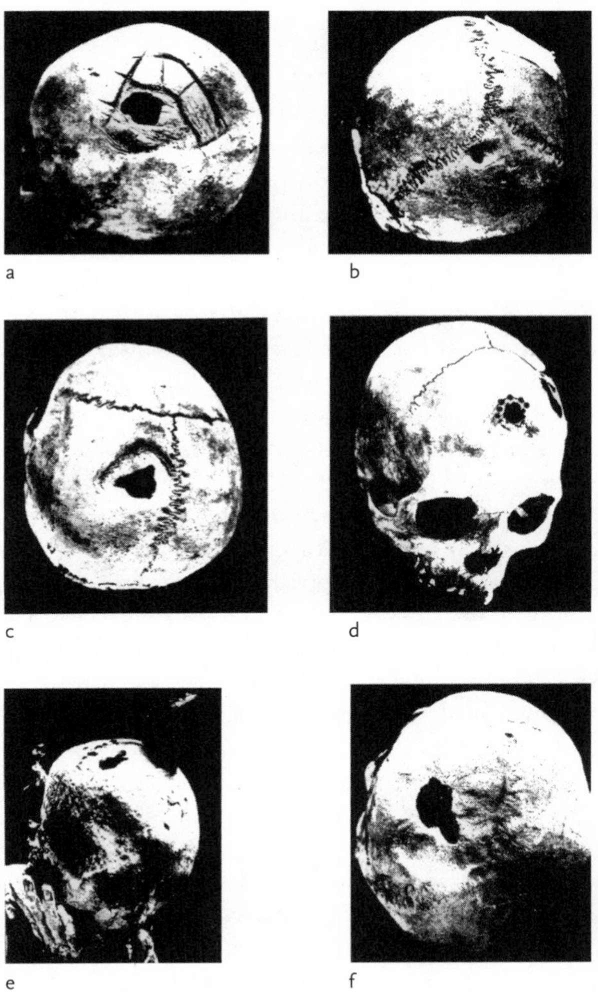

*7.4. Trephined skulls from Yauyos, Peru.*

exactly over its middle part. We shall study successively several small circular hollows, the depth of which only reaches to the diploe, and which limit the operating opening toward its upper part. A curvilinear incision joins the above-mentioned hollows and the operating opening. Portions of bone still remain of the fragment which it was proposed to remove. The hollows are six in number and have an average diameter of about 5 mm, except the lowest to the right, which is only 3 mm in diameter. This leads us to imagine that the operating instrument must have been conical and slightly pointed, perhaps one of the little copper rods which are found in abundance in the same tombs. The regularity of the markings of the hollows and the absence of any scratch round them make it probable that one of these rods acted perpendicularly by percussion (fig. 7.3h), causing only the breaking of the outer layer. A stone instrument acting as a drill could not leave a trace of this nature, but would necessarily produce the preliminary markings which this species of instrument always leaves before going beyond the surface. This induced the writer to repeat the operation, by way of experiment, with one of the copper rods on a fresh cranium. The result obtained by percussion was an incision identical to that presented by the cranium now before us. In this specimen a curvilinear incision has been traced in order to wear away the intermediary bridges between the hollows. The incision was not very deep, as it has only reached the diploe over a short extent. The instrument slipped when working at the right extremity of the incision, which was intended undoubtedly to eliminate the fragment circumscribed by the aforesaid hollows. The opening is of an irregular form, and its average diameter is 14 mm. The upper posterior edge appears in a polycyclical cutting, which shows that four or five hollows had been made, in every respect similar to those described, which occasioned the loss of substance observed at this place. The remains of bony substance left in this incomplete operation show that they were the seat of an osteitis which formed the motive for the operation.

## III

What is undoubtedly most surprising in the study of the trephinings which the ancient Yauyos carried out is the frequency of successful results obtained in the practice of such operations.

In the presence of a cranium which shows an artificial opening, more or less cicatrized, it is difficult to make a differential diagnosis between an opening by trephining and another produced by a simple depressed fracture. Cranial fractures were the most frequent motives for surgical operations, and therefore in the presence of certain losses of substance which at the same time present old fissures, it is almost impossible to define their true origin. The crania in Figures 7.4e and f are specimens of a group of typical cases of cicatrices following trephining. It is worthy of note that in a collection of 400 crania with artificial openings in the dome, 250 had more or less advanced cicatrices, thus revealing the survival of the patients, and the astonishing success obtained.

*Proceedings of the Seventeenth International Congress of Americanists*, pp. 75–83. London, 1912.

CHAPTER EIGHT

# The Discovery of the Chavín Culture in Peru

**THIS PAPER IS A SUMMARY** of the studies and surveys made in recent years to acquire knowledge of the characteristic features of the Chavín culture, and to determine its zone of diffusion in the territory of the Incas, or Tawantinsuyo.

## Introduction

In 1919, while exploring the basin of the Mariash, or Pukcha, River, one of the upper Amazon affluents, I found in Chavín de Huantar evidence of a culture that, up to then, had not been given due recognition. I proved that certain buildings and other products of aboriginal art found there belonged to a quite distinctive cycle of culture—that of the Chavín stone culture. Monolithic figures of serpents and felines, representing human heads, and stelae, obelisks, sundry utensils, and other objects decorated with incised or carved figures in plane, high, or low relief, representing grotesque felines, serpents, fish, lizards, and birds, are the main features of this culture, whose area of diffusion had then been reconnoitered only in the provinces of Huari and Pomabamba.

Subsequent to 1919, I recognized in collections of Peruvian antiquities, in Peru and abroad, a few examples of pottery and gold-work decorated with Chavín motifs; such as a jug in the Elías and Elías Collection made at Morropón in the Piura Valley; another in the Ramón Muñoz Collection from Cajamarquilla, Department of Ancash; a gold plate in the Dalmau Collection at Trujillo; two jugs in that of Lizandro Velez López Collection at Trujillo; a jar in the Máximo Neira Collection in the same city; a jug in the Antonio Raymondi Collection, now in the San Carlos University Museum; a picture of a jug published in the well-known works of Charles Wiener, Arthur Baessler, and Max Schmidt; a broken jug found by Max Uhle in one of the graves opened by him in front of the Huaca of the Moon in Moche; and various specimens, for the most part published by me, in the Trujillo Collection of the brothers Victor and Rafael Larco Herrera. I also recognized clear evidence of Chavín art in various gold pieces discovered by the Galloso brothers at Chongoyape, and in a specimen of the *Strombus* conch recovered by Abraham Pickman during work near the Chiclayo air base.

In the middle of 1925, I discovered in the rubbish heaps and burial caves of Cerro Colorado, in the Paracas Peninsula, a new kind of pottery ornamented with the same motifs and worked with the same technique as in the Chavín art, though with the addition of new typical features that linked genetically with classic Nazca pottery, such as the globular shapes derived from the gourd, tubular necks imitating the bones of birds, and polychrome painting with oil or resinous color.

In 1926 and 1927, while reviewing the works of Max Uhle for the purpose of appraising the foundations for his theory of the origin and development of Peruvian cultures, I was surprised to find that the remains of pottery he found in the Ancón and Supe rubbish deposits were none other than remains of classic Chavín pottery. Uhle believed that these pottery remains belonged to a primitive culture of cannibal fishermen who, according to him, were settled on the coast prior to the appearance of the people who brought from abroad the advanced proto-Chimú and proto-Nazca cultures.

The Chavín culture, despite these dispersed finds, had not yet achieved a separate existence as a true cultural entity. Its sparse and sporadic components seemed to lack direct or immediate sequence. For this reason, the few known proofs of Chavín art were regarded as coming with the domain of Tiahuanaco culture, or within that of Nazca, but always as expressions of other cultures already identified.

## Nepeña Valley: Cerro Blanco and Punkurí

In 1933 I discovered in the Nepeña Valley two splendid examples of Chavín art: the temples Cerro Blanco and Punkurí. For the first time, I proved that remains of Chavín civilization lay buried under the debris of buildings belonging to cultures hitherto considered to be the oldest and most advanced on the Peruvian coast.

Excavation of these monuments furnished fresh data on the characteristic features of Chavín culture in its adaptation to the physical conditions of the coast, on its two phases or stages of development, and on its great antiquity. The Cerro Blanco temple had been buried under a thick layer of mud, remains of old floods, upon which sugarcane is now being grown. In some areas, the temple was covered by two different types of structure—one that seemed to be merely a new local phase of Chavín proper, and another corresponding to the buildings, graves, and rubbish heaps of a people who lived there later. On the lower level, the buildings were of stone; the walls were plastered with mud and decorated with figures in relief, admirably modeled in fine clay and painted in a variety of colors imitating the stone sculptures of Chavín (fig. 8.1). In the fill of buildings destroyed and utilized as foundations of other buildings were found a few fragments of black vessels of the classic Chavín type (fig. 8.2). On the second level, the construction was of stone and small conical unbaked bricks, the walls plastered, smooth-finished, and painted. No fragments of pottery were found in the debris that filled the rooms of the buildings erected above this level. On the upper level were found remains of the dwelling houses, rubbish, and graves of a population that lived there and utilized, in their construction, the materials employed by their predecessors. These people belonged to the culture represented by the multicolored vessels of the Santa and Late Nepeña type, being contemporaries of the Chimú.

In the Punkurí temple, conditions were almost wholly repeated. The *huaca* has at one time been buried in great part under a mass of mud that seems to have spread over the entire valley. The lower level contained stone structures with walls decorated in the classic Chavín style. These buildings were knocked down and used later as foundations for the new buildings of the middle level, and this, in turn, served in similar fashion for those of the upper level. As at Cerro Blanco, in the two lower levels, remains of Chavín culture were found: an idol made of stone and mud, representing in high relief the figure of a feline painted in different colors; a grave containing the body of a sacrificed woman, together with a spiral conch (*Strombus galeatus*), a handkerchief embroidered with turquoise sequins, and a mortar and pestle, both of diorite, polished and engraved with figures in the classic Chavín style (fig. 8.3). In the middle level, the building had walls of conical mud bricks and were decorated with incised figures on a

*8.1. Cerro Blanco temple, Nepeña Valley. The inverted Ls and the frames of the upright elements on the back wall are brick red; frames on the lower elements are greenish yellow.*

*8.2. Cerro Blanco temple, Nepeña Valley. Fragments of monochrome incised pottery. Red pigment or traces of graphite in some incisions.*

previously plastered surface. Above this level were also found remains of dwellings, rubbish, and graves of the Late period of Santa, Nepeña, and Chimú (fig. 8.4).

Consequently, we have ample proof in Nepeña that the Chavín culture had spread to the coast and had become adapted to the conditions peculiar to its new medium. In the first stage of such adaptation, it had faithfully preserved the characteristics of the original culture; by the second, it had undergone considerable modification. For instance, the structures of the first stage were exclusively of stone, and were ornamented with figures that accurately reproduced those of the temple at Chavín. In the second stage, the buildings were of conical unbaked bricks plainly imitating the cuneiform stones used in the previous level, and painted figures copied the incised and relief figures of the original stone art. In the third stage, all features of both phases of the earlier art disappeared completely; the buildings were now of rectangular unbaked blocks, with plastered walls adorned with figures corresponding to an entirely new style. The structures of this period no doubt lasted until the Spanish Conquest.

Exploration of the Nepeña Valley, from Samanco Bay to the limits of the cis-Andine zone, permitted a fairly complete survey of the principal features of the cultures existing there. Among these are the following: (1) Ruins of towns, with burial grounds in the outskirts with more or less uniform contents, some built with rectangular mud bricks

*8.3. Stone vase with engraved figures, Huaca Punkurí, Nepeña Valley.*

*8.4. Stone vase with engraved figures, Huaca Suchiman, Santa Valley.*

made in a mold, others with small stones and mud, all belonging to the last stage of occupation of the valley and situated at intervals along the side valleys. (2) Pyramids in tiers, associated with other structures with large rectangular rooms built of mud bricks, and decorated, for the greater part, with multicolored frescoes representing warlike or mythological scenes, similar to those on Muchik vessels; also burial grounds in the outskirts with overlying graves and more or less uniform contents, hard to differentiate in respect of their two stages of development, for the later one seems to be simply a continuation of the preceding one. The same type of pottery runs through the two stages, retaining its morphological and decorative features with the sole difference of a falling off in the art quality of the latter stage. (3) Stone structures completely distinct in style from the above, but similar or identical to Andean megalithic constructions, such as those of Kusi Pampa, Pincha Marka, Kiske, Huaca Partida, Paña Marka, and the second *huaca* of Cerro Blanco. In the lower part of the valley, these buildings are found buried by others of a later age, and in the upper part they are uncovered and of such pure style that they continue without any apparent differentiation up to the Callejón de Huaylas. In the structures of this archaic style situated in the lower valley, the characteristic style of Chavín architecture stands out clearly. These *huacas* have platforms at different heights, communication between platforms being by shafts, and remains of altars, columns, and walls profusely decorated with figures modeled or painted in mud in the style of those carved in stone at Chavín de Huantar. In these *huacas*, use is made of conical mud bricks of different sizes, from 20 to 80 cm high, for the building up of the walls and the filling in of the platforms.

Before discovery of the Chavín culture in the Nepeña Valley, it might have been thought, judging by the few isolated finds of potsherds, that the old trans-Andine populations had filtered in, in a casual manner, by the lowlands of the coast or the *montaña*, in the fashion of temporary or migratory colonies. The Nepeña discovery definitely cleared up the true character of the Chavín culture on the coast. In the first place, it was now proved that this culture was rich in representative material, that it was unmistakable in its distinctive features, and identical to the trans-Andine culture in its essential characteristics. In the second place, it was demonstrated that its remains occupy a lower stratum than the cultures regarded by other investigators as the first and oldest in Peru. The Chavín people developed on virgin soil in the Nepeña Valley a civilization without precedent in respect to both originality and excellence of artistic production. The same architectural style, employment of the same kind of decorative and symbolic motifs, and particular methods of utilizing local materials, adapting them to preestablished standards, give the Chavín culture features of its own.

In possession of material that permitted us to differentiate the above culture, we then found it necessary to direct investigation toward broadening our knowledge of its characteristics and inquiring about its original sources of diffusion. These considerations, in the first place, made it necessary to explore Casma Valley, on account of its special geographical situation, and, in the second place, made equally essential the intensive exploration of the watersheds of the Cordillera Negra and the Callejón de Huaylas; for, in both regions, the remains of Chavín culture must lie beneath the strata corresponding to the cultures that had so far appeared there to be the predominant and oldest ones.

## Casma Valley: The Cerro Sechín Temple

In the second half of 1937, I was commissioned by San Marcos University in Lima to undertake an archaeological survey of northern Peru and to study by preference the remains of the oldest civilizations found throughout that territory, between the coast and the Amazon frontier. The expedition equipped for the purpose was made possible by help lent by the Institute of Andean Research in the United States and by Nelson A. Rockefeller.

*8.5. Moxeke, Casma Valley. Lower portion of idol made of stone, conical adobes, and mud, faced with clay and decorated with white, yellow, black, and red pigment, and placed in one of the niches running the length of the outer terrace.*

Throughout the trip I was accompanied by Messrs. Toribio Mejía X., Pedro Rojas, and Hernán Ponce, employees of the San Marcos University Museum, and by Miss Honour McCreery and Miss Barbara Loomis of the University of New Mexico, and for three months by Donald Collier of the Institute of Andean Research. Also for two weeks the expedition was joined by Edward McCormick Blair and Deering Danielson.

Among the more important sites surveyed by this expedition were the ruins of Sechín, Moxeke (fig. 8.5), and Pallka (figs. 8.6a–c, 8.7, 8.8), situated in the Casma Valley and identified as belonging to the Chavín culture; the megalithic aqueduct of Kumbe Mayo, near Cajamarca; the Yanakancha megalithic mausoleums near Hualgayoc; the Cochabamba megalithic ruins in the province of Chachapoyas; the Chokta ruins in the province of Celedín; and the Nunamarka ruins close to Chilia in Pataz Province. Except for Casma Valley, these are all within the Marañon basin.

The final report of the explorations carried out by the Marañon Archaeological Expedition, which is still in preparation, will contain the evidence to prove the wide zone of diffusion of the Chavín culture in the sierra and coast of Peru. For the time being I will confine myself to recording the discovery of the Sechín, Moxeke, and Pallka temples in Casma Valley, some of which, like that of Sechín, are adorned with sculptured monoliths in the Chavín style.

On my first visit in 1937 to the Cerro Sechín *huaca*, lying at the foot of the northern slope of the rock called "Los Corrales" or "Cerro Sechín," some 7 km to the east of the town of Casma, my attention was called to five stone posts on the edge of the side valley in which the *huaca* stands, standing in an almost straight line, barely emerging above the surface. Three were close together toward the east, and two, separated from each other, toward the west. Inspection of the surroundings of the *huaca* disclosed the existence of other stones, lying half buried in the fields and displaying carved figures on one face.

The posts turned out to correspond to other and larger units buried under a thick bed of loose earth; all showed, on one face, carved figures that were in turn part of other larger figures lost in the depths.

In order to gain more concrete information about the presence of these stones in such an unfrequented spot, I directed preliminary work toward digging out all stones in the loose soil.

My first impression was that these stones had been hauled from some other older building, from the Sechín Alto Temple, for instance,

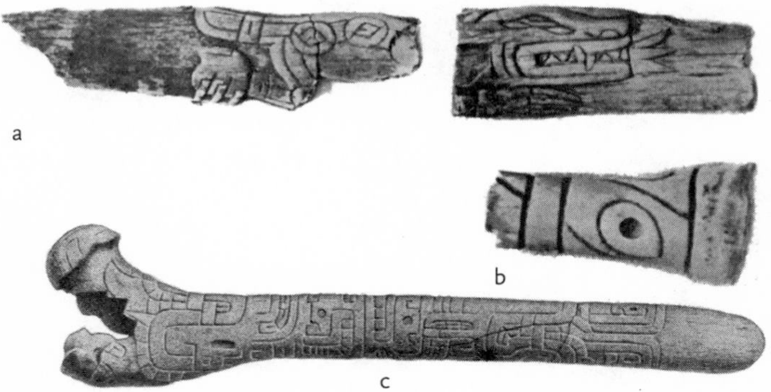


*8.6. a, fragment of bone spatula with engraved figures; b, fragment of the tube of human bone; both from rubbish heap in subsoil, Pallka, Casma Valley; c, bone spatula, Chicama Valley (private collection).*

*8.7. Pallka, Yautan District, Casma Valley. Potsherds from rubbish heap in subsoil beneath ruins.*

*8.8. Pallka, Yautan District, Casma Valley. Potsherds from ash heaps in ruins. Decorations done with sharp instruments.*

being brought here by another people for reuse or a new type of use. I was soon convinced, by the discovery of additional stone posts, that they followed a continuous line, with short empty intervening spaces. I then thought they perhaps formed part of a monument resembling the square precinct of Kalasasaya at Tiahuanaco. This forced me to deepen the excavation on the north side of the row, in order to reach the level on which they stood. For this I divided the ground of operations into 4 m sections, in order to examine carefully the details of position, shape, size, and ornamentation of the stones, and at the same time secure data about the terrain in which they were interred. While carefully removing, on one side, the layer of loose earth on the top level, which contained no archaeological remains at all, I had a vertical trench cut around the stone at the western end, following its sides very closely. I chose this spot because, behind this stone, there was a big depression in the ground about 2 m deep and from 3 to 4 m across. The earth and stones covering the monolith in front and behind were easily removed, and its base was reached. It was lightly propped against a pile of stones placed in front like wedges; and it contained a figure cut in plane relief, a half-human, half-feline monster, to judge from its features (figs. 8.9, 8.10). Because of its bristling disheveled locks, no doubt, the inhabitants call this the "*Huaca* of the Fierce Idol."

Excavation was easy behind the monolith. The stones piled there, and the loose soil, were taken out for a depth of 2 m, down to the base. At the front face, and the left and right sides, the job was harder. In front, the stone rested on mud hardened to the consistency of concrete, with a few stones embedded in it. At the sides, the base was likewise wedged by a number of small stones driven between the monolith and the adjacent large stones. To lighten the task and secure complete isolation of the monolith, we proceeded to straighten it and incline it slightly backward. Only then could we separate the pile of stones against which it lay; this pile, in turn, hid another, small monolith. Extending the excavation from east to west, we found on either side of the monolith of the Fierce Idol three more monoliths of the same shape and size as the small one. All four displayed human heads cut on one face.

Though two small monoliths were found at the very bottom of the excavation standing upright and in line with the larger one, no important fact was observed explaining the curious position of these stones. However, one of the smaller ones had left a clean-cut impression of its carved face in the mud on which it had fallen. This revealed that the monoliths at this site had been thrown forward, turned over, and dragged for a distance by a mass of mud originating in and traveling

8.9. Cerro Sechín. Engraved monoliths.

from the upper part of the side valley. For the rest, the ground consisted of a conglomerate of small stones cemented by a very hard, dark brown clay.

Work was proceeding simultaneously in other sections, for the sole purpose of removing the surface layer and locating the existing monoliths. Some others were uncovered, it being noted that they preserved a uniform, marked forward inclination. Digging was continued down to the level corresponding to the platform on which the wall of monoliths had stood. Toward the east, excavation was a laborious job, on account of the great amount of loose earth piled up there. To get at the base of the stones, it became necessary to move this earth in considerable volume, increasing in proportion as the digging advanced toward the west. Furthermore, a short way down, a multitude of

*8.10. Cerro Sechín. Engraved monoliths.*

stones appeared, almost completely covering the monoliths. Just as at the opposite end, the major and minor monoliths kept the same relative position, the first leaning or lying in a forward direction, the second intercalated between them. Among the latter, those at the lowest depth were standing upright or leaning forward slightly, and those that had without doubt been on top of these were found 1, 2, or 3 m ahead—minor monoliths underneath major monoliths, as if an earthquake had shaken the monument with such force that the wedges at the sides and below each monolith had been displaced, allowing it to fall. The solidity of construction on this side must have been much greater than on the other, for here there are still to be found remains of the primitive well-made wall. Though all the upper stones are out of position, the lower ones seem to be firmly set, especially in the section corresponding to the intervals separating the major monoliths. Moreover, the destructive force must have acted with greater intensity in the upper portion than in the lower, for only so can the falling or leaning forward of the majority of the major monoliths be explained.

On the western side, more so than on the eastern, the digging provided very illuminating data as to the formation of the exposed ground. At a certain depth, after getting rid of the layer of loose earth mixed with gravel and sand, a thin bed of rubbish was found running obliquely in front of the wall. Within this bed appeared fragments of multicolored pottery and skeletons of human beings and dogs. This bed thickened and assumed a frankly horizontal position as the trench advanced above and behind the row of monoliths. As soon as it was noted that the ground in this spot retained its stratified character, we tried as far as possible to avoid any falling-in of the upper layer and to deepen the trench in front. By this means it was possible to carry on excavation for 23 m, from a hollow that apparently marked the eastern limit of the wall, to the stone that stood out upon the highest part of the loose earth.

In the course of excavation, it was observed that the monoliths discovered on one side seemed to be twins of those on the other, so that the building may have had two symmetrical sides, left and right, with perhaps an entrance in the center marked by the tallest stone. This induced me to continue the work on the left, or eastern, side, and determine definitely the course of the wall. Excavation on this side proved as interesting and full of surprises as on the other. To get fuller information on the structure of the ground and the exact placing of the carved stones, I had the field of operations enlarged both areally and in depth. Not to lose any important detail, we at first removed only the loose surface earth; then we continued examining the ground as it was cut into along the trench opened from east to west.

The loose surface earth having been removed, there came into view, just as on the other side, the compact mass of stones and mud, and, in this, the carved stones. It was a hard job to remove this conglomerate in order to uncover the monoliths. Here, better than on the right-hand side, the stones that fell in the mud left the impression of their designs; and here also the evidence revealed by the excavation was far more illustrative and attractive, since it was possible to contemplate the ravages and magnitude of the earthquake.

The major and minor monoliths were found one after the other, the former lying down or leaning heavily forward, the latter thrown 2 or 3 m away from the wall. Some of the major ones were fractured in the upper third, and some of the minor ones were found under these. The falling flat of the bigger ones permitted examination of the ground on which they had been set up. The stones, strictly speaking, had had no foundations; they were placed directly on the hard stony floor with a few wedges at the sides. One of the monoliths had been placed on a heap of water-borne stones.

We next proceeded to excavate the central section, in order to join up the side trenches. This task was somewhat difficult, owing to the accumulation of loose earth that at this spot reached a greater volume, and to the need to extend the digging over a greater area in order to avoid slides. Five meters down a large stone was uncovered, the twin of the one on the other side. It was lying face down and was completely covered by a thick layer of stones and mud. This monolith has its top worn away, as if it had been exposed for a long time, and is broken in two at one-third of its height, as if in falling heavily it had hit against a projecting stone that acted upon it like a wedge. Toward the east of this long stone were found two minor monoliths, as if violently displaced from the wall. The space between the two large stones measures 9.7 m, and excavation here down to the level of the base or foundation of the wall showed that the two tall monoliths had been stuck into the mass of stones and hardened mud to a depth of 2 m. Above this mass was found a row of stones, almost all of the same size, covered by a thick bed of rubbish. This is the same bed that appears in the trench on the eastern side and continues along the western trench. The composition of this bed of rubbish is not uniform; in the lower half it is much mixed with earth and sand, and in the upper half it contains fragments of household pottery and many organic remains. Over this stratum is the loose earth of the lower level.

Observations made during the course of excavation, and the type of archaeological material obtained, furnish information regarding the sites occupied by the buildings adorned with engraved monoliths, the structure of the adjacent terrain, and the agency that disturbed the monuments, breaking up some and burying others, and thereby compelling the erection of fresh buildings upon the remains of the earlier ones.

The attached diagram (fig. 8.11) illustrates the outcome of our observations in respect to the excavations carried out in the eastern half of the temple facade. In the figure, letters mark the sections into which the terrain was divided in order to facilitate a methodical plan of excavation. The major and minor monoliths have below them letters and roman numerals for their better identification, and behind the row of monoliths are seen the layers or strata corresponding to the three

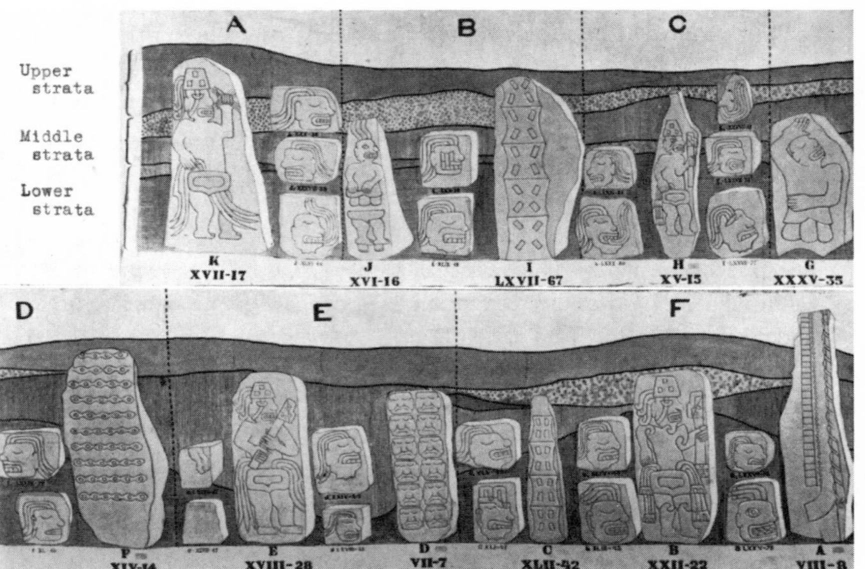


*8.11. Cerro Sechín. Eastern half of temple facade.*

stages or periods of occupation of this important construction.

The strata present an undulating surface, with easy rises and low depressions, at times of a considerable width. It is evident that the continuity of these strata, along the line of the facade, was broken by subsequent excavations, and mainly by streams of water or mud descending from the slopes of the neighboring hill.

Three main strata or levels are clearly distinguishable: the lower, the middle, and the upper. The first is formed by a mass of dried mud of a compact nature, in which are embedded large quantities of cobbles and medium-size stones with sharp edges, doubtless carried along by the mud. This mass of hardened clay forms one of the many strata of valley fill resulting from floodings by the river that even today wanders across the countryside without any definite bed. On the surface of this layer, or set inside it, is the row of engraved monoliths. A layer of rubbish of varying thickness and broken up into different patches occupies the depressions of this level. In it are found potsherds of the sub-Chavín type, kitchen midden remains, and other material, in every way resembling that discovered in the Teatino cemetery, in the Supe burial ground near the Faro where Uhle labored years ago, in various Nepeña and Santa cemeteries, and in the lowest layer of a cut made by the La Leche River close to the Batan Grande Huaca (Lambayeque). This rubbish, judging from the pottery, belongs to the Chavín culture in its second period, called by the writer sub-Chavín, to which also belong the vessels found by Bennett in the Gallinazo cemetery, in Virú.

The middle level is formed by another thick layer of hardened mud containing bits of conical adobes, stones, and even lumps of plastered walls painted with polychrome figures. It has a very unequal depth. Near the center its depth reaches to as much as 2 m and, at a distance from the center, to only 20 cm. The direction of this mass, the remains of old inundations, is distinct from and opposite to that of the previous inundation. In the latter, it runs from the river toward the foot of the hill, and in the former from the foot of the hill to the river. In all probability, torrential rains running down the hillside flooded the built-upon area, brought down the buildings, and, aided by the impermeability of the granite rock of the subsoil, swept toward the valley bottom, overturning and dragging the monoliths from their foundations, at times, for a distance of 2 to 3 m. The mud covering these monoliths, the impression left in the mud by each one at falling, the disorderly, inclined position, and signs of dragging in nearly every case lead to the conviction that in an extremely remote period, the building decorated with the monoliths was buried by an avalanche of alluvial matter. As in the case of the lower level, on the surface of this middle level we come across an abundance of rubbish and several graves containing pottery of the Santa or Huaylas-Yunga type. This differs from the sub-Chavín type, though retaining certain features of resemblance, and differs still more from the classic Chavín type.

The upper level has a different makeup from that of the former. The ground is relatively loose earth, sand, gravel, and cobblestones. Upon it are found remains of terraces and other roughly made stone structures and rectangular adobes; burials with pottery of the sub-Chimú, sub-Santa, and Inca type; and a new kind of incised pottery known from surface rubbish heaps in almost the entire Casma Valley.

Having satisfactorily proved the straight course of the monoliths from one end of the row to the other, or between the hollows that apparently served as side boundaries to a platform, I proceeded to explore the terrain immediately behind the central portion of the wall and its eastern and western ends. For this purpose I made several soundings on the presumed platform, with the following results:

1. The main wall, 52 m long, turns back at both ends, forming a curve at the corners. It maintains the same level for the whole distance, penetrating below the thick beds of rubbish and the buildings subsequently raised over them.

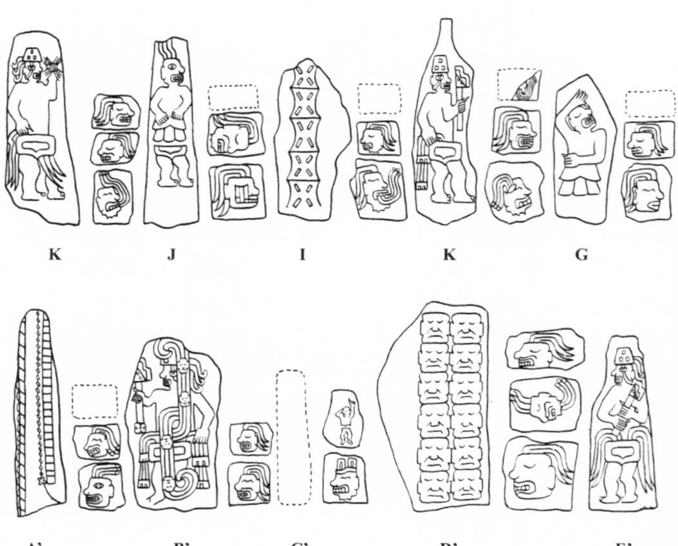


*8.12. Arrangement of the monoliths decorating the principal facade of the temple of Cerro Sechín. The upper row represents those on the eastern half of the front, the lower, those on the western half.*

2. Though the side walls are well preserved, it can be asserted that they are made of reused material, carved stones to which the builders attached no significance, utilizing them merely as building material, or perhaps as ornamentation. The major and minor monoliths were carelessly placed, and at different levels in the structure of the wall. Some of the human heads were reversed, and, in one instance, instead of a major monolith, a large plain stone had been set up.

3. On the eastern side, it was found that a thick wall of stones and mud had been built perpendicularly against the side wall of carved stones. This wall is nothing but the support of a terrace added to the main platform sustained by the wall of monoliths. The two structures must be of the same age.

4. Test excavations on both banks of the platform showed, finally, that the wall of carved stones is underneath a thick layer of stones and hardened mud, on which were raised the terraces, which, in turn, served as a floor to the numerous dwellings of the population that established itself in this place long after the builders of the wall had disappeared.

In the Cerro Sechín *huaca*, ninety-six monoliths were discovered altogether; eighty-nine alongside the wall or at a short distance in front

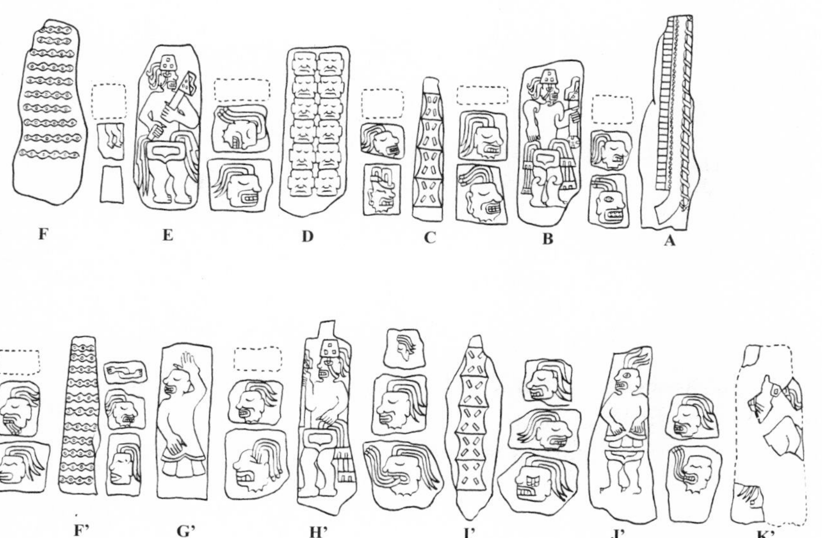


of it, and 7, 30, or 40 m to the northwest, scattered, turned over, and half-buried (fig. 8.12). There are two types of monolith: one, long, tall, and prismatic, like an obelisk, or in the shape of a tablet or flagstone, like a stela; the other, irregularly cubical. The first is here called a major monolith, and the second a minor monolith.

The stones apparently come from the quarries adjoining the *huaca*. The whole of Cerro Sechín is of granite formation. At the foot and on the slopes are heaps of stones broken away from the ledge, in the shape of thick slabs or large prismatic blocks. This material has been used by the ancients in their building and sculptures.

As a rule, on each minor monolith there is found a fracture face corresponding to the breaking away of the large block subsequently split to the required size. Major and minor monoliths were chosen in accordance with what they were to represent. On the faces and edges, no trace of preliminary working or of adaptation to a predetermined shape is found. There is no dressing or polishing of the stone. Even on the flat side where the carving comes there are no signs of previous smoothing of the surface. Some stones exhibit uneven sides, due to flaking or fracture; yet the figure appears carved on them, regardless of flaws that could easily have been eliminated. The major monoliths have a height of 180–440 cm, the minor ones, 60–120 cm.

The major monoliths were found face down or leaning forward. Four of the shortest of these were found in an almost vertical position, one to the east and three to the west. The minor monoliths were in some cases in their original position in the wall, standing upright or inclined slightly forward, in other cases a meter or a meter and a half away, as if they had been thrown from the top of the wall prior to the fall of the major monoliths.

## The Sculpture Cerro Sechín Monoliths

The monoliths show signs of lengthy exposure. Old breaks in the surface of the principal face have, as a general rule, destroyed the continuity of the figure represented on it; much, and in some instances widespread, erosion and scaling have eliminated the angles or worn them down. Such erosion also appears, in some examples, on the surface of the principal face, at intervals, as if the stone, after being carved, had been dragged over other stones. Among the fractured stones it is seen that, in some, the fracture took place before the falling of the stone, for, at the top, the carved figure is incomplete through the breaking away of one or two bits. In others, the fracture is the result of the stone falling and knocking against other stones. In this case a comminuted fracture appears at the top end, through the stone having split into pieces. In one instance, the carved stone in falling collided with another of the same kind. The principal face of almost every stone exhibits a layer of yellow patina, which spreads uniformly over the raised parts, the hollows, the grooves, and the deep cuts.

The technique employed in presentation of the carved figures is uniform throughout (figs. 8.9, 8.10). No fundamental differences are to be found. All seem to be the work of one artist, or of artists trained to standards of the same school. The grooves, hollows, and flat surfaces show no traces of a cutting tool. The grooves are few. The broad hollowed-out parts have been produced by an abrasion tool wearing away the surface to the required depth; the bottom and sides of these hollows reveal the delicate work of friction by a tool that wears away the stone gently and slowly. It is possible that this work was done with the help of water or some other substance giving cohesion to the abrasive sand inside the cut and facilitating handling of the tools.

No difference is noted, either, in the removal of the background of the figures. The same instrument scrapes and smooths the edges of the hollows. Work is not carried very far on the background, and this is what produces its rounded or curved aspect, similar to that of the cushion-shaped stones with rubbed-away angles found in the seats in the Cuzco ruins.

The operation of slow abrasion of the stone must have been preceded by the incised drawing of the outline of the figure. This is pertinently illustrated in the carving of one of the big monoliths in the central portion of the wall. This stone was selected because one of its faces afforded an almost black polished surface due to a layer of mica, perhaps a leaf from a fault, upon which the figure was drawn by incision, without reduction of the background, as if the job had been left unfinished.

To facilitate study of the monoliths that adorn the wall, a capital letter was assigned to each, starting, in each half, from the column marking the entrance, which is also the tallest.

The right- and left-hand, or eastern and western, halves consist of ten major monoliths and ten groups of minor monoliths placed above and intercalated between the major ones. These minor stones have been assigned small letters.

The figures represented on the monoliths, with the exception of the two tallest in the center, are of the same nature. They all show the human body, fully or partially, with certain feline features, and can be classified under three types: (1) full-length human figures, naked or provided with a simple headdress, a belt, and a tool or ceremonial branch; (2) human figures cut off at the waists; (3) bits of human anatomy—heads, eyes, vertebrae, hands, and feet.

Desiring a close acquaintance with the archaeological site discovered at the foot of the north side of Cerro Sechín, I did some exploratory work within the area of cultivated land comprised between the building discovered and the Sechín River. This reconnaissance led to proof of the existence of a wide depression that must have been a water reservoir, a little less than 25 m to the north of the temple. On the banks of this reservoir were found remains of stone walls, buried under deep layers of rubbish, and many fragments of monoliths with engraved figures. The rubbish occupies an extensive area within the cultivated fields, and in certain spots forms low hillocks or platforms partly destroyed by floods. Everything causes one to think that a building of engraved stones, similar to that at Cerro Sechín, stood on the level ground between the river and the foot of the hill almost on the edge of the above reservoir. This building must have been flooded, swept away, and buried in one of the many spates of the river.

Figure 8.13 I shows the first monument, X, erected facing Cerro Sechín. Around this there must have existed many dwelling houses, Y, and perhaps other larger buildings.

An inundation of this side of the valley must have taken place subsequently (fig. 8.13 II). The mud, laden with stones, swept forward and filled up the main hollow at the foot of the hill, and the ground resulting from this inundation, D, buried the primitive building X.

Later on, another building, X' (fig. 8.13 III), was erected on a higher level and closer to the hill, using for the purpose the materials, chiefly dressed stones, that at the beginning formed part of the building X. In this second building stage, a new material was employed in

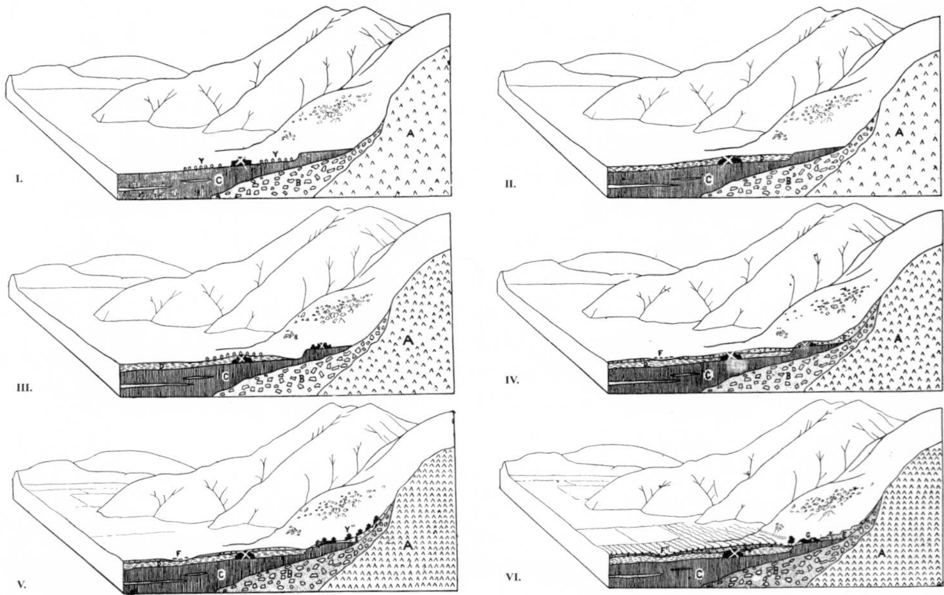


*8.13. Sections through Cerro Sechín Valley. A = Granite rock; B = Scree, formed of debris from weathering of granite rock, gravel, hardened earth, and angular cobblestones; C = Alluvial deposits forming part of filling of valley; D = Ground made by old river floods; E = Landslide from slopes of Cerro Sechín; F = Cultivated ground with rubbish; X = Remains of old buildings of Chavín type; Y = Remains of old dwellings.*

*I. The structures of the first period of Chavín culture.*

*II. Subsequent burial and destruction of these buildings, by alluviation and deposit of D.*

*III. Structures of second period of Chavín culture built on alluvial deposits.*

*IV. Destruction of these structures resulted from landslide, E, loosened from mountainside by torrential rains.*

*V. Third period structures were built on layer E.*

*VI. The present time. Modern cotton fields appear on the valley floor, while treasure hunters have sunk pits into the remains of buildings.*

the form of the conical adobe, and the technique of plastering and painting the walls of the chambers built within the enclosure of graved stones. A long period must have elapsed between the erection of one building and the other, because in the vicinity of X appear remains of pottery of the classic Chavín type, and in that of X' sub-Chavín-type sherds. This classic Chavín type, probably imported from the Sierra, becomes considerably modified to form the second type.

A further inundation, or rather slide of a great mass of earth and gravel from the hillside, took place later. This mass E (fig. 8.13 IV) buried and destroyed the second building X', filling up its different compartments and the passages and courtyards protected by the enclosure of monoliths. It came down with such force that it moved the great monoliths out of their vertical position, inclining them forward and in certain instances dragging them 3 m beyond the line of the enclosure. In this second layer of alluvial earth are remains of the sub-Chavín culture, fragments of conical adobes, pieces broken from the painted walls, and potsherds, all embedded in the compact mass of mud. Remains of this inundation appear outside the wide depression of ground, F, that to this day is marshy land and in other times, as has been said, must have been a reservoir.

On the layer thus formed various terraces that served as platforms, Y" (fig. 8.13 V), for dwelling houses later were built. The ruins of the latter are today buried under great accumulations of rubbish covering graves containing ceramics of the classic Santa or Huaylas-Yunga type. The torrential rains that fell on the coast of northern Peru in 1925 gave rise to streams on the hillsides that cut through the layers of rubbish, washing them for a considerable distance to the riverbed. And the *huaca* and treasure hunters have utilized these cuts in order to exploit the graves in the subsoil. The cropping of some stones of the enclosure, which served us as a guide in carrying out excavations in that place, is also due to this last inundation. Figure 8.13 VI illustrates the general disposition of the different strata that constitute this archaeological site, and has been drawn in the light of the knowledge obtained by means of multiple exploratory excavations.

## Types of Chavín Structures on the Coast

Little is known of the minor structures. Chavín potsherds appear in certain ash heaps that are the only evidence of human habitation. Possibly dwellings of huts of perishable material, with small stones and mud, formerly stood over or near to the area occupied today by the ash heaps. In some cases, heaps of rectangular or circular stones, or small terraces, seem to point to the remains of dwellings that might be assigned to the Chavín culture, since pottery remains of this type are exposed on the surface. But the most interesting point is that beneath these remains of buildings and dwellings, and hidden, as a rule, by the rubbish and accumulations of stones, are found graves of the Chavín type. Consequently, the custom widely generalized on the Peruvian coast, of burying the dead near the towns or even inside them, must be of great antiquity.

With respect to the major buildings, there is found to be a more or less uniform type, easily recognized throughout the Peruvian coast. A wall or rectangular fence, serving as a defense or protection to a main building that almost invariably occupies the center, and to other small structures alongside this, is associated with graves. The main structure of stone or sun-dried brick is formed of two or more terraces or small platforms, rising one above the other, there being on the top terrace a building almost always made of conical sun-dried bricks. It is not yet possible to determine the structural style of this main building, as it is completely demolished as a result of having been, for the greater part, despoiled by treasure hunters. It is only just possible to identify the platforms, the stonework of the revetment or supports of these platforms that form fairly high and level parapets, and the heaps of mud bricks constituting the remains of the temple proper. Likewise, little is known of the minor structures, beyond the scanty debris strewn inside the fenced area. On the coast, the wall is of stone and mud.

This type of major structure, involving a rectangular fence and smaller buildings among which stands a larger one that is, properly speaking, the temple, is characteristic. Its plan was so deeply ingrained in the mind of the ancient builders that in some instances, where the terrain was too broken to allow the building of the fence, this, in keeping with the preestablished plan, was even built on the side of the hill.

After the fact of the diffusion of Chavín culture on the coast was confirmed by the above finds, an important problem still awaited solution. The distribution of the classic Chavín-type pottery found on the coast was not well defined. Since, from time to time, isolated and sporadic specimens were found, it was thought that they might belong to colonies of people from the other side of the Andes that had occasionally settled on the coast, bringing their products from the interior. Beyond the Cordillera Negra, however, this kind of pottery was nowhere to be found. Was the Chavín pottery on the coast perhaps older than that in the highlands? Was the Chavín stone culture perhaps of less age than the conical mud-brick culture of the coast? Here are a few facts that partly help to clear up these doubts.

## Subsoil Pottery at Chavín de Huantar

In 1919 I recognized in the cultivated fields under which the great Chavín de Huantar temple is buried, and in the earth removed in order to uncover the steps of the main wing, a large quantity of black, brown, white, and red potsherds very similar to the household pottery appearing on the surface of the ruins in the Callejón de Huaylas. I failed to find one single specimen of Chavín pottery, either there or in the widespread rubbish heaps stretching toward the northern side of the Chavín ruins and close to the Wacheska River. In August 1934 I made a second visit to Chavín. The torrential rains that had fallen periodically in the years subsequent to 1919 had changed the bed of the Mariash River (Mosna River), on whose left bank Chavín stands. The fierce current of this river, after reaching the ruins, had destroyed and swept away a large portion of the main wings (fig. 8.14). After years it continued undermining the temple and deepening its course below the level foundations of the building. A third of the monument, intact in former years, had thus been destroyed; the debris had been swept away by the river, and the foundations badly undermined.

*8.14. Cut across east face of Chavín de Huantar made by Mariash [Mosna] River.*

*8.15. Chavín de Huantar. Potsherds from subsoil.*

While contemplating the damage done, I received a pleasant surprise. In the lowest beds of the riverbank I discovered a thick vein of rubbish containing a multitude of fragments of human and llama bones, and an abundance of sherds of the pottery so often sought in the Andean zone and only found as stray specimens on the seaboard. I took out of this vein of rubbish, and from other lower levels in the subsoil of the megalithic structures, a rich and instructive collection of classic Chavín pottery: black pottery, well polished and with a gloss with incised and carved decorations like those found in the best stone carvings of this marvelous Chavín art (figs. 8.15, 8.16). All this material lay buried under thick beds of gravel and mud washed down from the neighboring hillside.

This find contributed to a better knowledge of the characteristic features of Chavín culture, and to greater familiarity with the technical, morphological, ornamental, and representative aspects of its ceramics. It also permitted us to appraise certain data related to its high grade of workmanship and extreme age. The pottery is found beneath the alluvial level on which the megalithic structures of the temple were erected, which leads one to think that there is here also an overlapping of buildings belonging to other periods, and that the structures on the

8.16. *Vessel found in lower layers of cut shown above.*

lower level had been erected by people who were at once sculptors and potters, whose ruins were later buried under the layers of alluvium and new buildings raised upon them.

## Mocán and Kotosh

Fresh finds have, to a certain extent, helped to widen the horizon of this culture. While I was exploring Chavín, Toribio Mejía Xesspe was uncovering a small "*paskana*," or stopping place, close to the old road running up to the Contumazá highlands, at the foot of Cerro Colorado, 15 km north of the Mocán estate, in the Chicama Valley. At this halting place, he found sprinkled on the surface a quantity of Chavín potsherds mixed with others of the Chimú household type. This pottery, though less rich in ornamentation than the classic, is uniformly black and grayish like the former, and its style is markedly Chavín.

Among the potsherds taken out of the subsoil of the Chavín de Huantar temple were some resembling the incised and carved types of the Amazon country, which Nordenskiold considers to be the oldest there. This fact, added to the reports of the Franciscan missionaries of the existence of black, fine, carved pottery in the outskirts of San Luís de Shuaro, in the Perené basin, induced me to make an archaeological inspection trip in 1935 to the headwaters of the Marañon, Huallaga, and Ucayali rivers. In the surroundings of Huánaco, I found several artificial hillocks on whose surface appeared a few Chavín potsherds. In one of these, called the *huaca* Kotosh, dug into in past years down to its base by treasure hunters, I found in the upper beds of the cutting an abundance of Chavín potsherds mixed with other types closely resembling, on one hand, incised and painted pottery of the Paracas caves, and, on the other, incised and carved Amazonian pottery (figs. 8.17, 8.18).

## Pukará

In October 1935 I spent a few days in Pukará, a village in the province of Lampa on the right bank of the headwaters of the river of the same name, a small tributary of Lake Titicaca. This place is an old pottery-making center, famed for the antique stone sculptures, statues, and reliefs existing in the vicinity.

*8.17. Kotosh near Huánuco, Huallaga Valley. Pottery from rubbish layer.*

The modern village of Pukará stands on a wide alluvial terrace that partly covers another town of greater area, the remains of which are evidenced by hillocks and rows of stones, disposed in circles and rectangles scattered over the plain. Some of these stones are dressed, polished, and carved with figures in great part analogous to those appearing on the Chavín monoliths. The natives of Pukará now make earthen vessels; in their huts are found in actual use the implements and material of this craft. The earth used in preparing the mud and unbaked bricks of which they build their houses, and the soil cultivated for their crops, contains a large assortment of pottery of the classic Inca type. The plow turns up pottery mingled with earth and gravel. Strolling through the narrow village streets one observes that the walls and fences are plastered with beautiful multicolored fragments of Incaic ceramics, exposed and cleansed by the rains. If one attempted to fix the age and culture of the Pukará monuments by relying solely on the type of pottery appearing on the surface or in the subsoil as turned over by the plow, one would say that they belong to the time of the Incas. But what appears on the surface is completely different from that lying at a greater depth.

*8.18. Kotosh near Huánuco, Huallaga Valley. Potsherds from rubbish layer, red pigment in incisions. This pottery was found intermingled with classic Chavín pottery in the same deposit.*

The river, in its incessant task of seeking a bed, has gone first meandering over the plain, and subsequently deepening its bed. In the course of erosion and transportation of the sedimentary formations produced by nature and man, the river at times lays bare material hidden in their depths. The geographical situation of Pukará somewhat resembles that of Chavín; both are overlaid by thick beds of clay and fine gravel brought down from the sides of the nearby hills, and both are threatened and at times undermined by the river. In Pukará, the case may very well be the same as at Chavín; that is, that the buildings and the carved monoliths do not belong to the same era as the pottery found on the surface, that they are only survivals of the culture buried beneath the alluvium. These considerations, after my arrival in Pukará, led me to make a careful examination of the riverbed in the portions nearest to the ruins. There in the steep banks I discovered, as was to be expected, several superimposed layers of rubbish containing rich archaeological material of the same kind as that found at Chavín and Kotosh; a multitude of fragments of the finest pottery, incised, carved, and painted; as beautiful as and, in certain aspects, superior to the best specimens of Chavín pottery. This abundant material gathered at Pukará affords a fresh and illuminating contribution to our knowledge of Chavín megalithic art. The Pukará pottery is one of the best manifestations of the Chavín art proper; in it appear, as predominating ornamental motives, figures of the jaguar, the owl, the fish, and the serpent, modeled, carved, and drawn in the Chavín style.

## La Ventana

At the beginning of 1937, I explored the archaeological zone of the Department of Lambayeque, and, in the district of Illimo, in one portion of the La Ventana graveyard, eaten away by the La Leche River, I was able to prove the existence of three levels of strata formed by the refuse of human activity: an upper one, belonging to the last Chimú period; an intermediate one, belonging to the pre-Chimú period; and a lower one, corresponding to the Chavín era. In this last stratum I found remains of incised and carved pottery of the Chavín and Huallaga (Kotosh) styles.

## Ecuadorean Relations

Uhle, who in late years toiled solicitously on solving the problem of Maya expansion and colonization in South America, thinks that the high cultures of North and South America are simply branches of the Central American trunk. For him, the Ecuadorean and Peruvian cultures, in their more advanced phases, are so many outlying branches of the old Mayan tree. In my opinion, the problem of Central American origin of the Andean cultures can no longer strictly be linked with the second-age cultures, such as Muchik, Nazca, and classic Tiahuanaco, that do not offer the remotest resemblance to the Central American cultures, but do offer resemblances to the Chavín stone culture. And the fine, incised, and painted pottery of the Ecuadorean Sierra that Uhle looks upon as genuine Maya is none other than Chavín pottery.

## Characteristics of the Chavín Civilization

The research work so far done in connection with the Chavín megalithic culture gives some idea of its main characteristics and broadens the horizon of its area of diffusion throughout both the inter- and trans-Andean regions and the Pacific seaboard.

Within the domain of the Andes, no civilization has such well-defined and peculiar features as the Chavín civilization. Its most important center is the upper Marañon basin, and its widespread area of dispersion crosses the frontiers of the northern Andes. Where remains are found, whatever the example of building or handicraft, or whatever the material employed—stone, metal, bone, clay, or any other that has withstood the action of the weather—there appear the vigorous unmistakable architectural, sculptural, or pictorial creations of an extraordinary race. Its name and recollection have been erased from man's memory with the passage of centuries, but it has left behind undeniable traces of a civilization of such peculiarity and originality that it has no equal in other South American prehistoric cultures.

The following are regarded as typical manifestations of the Chavín civilization:

1. Stone buildings grouped within walled enclosures. Pyramidal temples formed of one or more tiered platforms, with interior galleries and rubble and earth fill. Special chambers or, properly speaking, places of worship in the upper portion, are reached by underground stairways. The inside walls of the chambers of worship and galleries sustain rubble and earth fill. The inside walls of the chambers of worship and galleries are frequently plastered with a thick layer of fire-hardened clay. This surface of burned earth is also applied to the stucco and modeled reliefs decorating the faces of the chambers

*8.19. Part of main front of Chavín de Huantar temple after 1940 excavations.*

and altars. The front of some buildings, like the Chavín de Huantar temple, is protected by a high wainscoting of dressed and polished flagstones (fig. 8.19), and the face of the whole building is lined with rectangular stones disposed in horizontal courses in which two courses of thin stones alternate with one of broad (fig. 8.20).

In the buildings discovered in the Callejón de Huaylas, such as those at Pomakayán near Huaraz, the real Chavín structures are hidden under Recuay structures, which proves the superimposition of buildings in some remote epoch. In others on the coast, like those at Sechín Alto and Moxeke (fig. 8.5) in Casma, and Cerro Blanco (fig.

8.1) and Punkurí in Nepeña, conical mud brick is used for filling in the understructure, while earth is used for constructing the large idols placed in the niches and for modeling the arabesque decorations of the inside of the chambers and paint for the mural frescoes.

The mud brick and plastic sculpture, apparently originating on the coast, do not exclude the lithic sculpture so characteristic of Chavín art, displayed, in the case of Cerro Sechín, in the numerous monoliths enclosing the great platform or foundation of the temple.

2. Sculptural work exemplifying an advanced stone art, displayed in figures carved in high and low relief, statues used for temple adornment, and a multitude of stone utensils found in graves. In this art, the outstanding features are the stelae and obelisks, and the knob heads reproducing fantastic beings (figs. 8.20, 8.21a–d), and monsters in the form of animals or birds, of which finds have been multiplied lately both in the Sierra and on the coast. Within this category are the Cerro Sechín reliefs representing human corpses, quartered human bodies, heads, eyes, arms, legs, and parts of the spinal column.

3. Pottery consisting of monochrome containers in black, red, or gray that at first sight give the impression of being wooden or stone vessels, or of having been made with a hard material and tools adapted to drilling, cutting away, incising, and generally sculpturing the figures adorning them. The body of the jug is solid, with pronounced curves, globe shaped, or, in some cases, with faceted

*8.20. Chavín. West side of main temple, 1940.*

*8.21. Chavín. a, head from west wall, 14.9 inches high, 15.7 inches broad; b, head found in thick layers of rubble and rubbish on south wall, 13.8 inches high, 11.7 inches broad; c, head discovered in wall around cultivated field adjoining temple, 16.9 inches high, 20.5 inches broad; d, head found in subsoil of cultivated fields facing main facade of temple, 16.9 inches high, 20.5 inches broad.*

surfaces and salient angles; the base, flat; the neck, thick, tubular, and arched; the rims, with an outward curving lip in imitation of wood or stone carving; the edges of the plates and the lips of the pots, thick and beveled. Vessels of this description carry an ornamentation of straight or curved incised lines, with a touch of graphite, in the case of the red-colored ones, at the bottom of the incision in rows of triangles in lines, or crisscrossing in a network pattern, perhaps a survival of the agave net or meshing that used to protect the original type wooden containers. They have tracery incised in the clay, prior to and after firing, fluted and pleated decorations, pitting and scratches, and plane, high, and low relief, imitating wooden vessels in shape, technique, and ornamentation.

4. Representations of demoniacal or mythical beings, based on one fundamental theme, the head of the feline (figs. 8.22, 8.23). Such are:

a. A long-bodied dragon, with a snout armed with big fangs and feet with claws, that resembles a crocodile (figs. 8.6a, 9.17).

This monster is hermaphrodite, and carries an enormous fanged mouth in its belly and a handful of yucca and red peppers in its feet. Associated with it in the same allegory are three animals, a feline, a fish, and a bird, either vulture or owl. The best existing example is the one adorning the obelisk found years ago in the middle of the main square of Chavín temple, now in the University Museum.

b. An anthropomorphic felinoid monster that has for archetype the feline accompanying the dragon. It is best illustrated by the figure appearing on the Raimondi stela now in the Museum of Peruvian Archaeology (fig. 9.51).

c. A humanized, birdlike monster, which is the same bird that accompanies the dragon. The body is built up by transformation of the morphological details, such as the wing and tail quill-feathers, the face and claws, into serpents and wholly or partially reproduced feline heads. Fine illustrations of this winged monstrosity are found in various entire or incomplete Chavín stelae, now reproduced in plaster of Paris and exhibited in the Anthropological Museum.

d. A fishlike monster which is likewise an idealized representation of the fish accompanying the dragon. As in the previous instance, the morphological details of the animal, the face, scales,

*8.22. Chavín de Huantar. Decorated stone cornice slab from temple.*

*8.23. Chavín de Huantar. Stone idol in shape of a spear head. Located in one of the dark inner chambers of the temple, uncovered in 1919, it is 17 feet 10 inches high.*

and fins, are transformed into feline heads. The finest example is in the great stela found in 1919 at Yauya, on the right bank of the Yanamayo, of which a replica is on exhibition in the San Marcos University Archaeological Museum (fig. 9.41).

e. Humanized felines, of simpler composition and with more human, though cadaverous, general features; strange beings, dismembered heads and limbs lacking the lower extremities, associated with arms, feet, heads, eyes, and vertebrae, as if these parts of the human body had been endowed with life. These fantastic beings are found in Cerro Sechín temple reliefs, and on tablets discovered in various sites in the outskirts of the Pukcha basin. In some instances, they wear long crimped locks, have the head covered with a helmet, and are armed with clubs or hatchets.

In the decorations of the ceramics, the gold and silver work, the bone carvings (fig. 8.6a–c), and the many stone utensils, we find motifs derived from the head of the feline or from the monsters described above.

It is remarkable that this Chavín art should be such a typically uniform style and in so many different manifestations, in places far removed from the centers of greatest development, preserving the characteristics of a mature industry based on fixed standards, and free from the substantial modifications so common in other arts that have likewise been propagated at a distance from their centers of origin.

Strictly speaking, there is no fundamental difference between a Chavín-type piece of pottery found at Chavín and another found on the coast, on the Huallaga, or in southern Ecuador.

## Summary

To sum up, very little was known about this civilization prior to 1919, in which year the first San Marcos University expedition was made to the important archaeological center of Chavín de Huantar. In subsequent years, a series of explorations covering different parts of the country have resulted in the discovery of other sites pertaining to the same civilization, as important as Chavín itself.

Temples and extensive beds containing Chavín pottery have been identified in the Callejón de Huaylas, at Inka Wain and Pomakayán; in the Santa Valley, at Ipuna and Suchiman; in the Nepeña Valley, at Cerro Blanco, Punkurí, and Kusi-pampa; at Pinchamarka and La Carbonera; in the Pativilca and Supe valleys, at Puerto de Supe and Chimo Kapak; in the Huaura Valley, at Choka Ispana; at Lachay, Chavín graves in the Teatino cemetery; at Ancón, extensive rubbish heaps with pottery considered by Uhle as belonging to the early fisherfolk; at Bellavista, Pachacamac, Cruz de Hueso, and Pucusana, rubbish heaps with Chavín pottery; and finally, in the Paracas caverns and at Ocucaje. Going east, in the Huallaga basin, chiefly at Kotosh, the outskirts of Huánaco, San Luís de Shuaro and Satipo; and, on the Marañon, in the basins of the Yanamayo, Pomabamba, Crisnejas, and Chotano rivers, where Pasa Kancha, Yauya, Chakas, Kumbemayo, Hualgayoc (fig.

*8.24. Small stone pot from graves, Lives Farm, San Gregorio District, province of Hualgayoc. Found by Germán Luna Iglesias.*

8.24), Huambos, and Pakopampa are to be found. To the south, in the basin of the Pukará. To the north on the seaboard, Mocán, Sausal, and Barbacoa in the Chicama Valley; La Ventana, Chongoyape, and Chiclayo in the Lambayeque Valley; and Moropón in the Piura Valley. In the southern region of Ecuador, Cerro Narrío, Alausi, Puntos de Mar, Cuenca, Sigsig, Chordeleg, Saraguro, Chinguilanchi, Rircay, and Uchucay, all places mentioned by Uhle but regarded by him as sites of Maya propagation.

Remains of the Chavín civilization are found everywhere buried under later remains as different in type as if they were completely unrelated. Yet certain facts given below lead to the presumption that a stage of transition once existed between the Chavín and the Recuay-Pasto civilization. In some aspects they seem to prove that the latter is derived from the former, or that, having had different origins, they for some time were contemporaneous and intermingled.

In the Sierra adjoining the forest lands, just as on the upper Huallaga and upper Marañon, Chavín remains are found in their classic shapes with all their wealth of variety of style. Apart from the stone sculpture, vessels are met with in these centers decorated by engraving that runs from mere incised lines or pitting and scratches to high and low relief and sculptured figures (fig. 8.24). This eastern Sierra art is also represented on the Pacific seaboard.

A general study of the coastal Chavín pottery from the standpoint

CHAPTER NINE

# The Feline God and Its Transformations in Chavín Art

**ABORIGINAL ART REACHES** its maximum degree of development in the North Andean region. Chavín art, characterized by its perfection of line, its richness of fantasy, the symbolism of its representations, the proportion and harmony of the whole, and the material used, which is nearly always hard stone, is the richest historical source and the best evidence of the high degree of civilization reached by the Peruvian race. The significance of its sculptural and pictorial works and the mastery with which they were executed all lead us to suppose that the culture of Chavín, illustrated in its art, is the product of a long process of gestation and elaboration, which must have been intimately bound to the material, emotive, and intellectual history of man, perhaps since his appearance on this part of the continent.

The culture of Chavín, along with almost all the cultures of Peru, is only one of the better-developed phases of the Andean Archaic culture, and surely the most advanced of them all. The best-developed cultures of the North have at all times received the influence of Chavín. The best examples of Chimú pottery, including under this rubric Tallanes and Mochicas, conserve in all their clarity the characteristics typical of Chavín art. For this reason, the geographical area of Chavín culture is not limited to the space occupied by its ruins situated on the edges of the streams named Mariash, Mosna, and Tungurawa Wacheksa, but rather it extends over almost the entire region of the northern Andes. Engraved stones and those with figures in relief in the legitimate Chavín style have been found in numerous ruins in almost the entire province of Huari and in the more distant provinces of Pomabamba and Pallasca. Ceramics with relief drawings of the same style have been found in some ancient cemeteries of Morropón and in almost all the non-Christian cemeteries of the North Coast of Peru.

Almost all the material known from this culture was acquired during the work of archaeological exploration carried out at the beginning of 1919 by the author, who stayed in the Department of Ancash a very short time. New explorations and excavations in this important region surely hold great surprises for Peruvian archaeology. Given the monographic character of the present work, of all the numerous and interesting material gathered, only that which illustrates the theme in question will be included here.

As in cultures studied previously, the fundamental motif of almost all artistic representations, sculptural as well as the pictorial, is the jaguar. The jaguar appears illustrated in its three principal aspects: realistic representations, those idealized or conventionalized to a lesser degree, and those conventionalized or idealized to a greater degree and anthropomorphic. These, in turn, give rise to more complex representations of symbolic and decorative character.

## Realistic Representations

These include representations of the entire body or only the head of the animal sculpted in high relief or in three dimensions. Sculptured portrayals of the feline are not rare; they appear generally in high, low, or flat relief. It has already previously been said that feline representations in high relief generally adorn porticoes of temples and entrances to fortified towns. Statues of felines are sometimes found in the Andean region, such as the two which form part of Sra. Centeno de Romanville's collection of antiquities in Cuzco, which Squier[1] made known and which still today remains in that city.

Much more frequent are the statuary representations of the animal's head. Feline heads, in the form represented in figure 9.1, are found in profusion in almost all the ruins of the Andean North, and in Tiawanako, Cuzco, Huánuco Viejo, and other archaeological centers of the highlands. They always appear decorating the walls of buildings, principally interior and exterior walls of temples. These heads are made up of two parts: the first part, the head proper, squared or rounded in form, carved more or less realistically, with the different parts of the face well defined; and the other part, corresponding to the neck, elongated, prismatic, or conical in form, which is inserted into the wall. Feline heads

9.1. *Monolithic jaguar head. Museo Arqueológico de la Universidad.*

modeled of clay are also frequently found. Sometimes they are independent, the head itself forming the entire vessel; at other times they appear as symbolic or emblematic figures decorating the most visible part of a vessel. These more or less realistically modeled feline heads constitute one of the specific characteristics of the pottery corresponding to the Inca period. They always appear as ornaments on Inca *aryballos.*

### *Representations of Feline Heads Idealized or Conventionalized to a Lesser Degree*

Idealized feline representations of the head as well as of the entire body of the animal appear both pictured and sculpted on pottery objects and carved on stone in high, low, or flat relief. Representations sculpted of stone are most numerous in the highlands and those of clay on the coast. However, feline figures are not rare in the pottery which comes from ruins situated not only in the Callejón de Huaylas but also from the eastern and western slopes of the Cordillera Blanca and Negra in the Department of Ancash.

The process of idealization usually follows a dual direction. Sometimes the animal is transformed by means of an aggregate of certain symbols or attributes. Different parts of the anatomy are made to stand out in an exaggerated manner, or the undulations, wrinkles, or profiles are modified, becoming converted into strips or thick cords like serpents. Others are dressed with objects typical of human clothing; the horizontal posture changes to a vertical one, and the anatomical or morphological parts smooth out, transforming the animal into an anthropomorphic personage.

This dual aspect of the evolution of art, determined by religious sentiment, is manifested in Chavín art in representations solely of the head as well as in those of the entire body of the animal.

*9.2. Feline head modeled in clay in typical Chavín style. Kuchi Machay, Carhuaz. Museo Arqueológico de la Universidad.*

The rude or embryonic forms of Chavín art appear in Archaic ceramics of the Callejón. Fragment 1050 of the University Museum reproduced in figure 9.2 comes from the cave of Kuchi Machay, Carhuaz. It is a magnificent example of porcelainized pottery in Andean art. The different parts of the head are modeled in high relief and painted red so that they stand out against the white ground of the vessel. Around its neck, it is wearing a wide black band on which appear emblematic white feline figures. The eyes are represented by two discs provided with a central or pupillary perforation, the nose by two small rectangular prominences, and the nostrils by another two circular perforations. The wide, open, rectangular mouth, displaying a line of teeth and prominent large canines, is outlined by a band or strip which is uniformly thick and prominent in the parts corresponding not only to the upper and lower lips but also to the corners of the mouth. On top of the head are four symmetrically placed protuberances: two small posterior ones, fragmented and eroded, the remains of ears; and two larger anterior ones, also fragmented and eroded, with incisions, dots, and red and black lines, which are surely remains of cephalic appendages.

The peculiar manner of representing the different parts of the face should be pointed out. Eyes, nose, lips, and teeth project their contours in high relief as if the artist had the intention of making the action of certain facial muscles—particularly the constrictors, palpebrals, and labials—stand out, with the aim of giving the countenance a greater ferocity. This peculiarity of Andean art acquires considerable development, as will be seen shortly in the art of Chavín.

The small stone head 785 of the museum, found at the foot of the principal temple of Chavín and reproduced in figure 9.3, represents the simplest form of the representations of the feline head in Chavín art. Like the realistic ornamental heads already described, this is made up of two parts. One, the head, properly speaking, is rounded. The other, elongated, corresponds to the neck or sleeve, which serves for setting it into the wall. Of this last portion, only a small part remains in this example. The eyes are rectangular, and the pupil is formed by a depression, which is also rectangular. The upper eyelid is in the form of an upside-down U, the inner end beginning next to the nasal lobe, and the outer end stopping at the level of the cheekbone. All the characteristics of the nose, which is wide with a supranasal prominence and large apertures, are remarkably human. The mouth is partly open; the lips, as in the previous case, indicated by a projecting strip or band, are drawn together near the corners of the mouth delimiting a rhomboidal space behind the canines. The teeth are triangular. The large canines protrude over the lips. The lower lip almost reaches the lower orbital rim, and the upper lip almost to the lower edge of the jaw. Behind the cheek appears a rectangular figure divided by two vertical intermediate lines, very eroded remnants perhaps of ears and earrings. There are four partially eroded prominences on the head. One, the largest, is situated in the middle part of the forehead and adorned with some volutes in relief. Two smaller ones, also of rectangular form with

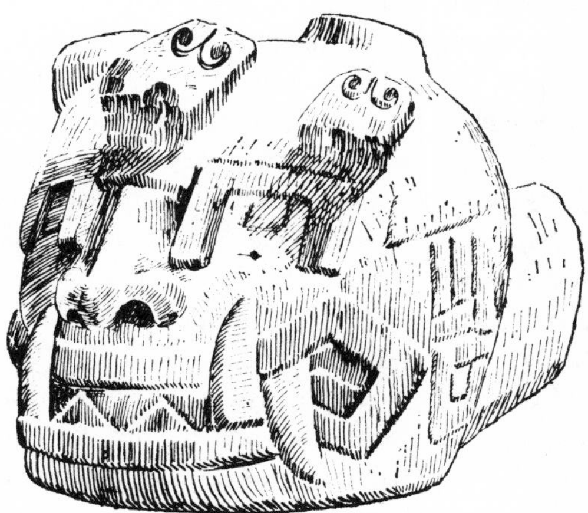

*9.3. Jaguar head in Chavín style. Chavín. Museo Arqueológico de la Universidad.*

9.4. Monolithic jaguar head. Chavín.

the same volutes, are situated one on each side of the middle one. The last is on the rear part of the top of the head, very eroded, and must, like the other three, be the remains of cephalic appendages.

Heads similar to that described are found in some profusion in many of the modern towns built near ancient ones in the Department of Ancash. Some serve as decorations of doors and walls of dwellings and others simply as building materials in the foundations and walls of buildings, churches, and cemeteries.

One of the stone heads is that seen in figure 9.4, which was found forming part of a wall in the new town of Chavín. Like those formerly described, it has a rounded form and measures about 0.70 m in diameter. The part corresponding to the neck has not been preserved. The different parts of the face have been carved in high relief. The eyes are circular, the part corresponding to the sclera, crescent-shaped. The pupil is indicated by a depression or circular cavity. The eyelids are transformed into serpents whose tails appear to adhere to the inner corners of the eyes, their bodies curved, their heads directed toward the temples. The forehead is decorated by two symmetrical serpent-shaped figures. The mouth is closed, stretched wide, with a circular extension at the corners. The projecting lips are well circumscribed and carved in the form of a wide strip or band. The prominent upper canines turn down and back. This is one of the typical forms of the idealized feline representation in Chavín culture. Its different parts are repeated, as will be seen later, more or less differentiated in the complex representations of this art.

The style of Chavín art is found equally illustrated in the ceramics of the North Coast of Peru. The vessel represented in figure 9.5 is one of these typical examples. It is a black vessel with a cylindrical handle and spout. The entire body of this piece has been adapted to the form of the head of the animal. This seems to be placed on a crescent-shaped base or support. The face has the morphological characteristics of felines. It is projected forward and forms a narrow muzzle. The eyeball is projected outward and is hemispherical. The eyes are decorated with a bicephalous serpent, which crosses the root of the nose, circles the eyeballs, and makes its way to the temples. The nose is small and flat, with the nasal openings in a scenting pose. The partially open mouth is identical in shape to that in figure 9.4, the lips well delineated, with interlocking triangular teeth, the prominent upper canines protruding over the level of the lower lip, and a hoop or ring in the center of the mouth. On the head are two appendages formed by a row of volutes, which issue from the forehead and fall over the temples and in front

*9.5. Head of the Jaguar-God represented on a black Chicama vessel. Museo Larco Herrera.*

of the ears. Vessels of clay similar to this one are still used in magical practices in the North of Peru as ceremonial rattles called *chunkanas.*

Other heads have been found, intimately related to these, in the form of mummified heads of the deceased. These should be considered as sacred objects or attributes symbolic of the gods since their use is found widely dispersed throughout ancient Peru. They almost always accompany divinities, great personages, priests, or chiefs. Sacred human heads, whether in the form of portraits of heads of mummies or the dead, appear modeled in clay or admirably engraved or carved in relief or into statues. Like the feline heads, they are also used to adorn temples. These heads serve as the tie between the feline heads and the realistic anthropomorphized heads. Wrinkles or creases produced by the drying out of the face and the curving of these wrinkles probably suggested the idea of the serpent. Then, if the artist believed that the head represented the new sacred being resulting from its transformation into a divinity by means of death, it is not daring to suppose that there existed an identification of these mummified heads with the sacred heads of felines. This is, without doubt, due to the desire of the artist to highlight and give life to certain morphological characteristics of the dead. Thus, the creases and wrinkles of the face are frequently transformed into serpents. Other parts of the animal itself, such as the nose, the mouth, and the eyes, acquire remarkably anthropomorphic characteristics. Figure 9.6 represents one of these transformed heads. The head is presently found on one of the pillars at the entrance to the stone bridge built from materials transported from the ancient temple over the stream which separates the temple from the town of Chavín. The head is large and oval (0.60 x 0.42 m). The face is dried out. On the forehead and cheeks it has numerous very obvious furrows and folds in the skin. The eyeball is large, round and protrudes. The nose is wide and flattened. The mouth is closed, the lips carefully joined, with various parallel sutures or furrows which radiate and diverge from the center part and the corners of the mouth. Possibly the eyeballs are artificial, or perhaps the desire was to represent feline eyes, and the grooves of the mouth could be the impressions of sutures produced when the mouth was sewn in the process of preparation or artificial mummification of the human head. This is one of the most important specimens of realistic representations of mummified heads in stone. This type of sculptured head becomes, as has already been said, like a bridge which connects the representations of idealized feline heads to those of properly human heads.

Figure 9.7 is of a human head of stone which is presently found on another pillar of the Chavín bridge. Its form is almost spherical;

*9.6. Mummified human head carved in stone. Chavín.*

*9.7. Human head of stone with the hair and muscles transformed into serpents. Chavín.*

its diameter is approximately 0.35 m. The face is markedly human. The eyes are elliptical, and the eyeball, eyelids, and eyebrows are well represented. The different parts of the wide nose, the lobes and the large nostrils, and similarly the septum and the bridge of the nose, are well modeled. The mouth is handled with great mastery, the lower lip slightly drooping, which gives the face a pleasant look. The facial muscles have received special treatment. Some of them, such as the constrictor muscles of the mouth, appear thick and curving. Others, such as the palpebral muscles, not only stand out like a cord but have been idealized by being transformed into a bicephalous serpent. The body of the serpent circles the eye, with the heads falling, parallel, on the cheek in such a way that they give the feeling that the eyes open and close through a contraction or relaxation of the serpent's body. Over the forehead is worn, as is customary in idealized representations of feline heads, two long appendages represented here in the form of serpents whose heads join in the center of the forehead. Their bodies cover the supraorbital portion and fall in a curve over the temples and the temporal region in the form of a volute. Similarly, the hair is transformed into a multitude of serpents which interweave in a compact entanglement from which project, here and there, some of their heads. Furthermore, the muscles of the cheeks have been transformed into serpents.

This human head presents the muscles and the hair in the form of serpents. In certain cases, the muscles appear under the skin like worm-shaped bulges; in others, the serpent muscle projects outward, lacerates the skin, and shows part of its body and head. The hair is also of snakes, which come out of the scalp and become twisted, tightly enmeshed on the surface. This head also displays the symbolic appendages covering the forehead in the form of large serpents, appendages which are characteristic attributes of the idealization of the feline. Consequently, two principal elements are found on this head: one, typical of the head representations, which consist of the transformation of the folds or wrinkles of the face into serpents; and the other, the cephalic appendage, which is characteristic of the idealized feline. Nonetheless, this example cannot be considered as a representation of a dead person's head because its different anatomical parts are treated with marked realism, and impress one with a physiognomy full of life. The relationship existing between the head and the facial serpent is not then clearly explainable. If the serpents replace the folds and wrinkles of the face during death, why do they give life to the face in this representation? The personage who died, the priest or chief, did not, in the concept of the indigenous artist, have to completely disappear from this life, but rather became transformed and enjoyed the exalted life of the gods, that is to say, those attributes characteristic of the gods; perhaps the individuals sacrificed or offered to the gods according to indigenous philosophy had become transformed or identified with the divinities themselves. This is, without a doubt, the reason why the wrinkles and contractions produced by the face of death were enlivened and converted into serpents that animated the features. The individual represented in this stone head could not have been a common man, but rather a superior being, idealized or identified with the divinity, and, as such, endowed with the appropriate attributes. This explains the physical features of the countenance and the presence of the cephalic appendages, which are luminous flashes or symbols of power. These heads were sacred, they represented the deified high personages; for this reason they adorn sanctuaries and all sacred places. There they are found together with the mummified human and feline heads. They all belong to the same religious cycle, and they are at the same time exponents of the degree of artistic advancement achieved by the primitive Andean inhabitants.

The Chavín style, characterized by the projections or enlarging of different anatomical parts of the feline in the form of sinuous or snake-like fillets, cords, bands, or strips, is unique and unmistakable in Peru. The fundamental motif, the root or base of all the art in this culture, is the representation of the head as seen in figure 9.2. It is not only found carved in stone, but as an ornament on vessels, in high and flat relief. Thus, the globular jar with cylindrical handle and spout, found in the Chicama Valley (fig. 9.5), is decorated with two of these heads in profile, located symmetrically on each side of the body of the vessel. Figure 9.8 is a faithful copy of this head. The different anatomical parts may easily be recognized on it, namely, the eye, the turned-up nose, the mouth, the teeth and large canines, the ear, and the appendage which seems to issue from the nose, covering the head like a band which follows the convexity of the head. Ending at the ear, the band is divided into three rectangular sections by means of two incisions cutting across the middle. With the aim of making the different parts of the face stand out with clarity against the light ground of the jar, the artist painted them dark red. Vessels from the Chicama Valley with this type of drawing are also found in the University Museum, and one of them was made known by Wiener[2] as coming from Chavín de Huantar.

The beautiful example of figure 9.9 is also adorned with the head of a feline, drawn in profile, looking to the right. This head is reproduced in figure 9.9. Here, as in the previous figure 9.8a, it is easy to identify the different anatomical parts of the face: the elliptical eye, the turned-up nose, the trapezoidal ear, the partially open mouth, the lip formed by a serpent-shaped band, the teeth and large canines. Over the head are three beautiful plumes formed by waving bands, which soften as they go up and forward like bursts of fire. Baessler[3] also reproduces a vessel adorned with one of these heads as coming from the valley of Chicama.

Another interesting example belonging to the culture of Chavín which presents the characteristic feline head as an ornamental motif is

*9.8. Globular vessel, adorned with stylized feline heads. Museo Larco Herrera.*

*9.8a. Stylized feline head, reproduced from that which adorns the vessel. It shows the cordlike peculiarity of representations in Chavín art.*

a small vessel of turquoise reproduced in figure 9.10. The exterior face of this vessel is found to be completely covered with figures in relief, consisting of a meshed network which leaves quadrangular spaces within which appears the feline face seen in profile. Here also it is easy to identify the eye, the turned-up nose, the bilobed ear, the serpent-shaped lip, and one of the large canines.

But, without a doubt, the most beautiful example of Chavín art

*9.9. Cylindrical vessel decorated with two idealized feline heads in high relief. Museo Larco Herrera.*

to date found on the coast is that reproduced in figure 9.11. It is a large spherical vessel, black, with a shining, porcelainized surface. The spout and handle are thick and cylindrical. Not only the surface of the body of the vessel but also the handle is decorated with frontal views of felines in high relief. The eyes are represented by two small hemispherical prominences, the nose by another, larger, elliptical one. From its upper edge issue appendages which surround the eye and fall on the temples and cheeks in the form of serpents. The mouth is represented in the same way as in figures 9.4 and 9.5, which is to say stretched toward the corners from which come the canines in the form of hooks pointed downward and backward. The teeth are represented by two small prominences, the tongue in a triangular shape, and the hanging lower lip divided into two almost rectangular prolongations.

In the Elías Collection of Morropón, there is also a beautiful vessel which was considered by Means[4] as belonging to the culture of Tiawanako; but the drawings which it has near the base and the thickness of the handle and the spout and other ornamental details are characteristic of Chavín style.

*9.10. Turquoise vessel adorned with feline heads in high relief (natural size).*

*9.11. Globular vessel decorated with stylized feline heads in high relief. Museo Larco Herrera.*

*Representations of the Feline Idealized to a Greater Degree*

Chavín art is almost always sculptural; line drawings are very rare. The figures always appear carved or sculpted in high, low, or flat relief, or modeled in three dimensions. The central archetypical figure or primordial element, the base of every representation, even of the most complex, is the feline head, just as it has been characterized in the preceding paragraphs.

It has already been shown that the archaeological centers where Chavín culture predominated, such as the ruins in the provinces of Huari, Pomabamba, and Pallasca, have not yet been duly explored. Studies and excavations have not been carried out in those places. The few pieces of pottery which are known to belong to the culture of Chavín come, for the most part, from places far away from those centers, principally from the cemeteries of the valleys of the North Coast. Chimú culture must have been influenced by the Andean at all times. This explains the frequent finds, on the coast, of archaeological objects belonging to the diverse stages and cultural aspects of the sierra.

Besides the representation of the head, the representations of the entire body of the feline are not scarce. Following are some examples.

Figure 9.12, which appears in the work of Baessler[5] on a vessel coming from the valley of Chicama, has all the characteristics of the Andean Archaic style out of which originated the style of Chavín. The feline appears seated. The head is large, the muzzle elongated. The partly open mouth shows the upper canines and the tongue. The nose is turned upward and back. The elliptical eye is surrounded by the palpebral appendage, which appears in the form of a large volute which not only surrounds the upper part of the eye but coils around, covering part of the face. Out of the upper part of the head issues the symbolic appendage, which is most similar to decorations on the idealized feline of the Archaic culture. The appendage, vertical in the first portion, bends at a right angle, becomes horizontal pointing backward, and, finally, terminates in a volute twisting once again toward the front. The tail is in a symmetrical position with the cephalic appendage. It extends horizontally, bending in the middle part upward and toward the front at a very acute angle and terminates in another volute. The fore and hind paws are provided with five claws. This figure is evidently analogous to the same animal in the Archaic culture of the Callejón and, at the same time, has elements characteristic of the style of Chavín proper.

Also, the feline represented in figure 9.13,[6] which, like the previous feline figure, is a frequent decorative motif in Chimú pottery, has

*9.12. Idealized feline in high relief which decorates a Chicama vessel. Reproduced from Baessler,* Altperuanische Kunst.

*9.13. Idealized feline which decorates a vessel from Chicama. Reproduced from Baessler,* Altperuanische Kunst.

certain markedly Andean characteristics. The animal is presented in profile. It is drawn with a certain realism: the large head, the elliptical eye with a palpebral volute which falls to the cheek, the partially open mouth showing the dental arches, the triangular ear falling back. The nose is transformed into a long appendage, vertical for the first part, the second part horizontal, turning back and adorned with some stepped figures. The tail is long, curved, turned upward and forward, and decorated with the same motif seen on the cephalic appendage. The whole body of the animal, excepting the hind extremity, is decorated with parallel vertical lines which leave equal spaces in which other small horizontal lines of different shapes (curves, hooks, etc.) appear. Furthermore, on the fore extremity and on the face, one sees numerous circular spots.

This figure is thus related as much to the Andean Archaic culture as to that of Chavín through its cephalic appendage, which is presented in the simple form as it appears in the Callejón and on the oldest ceramics of Chavín. These simple or elemental representations of the feline have great importance, as has already been mentioned, when it comes to trying to interpret the complex representations of Chavín art. It is advisable always to keep them in mind, because they constitute the primordial or embryonic type, which, through multiple differentiations, forms the elevated art of that culture.

In the doorsill of the new jail in Chavín is found a rectangular-shaped stone which measures 1.20 m long by 0.39 m in width, and 0.23 m thick. This stone presents numerous facets of fractures which appear to be recent. It was probably adapted, as many others like it, to the conditions required by the humble uses to which they are assigned.

Well, let it be kept in mind that, in Chavín, as in the majority of archaeological centers of the North of Peru, these objects of incalculable scientific and historical value are used as building materials and split with the idea of making them into lintels and doorsills of churches, houses, huts, and corrals or to fill other modest functions. The stone of the doorsill of the jail of Chavín presents on one of its faces the carving reproduced in figure 9.14, which has been traced from the original. In it, the head and part of the body of the feline are recognized. The head, which is to the left, has a rectangular shape and thus occupies half of the figure. The different parts are discovered with a certain facility: the semicircular eye; the pupil represented by a depression; the upper eyelid by a cord or fillet which, in front, hangs behind the nasal lobe, and behind, expands on the cheek in front of the ear. Over the large nose with a deep nasal opening is seen the ring inside a trapezoidal background which is always present as a supranasal accessory. The mouth is partially open; the lip, as usual, is represented as a band or strip. The teeth are triangular. Three large canines, two behind and one in front, protrude beyond the limits of the lips. The ear has the shape of a hook. Moreover, there are several claw-shaped prolongations in front of the face which may be purely ornamental. On the head at eye level are two parallel protrusions, perhaps remains of the cephalic appendage. The body has a skeletonized look; the part corresponding to the vertebral column is formed by a feline mouth, partially open, showing triangular teeth and large canines in pairs. As the canines break through the lips, they lift the lips slightly, making small notches. In front of and behind the first pair of canines, as if inserted in the spine, appear slightly curved bands like ribs curving toward the rear, with several anomalous figures in the intermediate spaces. Was this figure meant to symbolize death? If it were, this example represents one more tie between the corpse and the idealized feline.

*9.14. Idealized feline seen on a monolith found in Chavín.*

Figure 9.15 faithfully reproduces and presents one of the faces of another stone which, simply as building material, forms part of a chapel situated at the entrance to the town of Chavín. The stone has a rectangular shape, measuring 0.64 m long by 0.56 m wide, and its thickness is approximately 0.35 m. On this appears the feline in its natural position: the body horizontal and facing straight ahead. The head is large and rectangular. The eye is elliptical, the sclera crescent shaped, and the pupil almost circular. The eyelids are cordlike; the upper one springs out of the inner corner of the eye, passes the outer corner of the eye, and falls upon the face. The lower eyelid follows toward the inside along the edge of the symbolic supranasal figure, which is not clear here due to the erosion experienced by the stone. The mouth shows the thick lips clearly delineated, the teeth triangular, and the large canines, only three of which are preserved, on the stone. One of the canines cuts the upper lip and penetrates to the nostrils, and the others similarly cut the bottom lip and part of the chin. The nose is wide, and the lobes are small. The chin is thick; on the middle part of it is an ornament-like feline face shown in profile, looking downward; on its head, one can distinguish an almost circular eye, a turned-up nose, and a cordlike mouth. The line of teeth, the canine, and the

*9.15. Idealized feline, reproduced from a stone found in a chapel at the entrance to Chavín.*

tongue are converted into a serpent. And, toward the gonio or angle of the mandible, there is another eye identical to that just mentioned. The ear is small and bent upward. On the forehead, a tuft or bundle of cordlike appendages runs first upward and then horizontally, parallel to the head to the level of the neck. Each of the fillets or cords which is formed has a small notch or crease at the level of the eye. Adorning the neck of the animal is a collar formed by three [human heads] held by the hair to an armature in the shape of the feline mouth motif. Easily distinguishable are the wide cordlike lip, the teeth with convex edges, and the large upper canines. One canine is small and wide near the right corner of the mouth, which exceeds the lip and falls over the arm. The other, long and slender in the middle of the mouth, makes a notch where it comes out from the lip and then falls to the upper part of the corpselike middle head.

The body, of which, unfortunately, only a part has been preserved, in its middle portion, also presents the feline mouth motif as in the figure previously described. Here, the lips and two canines appear clearly. The ventral section is adorned with another feline head in frontal view; in the figure, only the right side of the head is seen. In it are distinguished: the elliptical eye, the nostrils, part of the mouth, and one of the canines. On the back of the animal, which appears very worn down in the stone, there remains some volutes and elliptical figures which are possibly remainders of some other decoration based on the feline head. The fore extremity is well treated: the hand has three long claws, and a bracelet made of a band provided with a large flap which falls or extends over the arm and adorns the wrist. Of the hind extremity, there only remains a part of the paw, and this, like the hands, has three large claws.

### *The Feline Huari, God of Agriculture, Associated with the Serpent, the Condor, and the Fish, Symbols of Lightning, Sun, and Moon, Respectively. The Obelisk of Chavín.*

The most important representation of the feline in its natural position is that which is found carved on the four faces of the obelisk reproduced in figure 9.16. This obelisk was found at the beginning of 1919 by the author in Chavín, and today can be found in the University Museum. Its form is not geometrically prismatic; on one of its narrow faces appears a slight depression, and in its upper fifth, a segment has been cut out. It measures 2.52 m high; at its base the maximum width is 0.32 m gradually diminishing to 0.29 m at the level of the cutout, and 0.26 m at the top. There is no doubt that the stone is not complete because the upper

*9.16. Obelisk found in Chavín. On it is carved the jaguar divinity associated with the serpent, condor, and fish. Museo Arqueológico de la Universidad.*

facet is rough, uneven, and recently fractured. It is split in its upper fifth. As for the rest, except for small erosions, the stone, in general, is well preserved. The obelisk probably had the shape of a flint, a point of a lance or arrow, and this form, as will be seen later, was what suggested to the artist the idea, apparently strange or capricious, to carve on this kind of stone of such an irregular shape the figure of his divinity.

Upon the surface of the stone are carved two felines who flaunt complicated and luxurious finery. They are arranged along the length of the stone with the heads upward. The body occupies the wide faces, and the extremities occupy the narrow faces of the stone. Both differ only in the manner in which the genitals are presented, the lumbar or rear section of the back, and the ornaments which they wear on their extremities.

The drawings which represent the two felines (fig. 9.17) have been traced from the original stone; the two are very similar. One of them, divinity I (fig. 9.17a), is in the attitude of devouring three animals: a condor, a fish, and a serpent-shaped monster, which appear in the space in front of its face. The other, divinity II (fig. 9.17b), appears to have already devoured the aforementioned animals because only a few fragments of them remain in the space in front of its face. In order to proceed in an orderly manner, the principal figure will be described first of all and, afterward, the secondary figures: X, Y, and Z.

## Principal Zoomorphic Figures

These will be studied successively: A. the head and its accessories, earring, and cephalic appendages; B. the neck; C. the body with its two portions, dorsal and ventral; D. the rear part of the animal in which are included the hindquarters and the tail; E. the genitals; and F. the fore and hind extremities.

### *A. Head (fig. 9.18)*

The head in divinity I (fig. 9.17a) is almost identical to that in divinity II (fig. 9.17b). The slight variations discovered are due to factors beyond the representation itself, such as the narrow field to which the artist had to accommodate this complicated drawing, or to the technical slips explicable in the repetition of the same figure when the necessary measuring instruments were not available. The eye is elongated and of an irregular shape, the eyeball slightly arched, the pupil marked by a rectangular depression. The double, cordlike eyelids are born from

*9.17a. Divinity I. The feline god Wari associated with the serpent, condor, and fish, personifications of lightning, the sun, and the moon, respectively, adorned with fruits, flowers, and seeds, symbols of the fertility of the earth.*

*9.17b. Divinity II. The feline god Wari devouring the three symbolic animals, the serpent, condor, and fish.*

*9.18. The head and its accessories: earrings and cephalic appendages.*

the internal corner of the eye, run parallel over the back of the eye, present a small crimp in the middle part, and, upon arriving at the external corner of the eye, make their way downward and backward. They perforate the earflap and form a handle behind it, from which hangs an earring. The mouth is partially open, elongated, with double lips, the inner ones wider than the outer ones. The canines are prominent and striated. One of them produces a notch in the upper lip. All the canines cut both parts of the lower lip. The nose is identical in both figures, as is the small supranasal figure, which, as will be seen later, is always found located at the level of the space between the eyebrows.

### EAR AND EARRING.

The ear is small, pierced, as has been said, by the palpebral cords which form a handle and must represent the earlobe from which hangs an earring, shown as a star-shaped figure.

### CEPHALIC APPENDAGE.

From the upper back of the head and almost at the root of the ear spring forth three appendages. The lower one runs immediately above and along the length of the head. It bends downward at the level of the nostril and ends in a small feline head. Its body is found divided in small rectangular sections, each of them decorated with a single, central longitudinal line. Another middle appendage, also serpent shaped, runs above the first, and ends in a star at the same level as the head of the previous appendage. The third upper appendage does not differ from the first, except in the motif which decorates its body, which here is formed by little triangles. The three appendages fall in front of the face.

*9.19. The neck adorned with feline heads and serpents.*

Furthermore, an important accessory to the ornamentation of the head is the stellar figure, which appears above the appendages in I. It is possible that this same star existed in II because the corresponding site is worn away on the stone.

### *B. Neck (fig. 9.19)*

The neck is adorned with a figure which occupies part of the upper portion of the back and part of the throat in the manner of a collar or piece of clothing. It is wide on the back and narrow at the throat. On the wide part appears half of a feline face, placed looking straight ahead. It covers the animal's nape. In II, the eye is distinguished; half of the nose, the corner of the mouth, and the corresponding canine are decorated with transversal furrows or striations. On the narrow part, there is a strange figure with the face of a feline or serpent. In I, the eye is not carved, the nose is barely sketched, but the corner of the lip and the left canine stand out well. In both representations, the head is provided with various appendages or with a very long one that is coiled like a serpent.

### *C. Body (figs. 9.20–9.25)*

The body is composed of three main sections: a front section which corresponds to the shoulder and upper portion of the trunk, a ventral section, and a dorsal section. In the first, which corresponds to the shoulder of the animal, appears the upper half of a semianthropomorphic personage, Ca, with the head, which is markedly feline, downward and covered by a cap which might be the cephalic appendage coiled up. The body is human with a band which crosses the back and

*9.20. (Ca) Feline which adorns the shoulder of the divinity.*

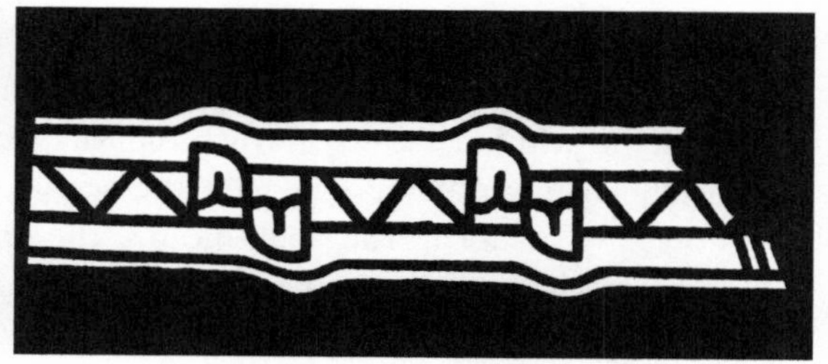

*9.21. (Cb) Feline mouth motif which replaces the stomach of the divinity.*

*9.22. (Cc) Glyph which is seen on the fore section of the back.*

*9.23. (Cd) Feline head which adorns the middle part of the back.*

*9.24. (Ce) Feline head adorned with flowers and fruits which occupies the rear or lumbar section of divinity I.*

*9.25. (Cé) Small feline head which occupies the rear part of the back of divinity II.*

disappears at the armpits. The arms are also human, well drawn with five fingers provided with their respective fingernails and a band or bracelet around the wrists.

In Cb, the ventral section is formed by a feline mouth, seen from the front. This appears with a double lip, the inner one thick, the outer thin. The teeth are triangular; the large striated canines raise the lips producing in them an undulation.

The dorsal section is, in turn, made up of three sections, front, middle, and rear. The front section, Cc, is occupied by a strange figure, enclosed within a frame of which the top part is missing. It has a feline head. Distinguishable on it are the semicircular eye, the pushed-up nose, the small ear, the open mouth, the lips, and the dental arch. It displays a cap or bow formed by a cephalic appendage which is twisted and knotted. The form of the body is very irregular. The forced vertical position, the figure resting, is supported by the hind paw with the hand pointing upward. Human fingers or perhaps arrows shoot out from the back, which spread out in the form of wings and are grouped in two branches, an upper one which forms the wings and a lower one which forms the tail.

The middle portion, Cd, is occupied by a large feline head, seen in profile. Distinguishable are the elliptical eye, the nostril, the supranasal figure, the small ear, the double lips, triangular teeth, and a large canine which cuts the two lower lips and part of the chin.

The rear is occupied in I by Ce, a head adorned with flowers and fruits, and in II by Cé, a small head on top of which is being carried a plant with wide leaves, held on by means of a bow. In both can be distinguished the semielliptical eye, the nose with the enlarged nostrils, the partly open mouth, the lip, and the dental arch.

### *D. Hindquarters and Tail (figs. 9.26, 9.27)*

The hind part of the animal is divided, as has been said, into two sections: a front part and a rear part. The front part corresponds to the hindquarters and is occupied by a semianthropomorphic Da, which is stretched out in a flying position, the body bending upward, the legs raised, and the hand closed beneath the chin. This is a position frequently taken by the feline, as will be seen later. The head is large, the eye semicircular, the pupil represented by a circular depression; the nose is large, the lips thick, the canine prominent. The ear is represented by a small hook, from which hangs a large fan-shaped ear ornament. On the head is worn an elegant crown, adorned with a plaque which seems to represent a human face, from which issue several emanations which could be luminous bursts. On the elongated body, the back decorated with the feline mouth motif and the belly is formed by a large head. In addition, it wears a sort of loincloth or trunks, and bracelets and anklets. A cord around the forehead runs the length of the trunk; it disappears and reappears at the waist. This cord is the same that adorns the feline heads in the Chimú culture.

9.26. *(Da) Monster which appears on the hindquarters of both divinities.*

9.27. *(Db) Feline head which forms the train of the divinity.*

The rear, or the train, figure Db, is formed by another large feline head. On it are distinguished the semielliptical eye, the rectangular pupil, the large nostril, a supranasal nipple-shaped prominence, the pushed-back ear, the partially open mouth with the wide inner and thin outer lips, and two large canines with numerous striations near the root. In addition, under the lower jaw there are three unequal appendages, a wide middle one divided into two parts, each one decorated with a rectangle, and two narrow ones at the extremes with transversal striations at the root.

### *E. Genitals (figs. 9.28, 9.29)*

The part corresponding to the genitals is found occupied in I by a fruit or seed, Ea, and in II by another feline head, Eé, which issues from the body by means of a thick cord formed by five filaments, united by another transversal cord. The head is well represented. The different anatomical parts of the face are distinguishable, and there is also a folded and knotted cephalic appendage which covers all of the upper portion. The feline tongue is projected outward in the form of a plant, with a fleshy stalk and leaves, provided with several buds or small eyes.

9.28. *(Ea) Genitals of divinity I.*

9.29. *(Eé) Genitals of divinity II.*

9.30. (Fá) Fore extremity of divinity II.

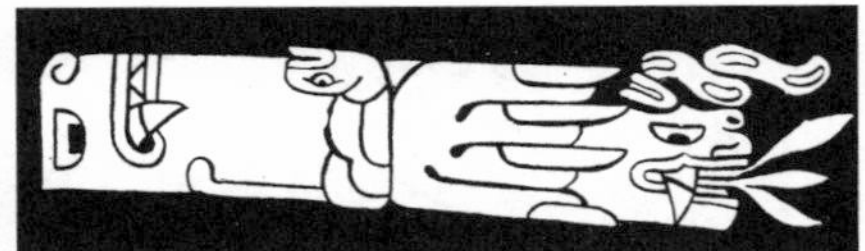

9.31. (Fc) Hind extremity of the divinity. It carries a feline head in its claws adorned with fruits.

### *F. Extremities (figs. 9.30, 9.31)*

In II, the front extremity Fá is well represented. The hand has four claws, and the wrist is adorned with a bracelet in the shape of a serpent, artistically and capriciously drawn. This is united by means of a band which runs along the inner arm to another feline head which adorns the elbow. This head has the semielliptic eye, the large nose, the thick lip, the canine with transverse striations, and the semicircular supranasal figure. In addition, in the middle part of the head hangs a serpent head, Fb, which is rolled up into a spiral and which assumes the form of a snail.

The hind extremity, Fc, is likewise well drawn. As in the previous figure, an anklet is worn at the level of the malleolus which is in the form of a rolled-up serpent tied by means of a cord which runs along the inner face of the leg with a feline head adorning the knee. The claws clench a feline head ornamented with fruits and seeds which hang from the nose and from the mouth.

### *Different Characters of the Twin Divinities (figs. 9.32, 9.33)*

Divinity I, as has been said, hardly differs from II in the ornamentation of the sections corresponding to the genitals, to the elbow, and to the dorsal or lumbar region. In place of the feline head with the tongue transformed into a plant which adorns the genitals of II, in I there appears a fruit or a seed Ea, which will be dealt with later. In place of the small head ornamented with a plant with long, wide leaves which adorns the lumbar section of II, a feline head Ce appears in the corresponding section of I, almost identical to the one represented on the genitals in

9.32. (Fa) Monstrous figure formed by feline and serpent heads which adorns the elbow of divinity I.

9.33. (Fb) Head of the serpent which divinity II wears hanging from his elbow.

divinity II. Here it appears adorned with flowers and fruits which issue from the nose and mouth by means of long peduncles such as are on the head which divinity II carries in its hind extremity in Fc. Instead of the viper head which adorns the elbow of II, in I, Fa is found adorned by an ornament formed by a feline head whose tongue is projecting out in the form of a viper, and which inserts into, by means of a long cordon, another feline head which has a single arm.

## Secondary Zoomorphic Figures (figs. 9.34–9.38)

In front of feline I, three accessory figures are represented with clarity: a divinity X, in front of the forehead, and two more, Y and Z, in front of the mouth.

The serpent-shaped monster represented in X is found mutilated due to the erosion suffered by the stone in this spot. However, two feline heads can be recognized in it: one at the front, very well drawn, facing right, and the other behind, which seems to correspond to the body of the animal, facing upward and backward. Coming out of the

*9.34. (X) Serpent-shaped monster, symbol of lightning, associated with divinity II.*

*9.35. (Y) Condor, symbol of the sun, associated with divinity II.*

*9.36. (Z) Fish, symbol of the moon, associated with divinity II.*

*9.37. Fragments of serpent devoured by divinity II.*

*9.38. Fragments of bird devoured by divinity II.*

mouth of the latter figure in the manner of a tongue is a serpent whose body is ornamented with parallel sinuous transverse lines arranged in pairs and intermediate spaces decorated with other, rhombohedron-shaped figures. A representation similar to this is worn or carried by animal I, hanging from its elbow, Fa. Here, the feline face as part of an arm looks toward the genitals, and both seem to be just appendages of another feline head found immediately to the right which is provided like the previous one with a tongue transformed into a feline head. As can be seen, this is the same figure as that represented in X. The long-tongued feline head is reproduced on the genitals in Figure II in which the head is provided with a long tongue, transformed into a plant. It is reproduced in the faces which are seen in the claws of the hind extremities, in which the tongue has similarly been transformed into fruits. Effectively, there are connections between this long-tongued head and those in which the tongue appears transformed into plants and fruits.

It has already been shown upon several opportunities that the most common manner of representing lightning is in the form of a serpent. If the head with the viper tongue symbolizes lightning, there must exist some connection with the power of procreation or of fertility, since the presence of the fruits could signify nothing else. It must be remembered that lightning has always been considered to have procreative powers, as in the legend of the Amuesha, it is lightning which fecundates a woman, who wore some flowers on her breast. All over the North of Peru, lightning was generally considered to be the progenitor of humanity. According to the sermon of Father Avendaño, cited by Tschudi,[7] some elderly Indians recounted "that after the flood, lightning fell in a mine on the hill named Raku, where he urinated. From the urine of this lightning were formed the Lakwases Indians. He immediately asked his listeners if they were not ashamed to be sons of urine and how was it possible that urine produced men, given that everything procreates the same as himself? The horse procreates the horse, the dog procreates the dog. How was it then that men could be born from urine?" Tschudi believes that this legend is only a fragment of a more vast cosmogonic myth, and that it probably had a very profound meaning.

Those who are born when lightning strikes later become priests or privileged personages who participate in certain supernatural powers. In indigenous beliefs and superstitions, twins are considered still today to be the sons of lightning, and exceptional powers of reproduction or fertility are even attributed to paired or twin grains and roots. These roots, represented in the conopas which are frequently found in the ancient cemeteries accompanied by different ceremonial objects, fulfill an important role in witchcraft rituals, especially in those which are carried out in order to obtain an abundant harvest.

Y represents a condor and Z a fish with a feline head. The condor is posed flying: it has a long, thick beak, the crests are large, the wings open, the claws extended. In short, it exhibits the morphological characteristics typical of this animal.

The fish is elongated. It has a feline face. It is provided with a kind of necklace at the level of its gills. It has a dorsal fin, a ventral fin, and two tail fins. It seems that the whole body is formed by two cords bent into handles, united at the tail by means of a transversal cord.

## Analogies and Differences That Exist between the Two Principal Twin Zoomorphic Figures and Ancillary/Supplementary Figures

Figures I (9.17a) and II (9.17b) are, as has been said, very similar: they differ only in some of their attributes and ornaments, as follows:

1. In front of the face of animal I appear three symbolic figures represented with marked realism: a serpent which issues from the mouth of a feline X, a condor Y, and a fish Z. In front of the face of the animal II appear only fragments of these animals: feathers Y' and pieces of the skin of the serpent X'.

2. The part corresponding to the genitals of animal I is occupied by the Ea, which has the aspect of a seed and which, at the same time, is one of the markings of the serpent, just as it is presented in X and X' and in the fruits which it carries in its hind claws, F. The part corresponding to animal II is occupied by a feline head with the tongue transformed into a plant with fleshy stalk and leaves and provided with numerous buds or laughing or sparkling eyes which have a great similarity to the elliptical eyes of the serpents which appear in Y', in front of the face of II.

3. The rear section of the dorsal or lumbar region in I is occupied by a head Ce, very similar to that represented in the genitals of II; it is well formed in this figure, as are a bundle of cords or filaments which bend upward, and in front of the head, a bed upon which lies one of the fruits projects from a long peduncle from the nose. In II, this section is occupied by the small head of feline Cé, adorned with a plant with wide leaves, attached to it by means of a bow.

4. Animal I has hanging from its elbow Fa, similar to the figure

which X carries in front of its face. The general aspect of animal I is that of a feline whose body is constituted almost entirely of a feline head out of whose mouth in the manner of a tongue emerges a long serpent which in turn is the tail of the animal, Fa. The two feline heads, that is, that which corresponds to the head properly speaking of the animal and that of the body, and the serpent of X, are found represented in the ornament or attribute which the animal has hanging from its elbow. On the ornament, the head of the serpent is large and is looking at the elbow of the animal. The body is not seen, but seems to be hidden inside the mouth of the feline itself; in addition, it has an arm adhering to it. From the elbow of animal II hangs only the head of the serpent, and the threadlike body seems to be twisted into a spiral at the nape of the neck like a cap, Fb.

5. Finally, animal I carries in the claws of its hind extremity a destroyed feline head, from whose mouth and nose issue different fruits provided with long peduncles. And in II, also carrying in its claws another feline head, Fc, with fruits or seeds similar, as has already been said, to the spots of I that adorn the skin of the serpent X.

The analogies of divinities I and II are so obvious that it must be supposed that it is not a question of the representation of two divinities, but rather of two aspects or two phases of the same divinity.

It should be noted that the differences which have been stated are not due to the introduction of alien motifs which modify or displace those which constitute the structural base of the representations in Chavín style. The monster, X, with feline head, body replaced by another head of the same animal from whose mouth like a tongue issues the serpentine tail, surely constitutes an agent or attribute of the animal god, not only of importance, but superior to that of the other symbolic figures, condor and fish, which appear together with it. If, as has already been suggested, this monster symbolized lightning, here would be a figure that could serve as a guide to the interpretation of this mythological personage, given that it is repeated, more or less modified, in different parts of the anatomy of the animal. It is possible through these modifications to know the connections it has with the powers of the principal divinity. Animal I has in front of its face the three mythological personages: serpent, condor, and fish. Animal II has in front of its face only fragments of these three, which makes one think that they have been devoured. And, if this is so, what is being dealt with here are the peculiarities of the same divinity; it is of major interest to make note of the changes that the different organs and ornaments of Animal I undergo after having devoured those mythological personages.

Animal I carries in its hind claws peduncular pear-shaped fruits, perhaps hot peppers. Animal II carries elongated plant products, perhaps roots of yucca or manioc and, in addition, others, elongated and undulating, perhaps the products of leguminous plants.

Animal I wears hanging from his elbow the snake-shaped monster X itself, more or less modified, but provided with its various constitutive parts Fa: the serpent-shaped tail, the body replaced by a large feline head, and the animal's own head with an arm or appendage joined to the neck. This figure is reduced or simplified in Animal II to a serpent head whose threadlike body seems coiled into a spiral at the level of the neck, Fb.

Inside the body of Animal I, there is a feline head adorned with flowers and fruits. Inside Animal II there is also a feline head adorned with a plant with wide leaves. The genitals in I are a leguminous plant product; in II, they are a feline head whose long tongue has been transformed into a plant.

In other words, the figures represented in the obelisk are of two different aspects of a divinity whose power or principal attribute is to give food plants to humans; for this reason, it carries the aforementioned products in its claws. In its first aspect, I carries, for this reason, the fruits inside its body, and in its genitals, the seed which should reproduce them. Under the action of other powers of nature symbolized by a condor, a fish, and a serpent-shaped monster, this divinity wastes fruits and seeds. But when the animal destroys or devours the secondary animals which symbolize the aforementioned powers, then the seeds germinate, grow, and flower, without doubt because it has diminished or dulled those powers. The first aspect of this divinity can signify the agent that creates the dry or hot period when the flowering disappears and only seeds are left; the second, the dark and rainy period of winter in which the seeds germinate and grow. Does I represent the agent or cause of summer and autumn, and II the agent or cause of winter and spring? Is it a question of a god who controls agriculture? Whatever the meaning is, it is remarkable that almost all the modifications noted are principally due to the treatment of the tongue of the feline of the accessory X. Is it this tongue that is transformed into a plant provided with numerous buds, or small eyes, and which forms the genitals of II? It is the serpent transformed into fruits which it carries in its claws. And finally, it is the markings that ornament the skin of the serpent of the same accessory figure (which come to form the genitals in I). All these different elements which appear reunited here in a complex and mysterious whole surely form part of a mythological cycle that is related to the powers of nature which directly influence the preservation or destruction of the socioeconomic values of humanity.

## Secondary Divinities Associated with the Principal Divinity: Serpent, Condor, and Fish

Besides the principal divinity already described, there are, as has already been shown, three secondary personages that are presented in various degrees of idealization and which must symbolize certain powers in nature. Lightning, figured as a serpent associated with the feline head or heads from which it issues, emanates sometimes from the forehead, sometimes from the neck, and sometimes from the mouth of the feline. It is one of the most important gods, and this will again be dwelled upon in the course of this work. The condor, symbol of the sun, follows it in importance and is the basis for a group of ornithomorphic representations. Finally, the fish, symbol of the moon, occupies third place which, in turn, is the origin of another group of ichthyomorphic representations. These three new personages who appear as secondary agents accompanying the principal divinity are, in reality, derived or emanated from it. It could be said that the soul of its composition is the feline itself; for this reason, the head of this animal is the structural cell, and the various forms which it assumes are simply variations of this archetypical element. Perhaps in no other manifestation of indigenous art is this intimate association between the principal and secondary personages better illustrated as in Chavín art.

Realistic figures of animals constituting the physical base of the representations of the gods or personifications of certain powers of nature appear with some frequency in ancient Peruvian art. When the divinity, whose physical base is an animal, loses its zoological characteristics to such a degree that its identification becomes impossible, then it almost always appears occupying the most important place in the ornamentation of the divinity as the realistic figure from the symbolic animal in varying degrees of conventionalization.

### *The Condor, Symbol of the Sun, Incarnation of the Feline God*

In Y, the condor, which, as will be seen later symbolizes the sun, appears represented with marked realism (fig. 9.35). Identified with the condor are: the round head; the long, thick, curved beak; the circular eyes;

the crest divided into three large lobes; the circular ear; and the wings, tail, and legs extended in an act of flying.

The representations of the condor, like those of the feline, appear in profile as well as from a front view. Figure 9.39, which represents a condor in profile, has been traced from a fragment of rock found in one of the walls of the new town of Chavín. It is now in the University Museum. The head is that of a feline with the different parts of the face represented in it: elliptical eyes with the pupillary depression also elliptical, crescent-shaped sclera, thick protuberant upper eyelid, flattened nose, small nostril, supranasal prominence, partially open mouth, thick lips, triangular teeth, and large canines that exceed the lip line. The lower canine cuts the cheek and almost reaches the orbital rim. The upper canine cuts the lower lip and half of the lower jaw. The ear is large and bifurcated into two hook-shaped portions, one above and the other below. It wears on its head an elegant crest formed by four isolated volutes that alternate with others adhering to the head itself. The beak of the condor appears juxtaposed in front of the face.

The condor displays an elegant necklace ornamented with the motif of the feline mouth. One sees not only a row of triangular teeth but also the large canines which exceed the lip line. This mouth forms a sort of armature from which the feathers are held that make up the wing, of which only a few portions remain in the stone.

A still more interesting representation of the condor is that which appears carved on one of the faces of the large stone, which is presently

*9.39. The Condor-God as it appears in a relief of Chavín. Lateral view.*

*9.40. The Condor-God as it appears in a relief of Chavín. Front view.*

found in the cultivated plot of land or plaza situated across from the principal temple of Chavín. The stone is very eroded. Two similar figures appear on it. In one of them, the drawing has not been finished, and, in the other, the central part has disappeared due to recent damage (fig. 9.40). Representations of condors of this style must be frequent, because the same figures also appear on other stones found in the houses of the inhabitants of the present village of Chavín, but so eroded that it has not been possible to reconstruct a complete figure. Due to the polishing, which these stones show on the face on which the figure is outlined, these have been preferentially used by the natives of those places for various domestic purposes, mainly to grind grains. This work of constant rubbing has worn away the surface of the stone and caused the drawings to be lost.

Figure 9.40 has been traced from the stone found in front of the principal temple at Chavín. The different parts of the condor can be clearly distinguished in it. The condor is presented with its wings and tail widely extended, talons on its feet, and its head pointing upward. As has been said, the structural cell of this presentation is the feline head. It is the motif which constitutes the basis of the ornamentation. The head, seen in profile, shows all the animal's morphological characteristics: the circular eye, crescent-shaped sclera, circular pupil, eyebrows formed by a protruding knot which is also circular, partially open mouth, triangular teeth, large canines which protrude beyond the lip line, a volute-shaped nose with a supernumerary nostril, a small hook-shaped ear, and a crown or crest formed by three plumes, each one of which is made up of stylized figures of the same feline heads. The beak is juxtaposed in front of the face.

The wings have four sheaves of feathers which issue like tongues from a kind of armature which decorates the scapulas. The armature is formed by a feline mouth, which is composed of the cordlike upper lip of which one sees only the middle part and the right-hand corner of the mouth; teeth occur on the curving edge, and a large canine curves toward the corner of the mouth. In addition, there are three little tongues interspersed in the intermediate spaces between the sheaves of wing feathers. The upper two of these little tongues form as they issue from the lip, two folds or creases which divide the space corresponding to the back into three sections adorned with drawings also derived from the feline head, seen in profile. In each one can be seen the round eye with the crescent-shaped sclera, half of a curving lip and teeth. An appendage, coming from the front part of the scapula, forms the upper front edge of each wing ending in a feline or serpent head with a small rectangular figure in front of it. Each sheaf of feathers is decorated with two extremely stylized feline heads in profile. In the first, the interior head, can be identified the eyes, lips, and teeth, represented by almost geometric figures. In the second, the exterior head, the same motif is enlarged and repeated. The eye which occupies the tip of the feather has a rhomboid shape, the sclera is angular, and the pupil is lozenge shaped. The mouth is recognized by the upper lip in the shape of an S. The lower hook forms the nose and the upper one the corner of the mouth. In addition, two teeth and a canine are distinguishable. The feathers of the tail also issue from another armature which has the shape of a feline mouth. This one displays both lips and both corners of the mouth, rectangular teeth, curving canines near the corners of the mouth, and three little tongues, which, like those previously described, raise the upper lip at their base. These are interspersed in the spaces between the sheaves of feathers, each one of which, like the sheaves of the wing, is similarly decorated with drawings derived from the feline mouth motif.

The lower extremities are semiflexed, the feet with three large talons, the thigh decorated with the feline head motif, and the tarsal with a band likewise ornamented with the same head. The first head shows: a circular eye with crescent-shaped sclera, a mouth with rectangular teeth and a canine, the nose in the shape of a hook. The second is formed almost entirely of the mouth fitted with rectangular teeth, a small central tongue, two volutes above the lips, and another at the level of the knee.

### *The Fish, Symbol of the Moon, Incarnation of the Feline God*

Another of the animals that plays an important role in the mythological representations of Chavín art is the fish, or rather the ichthyoform monster with a feline or condor face. In this form, it figures in pottery from the coast as well as in the sculptured works of the northern Andean region. In describing the fish represented in Z (fig. 9.36), it was said that this mythological animal probably symbolized the moon. Thus, in the idol represented in figure 9.41, the symbolic personage appears associated with the fish and with more realistic characters (fig. 9.42). The

*9.41. Fish-God in a stone from Yauya.*

*9.42. The fish with feline head, symbol of the moon.*

head keeps its feline character, but the body is that of a fish. On it are identified the parts corresponding to the gills and the dorsal, ventral, and tail fins. Furthermore, there is a longitudinal band above the body and another transversal one, between the body and the tail. These different parts appear further developed on the divinity represented in figure 9.41, which is none other than an idealization of this original animal; the figure also has as a structural or representative foundation, the sacred figure, the feline head, transformed or differentiated into a fish-God, in every way comparable with the condor-God previously described.

The important monolith on which the fish-God is carved was found by the author in the doorsill of the ruined church in Yauya, a town in the province of Huari. Its provenience is unknown. It is a rectangular granite slab, fractured, no doubt, in order to adapt it to the dimensions of the doorway. To do this, several pieces were separated from the stone, some of which were found at a short distance away; however, it was impossible to use them to reconstruct or to infer the original dimensions of the monument, not to mention the accessory figures that adorned the head of the idol.

The stone is a parallelepiped. It has three of its polished faces: the two narrow laterals, and one of the wide ones. It measures 1.65 m long, 0.57 m wide, and 0.15 m thick. The divinity reproduced in figure 9.41 is carved on the polished faces.

It consists of a monster which seems to be seated. It has its arms open and its hands directed upward. The body is elongated and occupies the wide face of the stone, while the extremities occupy the narrow lateral faces. In order to identify the various constitutive parts of this divinity and its ornamental details, the following will be described: A. the head, B. the neck, C. the thorax, D. the abdomen, E. the tail, F. the fore extremities, G. the hind extremities.

## A. THE HEAD (FIG. 9.43)

The head, which in appearance has an extremely complicated form, is the result of nothing more than the combination or union of two feline heads, in lateral position, by means of the mouth in the way that two

*9.43. The monstrous head of the Fish-God.*

lateral heads commonly comprise a single monstrous head in a frontal position. In each one of the halves of this head, it is relatively easy to distinguish the different constitutive parts: the eye, large, round, formed by the body of the fish in figure 9.42 which appears to be bending with the head up and the tail down; the large and flattened nose; the hook-shaped ear; the mouth with double lips, the external of which are divided into triangular sections; and the triangular teeth, whose long canines cut the lips and part of the cheek. In addition, the head has two wide tufts of feathers or appendages which soften as they go upward like bursts of flame. The union of these halves form the head of the monster, and that is looking upward. It has a large mouth fitted with teeth and canines, and two noses and two eyes which are simply variations of the fish; they indicate that the animal being dealt with symbolizes a luminous body connected with the light that radiates from the eye of the feline. Its two ears are shaped like hooks. Four lateral appendages or bursts of fire radiate from the head. Two large canines also radiate from the corners of the mouth, and a small tongue with two wide appendages form the central part of the already mentioned corner of the mouth. These different parts constitute the monstrous head. Perhaps the figures which appear to either side in the form of stars or hooks also form a part of it.

### B. THE NECK (FIG. 9.44)

The neck is made up of two parts, an upper and a lower. The first is formed by the feline mouth motif with its lips, triangular teeth, large canines, and tongue. This figure occupies the neck, properly speaking, and, from the lower edge which corresponds to the chin, issues a wide band which hangs on the chest like a shoulder cape. This is ornamented with geometric figures, which, as will be seen later, are also derived from the feline mouth motif. They are arranged in three groups: two lateral and one midcenter.

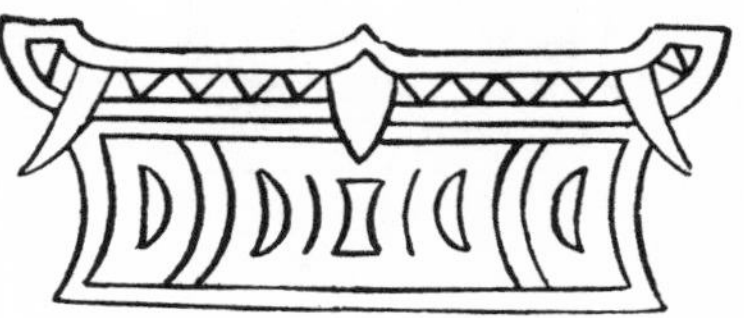

9.44. *The necklace or shoulder cape of the Fish-God.*

### C. THE THORAX (FIG. 9.45)

This is made up of three sections, a middle, an upper, and a lower. The middle portion is occupied by a feline mouth; in it, thick lips, triangular teeth, and the large canines can be distinguished. The upper portion is formed by five figures, two at the ends which are eyes and three in the middle which are conventionalized figures of the mouth motif. The lower portion is similarly occupied by five figures: two end figures from which, due to recent fractures, remain only some parts of geometric feline head figures; and three in the middle, which are identical to those to which they correspond in the upper band.

9.45. *Figure derived from the feline mouth motif which adorns the thorax of the Fish-God.*

### D. THE ABDOMEN

This part of the monster is covered by a grotesque mask (fig. 9.46) which displays a feline mouth on the forehead. Under it are distinguished in great clarity the nose and the eyes, with upper eyelids transformed into serpents that emerge from the inner corner of the eye and make their way toward the outside. The supranasal elements adorn the space between the eyebrows. Furthermore, the motif derived from the feline mouth is on the parts corresponding to the ears. And, finally, a large serpent head appears on each side of the mask, as if it hung from the ear.

9.46. *Monstrous head which ornaments the abdomen of Fish-God.*

### E. THE TAIL (FIG. 9.47)

This is formed in three sections, a middle and two lateral. The middle is formed, in turn, by four geometrical motifs derived from the feline mouth, which are placed one on top of the other in a line, and the side sections, which are wide, by two other figures which are also derived from the feline mouth motif.

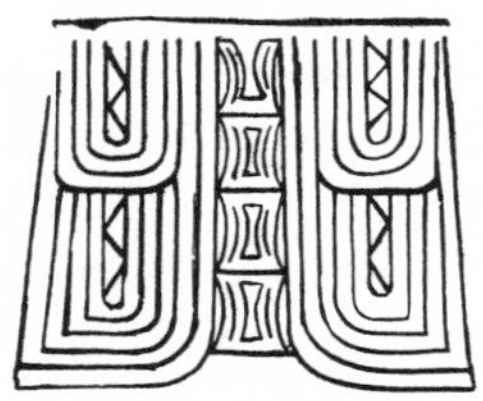

9.47. *The train of the Fish-God.*

### F. THE UPPER EXTREMITIES

The upper extremities (fig. 9.48) are found, as has been said before, in a semiflexed position, with the hands directed upward. These are fitted with three large claws, and the wrist is adorned with a band or bracelet which is also formed by a conventionalized feline face, in which are easily distinguished the eye, the nose, the canine, and the teeth, like a cord or band which runs along the internal edge of the arm and which seems to hold two fish, which are clearly represented under the elbow of the animal. Both seem slightly curved, the upper with head outward, the lower inward.

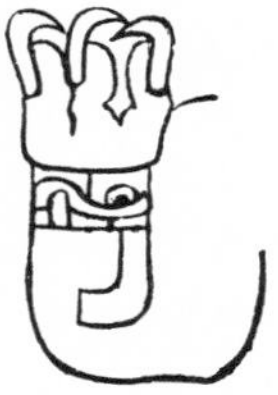

9.48. *Fore extremity of the Fish-God.*

### G. THE LOWER EXTREMITIES (FIG. 9.49)

These are much thicker than the upper extremities; they, too, are semi-flexed. The feet have three large claws. At the level of the ankle is worn a band also adorned with a figure derived from the treatment of the feline mouth. On each side of the leg once again is reproduced the S-shaped figure, which is the same as the one seen on the sides of the head of the monster.

The different parts of this divinity are simply modifications of the anatomical parts of the fish with the feline head. Like that figure, there is the feline head, the neck, and the part corresponding to the gills, the elongated body divided into three portions, a middle and two sides, and figures with curvilinear edges which could correspond to scales. The tail in figure 9.41 is just a modification of the tail like appendage (or cauda) of the fish, and even the band which separates the body from the caudal train appears on the monster represented by the belt. And, finally, possibly the fore and hind extremities of the monster are simply transformations of the fins corresponding to the fish.

For these reasons, this divinity is considered to be derived from a fish. According to this, an icthyomorphic god linked to the feline god is perhaps an agent of the feline god who must personify or symbolize some of its powers. The fact already noted that the fish constitutes the eye of the monster is very significant. It is the eyes of the feline which emit luminous rays on dark nights. This fish god symbolizes the moon; it is one of the aspects of the principal divinity. This new fact will be focused on in due time.

## Anthropomorphic Representations of the Supreme Divinity

The simplest forms of the semianthropomorphic representations of the feline are found in the pottery of Chavín. The representation of

*9.49. Lower extremity of the Fish-God.*

the feline god in Chavín style also appears in the coastal valleys. The majority of vessels of this style, found in Chicama, are wrinkled looking and are made with a cylindrical handle and spout with a thickened or flanged lip. The predominant clay color is dark gray, and then black and reddish brown. The vessels are small, and beautiful, with polished and glazed surfaces. The figures are almost always modeled in relief, repeated, and placed symmetrically in panels. One or more personages appear; even in these scenes, the principal figure is always an anthropomorphized feline. The infiltration or establishment of Chavín art on the North Coast of Peru is so obvious and so profound, that it is not possible to determine the limit of its radius of dissemination. It has already been shown that Andean art radiated toward the coast since the Archaic period. Everything leads one to suppose that the most advanced of the cultures of the North Coast are derived from that of Chavín. Another type of vessel also characteristic of Chavín culture is that in which the feline god has been sculpturally represented. These semianthropomorphic vessels are not scarce in the Chicama Valley. They have different dimensions. Some are large with a bell-shaped neck with a wide mouth. Almost all assume the form of the semianthropomorphic vessel (fig. 9.50). The jaguar-God appears seated here with his hands on his knees. The large head is rectangular and modeled in the characteristic Chavín style: semicircular eye, pushed-up nose, triangular appendages over the forehead, partially open mouth, large

*9.50. Anthropomorphic divinity in Chavín style.*

canines, and triangular ears. He wears a white tunic or long shirt which has a wide brown collar or shoulder cape, decorated with wide transversal white lines and a wide band, also brown, on his wrists.

## The Raimondi Monolith (fig. 9.51)

The most important representation of the principal divinity in the region of northern Peru is that which appears on the monolith found and made known for the first time by Antonio Raimondi. This enormous statue had been found in one of the compartments of the Chavín temple. Raimondi encountered the monolithic stone in a house in the town of Chavín, where it had been taken on its removal from the temple or *castillo*. According to Polo in 1840, Don Timoteo Espinoza, a native of the town of Chavín, found it while turning over land for cultivation near the temple or *castillo*.[8] In 1874 it was taken to Lima, where it is presently to be found in the National Museum. It has the form of a rectangular prism. It measures 1.95 m long, the upper part measures 0.73 m in width, the middle 0.74 m, and the lower 0.76 m; its thickness is 0.17 m. According to Raimondi, "the drawing is the caricature of a man; in each hand he is holding a sort of scepter, formed by a sheaf of small snakes, and on his head a great ornament, made up of numerous small snakes and large mouths with fangs analogous to those of the column already cited. The individual who worked this stone seems to have had the idea of representing the Evil Spirit."[9] Polo, after a long and interesting dissertation on the ruins of Chavín, on the use of the snake as a symbol, on the cult of the god Kon, and of the sun god, gives the opinion that: "the god with the face of a man or rather of a buffalo or bison (*Bos americanus*), with claws on its feet and hands, with anklets on the lower part of his legs, grasping the columns, seems to be the god Sun, with his head crowned with rays."[10] According to Markham, "the personage represented on the stone of Chavín is the same who appears on the monolithic doorway at Tiawanako. It represents the genius of the same people and the same civilization, although in different periods. Of these, the latter one corresponds to Chavín. In Tiawanako, everything seems to hide an intention or a meaning. In Chavín, the conception is more confusing and the execution more overloaded; they seem conventional and without symbolism."[11] Also, Joyce considers this figure related to that of Tiawanako, although its style is very different. "The attitude," he says, "of the personage portrayed and his attributes, seem related with the god of the skies, the rays could be those of the sun, the scepters,

*9.51. The supreme divinity in the Raimondi monolith of Chavín.*

lightning; the inverted position of the multiple heads could indicate in a conventional form that his gaze is turned toward the sky."[12] And, following Uhle, Joyce further relates this figure to certain representations on Nazca pottery, "where appears the same multiplication of heads, surrounded with the rays in form of hooks or ostrich plumes." "On said pottery, as in Chavín," he says, "the god is also presented in an inverted position and the human heads come out of the mouths of other heads. In addition, he carries in his hands two serpents that probably personify the lightning."[13]

According to Uhle, the relief at Chavín belongs to the proto-Nazca style. In a certain way, it forms one of its best manifestations. "In the entire relief, only the motifs of the scepters and of the serpent seem of strange origin, perhaps representative of some not very important relationship with the neighboring proto-Chimú style." Does the relief represent, he wonders, the combination of a cat (tiger), wildcat, or a centipede? The usual form of proto-Nazca representations, he adds, makes it easy to be convinced by the illustrations in all the publications about this strange style that it "is nothing but the stylistic predecessor of the great doorway at Tiawanako." "The relief of Chavín apparently represents the monster who in eclipses devours the Sun or the Moon."[14]

## The Supreme Divinity in the Raimondi Monolith

The semianthropomorphic idol of the Raimondi stone is shown standing in a majestic pose, the face forward, the body vertical, the arms open and slightly flexed, and a scepter in each hand. All of it rests firmly on the muscular lower extremities whose large curved claws are turned outward as if the feet had rotated on the heels. On its head it wears a high, sumptuous miter. With the objective of studying all its representative details, the following will successively be described: (A) the idol, properly speaking; (B) the tiara; and (C) the scepters.

### *A. The Idol*

The constitutive parts of the idol are: the head, the trunk, and the extremities. The head is large and square, occupying almost half of the mass of the figure, excluding the ornament on the head. The hair, transformed into serpents, appears at the sides of the temples. The large eyes are elliptical. The sclera are crescent shaped, the pupil is circular, and the upper eyelid is cordlike. The large nose is flattened and situated in line with the eyes. The mouth is partly open, the corners of the mouth turned down, the lip thick, the teeth rectangular and lined up in two rows. The triangular canines, in pairs, reach the outer edge of the lips. The lower jaw is formed by the combination of two feline heads in a lateral position; united at the mouth of the idol, they make up the monstrous head represented in figure 9.52. This peculiarity of combining lateral faces of feline heads and forming monstrous heads is a characteristic of Chavín art. Note has already been taken of the existence of this curious phenomenon in studying the composition of the monstrous head of the fish god. This strange manner of representing the head of divinities modifies the anatomical or morphological parts of the archetypical animal, and develops a group of teratological representations which, in appearance, have no connection with the representation of the head itself. The combination of two feline heads in lateral position or in profile into a single head completely modifies the original face of the animal. The muzzle widens, the nasal apertures appear adorned with one or more circumferences or volutes, no doubt remainders of the turned-up form of the upper lip as it currently appears in the profile of the feline head.

The idol displays the motif, B (fig. 9.53), on its forehead like an emblematic figure. B is part of the feline face, seen from the front, and shows a high degree of conventionalization. Possibly, this figure is the same that appears in the representations of the feline face above the nose which must symbolize some of the divinity's attributes. This face, B, is rectangular. It is probably this form which suggested to Polo the idea of the buffalo or bison when he tried to describe the kind of animal god which was represented in the Raimondi monolith. The mouth carved in this art style presents the thick, simple, cordlike upper lip, the corners of the mouth arched, and the teeth wide with a curved edge. The small, triangular tongue lifts the lip slightly. The long canines: two front ones which project forward and outward, coming out from under the lips at the level of the forward angles of the face; and two back ones which come out near the corners of the mouth projecting toward the outside, parallel to the front. The nose is represented by two small circular depressions adorned with two parallel curved ridges over them, perhaps wrinkles or folds.

A curved transversal line drawn from shoulder to shoulder passing under the jaw indicates a piece of clothing which adorns the neck. From the lower border of this hangs a wide band which covers the chest and which is joined to the belt like a breastplate. This band is likewise made up of a feline mouth motif, C (fig. 9.54). On it, also, appear the double lip, the rectangular teeth, four canines with the points hidden below the lips. The three adjacent volutes on either side of this mouth are perhaps derived from the turned-up nose.

Circling the waist is another band, D (fig. 9.55), which is also the representation of the upper jaw of the feline. On it are distinguished the horizontal upper lip, the corners of the mouth forming a hook

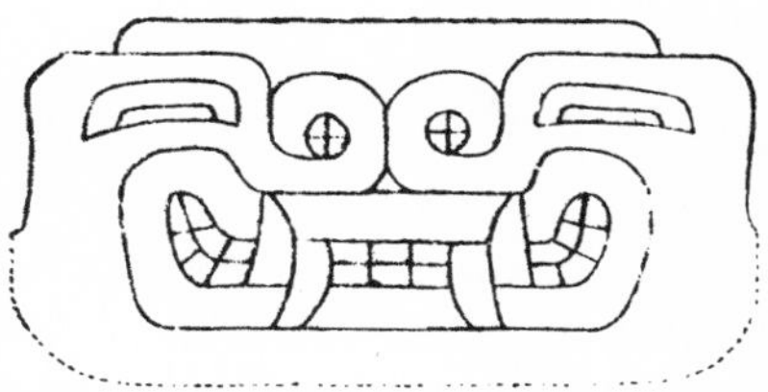

*9.52. Monstrous head formed by the combination of feline heads in lateral position which occupies the lower half of the face.*

*9.53. Emblematic figure derived from the feline head which adorns the forehead.*

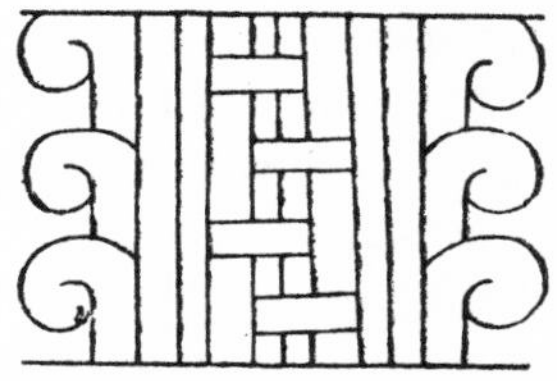

*9.54. Feline mouth motif which adorns the chest.*

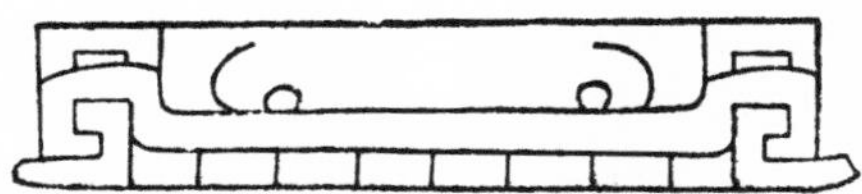

*9.55. Feline mouth motif which forms the belt.*

that hold the canines which are, in turn, hooks themselves, the row of rectangular teeth, the nostrils and nasal folds, and the rectangular eyes located just above the corners of the mouth. At each side of the belt hang a pair of serpents.

The extremities are thick and muscular. As Uhle has noted, the curves of the arms, the calves of the legs, and the three large claws with which the hands and feet are equipped, two in front and one in back, are characteristic of the feline. Bracelets and anklets in the form of bands or strips adorn these extremities.

### *B. The Tiara*

The tiara or miter which majestically adorns the head is the most important ornamental piece on the idol. Although, as will be seen, it is but the appendage of the principal deity, until now there has been found no other headdress like this which is as rich and complex in elaboration or with such multiple symbolic attributes. The tiara is strictly just the elaboration of the cephalic appendage, the symbolic element of greatest importance in the idealization of the feline. Uhle identifies this piece with the centipede. According to him, it always shows up associated with the principal divinity and is found well illustrated in the mythological representations on Nazca pottery. The centipede can be recognized on the monolith, says Uhle, "in the long, wide worm extended upward, the number of obliquely slanting feet which accompany it on both sides, symbolically expressed by halves of serpents, in a small centipede face, in the last upper part of the head of the monster, and in the numerous faces which in the manner of other proto-Nazca representations grow progressively along the length of the body of the worm, concluding with a final face which gives the impression that the critter wants to bite with its tail as well."[15]

The hypothesis of Uhle regarding the identification of the centipede in the cephalic appendage is not entirely acceptable. The tiara is the ornament of the head resulting from the elaboration of the cephalic appendage. This modification or transformation is shown in an immense series of representations that illustrate multiple and varied forms which evolve from the simplest, such as those which adorn the idealized feline heads in the art of the Callejón, to the most complex, such as that which forms this tiara. Flowers, fruits, arrows, and mummified human heads issue from the forehead, the neck, or the mouth of the feline god of Nazca. The tiara is the elaboration of the cephalic appendage formed by an interlinking of feline heads. These surely were attributes of the divinity; they are not always shown multiple and interlinked. Generally, the appendage ends in just a feline or serpent head. When they are shown interlinked, as in this case, only then do they assume strange or monstrous forms which can easily be confused with the figures of serpents or worms.

The miter is composed of an armature or cylindrical helmet adorned with volutes and serpents arranged in pairs and in line, eight in number, on each side of the helmet, irradiating outward and upward. The wide central band which longitudinally adorns the helmet is formed by the superposition of four heads or masks placed in file. It is inferred

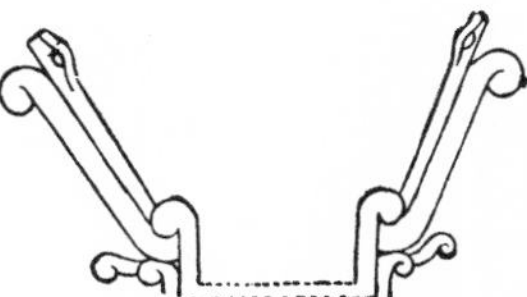

*9.56. Motif derived from the feline mouth. Reproduced eight times to form the headpiece of the miter.*

that the helmet or armature has a cylindrical shape by the arched manner in which the basal edge of the tiara has been drawn. This is formed by the superposition of eight pieces, crowns or rings similar to that reproduced in E (fig. 9.56) derived from the motif of the feline mouth. In each piece can be seen the corners of the lips and the large front and back canines: the first transformed into volutes and the second into serpents. The teeth are similarly transformed into small volutes.

The middle band is formed, as has already been said, by the superposition of the masks represented in F, G, H, and I (figs. 9.57–9.60).

In F (fig. 9.57), the face has a rectangular form, derived also from A and B. In it, the upper lip, the corners of the mouth, and the teeth with curvilinear edges are distinguished, as well as the back canines which project outward and to the sides almost at the level of the corners of the mouth. The front ones also project outward and forward at the level of the angles of the face. The front canines grow thicker and coil at their extremity like a volute. Furthermore, a small triangular tongue can be seen in the middle part. The central part of the face is decorated by a motif formed by two volutes united by means of a lattice marked with intersecting lines to form squares; it is repeated twice and arranged on either side of the face. This squared motif must surely have a religious significance because it is present in other representations of idealized feline heads, sometimes on the face, other times on the forehead. It is possible that it is derived from the grid square form which represents the nostril of the animal, seen in A, as well as in other representations of the feline.

The mask of G (fig. 9.58) does not differ from the preceding one except in a few details. Besides the rectangular face, the front canines transformed into volutes, the teeth with the curving edge, and the canines in the corners of the mouth, this figure displays the animal's eyes with eyelids in the form of volutes immediately over the corners of the mouth. The central part of the face is adorned with the feline mouth motif with double lips; the external one is divided into three

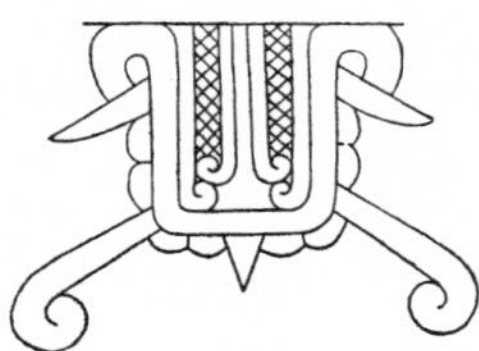
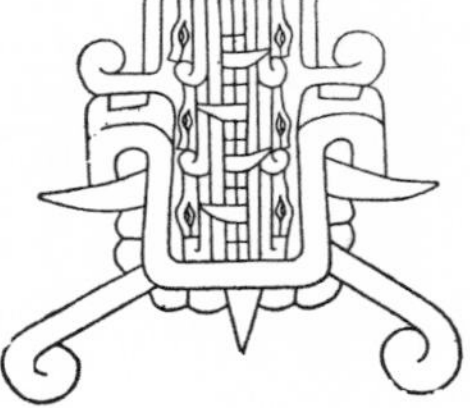

*9.57–9.58. Feline heads which form the lower links of the ornament of the tiara.*

*9.59.–9.60. Feline heads which form the upper links of the ornament of the tiara.*

parts, each one bending in one of its extremities, forming a volute, leaving three spaces that are occupied by serpent heads. The quadrangular teeth and the long canines reach the exterior edge of the lips.

H (fig. 9.59), in its general form, does not differ from the preceding figures. The face here features different parts: the nostrils, the folds or ridges which define the nose, the supranasal figures, the eyes, and the thick upper eyelids, undulating or sinuous, and coiled at the tips. Over the middle part of the forehead appear two condor heads, seeming to come out of the mouth of the previous mask. On each side, a volute falls vertically over the middle part of the eyelids.

I (fig. 9.60) differs from the previous figure only in the figure or sign which it carries on its forehead which seems to be inserted or juxtaposed in the inner corner of the eyelid. This sign, formed by two volutes united in the middle by a broken line or zigzag, is similar to that which is shown in figure F (fig. 9.57).

The figure shown in J (fig. 9.61), which crowns the tiara, seems to project like a tongue from the mouth of the previous mask. It is also derived from the stylization of the feline mouth motif. This is composed of a double lip; the inner ones, where they come together to form the corners of the mouth, twist around transforming themselves into serpents, and the outer ones volutes. In addition, an accessory figure formed by four small volutes or hooks is seen in the space left between the heads of the two serpents.

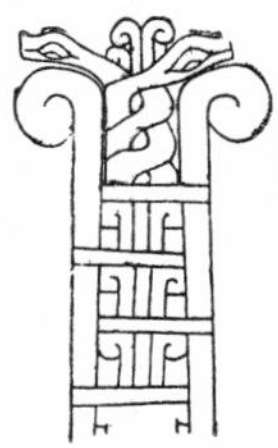

*9.61. Motif of feline mouth which forms the tip of the tiara.*

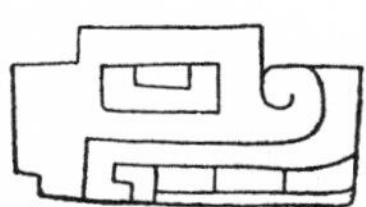
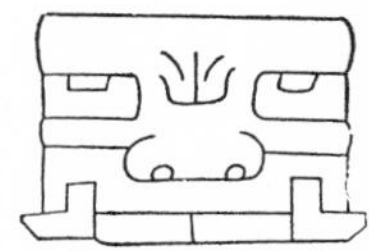
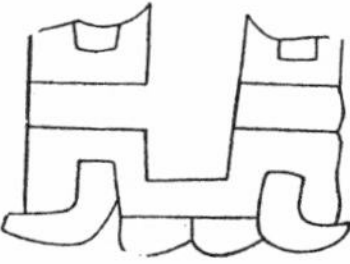

*9.62.–9.64 Motifs derived from the feline head.*

### *C. The Scepters*

The scepters the idol carries in each hand are identical and are formed by a sheaf of lances, clubs in the form of feline heads, and arrows in the form of serpents. K, on the lower part of the scepter, is attached to a cord composed of the bodies of two snakes which could represent a club or the *liwi* or bola (fig. 9.62). On this head are clearly distinguishable the rectangular eye; the pupil; the turned-up nose; the lips, the upper one thick and also turned upward, the lower thin; the rectangular teeth; and the canine. L (fig. 9.63) is another mask which appears below the elbow of the idol; here also the wide, flattened nose, the rectangular eyes, the space between the brows, and the mouth equipped with teeth with a curved edge, and sharply pointed canines turned toward the back can clearly be distinguished. M (fig. 9.64), which appears on the upper part of the scepter, is similar to the previous figure. Also distinguishable are: the mouth from which emanates the sheaf of hooks, lance, and serpents which crown the scepter; the rectangular eyes; the curved canines; and the teeth with curved edges.

The aforementioned idol is the representation of the supreme divinity, the jaguar, in its anthropomorphic aspect. Its feline character is manifested with almost no difference from the other morphological variations of this animal god, either as found on the monuments of Chavín or of other Peruvian cultures, except in its greater complexity and symbolism. More about the meaning of this representation, to the cephalic appendage, to its anthropomorphic character and symbolism, as well as to its connections with the supreme divinity represented in Tiawanako and Nazca—which the hypotheses already mentioned have suggested—will be focused on to a greater extent in the course of this work.

## The Monolithic Lanzón

In the center of one of the chapels or compartments in the middle section of the temple of Chavín, the walls of which are adorned with large, deep, rectangular niches, a monolith, which is the statue of the supreme divinity, is to be found. Its four faces are represented in figures 9.65–9.68. The information which exists about the aforementioned monument is, in some cases, incomplete and defective and, in others, false, and gives but a vague or remote idea of what this piece of sculptural art is in reality. It is unique in its class in South America, in the quality of its workmanship and the material used, as well as in its great historical significance.

Without a doubt, the inconveniences inherent to this place for studying or for carrying out research, such as the absolute lack of light within the temple, and the constant threat presented by landslides which are produced when the earth is disturbed, make a thorough and therefore true study of this monument impossible. Raimondi reports that "at the crossing which is formed by two passageways in the central building is found this kind of column of granite, sculptured in low relief, with very capricious drawings. It is in the form of a triangular prism, 2.20 m high and of varying width."[16] According to Polo, the monolith "looks like a *lanzón* (lance) of 2.20 m in height, its base has three faces, it narrows in the upper part, it fits into the roof, and it is supported on a rounded stone which serves as a seat or support."[17] In their books, Middendorf,[18] Wiener,[19] and Polo himself provide imperfect drawings of the monolith which all correspond to only its upper half, which was the only part in plain sight until March of 1919, when the author discovered it in its totality.

The monolith is held by the enormous stone beams which form the roof of the chapel and it is suspended there, because while carrying out the excavations in order to totally uncover it, it was confirmed that its lower extremity ended in a point and had no base of support. The discovery of the floor of the room where the monolith is located was not achieved. Everything leads to the supposition that, after the Conquest, the room was filled with stones and clay perhaps with the intention of hiding the idol. It is quite possible that, in the lower part of the room,

*9.65–9.68. The monolithic Lanzón from Chavín de Huantar.*

other hidden sculptured stones exist which would have adorned the chapel. The monolith has the form of a giant dagger, knife, or lance point. Observed from the only door that exists, which is at the level of the floor of the entrance gallery, it gives the impression that, in becoming detached from the ceiling, it remained stuck into the ground with the point down and the handle up. The monolith has been damaged in its upper extremity. It must have run through the ceiling of the chapel to project or sit erect in the upper room of the temple, of which there are still remains of walls made out of polished stones. The floor of this room was reached by means of some admirably worked stone stairs which ascend from the platforms or plazas. The platforms or plazas, located in front of the temple up to buildings on top of it, have now been converted into cultivated fields of maize and potatoes. The Lanzón is oriented so that the cutting edge which corresponds to the face of the idol looks to the east, and the blunt edge which corresponds to the back of the idol to the west. The length of the monolith is 4.53 m.

Of the two parts which make up the giant spear point, the handle and blade, the handle has the approximate shape of a rectangular prism; the front and back faces are much narrower than the side ones. The blade is roughly prismatic; in its upper third, it presents four facets—two side ones, a front, and a back. The facet on the right side is flat almost all of its length, except near the base in which it offers a slight vaulting which is pronounced toward the front; the back facet is almost convex in the base and concave a few centimeters below this; the left facet has a slight convexity or bulging, and is almost uniform in the upper third. The back facet is very short, and almost all of its longitudinal extension converges with the left face.

In the middle third, the blade presents two lightly convex faces which join in front and behind forming projecting angles.

In the lower middle third, the left face shows a depression in such a way that two facets are formed. Finally, the two faces of the blade of the knife join a few centimeters above the point, thus having an effect on the elliptical form of the section.

The stone, then, has neither the form nor the dimensions made note of by Raimondi and by Polo, nor does the stone seat or support mentioned by the latter exist.

Despite the monolith having been discovered in its entirety and the drawings presented here have been made with the greatest fidelity to the original itself, through the help of numerous tracings (which today form part of the archaeological collection at the Museum), they cannot be considered to be perfect reproductions of this monument. This will only be achieved once the site has been put in order in such a way as to ensure faithful photographic reproductions. The different parts and decorations of this work of genius have been modeled with such a mastery of the art that it is impossible to imagine how it was done without the help of indispensable precision instruments. All this leads us to consider the Lanzón one of the most remarkable products of religious feeling and one of the masterpieces of American indigenous art.

## The Supreme Divinity in the Lanzón Monolith

It is on this granitic stone of such irregular shape that the statue of the supreme divinity has been shaped. This appears standing upright, looking straight ahead, with the left hand down, turned back, showing the back of the hand, and the right hand is held high with the fingers extended, showing the palm.

The head is enormous, occupying a third of the mass of the blade and almost half of the idol. The body is short and thick, and the extremities small. The idol as a whole, in both its morphological and its ornamental parts, is admirably sculpted in high relief. Everything about the work speaks of care and meticulousness; of a great expenditure of energies in the arduous labor of carving the hard stone; and, above all, of an outstanding artistic sense in order to adapt a religious concept so complex and fantastic to the raw material least appropriate due to its hardness, and the most difficult to work because of its form.

What the artist intended was not to portray either a human form or that of any determined animal. In that case, he would have tried to represent ideal forms of human or animal anatomy. As in Greek art, he would have tried to find the rhythm of the formal and structural whole and give expression and life to the objects represented. The artist, who knew how to draw and sculpt figures of serpents, mouths, gestures, feline claws, and condor plumages in the most beautiful and harmonious poses and movements, the way a talented artist of our epoch would, was capable of effortlessly finding the harmony in the anatomical or formal whole if this had been his artistic or religious ideal.

What the indigenous artist intended to represent was the way he conceived of this malignant spirit, the lord of the forest, progenitor of the most powerful animals of creation and of humanity. It was animal and man at the same time, the one who originated and controlled the great powers of nature. It was not his intention to represent the wild beast who caused harm and who could conquer and kill, but rather the powerful being that his imagination had forged and which existed solely in the world of his fantasy, for him a real world. The present-day artist sculpting a statue, for the most part, tries to faithfully copy natural forms, thus producing a portrait, or else tries to emphasize lines and beautiful forms from nature, aided by the skill of his hand and his cultivated artistic feeling. He copies, he combines, and, it could be said, he corrects through a process of the idealization of natural forms and subjecting them to the laws of art, which he discovered or acquired during his training. The indigenous artist, under the impulse of religious ideas, forges in his imagination an entity which does not correspond to anything in nature, which is the product of the combination of various real elements, symbols, and attributes which do not belong to a determined personage, nor do they represent a harmonious combination of lines and natural forms or the exaltation of these. His work is the product of a systematization of the religious ideas of his time. It is the crystallization of his philosophy, of his concept of the world and of life, and the objectification or materialization of the beings that his imagination creates. To this is due the apparently inexplicable fact of using the most inappropriate materials in terms of their nature and their form for representing his gods. As to the purely aesthetic feeling, the religious objective always comes first. The form of the lance point must have had some divine significance when it was chosen by preference to represent the supreme divinity. Perhaps here also is hidden a new link which connects death, symbolized by the lance, with the supreme divinity, the feline, that occurs as in another instance with the lifeless human head.

The enormous head of this god is clearly feline. Its hair is formed by bunches of serpents which detach themselves from the skin, coiling over the forehead and smoothly stretching out toward the back. The eyes are large, and their different parts are perfectly chiseled: the eye socket deep, the projecting sclera crescent-shaped, the pupil hemispherical, and the upper eyelid transformed into a serpent which emerges out of the inner corner of the eye and then encircles the eye and straightens out toward the temple. Another serpent also replaces the lower eyelid and falls upon the cheek, and a third detaches itself at the level of the cheekbone.

The muzzle is wide, prominent, grimacing with a ferocious look; a slight undulation or concavity appears above the nose. The nostrils are open wide; the facial folds pronounced by means of deep furrows, especially the fold above the nose. The contracted lips impart the irritable snarl to the countenance of the savage beast. The row of admirably worked rectangular teeth are arranged so that their cusps project forward. The large upper canines are two in number, one on each side up in the corners of the mouth. These canines cut into the lower lip and part of the cheek. Above the nose are two irregular figures in the form of symmetrically placed horns, the same which always appear in representations of the feline which have been designated with the name "supranasal figure." The ears are small, the earflap in the form of a hook. The perforated lobe sustains large earrings made in two pieces, an upper piece in the form of a lanceolate blade and a lower one in the form of a ring or hoop. The idol displays a necklace or band decorated with a wavy cord occupying the middle part with small rectangles interspersed within the hollows of the waves. A wide belt or loincloth, exquisitely decorated with a band formed by the interlocking of various feline heads and a wide scalloped border, circles the waist with the help of two cords or strips whose ends are also feline heads.

The upper extremities allow the palm, the ridges, and lines of the hand to be clearly seen. The lower extremities have the paws placed in such a way that the tips of the toes touch in front and the heels turn out. In addition, bracelets and anklets are worn by the idol.

A kind of miter or headdress, also decorated with artistically arranged feline heads, covers the head of the idol. On the point of the miter is a pair of feline or serpent faces, joined by two serpent-shaped cords which hang down the back, interlaced like a giant braid which ends near the lower vertex of the monolith.

On the frontal face of the handle of the monolith there also appears a furrow or groove which leads to a circular depression situated in the angle formed by the blade and the handle, and continues through the center part of the head. Without doubt, through this canal ran the blood of the victims sacrificed to the divinity in the contiguous upper compartment. On the floor of this upper compartment should have been the sacrificial stone, which was the upper tip of this monolith. The arrangement of the canal through which the blood ran permitted the blood to arrive directly at the mouth before it spread out over the surface of the stone.

## General Considerations on the Art of Chavín

Among the multiple and varied manifestations of aboriginal art, the art of Chavín stands out, ubiquitous, original, and unmistakable. It can be considered as a variety or derivation of megalithic art and, at the same time, as one of the highest expressions of the indigenous genius.

The fundamental facts which determine and define Chavín art are: the belief in a supreme divinity of animal nature, who was the origin and endless source of imaginary concepts about the world and about life; the mastery of stone not only in order to shape enormous blocks and to construct indestructible buildings but also to preserve indelibly through time the history of Chavín's physical and intellectual activities; and sculpture as a means of ensuring the fidelity and beauty of its religious concepts.

The feline is the fundamental base, the primordial cell, the structural unit of all the representations in Chavín art. This animal, which is surely no other than the jaguar, is the sacred symbol, the racial emblem, the prototypical animal which maintains and fixes the form and originating nature of the divinity through its transformations or incarnations. The statue of the feline adorns the walls of the temples and all sacred places. Its figure appears in the emblems displayed by divinities as well as personages, chiefs, or priests. The feline is the model which the imagination of the artist abides by when he is trying to represent the gods. It is the divine spirit which is embodied in other animals such as the serpent, the condor, and the fish, which symbolize the manifestations of its power, objectified in the lightning, the sun, and the moon.

In Chavín, as in Cuzco and Tiawanako, hardness, weight, distance, and height were not insuperable obstacles for the Indian when he wanted to make use of stone. He used granite and, in general, the hardest stones. He transported enormous blocks of stone over long distances, and elevated them to considerable heights. Finally, his mastery of stone was of such magnitude that he not only cut, worked, and polished stone in order to obtain geometrical surfaces, but also created objects of great beauty and instruments of ceremonial and domestic use. Everywhere in the provinces of Huari, Pomabamba, and Pallasca are found the products of this admirable art. The majestic temple of Chavín, the fortified town of Yayno, and the pyramidal temples of the Callejón de Huaylas are megalithic structures comparable with those of the Urubamba Valley. In many of the ruins of the province of Pomabamba, cube- or parallelepiped-shaped stone funeral caskets are found, the tops of which appear so carefully carved and polished that they surpass the best examples of worked stone from Tiawanako. The foundations and walls or ramparts of the great temple at Chavín are made of enormous blocks of stones which are not worked. But the most important parts of the building, like part of the facade and the lovely stairway which the author discovered in 1919, and like the upper compartments, are formed from worked stones so well fitted to each other that they could rival the best constructions in Cuzco.

Regarding the artistic character of Chavín culture, a marked tendency toward sculpture is observed, even in cases where the material used is not hard stone, but rather a malleable or plastic material. The figures, in some cases, appear carved by making simple incisions or grooves. In others, the background has been dug away or shaved off so that the figures stand out in bas-relief. Frequently, the edges are smoothed or the contours rounded and the background deepened so that the figures stand out in high relief, or else certain details are shaped even below the surface of the stone in such a way that they appear in low relief. And, lastly, the contour of the figure can be completely shaped in all dimensions, thus forming a statue. This tendency toward the sculptural is one of the most notable characteristics of this art, and it persists in the pottery of Chicama which seems to be its derivative. The portrait heads and reliefs, which are the most excellent sculptural examples found in this place, have the stamp of Chavín art. One could feel assured with no little basis that they belong to the same culture and the same epoch. One could even put forth the assumption that the key to a better future knowledge of Chavín art is offered in the interpretation of the many forms and mythological representations of Chicama pottery, today still wrapped in mystery and distant from Chavín. The more one studies and knows about the cultures of the sierra, the greater the analogies with those of the coast are found, and the hypothesis that the latter are only a reflection of the former is supported.

## The Determining Drives in the Evolution of Art

The genesis and evolution of Chavín art are due to the simultaneous action of two forces, feelings, or drives: the one idealistic and the other utilitarian; the one mythical or religious, the other ornamental or aesthetic. Both act upon the fundamental concept or primordial psychophysical element on that mysterious ideological protoplasm, the idealized jaguar, and originate and develop the art.

Religious feeling is, in primitive or embryonic societies, the most powerful drive which absorbs almost all the activities of man. The utilitarian, which seems to be inherent to human nature, always tends to orient these activities toward that which is simple, to that which offers least resistance, to that which offers a saving of energy, and reaches its equilibrium and repose in the balance, rhythm, and harmony of deeds and ideas.

In Chavín art, the first religious feeling manifests itself in the process of idealization; and the second, the utilitarian, is manifested in the double process of elimination and substitution. Both converge and act simultaneously in representing or forming their gods, that is to say in the architectural work of representing the creations of their fantasy. It is through these procedures that the mythical structural units are created, and that these are arranged and intertwined to form the most complex mythic entities. In accordance with this, first the processes of idealization, elimination, and substitution will be studied, and then the architectural composition of the gods.

## The Religious Drive
### *Idealization*

Idealization is carried out through different procedures which act in a simultaneous, a gradual, or a successive manner. In a first stage, a link between the feline head and the lifeless human head is established. It is well known that, in Peru, it is a very ancient custom to artificially prepare or mummify human heads for religious purposes. They were the objects of a very intense and generalized cult. They must have played a very important role in religious and magical practices. Perhaps they symbolized certain events or mysterious and transcendental phenomena, because they were not only preserved through artificial mummification, but they were also worked in stone and clay with such marked realism that, had the mummified heads disappeared, their morphological characteristics could have been studied from those worked in clay and stone. They show folds, furrows, wrinkles, and even the sutures of the lips; and these are the elements utilized in the idealization of the feline. The palpebral and orbicular muscles, the ears, the teeth and canines, the hair, and the wrinkles in the space between the eyebrows were highlighted and were converted into sinuous bands or cords and into hooks and volutes.

In a second stage of idealization, the hair and the cordlike muscles of the feline are transformed into serpents. The serpents replace the facial muscles which produce the undulations and folds. It is by their contracting and expanding that they seem destined to open or close the eyes and the mouth. Those which lacerate the skin of the head as well as of the face emerge undulating toward the surface, and they coil and interweave.

In a third stage, the feline is adorned with certain symbolic objects, such as mummified human heads, appendages which yield like bursts of fire, stars, fruits, flowers, seeds, etc., which surely must be the same attributes. Among the aforementioned objects, the cephalic appendages, stars and human heads are the ones which stand out and occupy a preferential place. The cephalic appendages almost always appear associated with the stars and must be the symbolic elements which link it to the sidereal world; the heads, without a doubt, symbolize its destructive power or death.

In a fourth stage, a marked tendency toward anthropomorphization is noted. The animal is shown adorned with objects and symbols which are characteristic of man, principally one who exercises spiritual or temporal power, such as miters, earrings, bracelets, anklets, belts, and scepters. Furthermore, little by little, the animal changes the horizontal position of the quadruped for the vertical position characteristic of man.

In a final stage, a maximum of idealization is reached through an amalgam or combination of two felines, or two parts of felines, which give origin to a teratological being of such extraordinary heteromorphism that it makes it impossible to identify by means of simple artificial observation. Only through careful analysis of its various parts can one succeed in discovering its composition and feline origin.

These stages of the process of idealization of the feline could be reduced to three: in the first, the hair, teeth, and muscles of the animal are transformed into serpents; in the second, the feline is bedecked or adorned with certain attributes or symbolic objects; and in the third, the animal is anthropomorphized and the head is transformed into another, monstrous one, resulting from the combination of two feline heads.

## The Aesthetic Drive

Under the impetus of aesthetic feeling the representations of the feline are found subject to a double process: elimination and substitution.

### *Elimination*

Through a process of elimination, different parts of the animal gradually disappear until at last it is reduced to the simplified representation of the mouth. This process, like the previous one, goes through several stages. First, the tail of the feline disappears. It gets confused with or merges with the cephalic appendage, or another feline head is provided or contributes to the formation of a serpent-shaped bicephalic monster. It would be very risky to try to identify the tail in the cephalic appendage, although it is certain that in some representations of the feline in Nazca art, the tail and the body are elongated and become serpent-shaped. When the extremities disappear, in some cases they become converted into an appendix of the head. In Chimú art, nearly realistic representations of the feline appear provided with a cephalic appendage like an independent body adorned with fruits and other symbolic objects. Sometimes this appendage is inserted in the base of the head or in the neck, in the forehead, between the eyebrows, or in the nape of the neck, and, at other times, it comes out of the mouth in a simple form or divided into two or three branches, and almost always adorned with flowers, fruits, arrow points, mummified human heads, etc.

The hind extremities are eliminated at once; this is what happens with the feline who adorns the shoulder of the divinity represented on the obelisk. Afterward, the entire body disappears, and only an extremity, a fore one, remains attached to the neck, as seen in the figure, which one of the divinities represented in the same obelisk carries, hanging from the elbow. And finally, the body disappears entirely, leaving just the head.

This is, as has already been said repeatedly, the fundamental motif in the art of Chavín. Simplified in its various anatomical parts in varying degrees of idealization, and represented from the front as well as in profile, the feline head always forms the primary element. It is the structural unit from which originates and with which are formed the most complex representations of the divinities.

The process of elimination does not stop at the head, but also acts upon it, so that the forehead, the ears, the eyes, and even the lips are gradually eliminated, leaving just the row of teeth and the canines. It stops only when the geometric motif resulting from the stylization and simplification of the various parts of the mouth have been reached.

The figures produced through the gradual elimination of the anatomical parts of the feline form independent ornamental motifs. These, when juxtaposed, form the organs and the various parts of the bodies of the figures of the gods.

It is almost unnecessary to illustrate these different phenomena with examples since they abound in this art style. The reader can find them with facility on reviewing the different motifs resulting from the dissection which has been made of the figures of the principal gods.

In the figures of the twin divinities which appear on the obelisk (fig. 9.17) and on the fish god in Yauya (fig. 9.41), there is a true sample book of motifs which graphically illustrates the different stages of idealization and elimination.

### *Substitution*

The process of substitution is as obvious as the previously described process. The different parts of the body of the animal are substituted for motifs derived through the treatment of the feline. This process is revealed from the instant the serpent replaces the muscle, and even the cordlike trait which the profiles of the head show might well be considered a phenomenon of substitution. In no example is this phenomenon better illustrated than in the twin divinities of the obelisk (fig. 9.17). In them, the different parts of the body have been substituted by motifs derived from the feline figure in different degrees of idealization and elimination. The shoulder, neck, back, stomach, hip, tail, genitals, arm, foot, finally, all of the morphological topography of the divinity, have been substituted with fragments of felines. If it were not for the care which the artist took to place the different structural parts of the divinity in a coordinated and symmetrical whole, it would have been impossible to recognize or identify the specific form of this animal god. The different parts which enter into the composition are juxtaposed, without any line whatsoever that delimits the general outline. It has been necessary to be guided by certain special sighting points, such as the size of the head and claws, and not consider the decorative figures in order to recognize the general profile of the feline god in this labyrinth of drawings.

## Architectural Composition of the Representations of the Gods, Their Figures Are Transformations of That of the Feline

The processes of idealization, elimination, and substitution, acting in conjunction upon the feline figure, modify it, and create other, monstrous figures which represent the divinities. At the same time, they form the different motifs that decorate not only the figures of divinities but also all the objects related to their worship, and they are the objective evidence of their civilization.

It is interesting to observe how the imagination of the indigenous artist works when one attentively studies the materials or products of his religious feeling and artistic genius. The head of the feline is the raw material, the central point, the inexhaustible source of his fantasies. The common head is made sacred from the moment the appendage is added. This would be the sacred sign, the *waka* or magical force which converts it into a dynamic element, charged with potential energy. It is the vital element or germinal cell, able to grow and differentiate, that is, evolve and turn into complex mythical organizations.

## The Serpent, Symbol of Lightning

A double process of simplification and elaboration is shown in the artistic treatment of this mythic cell. Through the former process, the head gradually loses its originating form, its different parts atrophy and acquire, bit by bit, the form of the serpent. The ears disappear. The face flattens. The eyes become elliptical. The turned-up nose becomes shorter. Even the canines disappear. The appendage bends into handles and coils around itself in a spiral or guilloche and, in not a few cases, acquires the markings of the coral snake and other ophidians. In the art of Chavín, as in Andean art as well as in its radiations, are found examples which illustrate these phenomena of idealization. Between the two large serpents represented on the Lanzón stone whose heads appear with feline characteristics on the peak of the tiara of the supreme divinity and whose interlocked bodies hang down the entire length of the tiara, and the almost realistic serpents which accompany the anthropomorphic divinities represented on the pottery of Chicama, there is an intermediate range of simplified representations.

The process of elaboration is similarly revealed. The feline heads join, link, and combine to form more complex or differentiated organizations. These combinations form, as will be seen shortly, organisms which have different functions from those characteristic of the feline. Here is confirmed that phenomenon which could be called, using the terminology of Bergson, creative evolution; that is, the creation of organisms which have distinct qualities from that or from those who have intervened in their formation. Two heads of felines of different sizes are combined: one, the smaller one, forms the head, properly speaking, of the monster; the other, larger one, the body; from the mouth of the larger head issues a large appendage or serpent, and there we have the serpent-shaped monster which accompanies the divinity represented on the obelisk. Two or more heads are interlinked in such a way that one appears to come out of the mouth of the other to form the symbolic figure which occupies the middle part of the tiara. Several heads are combined, merging their principal parts, the cordlike lips form a continuous cord which connects all the heads, and each mouth corresponds to two mouths; thus, a symbolic figure is formed that decorates the tiara and the belt of the supreme divinity represented on the Lanzón.

Cephalic appendages in the art of the Callejón de Huaylas appear lineal, sinuous, broken into zigzags, or forming hooks and volutes, simple or in chains, and almost always associated with stellar figures. In the art of Chavín, cephalic appendages appear more differentiated. They are wide, undulating, and multiple, and they issue from the cranium-like tongues or bursts of fire. The lineal or cordlike appendages are elongated and bend into a spiral, or form uniform handles and more or less geometric frets. With frequency, the appendages or aforementioned flashing tongues are formed by two or more parallel concentric lines that take different forms. Thus, they become triangular, lozenge-shaped, and, sometimes, the central line closes and encloses another line in a zigzag. In that case, it takes on the aspect of an elongated feline mouth with multiple cordlike lips and constitutes a motif which seems, from its appearance, to be derived from the mouth, but which, in reality, is nothing more than a differentiation of the cephalic appendage.

## The Condor, the Heliacal Symbol

In the evolution of art, the head of the feline and its appendage, as has been said, constitute a kind of embryonic organism. By virtue of the processes of conventionalization already noted, the head transforms into other mythological organisms, more complex and of greater functional differentiation. Thus, sometimes the head is modified, becoming more simplified: the muzzle becomes elongated, the eye becomes circular, the appendage becomes extremely long, twisting to form a multitude of handles which are grouped and lined up symmetrically, assuming, bit by bit, the shape of a bird, a figure which becomes completed by the attachment of talons and a beak. In a greater degree of differentiation, the handles expand, are symmetrically lined up at the sides and behind the head, ornamented with figures of feline heads in various degrees of conventionalization and thus form the wings and the tail of the condor, the figure of which is completed by the juxtaposition of talons, beak, and crest. In this way, the figure of the condor, the heliacal symbol, becomes established.

## The Fish, the Selenic Symbol

At other times, the head is hardly modified at all. The mouth maintains its feline character, the nose becomes elongated and twists upward and back like a volute, and the appendage is arranged in two long handles which are joined together by means of a transversal cord, thus acquiring the figure of a fish, which is completed by the addition of fins. In a greater degree of conventionalization, the head is transformed into another monstrous head through combining them with another two feline heads, and the handles expand tremendously; the different parts of the animal become ornamented with the feline head motif in various degrees of conventionalization. In this way, the figure of the fish, the selenic symbol, becomes constituted.

## The Feline God, Wari of the Pleiades

With a greater degree of conventionalization and idealization, the different morphological parts of the entire animal are transformed through the process of substitution, by virtue of which each of the principal organs is replaced by motifs derived from the treatment of the feline. Through the other process, the animal is replete with certain symbols or attributes which are peculiar to this divinity, the star that reveals its sidereal character (fig. 9.5) being one of the most important. Thus is constituted the figure of Wari, which is the feline which resides or is found alongside the stars of the constellation of the Pleiades which devours the sun and the moon, and who controls the great meteorological phenomena.

## The Supreme Divinity and the Lanzón Monolith

With a maximum degree of idealization, the feline itself abandons, as has already been mentioned, its horizontal position and acquires the vertical one of man, and, at the same time, the garments and symbols of his power, such as scepters, tiaras or miters, earrings, necklaces, belts, etc. Thus is constituted the figure of the supreme divinity. It is this, that almighty spirit, which almost never stops figuring either in the cosmogonic myths of the tropical forest or in Andean myths. As has been seen, all the other divinities are just derivations or transformations of the supreme divinity.

Regarding the representations of this divinity, there is still a fact of the highest transcendence which must be explained, which is the predilection of the artist for stones in the form of lances for carving the supreme divinity. The lance must have been, like the mummified human head, a symbol of war or of death, thus its connection with the evil spirit. But there is a fact which offers a more convincing explanation, and that is the relationship which existed between the wild forest tribes and the several tribes which made up pre-Columbian Peru. This fact impels us to search for the explanation of certain Andean mythological phenomena in the mythology of tropical forest cultures. Between the Muchika language, which was in other times predominant in the North of Peru, and the languages of the Carib Arawak trunk, certain evident lexical analogies are noted. These analogies also appear, as has been indicated, in the cosmogonic myths.

The well-known Father José Gumilla, in a passage about the Carib, says, "Not disagreeing much with this, the erudition of the Achagua Nation, protests that the Caribs are the legitimate descendants of Tigers, and, for that reason, they behave with the cruelty of their parents. Because of this, the name Chavi *signifies Tiger* in their language; they derive the word Chavínavi, which for them signifies as in Caribe, native of Tiger. Other Achaguas from other factions or tribes further explain the species and give it more soul in this way: Chavi is the Tiger in their language, and Chavína is the lance and, of the two words, Tiger and Lance, they take the name of the Caribs, calling the Chaví-navi, which is the same as *children of Tigers with Lances*, an illusion or simile very typical for the bloody cruelty of the Caribs."[20]

Here, I have expressed in synthesis the tropical forest origin of the Andean peoples who worship the jaguar and provided the explanation of the name *Chavín*, which the divinity originally had, and the form of the stone lance used to represent it.

The contribution that the art of Chavín brings to a better understanding of the religion of ancient Peru is of the greatest importance, since it is the foundation upon which the art of Peru, in general, has been built. Chavín represents one of the cultural pyramids of America. Further investigations will surely offer the solution to many problems and the key to many enigmas that are present in the study of Peruvian civilization.

1. Squier, 1877, p. 458.
2. Wiener, 1880, p. 603.
3. Baessler, 1902–1903, Vol. 2, Plate 70, fig. 258.
4. Means, 1919, p. 17. fig. 1a.
5. Baessler, 1902–1903, Vol. 2, Plate 60, fig. 239.
6. Baessler, 1902–1903, Vol. 2, Plate 59, fig. 238.
7. Tschudi, 1918, pp. 34–35.
8. Polo, 1899, p. 197.
9. Raimondi, 1873, p. 215.
10. Polo, 1899, p. 264.
11. Markham, 1910, p. 136.
12. Joyce, 1912, pp. 175–177.
13. Joyce, 1912, p. 181.
14. Uhle, 1920, pp. 53–55.
15. Uhle, 1920, p. 54.
16. Raimondi, 1873, pp. 214–215.
17. Polo, 1899.
18. Middendorf, 1893–1895, pp. 99–100.
19. Wiener, 1880, p. 575.
20. Gumilla, 1745, Vol. 1, p. 216.

## REFERENCES CITED

Baessler, Arthur
1902–1903 *Altperuanische Kunst. Beitrage zur Archaologie des Inkareiches.* 4 vols. Berlin.

Gumilla, Jose
1745 *Historia natural, civil y geográfica de las naciones situadas en las riveras del río Orinoco.* Vol. 1. Barcelona: Gilbert y Tutó.
Joyce, Thomas
1912 *South American Archaeology: An Introduction to the Archaeology of the South American Continent with Special Reference to the Early History of Peru.* New York.
Markham, Clement
1910 A comparison of the ancient Peruvian carvings and the stones of Tiahuanaco and Chavín. *Sixteenth International Congress of Americanists,* 1908, Vol. 2, pp. 389–394. Vienna.
Means, Philip Ainsworth
1919 Una nota sobre prehistoria peruana. *Mercurio Peruano,* Vol. 3, no. 13, pp. 14–19. Lima.
Middendorf, Ernst
1893–1895 *Peru.* 3 vols. Leipzig.
Polo, Jose Toribio
1899 La Piedra de Chavín. *Boletín de la Sociedad Geográfica de Lima,* Vol. 9, Nos. 5, 6, pp. 192–231, Nos. 7, 8, 9, pp. 262–290.
Raimondi, Antonio
1873 *El Departamento de Ancash.*
Squier, Ephraim George
1877 *Peru Illustrated or Incidents of Travel and Exploration in the Land of the Incas.* New York: Hurst and Company Publishers.
Tschudi, Johan Jakob von
1918 *Travels in Peru during the Years 1838–1842, on the Coast, in the Sierra, Across the Cordilleras and the Andes, into the Primeval Forest.* New York: Wiley and Putnam.
Uhle, Max
1920 Los principios de la civilización en la sierra peruana. *Boletín de la Academia Nacional de Historia* 1(1): 44–56. Quito.
Wiener, Charles
1880 *Pérou et Bolivie.* Paris: Librairie Hauchette et Cie. Paris. Gumilla, 1745, Vol. 1, p. 20.

Excerpt from "Wira Kocha," *Inca* 1(1–3) (1923): 256–320. Lima. Translated by Freda Wolf de Romero.

CHAPTER TEN

# The Remains of Three Different Pre-Columbian Cultures Have Been Found on the Paracas Peninsula

**RECENT WORK CARRIED OUT** by the Museum of Peruvian Archaeology on the Paracas Peninsula revealed the existence of important archaeological finds corresponding to three distinct pre-Columbian cultures. The first is represented by the Cavernas of Cerro Colorado, whose antiquity goes back to an epoch before the cultures of the Mochica in the North and of the Nazca in the South. The second, represented by the Sarcophagi of Paracas, immediately follows the first and is the origin of the well-known Nazca culture. And the third, represented by the cemeteries of La Puntilla, of Waka Blanca, and of the Upper Section of Paracas, corresponds to the last period of local Chincha culture, influenced by that of the Incas.

## I. First Type of Tombs. Andean Archaic Epoch. First Period: Pre-Nazca–Cerro Colorado.

Twenty-five kilometers to the south of the port of Pisco, following the beach and behind the bend or inlet of La Independencia, one sees a line of small, reddish-looking hillocks. On the upper part of this hill, outcrops of red porphyry stand out against the undulating field of the lower slopes with its depressions covered with clay and sand sprinkled with granite debris produced by the fragmentation and metamorphosis of that eruptive rock. This landscape disappears and is replaced by extensive wastelands of sands and layers of fossil-bearing clay, where one descends and crosses the neck of the peninsula of Paracas which doubtless was in other times, perhaps not so remote, a channel separating the peninsula from the continent.

On the lower slopes and depressions of Cerro Colorado, some fifty cysts have been discovered, only five of which have been excavated. It is not yet possible to know their exact number, distribution, or the area occupied by them.

Judging from those which have been plundered, the cysts were constructed adjacent to each other. Almost all of them belong to the same type, although they do not all have the same dimensions.

Removing the surface layer of clay, a thin layer of caliche soon appears. When this is opened, there appears a cylindrical construction of stone or *chullpa* 1 to 1.5 m in diameter and close to 2 m in height, which serves as an entrance or vestibule to the "cavern." It is filled with sand and sometimes contains human remains and yet another layer of caliche which it is necessary to break in order to reach the mouth of the tomb, which communicates by way of a tunnel 3 m long leading to the funeral chamber proper. The hard ground into which the tomb has been dug shows two layers of clay, the upper one of 2 to 3 m of a compact consistency through which the tunnel passes, and the lower one of a lumpy or cloddy consistency. The latter has a height of approximately 1 to 1.20 m and a maximum diameter of 3 to 4 m. On the walls of the tunnel appear some hollowed-out cavities or steps to facilitate the descent to the tomb. On the walls of the cavern almost at ground level are several depressions or niches occupied by the dead.

Each tomb contains approximately thirty to sixty bodies, of men, women, and children. Some are located in niches, others in the ground, others on top of the ground, and even along the tunnel until they reach the upper mouth of the cylinder. This is always closed by a platform or roof made of whale ribs and sleeping mats.

Examination of the archaeological materials extracted from these tombs permits the confirmation of the following facts:

The people buried in the caverns of Cerro Colorado belonged to the same ethnic group, perhaps to the same community. To judge by their skeletons, they were of medium stature, of a not very robust physical constitution, and of relatively poor muscular development. A predominance of the feminine population and a relatively low infant mortality are noted. All have the cranium deformed by a procedure which impressed it in a characteristic form: the cuneiform.

They suffered from certain illnesses which, except for isolated cases of infections, did not leave obvious traces on the bones, but were the reason for the bloody surgical treatment displayed on their crania.

They possessed abundant food resources, not only of marine origin such as fish, shellfish, and perhaps some mammals, but also and especially those of agricultural origin, such as diverse grains and roots. Even more interesting, they succeeded in preserving meat by means of special processes of drying and curing.

As for the products of industrial and artistic activities, the objects found show that they had achieved a culture not inferior to the highest of pre-Columbian Peru. They made narrow-mouthed baskets of totora reed for different uses; some were used as funerary urns and others to protect delicate and fragile objects.

In their ceramics, they make frequent use of the figures shortly to be described of thick resinous dyes of vibrant colors, such as canary yellow, green, red, and black. The majority of representations are realistic copies of varied fruits, artistically modeled, which contrast with the more primitively made human figures. In the decoration also appear the mythological personages which are the fundamental ornamentation of the ceramics from the valleys of the archaeological region of Nazca. The most general form of vessels is globular with double spouts and handle, imitative of cigars or the lagenaria gourds which preceded and from which originated the globular forms of Nazca ceramics.

Even though this pottery is not as primitive as the Archaic from the Callejón de Huaylas, nor as artistic as the sculptural Mochica or the pictorial Nazca, because of its technique, form, and decoration, it can be considered as an intermediate stage between the pottery of Chavín from which it comes or with which it has an intimate phylogenetic relationship and the Andean Archaic style, which in the Rio Grande valley is called pre-Nazca.

A special style is found in almost all of the examples of textile art. Nets, gauzes, and meshes were worked in a stitch that looks like crochet. Open work mantles and mantles displaying the most beautiful and complicated mythological figures were woven in the style of silk lace, of vicuña or llama wool, of cotton, and of a kind of vegetable silk, and constitute the most magnificent examples. They are used as napkins or protective cloths for delicate ceramic pieces, as containers for sewing utensils, as dressings and bandages of the wounds caused by trephinations, and as articles of clothing and headgear.

The mummies seem to correspond to different social classes. There are some very poor ones who are found almost naked, or wrapped in a shroud or thick cotton sheet. Others possess one or two ordinary robes and a few simple adornments, such as shell or bead necklaces. Finally, others have showy clothing: they are covered by two or three open-work robes, and in addition they are wearing turbans and a thin golden diadem on their heads. Everyone, poor and rich, always has at least an ordinary clay plate with food and one or two gourd containers. No objects of silver or copper are found.

## II. Second Type of Tombs. Andean Archaic Epoch. Second Period: Pre-Nazca-Paracas.

At a kilometer and a half to the west of Cerro Colorado, crossing the neck of the peninsula, one reaches the lower northern slopes of the Paracas Peninsula. This appears covered with sand over which, in the lower part, dunes stand out, and in the upper, prominences of clayey rock. A kilometer and a half of dry former seabed lies between the present beach and the rocky incline of the peninsula, formerly lashed by waves. Over many centuries the sea has been filling in with mud and slime the channel which separated the island of Paracas from the continent.

Careful exploration carried out by the Museum, extending approximately a kilometer into this first section of the lower northern slopes of the peninsula, has revealed the existence of some archaeological deposits: funerary chambers and other subterranean buildings, some of which seem to be dwellings, while others seem to be of a social or ceremonial nature, related, perhaps, to the cult of the dead.

On simple inspection nothing leads us to suspect that a population lies buried in the sand here, except for one or another obsidian blade found on the surface, and small regularly arranged rows of stones, forming rectangles corresponding to the walls of the funerary chambers and dwellings.

The special system of underground constructions buried at a certain depth by masses of sand carried by the *paracas* winds, the hot, dry climate, the general sterility of the land, and the atmosphere which incessantly renews itself, impeding the development of microbic flora and fauna, have been the factors which allowed all the products of human activity, biological as well as physical, the human bodies as well as the products of the arts and industries, to remain intact until our time.

Here also, as in almost all cemeteries in Peru, the treasure hunters have left the trail of their destructive acts. In 1910, one of the best cemeteries from which some regally dressed mummies were extracted was discovered and plundered. They were brutally destroyed, and the articles of clothing which adorned them were sold to various collectors in Pisco. These vandalized trophies made up the various lots of antiquities that would later arrive at national and foreign museums. In spite of inquiries on several occasions by both national and foreign archaeologists as to the exact provenience of this kind of object, no one managed to discover what today the Museum of Peruvian Archaeology has happily succeeded in discovering.

The work carried out by this author since last year in this region has demonstrated the following archaeological facts:

1. Groups or rows of subterranean rooms situated along the ancient beach. They seem to be dwellings.

2. Immediately behind them, a row of patios or corridors.

3. Another row of great funerary chambers or mausoleums, behind the former and parallel to them.

4. Garbage middens situated principally at a short distance away from the habitations, or covering the tombs.

It is not difficult after practicing a few prospector's tricks to locate these different constructions. Sometimes the investigator is guided by the darker appearance of the soil characteristic of the midden. At other times, it is by the rows of small stones, the remains of subterranean walls which announce the existence of the habitations. Finally, on other occasions, it is by the easy penetration of the steel probe into an outcrop of organic earth or *waka* earth, which betrays the tomb.

All the constructions are underground. The walls are from 30 to 40 cm thick and generally rest upon a hard granitic formation which is found at a depth varying from 2 to 4 m. Small, sharp-cornered stones, seaweed, sticks, whale bones, and a calcareous-looking mud which produced mud pies as hard as cement make up the principal construction materials.

Even though it is not yet possible to map out the general plan of the underground constructions, it can be inferred from what has been discovered that there are groups of compartments which must have been destined for particular functions. Nothing else would seem to be indicated by the fact of finding, with a certain uniformity, rows of rooms each provided with an antechamber constructed on a floor above through which access to the interior room is maintained by means of a stairway, and of other chambers similarly provided with their respective antechambers and which contain a small oven or stove and a large jar, perhaps destined for the conservation of food and drink, and, lastly, the row of patios which leads to the funerary chambers. A room associated with its respective stove, patio, and funerary chamber might be said to constitute the structural unit of the vast complex of constructions.

Notable is the presence, in the patios as often as in the chambers, of small *chullpas* or ovens with remains of ashes.

At first glance, everything makes one think of a town made up of dwellings provided with kitchens and patios. When the great funerary chambers are opened and the presence of richly adorned bodies and of the ovens comes into evidence, then, and only then, the researcher discovers that all buildings are subordinate to the funerary chamber. It would not, therefore, be too venturesome to affirm that we are dealing with constructions dedicated to the cult of the ancestors.

The exact dimensions of the chambers we have mentioned cannot be determined with any precision. Some are relatively small and contain the remains of one, two, or three individuals. Medium-size chambers measure from 6 to 8 square meters. Others are much bigger, in which the bodies are superimposed as they are in *wakas* from the Inca period.

In this kind of cemetery, the treatment which the body received is quite original. By means of a forced bending of the extremities and the vertebral column, the head has been placed between the legs. The extremities are strongly contracted, the inferior extremities are crossed over the nape of the neck, and the superior extremities are crossed over the chest. This peculiar position, similar to a ball of wool, has been maintained by strong bindings. The spaces have been filled in with their own clothing, which results in the spherical or ovoid form of the mummy.

These bundles have been covered with garments, located in narrow-mouthed baskets, or covered with skins of condors and foxes. Gauzes and very fine cloths adorned with mythological figures of vibrant, harmonious colors partially or totally cover the head. Generally, they are also wearing a turban made by a long woven band of exquisite beauty which forms a tassel or rosette on the forehead or on one side of the head. The entire body is wrapped in two or three mantles, one of blue with embroidered red fringe, and the others of different colors showing mythological figures. All of this, in turn, is protected by a thick sheet of cotton.

The base of the bundle shows traces of carbonization which sometimes involves only the surface layers or rises inside until it reaches a third of the way into the bundle. What is most notable is that the fire does not affect the soft parts, the bones, or the hair, whose integrity contrasts with the carbonized mass which is stuffed inside. The blackish look of the body reminds one of the mummified, shrunken heads of the Jivaros.

Whatever the cause which has produced this phenomenon, whether it has to do with a true cremation or carbonization in a slow fire or by the action of certain chemical substances, the fact is, that for the first time, we find testimony of a deliberate system of artificial preservation of the human body by means of a process of mummification based on drying and smoking.

There are two additional important facts which reinforce the hypothesis of cremation. The first is the rigid appearance of the external mantle, which seems to closely adhere to the embroidered mantle; this clearly indicates that it was wet with sea water while the bundle was burning. The second is the presence of the *chullpas* or ovens containing ashes, which suggests that they were used in the cremation.

Beside the mummies, and apart from the multiple objects of personal use, such as combs, necklaces, stone axes, sewing and weaving utensils, ceremonial wands, etc., are found some pieces of pottery. Among these are globular-shaped pots with double spouts and handle similar to those of Nazca: some ordinary plates, badly fired; and others which are black with an interior face decorated with figures of fish.

## III. Third Type of Tombs. Inca Epoch.

In the cemeteries belonging to this type, the bodies are found at a shallow depth in the sand. No kind of construction is discovered. They are indiscriminately scattered, some beside or on top of others in a contracted position, sometimes seated, sometimes lying down. Their clothing is known from the last coastal period for men: the chemise or *unku*, slings, striped woolen bags, sticks and fish nets; for women: the well-known mantles or *yacollas*, tunics, *tupus*, earplugs, headpieces of copper and silver, various objects of wood, shell, and bone, and utensils and instruments for pottery making and the art of weaving for women.

The position of the face and of the head do not conform to a determined direction. They generally carry a small sheet of copper in the mouth; but nothing helps to classify this class of tombs chronologically more than the undeformed heads of the individuals, which correspond to a well-defined Andean oblong mesocephalic type. They are wrapped in one or two cloths of white, darkish green or orange cotton; or they are placed inside a large, crudely made jar.

Almost all the mummies still conserve their soft parts and are relatively fresh, with the characteristic mummy odor. Not uncommonly, necklaces of blue or green glass beads of post-Columbian origin are found among their clothing. All of this confirms the opinion that they belonged to peoples of the Inca and even to the Hispanic periods. The pottery is composed of pots, plates of different sizes, and globular jars with long, cylindrical necks, painted black, red, and white with ornamentation in bands, derived from those used in textile art and generally consisting of motifs of animals or other life forms.

This type of cemetery has been identified in various places in the Valley of Pisco. There, as in other areas, they make up the most superficial archaeological deposits which the grave robbers call poor cemeteries. Because of their contents, they are considered to represent the results of contact or fusion of the final Andean cultural irradiation with the final period of local cultures. This is the reason vessels of the Cuzco type mixed with those of local style appear in the same tombs.

Other cemeteries belonging to this type are: the very extensive cemetery of Juan Gil, which is found some four leagues to the southeast of Pisco, next to a midden and very close to the roadway to Ica; those found in the highest parts of the Paracas Peninsula, close to the neck; and some four or five which follow one another in a line from La Puntilla to the foot of Cerro Colorado between the middens which border the beach to the west and the hills called Waka Blanca to the east.

## General Considerations

The archaeological materials of Paracas contribute a considerable contingent of knowledge to the solution of some fundamental problems of Peruvian archaeology, such as those relative to the antiquity and chronological succession of cultures, to cranial deformation, to trephination of the cranium, to artificial mummification, to the cult of the ancestors, and to nutrition and agriculture.

### *Antiquity and Chronological Succession of Cultures*

On the peninsula of Paracas, the presence of two cultures which correspond to two well-defined eras have successfully been recorded: the very old pre-Nazca, and the relatively recent Inca. Both have specific characters. None of the objects found in the caverns and funerary chambers of pre-Nazca appear in the Inca, and, reciprocally, none of the objects found in this latter type appears among objects found in the earlier cultures.

In turn, two periods are recognized in pre-Nazca: one older, that of Cerro Colorado, whose culture has clear affiliations with the Andean [culture] of Chavín; and the other later, that of Paracas, whose culture is intimately related to, without being confused with, that of Nazca, to which it surely gave origin.

Not the least vestige of the culture of Nazca, characterized by polychrome pottery, has yet been found in Paracas. In pre-Nazca, there is a predominance of the textile art. The ceramics have characteristics which oblige one to consider them as a stage antecedent to that of Nazca. All this makes one think that the peninsula has been inhabited since the epoch of the apogee of the Andean culture of Chavín by people who developed the art of weaving to an extraordinary degree, and who disappeared from this place for some centuries during the Nazca period. It is inhabited once again during the last pre-Columbian period by poor fishermen and agriculturalists belonging to the tribe of the Chinchas and by immigrants from the highlands. And, as the culture of Chavín is one of the most ancient and shows up in a considerable degree of development in the pre-Nazca culture, it can be assumed that many centuries passed in order that this culture could achieve such a high degree of development on the coast as it had in the sierra, thereby pushing back the antiquity of man in Peru.

### *Cranial Deformation*

The bodies extracted from Cerro Colorado all have heads deformed in the cuneiform style. Those extracted from Paracas are in the cylindrical form called *sayto* or *aymara* by the chroniclers. Those from cemeteries corresponding to the period of the Incas show an absolute lack of deformation, and it is well known that the Nazca are of the flattened or avocado type.

These distinct types of cranial deformation corresponding to different cultures contribute to the definition of the specific character of each culture as well as to determine the different stages through which the curious custom of head deformation has passed.

### *Trephination of the Cranium*

Almost 40 percent of the bodies found in Cerro Colorado present palpable traces of bloody operations carried out on the head. Frequent are trephinations practiced by the methods of scraping and of circular incisions and extensive resections which, at times, involve almost half of the skullcap. The magnificent state of preservation of these examples and, above all, the quantity and variety of objects related to these operations which accompany the body brings with them a whole set of teachings which illuminate many obscure or dubious points as to motives, methods, or operative procedures, surgical instruments, and postoperative treatment. Making use of these materials in this way, one can reconstruct almost with certitude the entire operative process and raise other, new problems derived from the deeper study of this important subject which, for the last several years, has been a lively preoccupation of anthropologists.

Up until now, no typical cases of cranial fractures have been found. Depressive fractures, comminatory, and irradiating are the principal motives which determined trephinations in the Andes. Many times, the operation consisted solely in careful elimination by scraping the external plate and the diploe, maintaining intact the vitreous shield. There is no trace whatever of periostitis or osteitis, either pre- or post-operative, in the injured area. If these crania had not been found with their respective dressings, one could suppose that the operations had been performed postmortem. Nonetheless, the absence until now of complete proof as to the local motive of determining the operation obliges one to remember the ancient hypothesis of trephination for cerebral disorders or for thaumaturgical causes.

But nothing has come to satisfy scientific curiosity more than the set of operative instruments. In one of the caverns was found a packet containing knives of obsidian with their respective handles stained with blood, together with a spoon or curette made from the tooth of a sperm whale, rings of cotton to protect the wound, cloths, bandages, and thread. The obsidian knives are of different sizes. Some are instruments for puncturing, as though they were to be used for bloodletting; others are true scalpels, with which one can admirably cut and lop off soft body parts; and others, larger and thicker, seem destined to work on bone. Without a doubt, the curette served to scrape the periosteum; the threads are the same as those which appear near the edges of the wound. And, as has already been mentioned, there were rolls of cotton and bandages to protect the wound.

### *Artificial Mummification and the Cult of the Dead*

It was not known until now whether a special mummification treatment existed since, with the exception of the artificially mummified human heads which are so profusely made use of in Nazca rituals, the preservation of bodies was obtained by means of simple desiccation produced by the dry air or by the sand. In some cases, as in the mummies of the Inca-Tiawanako period, the bodies were carefully wrapped in cotton.

The mummies coming from the caverns of Cerro Colorado seem

to have been dried, perhaps with the use of fire. This would explain the absence of larvae or other remains of the cadaverous fauna usually found, and even the fragility of the soft tissues and of the skeleton. The procedure of desiccation, of smoking, or better expressed, of carbonization, as has already been said, was evident in the bodies taken from the sarcophagi of Paracas. The existence of bodies, all with deformed heads, the majority of which have been trephined, of constructions which appear to have been solely destined for the cult of the dead, of rich and elegant clothing with colorful mythological figures, and all the complex of objects of symbolic or ceremonial character, such as rackets, ceremonial staffs, and tubes of human tibias, make one think of a complicated religious system related to the cult of the ancestors.

### *Nutrition and Agriculture*

What is most surprising in Paracas is the contrast between the presence of highly developed cultures and the absolute absence of the basic elements of life in any geographical environment, such as water and cultivable lands. The former is to be found at more than a league from Paracas, the latter at a little more than five.

Foodstuffs must not have been scarce, to judge from the remains of food products found in the tombs: maize, lima beans, various other kinds of beans, peanuts, yucca, sweet potatoes, and, above all, meat which had been pressed and preserved fresh using a resinous, antiseptic substance. All argue in favor of the existence of abundant and healthful foods. Moreover, one can add the presence of narrow-mouthed baskets of weavings of cotton, wool, and vegetable silk, and of a multitude of objects made of gourds taken out of the ground, together with the principal objects of their arts and industries. But something more invites reflection upon the economic condition of these people. At a short distance from Cerro Colorado, behind La Puntilla, stretches a wide depression which produces the effect of an ancient valley covered with sand. Here and there, the presence of a scarce plant implies that at a certain depth runs underground water. In the valley of Nazca, as is well known, man took advantage of this water by means of cleverly built canals, succeeding in irrigating large portions of land. Why not suppose that near Paracas, they also took advantage of underground water for the irrigation of great extensions of lands, today covered and sterilized by the sand?

*La Prensa*, June 7–8, 1926. Lima. Translated by Freda Wolf de Romero.

# CHAPTER ELEVEN

# A Modeled Clay Scene in Ancient Peruvian Art

## Introduction

I had the opportunity while on a trip to the Department of Ica in the summer of 1921 to look over the major private archaeological collections in that important region. At that time, I saw the collections of Cánepa of Pisco, Pellanne and Elías of Ica, and Perata and Benavides of the Ingenio Valley. They had been formed after 1901, the year in which Max Uhle discovered Nazca-type graves in Ocucaje, and also in which the finds of fine ceramics awakened the interest and avarice of the natives to the search and commerce of antiquities; an interest and avarice which intensified later on when the wealthy Victor Larco Herrera purchased antiquities to form a museum. Thus, in just a few years, thousands of pottery objects from different cultures and epochs were removed from the ancient cemeteries of that department. Today, those objects are disseminated all over the world.

The Cánepa collection was composed of several types of ceramics and textiles, corresponding to the Inca and Chincha cultures and to that of Paracas, confused at that time with Nazca culture. The Pellanne collection was composed of Nazca pottery, Inca mummies, and objects of carved wood and Chincha pottery. The Elías, Perata, and Benavides collections were almost entirely made up of objects of Nazca ceramics coming from the Cabildo cemeteries in the Ingenio Valley.

In the Benavides collection, I found a new object in Peruvian art consisting of a clay model (fig. 11.1), that illustrates a ceremony or an

*11.1. A modeled clay scene. Representing a scene of social life from ancient Nazca, in which is participating a family composed of father, mother, older sister, son, and younger son, and domestic animals, dogs, and parrots. Found at the beginning of 1921 in an ancient cemetery of Cabildo, Ingenio Valley, Department of Ica.*

aspect of the life of the ancient inhabitants of Nazca. This clay model is the subject of this article. It was found together with some sheets of gold and several ceramic pieces in a cemetery next to the house of the Cabildo ranch. Except for damage of the extremities present in two of the human figures, this image was found in a good state of preservation. By the time the government acquired the Larco Herrera collection in 1924 for the Museum of Peruvian Archaeology, it had been broken and repaired. The paint which previously had been of very intense colors had disappeared in some places, and the ancient damage had been restored.

## The Model Scene

The model is not an artistic work. Studying it, nevertheless, awakens extraordinary interest due to the originality and realism of the representation and because of the mystery shrouding its meaning. Models of sculptured scenes, known up to now, are almost exclusively from Muchik art, and all of them appear as decoration on vessels in the form of relief or sculptured figures. The model under study has no relationship with any such utilitarian object; it is merely a representational object. The figures have been localized and distributed at the will of the artist over a flat field or platform.

The platform is a rectangular tablet of clay of compact consistency, like that of baked clay, measuring 143 mm by 108 mm and 8 mm thick. It is fine-grained, reddish yellow, and has a tympanic sound when struck. The surface of the upper face is smooth and uniform; that of the lower, irregular, wrinkled, with traces of colloidal fracturing.

On the platform appear five human figures in the act of walking in a procession: a man, a woman, two boys, and a girl, some behind others, accompanied by four little dogs. All of them seem to be marching, reflecting joy in expression and in attitude. The man is playing a set of panpipes and carries another two on his head and a little dog under his arm. The woman carries panpipes in her hands and parrots on her shoulders. The girl carries a vessel under her arm, a parrot on her shoulder, and an undetermined object on her back. The dogs are going at a quick pace with their ears erect, their tails up and curled forward, as though they were walking attuned to the music. It could portray a family, composed of a father, mother, and children, going to a festival to put on an important performance or, perhaps, very happily returning home afterward.

## The Figures Represented in the Model

The figures represented in the model are distributed as indicated by the diagram in figure 11.2; the outlines of the places where the figures are affixed to the platform have been filled in with cross-hatching. They are:

Two boys, A and A', located in front, side by side, in line with each other, and almost at the front edge of the platform.

One man, B, located behind those in front in a middle longitudinal line.

A woman, C, located behind the man.

A girl, D, directly behind the woman in front of her and almost at the rear edge of the platform.

Two small dogs, located on each side of the man and on each side of the woman, on the lateral edges of the platform: P1, P2, P3, and P4. In order to facilitate the description, I will deal in succession with: I. the human figures, II. the animal figures, III. the figures of other objects.

## I. The Human Figures

In the study of the human figures I have included the data which make it possible to determine general features of the human characters

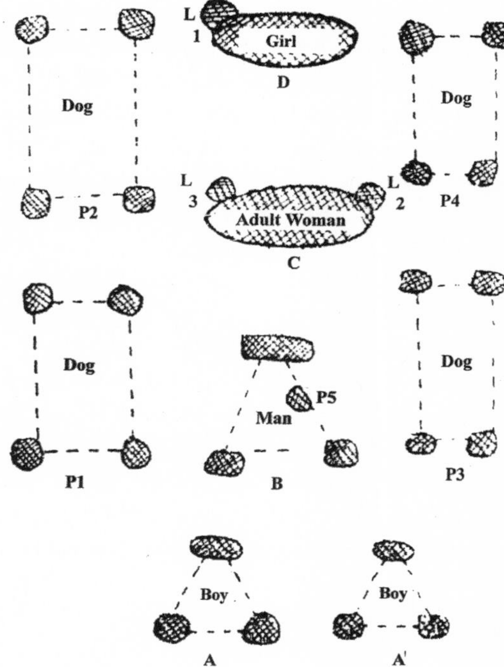


11.2. *Diagram indicating the position of the figures in the model.*

represented and those which permit us to examine the kind of clothing they are wearing.

## General Characteristics of the Human Figures

Figure 11.3 is a reproduction of the human figures A, viewed from the right side, and A', viewed from the front, in order to show the details of dress.

A corresponds to the figure which in the model is to the left, and A' to the right. Both personages are standing up; the lower extremities vertical and firm, the upper, loose and extended, hanging at their sides, the hands barely outlined; the torso is straight and firm; and the face is uplifted, looking straight ahead and painted yellow. The height of A is 55 mm, and of A' is 61 mm. The head is elongated by artificial deformation, like the elongated heads of the Nazca type; the nose is aquiline; the eyes elliptical and slanting; and the face small, full, oval and has an infantile aspect. They wear ornamental labrets, a and b, hanging from their lower lips. The clothing is masculine.

B (fig. 11.4) is likewise standing upright. The lower extremities are slightly separated, the right ahead of the left; the trunk and the head inclined somewhat forward. The upper extremities appear in action: he carries a small dog under his left arm, and with his hand he holds a panpipe close to his mouth. The head is elongated by artificial deformation. The cranium is flat at the forehead, and projecting considerably backward and upward, the face lean, in contrast to the bulging faces of the boys; the nose long and hooked, and the eyes elliptical and elongated. The height, including the headdress, is 80 mm. The dress is clearly masculine.

Figure 11.5 is a reproduction of the human figures C, viewed from the front, and D, viewed from the side. C is standing. The lower extremities are hidden beneath a long tunic. The body is thick and bulky, principally in the hips and chest. The head is inclined slightly forward. The arms are semiflexed, holding panpipes in each hand. The cranium is high, flattened from the front toward the back. The face is thin, painted in horizontal bands: the upper one yellow, the middle blue, and the lower one red, with parallel red lines on the cheeks like tears; the nose long and hooked, the eyes elliptical, elongated, and slanting; and the mouth with the lips withdrawn, as if there were teeth missing. The size is 59 mm. The dress is distinctly feminine.

D, likewise, is standing. The lower extremities are also hidden beneath a tunic. The body is straight and slender. The head small, the

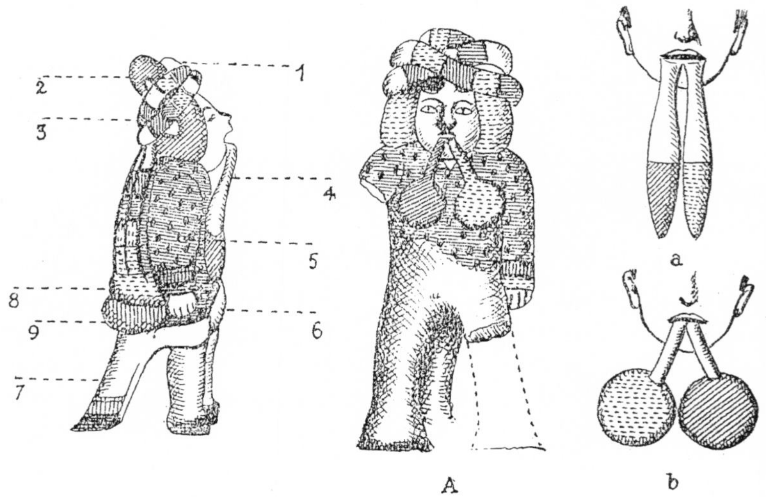


*11.3. Side view of Boy A: 1, frontal pad; 2, ring-shaped cephalic pad; 3,* llauto*; 4, lip ornaments; 5,* unku *(shirt); 6,* wara *(loincloth); 7, skirt; 8 and 9,* kipes *(bundles). Frontal view of Boy A: a, lip dowels of A; b, lip ornaments of A'.*

*11.4. Man B of the model.*

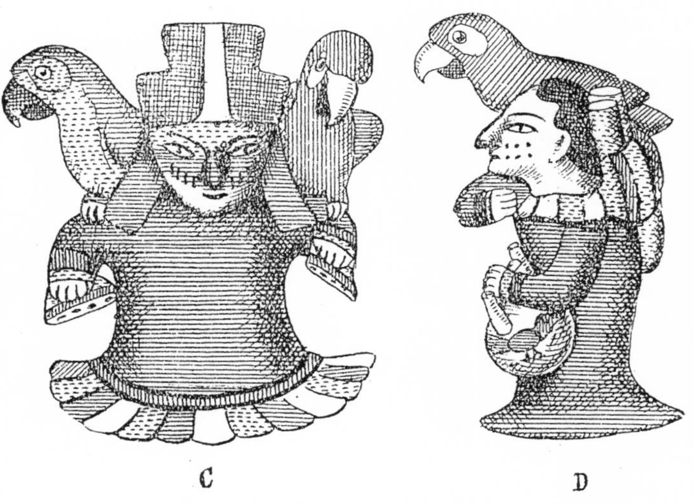


*11.5. The two women: C, adult, and D, girl.*

cranium deformed, the face full, painted yellow with black dots on the cheeks; the nose long and projecting forward; and the ears large. The expression is infantile. The arms are semiflexed; the right hand holds the ends of a sash or mantle which is worn on the back; and the left holds a vessel. The dress is obviously feminine.

The features indicated confirm the supposition that the figures A and A' are boys; B, an adult man; C, an adult woman; and D, a girl.

## The Clothing of the Human Figures

In order to facilitate the study of the dress of the personages represented in the model, I have imaginarily separated the different parts of the clothing of each figure. I have tried to reconstruct the entire distribution of the pieces recorded. Here is the respective inventory:

| **MEN** | | | |
|---|---|---|---|
| Headdress: | A | A' | B |
| *Llauto* | 1 | 1 | 1 |
| Frontal pad | 1 | 1 | 1 |
| Cephalic pad | 1 | 1 | 1 |
| *ñañaka* (headcloth) | | | 1 |
| Dress: | | | |
| Tunic or shirt (*unku*) | 1 | 1 | 1 |
| *Wara* (loincloth) | 1 | 1 | 1 |
| Skirt or short skirt | 1 | 1 | 1 |
| Adornments: | | | |
| Lip ornaments | 1 | 1 | — |
| Miscellaneous Objects: | | | |
| Carrying cloth or bundle | 2 | 2 | — |
| **WOMEN** | | | |
| Headdress: | C | D | |
| Head uncovered | | | |
| Hair | long | short | |
| Dress: | | | |
| Tunic (*unko*) | 1 | 1 | |
| Miscellaneous Objects: | | | |
| Carrying cloth or bundle | | 1 | |

### *Men*

#### HEADDRESS

The pieces which make up the headdress of the men, shown in figure 11.6, are the following: the *llauto*, a, b, and c; the ring-shaped or cephalic pad, e, f; the frontal pad, g, h; and the *ñañaka*, or headcloth, d.

The *llauto* a belongs to the boy A; *llauto* b belongs to A'; and *llauto* c, to the man B.

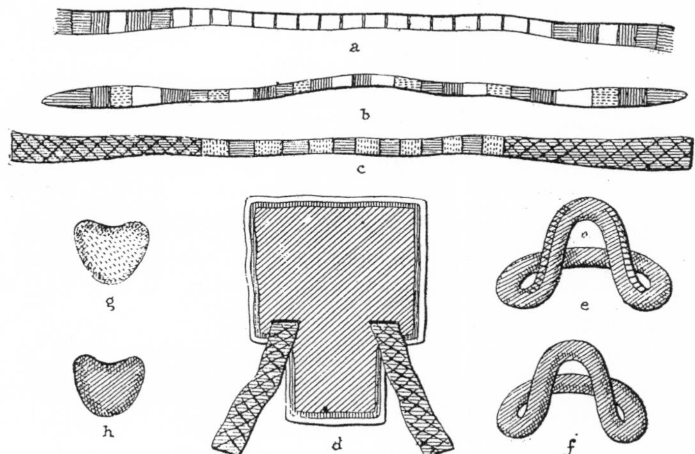


*11.6. Various articles of headgear. a,* llauto *of Boy A; b,* llauto *of Boy A'; and c, d, and e,* llauto, Ñañaka, *ring-shaped cephalic pad, and frontal pad of Boy A'.*

The *llautos* a and b are quite similar. They are made up of long narrow strips decorated with transverse bands of different colors. Example a widens at the tips and ends in abundant fringe, and b gradually narrows to pointed ends.

*Llauto* c is composed of a long, wide strip decorated with transverse bands of blue, red, yellow ochre, and white, and has terminal blue tassels crisscrossed by slanted black lines.

The frontal pad is round or half-moon shaped and lumpy, probably filled with cotton or totora reed and fit to the forehead; g and h reproduce those worn by the boys; g is yellow in color, and h is green. The frontal pad of the man is identical to these, but is painted with white and black stripes.

The ring-shaped cephalic pad, composed of a thick cord, of circular form, was probably flexible inasmuch as it fits the upper part of the back of the head. It is, perhaps, a cylindrical bag filled with cotton or totora reed. The ring-shaped pad f reproduces that which the boys wear; one is green, the other is yellow. The ring-shaped pad e reproduces that which is worn by the man. It is identical to the ones the boys wear in form, but it is of the color green decorated with transverse lines.

The *ñañaka*, or headcloth, d, is worn only on the head of the man. It consists of a rectangular cloth, the external face green and the internal face white, decorated with a red and white bicolor border on the external face and a border with vermiform or S-shaped figures in different colors on the internal face. The ends of the *llauto* apparently pass through openings made in the *ñañaka*.

*Tunics.* Males are dressed in tunics of the type reproduced in figure 11.7a and b. Tunic a corresponds to the type worn by the Boys A and A'; and b, that worn by the Man B. Both have the same form; they are rectangular, and provided with sleeves, which are short in a and long in b. Tunic b is red with wide yellow borders, with short fringe on the edges of the hem and the sleeves. Tunic a is blue sprinkled with circular red spots and has yellow borders on the sleeves.

*Wara, or loincloth.* Similarly, males wear *waras* of the type reproduced in figure 11.8b and d: *wara* b, corresponding to that worn by Man B, and *wara* d, corresponding to that worn by Boys A and A'. *Wara* b is large, white, and plain, probably made of cotton, and sprinkled with red dots. Those of the boys, d, are equally plain, white, and small.

*Skirt or short skirt (wairo).* Also, the males wear the skirts reproduced

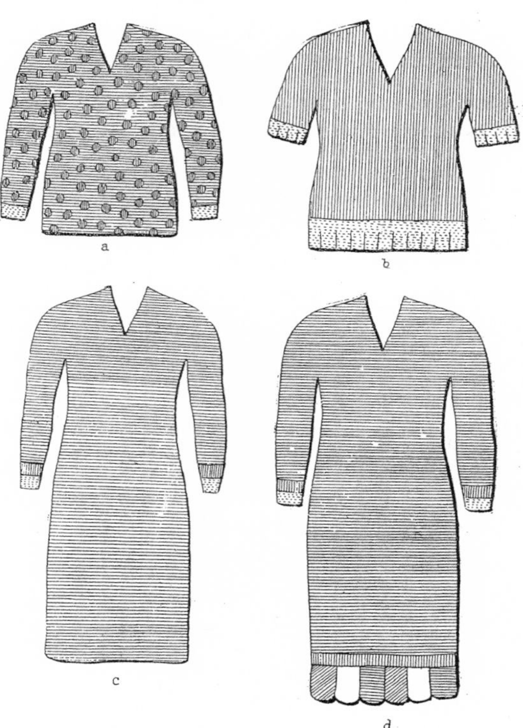


*11.7. a, b, types of tunics worn by men; c, d, types of tunics worn by women.*

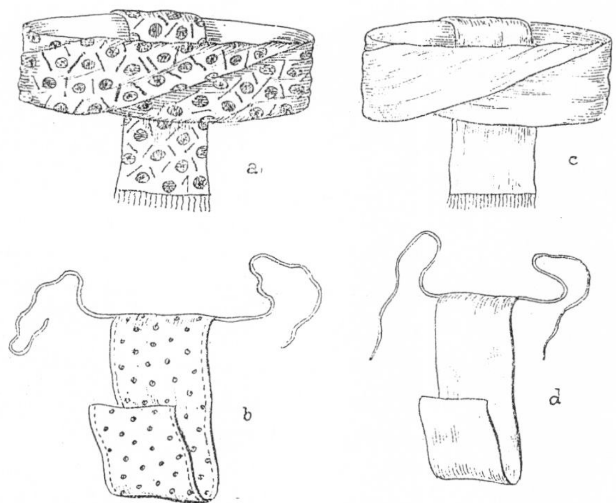


11.8. Skirts and waras (loincloths). a, c, type of skirt of the man and of the boys; b, d, types of breechcloths of the man and of the boys.

in figure 11.8a and c. The skirt a, corresponds to that which Man B is wearing, and skirt c to that which the Boys A and A' are wearing. All three are similar in form: two are small, plain, and white as in skirt c. One is large skirt a, which is also white; it is sprinkled with pupillary red, blue, and yellow spots interspersed with slanting black lines.

## ADORNMENTS

*Lip labrets.* The boys are the only ones who wear lip labrets, and they are of two types (fig. 11.3a and b). The first, a, consists of a pair of long spindle-shaped cords. Each cord is divided into two parts, marked by different colors. The longer upper portion is white; the lower of one, green, and of the other, yellow. Possibly the difference of color indicates a different material. What has been represented by the upper part is the cord which serves for inserting into the lip. The lip labrets themselves, which would be the somewhat conical colored tubes, make up the lower part. The second, b, consists of two circular discs, provided with slender insertion cords. The edge of each disc is marked with the perforation through which pass the insertion cords.

## MISCELLANEOUS OBJECTS

*Kipe or bundles.* These are three—figure 11.9: two red, a and c, and one yellow, b, which is smaller than the red ones. The body of the *kipe* is rounded or elliptic and narrow at the ends; a and b are worn at the waist by Boy A; and c, by Boy A'.

## *Women*

### HEADDRESS AND HAIRDO

The women, C and D (fig. 11.5), have their heads uncovered. The adult woman has long hair divided into two bunches which fall forward over her shoulders on each side of her face. Over the upper part of her head, her hair forms a kind of crest or bun, with a white band down the middle, which might only indicate the part in her hair or, more probably, a kerchief placed over her deformed head.

### DRESS

*Tunic.* The tunics of the Women C and D are reproduced in figure 11.7c and d. They are long, blue in color, and similar to the tunics worn still in the ancient way by Indian women in the sierra today. They differ only in that they have long sleeves, and polychromatic decorations on the edges of the sleeves and at the hem. The tunic of the adult woman, d, has as decoration at the hem, a sort of ruffle of small feathers with a red border and two bands on the sleeves, red and yellow. The only decorations on tunic c are the two bands on the sleeves.

### MISCELLANEOUS OBJECTS

*Kipe.* The *kipe* which Girl D carries on her back (fig. 11.5) is composed of the object being carried itself (fig. 11.10e) and of the carrying cloth

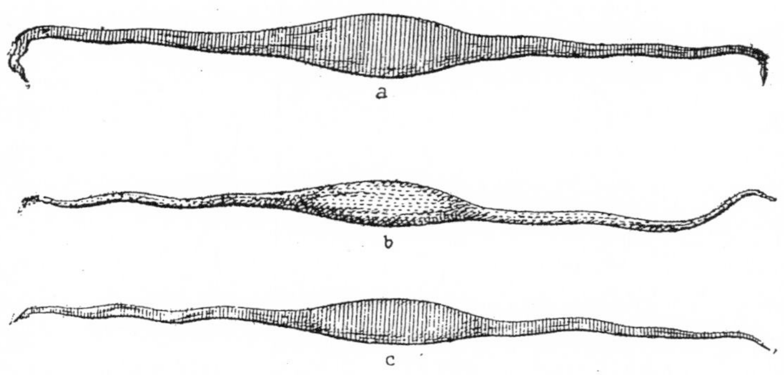


11.9. Kipes. *a, b,* kipes *worn at the waist of Boy A'; c,* kipe *worn by Boy A at the waist.*

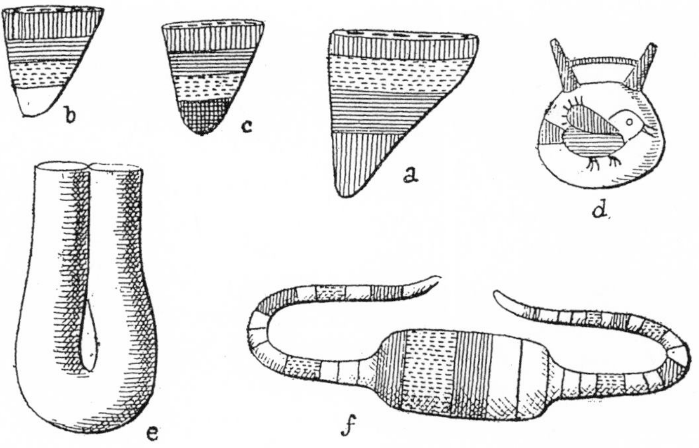


*11.10. a, b, c, panpipes; d, vessel of Nazca type; e and f, parts of the* kipe, *or bundle, that Girl D wears on her back.*

with which it is carried (fig. 11.10f). The cargo consists of a yellow cylinder, bent or folded, whose nature and use remain unknown; the carrying cloth is a striped, rolled-up piece of cloth.

## RECONSTRUCTION OF THE CLOTHING

*Headgear.* Nothing is to be learned from the headgear of the women except for the special form of the hairdo.

Since the heads of males are almost totally hidden by the headdress, it is impossible to determine their hairstyle. In figures of males represented in Nazca pottery, the hair always appears cut at the forehead in the manner of bangs and hanging at the sides of the face in two or three bunches of different lengths. This detail characteristic of representations of people of Nazca is not discernible in the figures A, A', and B, or figures 11.3 and 11.4.

The headdress is made up of three main parts: the frontal pad, the ring-shaped pad, and the *llauto*; and of one accessory, the headcloth, or *ñañaka*. In A and A', the headdress is composed solely of the principal pieces which are not very different from the headdresses of the anthropomorphic figures on Nazca pottery. On the pottery, the headdress consists of a turban, probably a long cloth given several turns around the head, and a big tassel made of threads of different colors sometimes fixed on the forehead and, other times, to one side. This cloth or turban is fixed on the head either with a headcloth, or *ñañaka*, with decorated borders, or with a ribbon, or *llauto*. The headdress, in its bulk and large size, has a certain similarity with the turban of Orientals.

In A and A', three parts of the headdress have been carefully modeled by means of using separate bits of clay, which helps to identify them.

The frontal pad is located over the fore part of the top of the head, in part supported by the head and in part by the ring-shaped pad. Figure 11.3A: the upper arch of the ring-shaped pad protects the sides and the top of the head, and the lower portion rests against the nape of the neck in such a way that it frames the face. Seen from the front, the figures seem to be wearing a helmet similar to Muchik helmets. It is likely that the material of the ring-shaped pad and of the frontal pad is cotton or totora, wrapped in rags like the material of the Muchik helmets or like the pads used for the deformation of heads found in Andean graves of Nazca. These two pieces of the headdress are secured by means of a *llauto* which is wound several times around the head and crossed over the frontal pad in order to support pressure in this zone, and the ends or tassels fall gracefully over the back. No original *llautos* have been found in the graves of Nazca. Those which appear in the model are, however, in every way like the *llautos* of Andean culture, contemporary with that of Nazca. They consist of bands or tapes worked using tapestry technique with geometric decoration. These are something like the *llautos* of the Cavernas [culture] of Paracas, but different from the *llautos* or turbans of the Necropolis. By means of this curious placing of the three parts of the headdress, the front of the cranium receives pressure helped by the resistance offered by the part of the ring-shaped pad which rests on the nape of the neck. This produces abnormal development of the cranium from front to back, since, under pressure of the apparatus, the cranium necessarily develops toward the upper front part of the head. It has not been possible for me to determine in a clear way if these three pieces are the deformation apparatus or if they are simply parts of the headdress. They are worn by the boys as well as by the man. At any rate, it is to be supposed that the headdress favors or adapts itself to the peculiar form of the head.

The man also wears the headcloth, or *ñañaka* (fig. 11.6d), which covers his headdress and falls down his back. This piece appears only in the headgear of women represented in the pottery of Nazca, and never in that of men. The *ñañaka* of Nazca consists of a very fine rectangular cloth or veil with welting formed by figures in high relief representing flowers, fruits, humans, and animals. The *ñañaka* of the man B (fig. 11.4) differs from those found in Nazca, but is similar to those found in Andean burials and in the Necropolis of Nazca.

## DRESS

The human figures depicted in the pottery of Nazca are important materials to study to gain a knowledge of pre-Columbian clothing. However, only three of the different pieces which make up the clothing can successfully be identified with any clarity from the figures on the pottery: the tunic, the loincloth, and the mantle.

The tunic of the man is shorter than that of the woman. The man's tunic scarcely comes to the waist. It is, without a doubt, longer than the archaic tunic of the anthropomorphic figures from the Callejón and of the Muchik, which are short, and the tunics of Paracas, which, although they are very wide, do not come to the waist. On the woman, the tunic is long and reaches to, probably, the ankles, although in the two women in the model, the tunic hides their feet. Apparently, the tunics are provided with sleeves, but sleeves are not clearly present in the clothing of anthropomorphic figures represented on Nazca pottery, or in the clothing found in Paracas. The sleeveless tunic in the style of the *kushmas* of the forest tribes or the Inca *unku*, on being placed on the body, form a fold at the level of the armpit along the internal face of the arm which looks like a sleeve. This is, perhaps, what induced the artist to represent sleeves in the five figures of the model. Nevertheless, I would argue in favor of the existence of the sleeves. The fact remains that the Man B is represented with his arms bare from the elbows while, in the others, the sleeve comes to the wrist. As for the rest, sleeves are not exotic in ancient Peruvian clothing. They appear in Andean Archaic culture and in Muchik.

The loincloth, or *wara*, is the same on the three males. It must be a simple undecorated piece, long and rectangular like those found in Paracas to judge from the manner in which it is presented.

Likewise, the skirt is probably of the same type as the skirts found in Paracas, inasmuch as the manner of wearing it is in every way similar to the way it is worn by anthropomorphic figures which decorate the cloths found in the Necropolis. All of the above permit us to infer that the skirt of the model is a long rectangular cloth decorated with geometric figures which was provided with tabs featuring large tassels. These wrap several times around the waist, the tassels of which hang at the sides or back.

The colors used in the decoration of the garments are sky blue, red, yellow, green, white, and black.

Lip labrets of the type used by the Boys A and A' have not yet been encountered among the archaeological objects of Peru. Max Uhle[1] reported two labrets or buttons of stone coming from Tiawanako; and Joyce[2] tells of lip plugs in the form of buttons such as those which come from Pernambuco, reproduced in the ceramics of the Peruvian coast. In the collections I have examined, I have not found examples of lip plugs such as those referred to by Uhle and Joyce. A single black anthropomorphic vessel from the Muchik culture represents a woman who is holding in her lap a child with an apparatus for deformation on its head. She has a lip plug in the form of a short pipe inserted in the lower lip.[3]

According to Nordenskiöld,[4] three types of lip plugs or lip dowels exist among South American tribes, not including among them the wooden peg or plug which serves to enlarge or maintain open the hole where the lip plug is placed: (1) the discoidal, which is a disc of wood, rounded and exaggeratedly big; (2) the button provided with a more or less long prolongation, like a nail; and (3) that of the form of a squashed cap.

Besides these three types, Sir Everard F. Im Thurn describes another type of lip plug used among the Indians of Guiana who have some similarity with that of Boy A' (fig. 11.3b). He says: "The men make a hole just below the middle part of their lower lip through which they pass a strand of thread which they secure inside the mouth and which they insert through an ornament in the form of a bell which hangs down on the chin."[5]

Herderschee[6] and Roth[7] report that Indians of both sexes among the Trio and Wayway have the lower lip pierced on ordinary occasions with a thorn or barb or a thin splinter of wood and, on festive occasions, with a small stick adorned with feathers or, perhaps, a disc also adorned with feathers. This fact obliges us to consider as a possible interpretation that the lip plugs or labrets of Boys A and A' are stalks and discs of wood covered with macaw feathers as are the lip plugs of the Indians of Guiana.

## II. The Animal Figures

The animals represented are clearly dogs and parrots.

### *Dogs*

These are five: one of them, P5, the smallest, is carried under the man's arm. The others, P1, P2, P3, and P4, which are almost identical in form, color, and size, accompany the procession. These are arranged in pairs on each side of the personages.

P1 is identical to P4, and P2 is identical to P3 (fig. 11.11). All of them, including P5, have common characteristics. They are probably small dogs, judging from their size compared to the size of the human figures, although ancient artisans do not always conveniently form figures in proportion to the scene. In this particular case, perhaps with the deliberate intention of representing persons of different ages and domestic animals of similarly different ages and sizes, such as the dogs and birds which form part of the planned scene, the artisan felt obligated to ensure the fidelity of his representation by maintaining the necessary proportions in modeling the figures so as not to detract from the meaning of the representation.

The size of the dog could not be established with precision, but, in height, he must at least reach the knee of the man. The head is small; the muzzle long and pointed; the ears small, triangular, and erect; the body thick and solid; the legs short and robust; and the tail bushy and curled forward over the hip. His hair, probably long to judge by the bushiness of the tail, is white with big black spots along the back, on the legs, and on the face: the stomach and the insides of the legs are white.

P1 and P4 (fig. 11.11) have certain characteristics which distinguish them from P2 and P3, the upper lip, or better, the nose is flesh

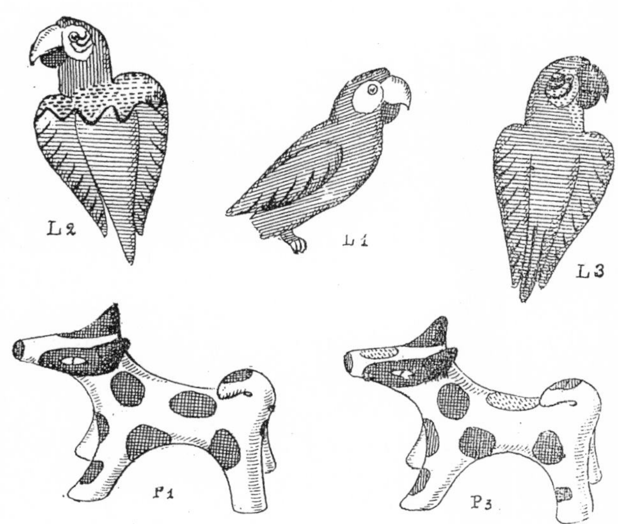


*11.11. Parrots and dogs. L1,* Psittacus; *L2,* Ara macao; *and L3,* Ararauna. *P1 and P3,* Canis ingae.

*11.12. Pictograph that adorns a Muchik vessel in which a dog similar to that represented in the model appears.*

colored, and they have a circular black spot near the anus; while in P2 and P3 the nose is black, and they lack the anal spot. And, reciprocally, P2 and P3 have other differentiating characteristics consisting of two large oval spots the color of yellow ochre: one in the center of the face and the other at the center of the back. The little dog, P5, has no distinguishing characteristics.

The figures of the dogs which most closely approximate those represented in the model are those which appear on Muchik pottery, commonly in pictographs and in relief, and in Andean pottery. Both are contemporary with those of Nazca.

Figure 11.12 reproduces the pictograph from the globular-shaped vessel with the arched tubular neck (Muchik Sp.1/477). It is the scene of a sacrifice of prisoners and homage to a chief; a dog almost identical to the one in the model plays an important role. The animal jumps very enthusiastically among the persons who carry offerings to the chief. In its idealized form and with human dress, it acts together with other dogs in the same pictograph in the scene to receive blood which flows from the amputated leg of a prisoner who is found naked, his genitals well-drawn, with a thick noose around his neck and manacled.

In figures 11.13 and 11.14, reproduced, in two positions is a zoomorphic vessel with a double spout and flat arched handle of Andean type, which represents a dog in the pose of gnawing a bone, very similar to the dog represented in the model.

As for the rest, the white dog with the black *muro-muro* spots is found

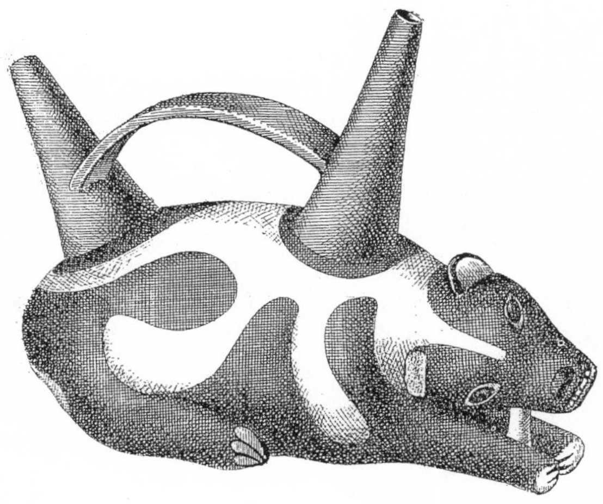

*11.13. Right lateral view of a vessel of Andean culture. It represents a dog in the pose of gnawing a bone. Sp. 4668 of the Museum of Peruvian Archaeology.*

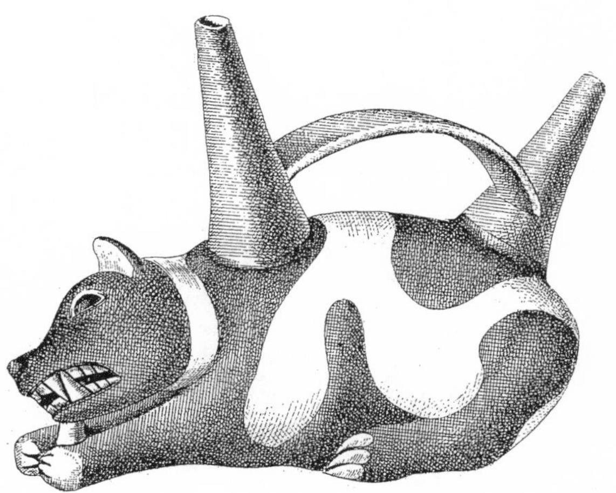

*11.14. Left lateral view of the vessel reproduced in figure 11.13.*

profusely represented pictorially and sculpturally in Peruvian ceramics in general, as often in its realistic form as in its idealized form. Figure 11.15 reproduces one of these dogs represented in Muchik pottery.

Skeletons or mummies of dogs have not been found which could correspond to the many varieties of dogs which appear in the pictographs and models in relief of Nazca, Muchik, and Andean pottery. This fact makes identification of the dogs in the model difficult.

Tschudi[8] was concerned about a variety of indigenous dog whose skeleton he found in ancient burials of the sierra from which he supposed was derived the sort of shepherd dog which exists today in the punas which is called *Canis ingae*. Nehring,[9] who studied the skeletons and mummies of dogs found in the Necropolis of Ancón by Reiss and Stübel, discovered another breed of dog which he called *Canis ingae pecuarius*. Allen[10] has compiled studies relative to the Inca dog. On the basis of the information he brought together, I infer that the dog in the model, if not a new variety of *Canis ingae*, is similar to that described by Tschudi. With the exception of the hair, which, according to him, is "rough, long and thick, yellow ochre in color, with wavy dark shadows," the other characteristics seem to correspond to it. To wit: "A small head; long, pointed muzzle; the upper lip is not split; small, erect, triangular ears; short, strong body, angularly built ("*untersetzt*"); legs somewhat short; the tail some two-thirds the length of the body, completely shaggy and curled toward the front; stomach and insides of the extremities somewhat lighter than the background color of the back."

### *Parrots*

There are three (fig. 11.11): one small L1, which appears on the girl's right shoulder; and two large ones, L2 and L3, which appear on the shoulders of the woman. The three are different.

*11.15. Vessel of the Muchik culture which represents a dog similar to the one which appears in the model 3/6782.*

L1 has green plumage over the entire body with darker markings on the flight feathers and yellow markings on the back of the wings. The thick beak is curved, the upper part light-colored, and the lower is dark, almost black. Possibly, it is the silly or deaf parrot, *Psittacus mercenarius* of Tschudi,[11] or *Chrysotis mercenaria*,[12] which the Indians call *q'alla*.

L2 is standing on the left shoulder of the Woman C. The plumage is red on the lower face of the body, the crown of the head, and the neck; it is orange-yellow on the upper part of the wings, and bordered by a black line. Flight feathers and tail feathers are blue bordered by black stripes, a white or nude face with curved black lines, drawn around the eye; and a thick, curved beak, the upper mandible, is white with the lower edge of the lower half black and the lower mandible black. These characteristics correspond to the macaw, *Ara macao*.[13]

L3 is standing on the right shoulder of the woman. The plumage is of a dark blue color, especially the upper part of the body, with some blackish markings on the tips of the flight feathers and the tail feathers. The lower part of the body is orange-yellow, which also extends to the auricular region and sides of the neck. The beak is thick and black, the upper part curved and sharp, and the lower short, wide, and somewhat flattened, which contrasts with the light color or white of the face, and the eyes are adorned with small curved concentric black lines. These characteristics lead me to identify this bird as the macaw of blue and yellow plumage, *Ararauna*.[14]

It should be noted that the colors used in the decoration of the clothing belong to the chromatic range of the multicolored plumage of the macaws represented in the model. There is a predominance of blue, red, and green. It is not improbable to suppose that the tunics, at least those of the males, are of feathers which imitate the plumage of the macaws, taking into account the peculiar decoration of the blue tunics of A and A' with red spots, just as those which appear in the macaws and the considerable development reached by the *ars plumaria* [art of feather work] in Nazca culture.

### *Other Objects*

The vessel the girl carries under her arm and the panpipes carried by the man and the woman (fig. 11.10a, b, and c) alone serve to identify the Nazca style of the model, since the panpipes are faithful reproductions of the clay panpipes found in Nazca graves. The vessel is equally typical in its form and decoration of the pottery of Nazca. The vessel is spherical, has two spouts, united at the middle by a flat arched strap-handle; the body is white ornamented with a bird-shaped figure; and the spouts and handle are a violet-hued red.

The panpipes are five in number, three carried by the Man B, and two by the Woman C. Of the man's three, one is big and two are small. The largest, a, has the form of a right triangle; the borders are thick and rounded; it is composed of six tubes, and its external face is decorated by three transverse bands, the middle one blue, and, of the bands at the extremes, the lower one is red and the upper yellow. The small ones are triangular, with rounded outlines, and composed of four tubes each, ornamented on the free face with four bands; the colors, from the base to the apex, red, blue, yellow, and black.

In summary, the characteristics previously discussed for each of the human and animal figures represented allow the following interpretation and identification:

| | |
|---|---|
| A, A' | Boys or adolescent males |
| B | Man of adult or mature age |
| C | Woman of adult or mature age |
| D | Girl or adolescent female |
| P1, P2, P3, P4, P5 | *Canis ingae mercenarius* |
| L1 | *Psittacus* |
| L2 | *Ara macao* |
| L3 | *Ararauna* |

In summary, the model depicts a family of ancient Nazca, composed of father, mother, elder daughter, elder son, and younger son, accompanied by domestic animals made up of five dogs (four big ones and one small), one parrot, and two different species of macaw.

## General Considerations on Modeled Clay Scenes in the Ancient Art of Peru

Models of groups or scenes such as the model under study are not rare in ancient Peruvian art.

An abundance of pottery types such as that possessed by the National Museum of Peruvian Archaeology, organized in series according to form, decoration, and composition, illustrates the principles which govern the development of these three factors of artistic elaboration.

Effectively, the form and the decoration are fundamentally derived from the form and decoration of the natural objects which serve as models. The archetypical forms and principal decorative motifs in sculptural ceramic where the material is more abundant and illustrative, as in Archaic from the North, Muchik, and Andean, are replicas made by molds, or imitations imperfectly modeled, of natural receptacles. A great variety of forms and decorations in Muchik pottery have their origin in the varied forms of the fruit of the *lagenaria* and *cucurbitaceae*, the gourds and squashes. Many geometric motifs are derived from the spots, stripes, depressions, or reliefs of these fruits. Other forms and decorations are partial or complete reproductions of natural or fantastic beings, such as the three-dimensional figures of animals which appear on the neck, handles, or body of Chimú vessels, or the representational drawings of crustaceans, fishes, birds, reptiles, or mammals which decorate bichrome Muchik and polychrome Nazca vessels. In all these cases, the object copied is a motif which is repeated in order to satisfy a merely decorative end. Moreover, on the light-colored field offered by the surface of the vessels, the artist paints or models in high or low relief portrayals of social life such as agricultural scenes, or those of hunting, fishing, battles between different tribes; homages to chiefs; various dances to the sound of flutes, panpipes, and drums; textile workshops; the slaughter of sea lions; the collecting of snails; the struggles of mythological beings; etc. These are illustrated in different degrees of elaboration, from the simplest scenes in which figure only two representational units, to the most complex in which intervene thirty and more such units, like the complicated scenes of human sacrifice, those of the treatment given those vanquished in war, and the dances in chorus of warriors and mythological beings.

When one studies carefully a collection of these scenes, one discovers a certain relationship among them, not only of similarity but of continuity. The pictographs contain portrayals of humans, animals, and mythological beings which are recognizable or identifiable throughout all of the representations. That is, certain figures have, according to the role they fill, a definite personality whose history can be followed through different scenes as one could follow the personages of a novel through the fragmented pages of a book, in this case, a book of aboriginal history the pages of which have been ripped out, disordered, and broken.

Figuration is distinct from decoration. Decorative figures in relief are superimposed on the body, neck, or the handles of a vessel without in the least affecting its form. In figuration, a gradual transformation of the parts of the vessel is brought about through the mere transformation of accessory morphological elements, such as the neck and handles, up to the total transformation of the entire receptacle. In figurative pottery, the form of the object depicted replaces the archetypical form of the vessel.

In the figuration process, there is a double tendency: one which maintains the form of the vessel, the utilitarian; and another, which tends to annul the form of the vessel for the sake of the likeness, of the figurative. Thus, the transformation undergone by the vessel is explained: first, of the neck of the vessel which the artist associates with a human or animal head and, afterward, the entire body of the vessel, through the successive modeling of the upper and lower extremities of the human or animal. That is to say, the artist considers the vessel as a living being, one of the natural or supernatural beings of his surroundings, since that is the only way to explain the abundant and varied figurative and semifigurative pottery of his artistic production.

Moreover, the artist takes advantage of the rounded, cubic, or parallelepiped forms of the vessel to model over it: first, individual images which appear in the manner of statues on the vessel which serve as their pedestal, such as the images of humans, mammals, and birds which pose or rest upon the vessel. Second are sculptured individual images which come to be part of the painted or modeled scene in relief which covers the surface of the vessel such as the example from Muchik pottery in which a three-dimensional figure of a bird appears on the upper pole of the spherical vessel and, on the body, a tree in which is perched a multitude of small birds and two nests full of little eggs, with the nests modeled in relief and the birds painted. There are many other examples in which the protagonist of the scene appears as a three-dimensional figure on the vessel and the scene itself on the surface. Third, finally, representational scenes in which all the personages appear modeled into the body of the vessel itself, in such a way that the original form of the vessel disappears and is replaced by the figures which make up the scene, leaving only its utilitarian character, the neck and the hollow interior. The most notable scenes of this type are the models of buildings, temples, dwellings, and boats. Thus, a Muchik vessel schematically reproduces a building similar to that of the fortress of Paramon'qa. It is modeled in the pyramidal form or truncated cone of the building—the terraces, the big patios, the *qoll'qas* (or granaries), the houses of a small town, the principal doorway of the building, and the contiguous room for the guard. In another model of Chimú pottery appears another similar building. On an elevated prominence there are several houses and patios and, at the entrance, a guard. Inside the houses, one sees women weaving with their looms held by posts and one of them in the act of emptying a vessel. There are, moreover, many other well-modeled simple scenes such as that of a man preparing a meal of fish in a pot; that of someone out of breath carrying an enormous stone worked in the Inca style on his back; that of one who is persistently working at pulling the halter of a llama who resists walking; that of one who is collecting shrimp using an *isan'qa*, or conical narrow-mouthed basket; and the numerous scenes of mythological beings who lead prisoners; that of condors who devour a human body; and that of complex representations of human sacrifices.

There is one kind of figuration which is not due to the drives or motives that determine the transformation from vessel into a three-dimensional figure. This happens with the human or animal figures, hollow or solid, usually small, which are frequently found in pre-Columbian graves corresponding to different cultures and to different epochs. Figurines representing men, women, or children are found in archaeological deposits in the oldest cultures as well as in the most modern. I have found them in Archaic graves in Paracas; in those of the Muchik, Nazca, and Andean of the second epoch; and in those of Chincha, Chancay, Chimú, and in Inca of the third. In the cemetery of Manache, Huarmey, explored by the University Archaeological Expedition of 1919, I found bodies in a horizontal position accompanied by black Chimú ceramics and at the head of the individual a clay figurine. In the Necropolis of Ancón in 1875, Reiss and Stübel found some of these figures almost always in the graves of children. In the excavations that I carried out in the Waka Malena in the valley of Asia in Cañete in 1925, I found two figurines, one of silver, the other of copper, from the period of the Incas, inside a pot containing objects of witchcraft or thaumaturgy. I also found, in 1927, many figurines of clay, some wrapped in rags, in graves of the Chincha culture of Ica, Pisco, and Nazca. In Paracas, I found similarly small bundles in the form of dolls, containing clothes in miniature, identical in their form and style to the clothes found in the Necropolises. In Nazca, one finds, with a certain frequency, human figures of clay meticulously modeled, solid, well polished and, in which, at times, the curvilinear or bulky outline of a figure was exaggerated, especially in the figures of women, those which had a marked obesity approaching a true steatopygia, similar to the human figures of Aurignacian paleolithic art of the Reno age. These figurines are even more abundant in the cemeteries of the Chancay culture where they are found of all sizes, some so small they fit in the hand and others up to a meter high. Human figurines of clay, silver, gold, but primarily of turquoise, are also found in Inca graves on the coast and in the sierra, such as those of turquoise in the collection of Emilio Montes, today in the Field Museum of Chicago, which came from Cuzco; those found by Roman Aparicio and Santiago Astete, in the ruins of Piki Lla'qta, near Cuzco; and those found by Victor Elías in the graves of Chulpaka, of the Chincha period. In general, these figures are considered to be idols, *konopas* (fetishes). Reiss and Stübel consider them to be children's toys.

The making of human figures is not limited to the mere representation of isolated objects, but several scenes can be represented on the same piece. Such is the case with the sculptured figures which decorate the handles of the Chimú *tumis* (knives) or the handles of Muchik spear throwers. Some of these scenes are very interesting and might be justly compared with the scenes on Muchik pottery.

Furthermore, an appreciation of the character of scenes must take into account other considerations derived from the study of the collections. The majority of archaeological objects in graves, principally the graves of the first and second epochs, show no sign of use. Similarly, the fine clothes which accompany the body are found to be currently new and, in certain cases, unfinished. The figurative Muchik vessels and the pictorial Nazca and Andean are delicate and fragile and of forms not adapted to domestic use. Domestic utilitarian ware is rarely encountered in graves and appears only in fragments inside the middens. Everything argues in favor of the ceremonial character of these objects. Moreover, they are not unique. They are found duplicated and multiplicated in the archaeological collections of Peru from different sites and from a single cultural region, and the same object is found duplicated in the same grave or others, identical or similar to it, in different graves.

In the existing archaeological collections in national and foreign museums, what is remarkable is the presence of similar and even identical objects, in form as well as in decoration, and in respect to simple figuration as well as the representation of scenes. Thus, there are known series or classes of ware in the form of fruits and grains, crustaceans, fish, birds, reptiles, mammals, humans, and mythological beings; these last divided into subseries or subclasses with respect to the particular manner in which they are depicted to the purpose or function they are fulfilling and, finally, to the common characteristics which individualize or define each representation within the complex and, at times, a chaotic set of representations. And just as there are series of similar individual figures, there are also models like the series of specimens which illustrate different and successive acts of human sacrifices. The figures depicted in pictorial or sculptured scenes also appear sculpturally or pictorially in other specimens of the individual style. The same figures, clearly distinguished by their physical type, dress, or personal adornments, act also in other scenes. Thus, in the majority of hunting scenes, the same personages are included, and something similar happens in the scenes of gathering snails, of fishing, of combats, or of homages to a chief.

Some scenes are identical in several representations as if they were made from a mold, and others are different parts of the same scene, parts which add to or clarify the complex representation. Thus, there are vessels which picture naked men with a noose around the neck and with hands and feet tied; there are others which represent birds of prey, anthropomorphized bats and other animals, and bearers of various objects: musical instruments, knives, offensive and defensive arms, etc.; other vessels, finally, in which two or more of these personages take part in the same scene, such as happens with partial or individual representations and with simple scenes related to certain ceremonies. These representations considered in isolation apparently lack meaning, and it is necessary to form a similar series with them in order to interpret them. Thus, a receptacle which depicts a leg, an arm, or a human cranium taken by itself on its own might be considered an artistic object. Nevertheless, it has a more profound meaning. There are vessels that represent with marked realism human arms and feet which have been severed by a direct cut through the bone or by disarticulation, to judge by the stump of the amputation. These facts obligate us to assign to each specimen a double value: an individual one, as an artistic piece, and the other, collective, by the relation each has within a group or series of similar specimens.

These considerations lead me to attempt a general explanation of the model scene in the light of what we have learned from scenes depicted in Peruvian ceramics. The first impression that the scenes preserved in the graves of ancient Egyptians share a resemblance to scenes found in the graves of ancient Peruvians could be because the motives which determine the making of them could be the same. From the first glance on, there is a marked analogy between the burial arts of ancient Egypt and the burial arts of ancient Peru. Here, as in Egypt, since primitive times it was a very widespread custom to bury the body together with offerings of food, clothes, and all those objects which, in keeping with their beliefs in immortality, would be needed by the deceased in the other life. It is well known that in Egypt during what is called the Dark Age which included the VII to the IX dynasties, from 2500 to 2000 B.C., the custom developed of placing together with the bodies not only the offerings necessary for the future life but also the servants of the deceased so that they should continue serving him beyond the grave. This peculiar custom, which was considerably widespread, culminated in the custom of placing in the tombs, particularly of great personages, complete groups or scenes of domestic life, those which, one might say, synthesized the multiple activities which the buried personage had to dedicate himself in the future life.

In the spring of 1920, American Egyptologists from the Metropolitan Museum in New York found a splendid collection of models in a tomb adjacent to Thebes. Few Egyptian finds before the tomb of Tutankhamen attracted as much attention as these models because a complete representation relative to the daily life on the estate of a noble of ancient Egypt was found. The tomb was of Mehenkwetre, chancellor and assistant of the royal palace during the reign of Pharaoh Mentuhotep, 2,000 years before Christ. The Egyptian models had a specific goal, the significance of which can be deduced from the representation itself and from the connection which these representations hold in the life of the deceased. The Egyptian models, strictly speaking, are nothing but the reproduction of activities of the royal life that the deceased had, exalted or improved in the model in order to be reproduced in the life beyond the grave.

For all the great similarity between the custom of interring bodies with offerings, with figurines similar to the Egyptian *ushabtis* and vessels with diverse scenes, however, in the light of what we have learned from the study of scenes in ancient Peruvian art, one cannot attribute their manufacture to the same causes which motivated the manufacture of Egyptian scenes. I have declared that Peruvian scenes have, as do the individual representations, basically a ceremonial character. They must have been manufactured periodically, and, for that reason, duplicates are encountered in different graves. All of this induces us to suppose that the different scenes and figures were periodically manufactured, used in ritual ceremonies, and distributed afterward as sacred objects and, as such, carried to the graves without having any relationship with the life of the personage buried.

## Conclusions

The preceding study permits me to formulate, for now, the following conclusions:

1. The model, the motive for this work, registered in the Museum of Peruvian Archaeology with the number 3/6782, reproduces an aspect of social life, perhaps religious, of the ancient Nazcas, in which figures a

family, some of whose members are perhaps principal actors in a ceremony of some kind, to judge by the animals and objects of symbolic or ceremonial character which they carry, such as the lip ornaments, the vessel, the panpipes, the macaws, and the dogs.

2. Whatever the motive or motives which determine the manufacture of models such as the one presented here, the scene cannot be considered as a whole or complete representation of a determined event or of a personal and individual character, but rather as a part or an aspect of a more complex representation and of a collective or social character.

3. Although it is true that the model cannot be considered in the same way as the models of scenes which decorate utilitarian objects, the model itself is alone in its category, as are the Egyptian models, and has no utilitarian character whatsoever. Nonetheless, one does not discover in the representation, as one does in the Egyptian models, the definite purpose of the artist in modeling it.

4. The model is an original specimen, new in ancient Peruvian art until now, unique in its class; but, given the scarcity of archaeological work which has been carried out until now in Nazca, it is assumed that other similar examples will be found in the future.

1. Max Uhle, *Kultur und Industrie Sudamerikanischer Völker*, Vol. 1, Plate 19, Figs. 23, 24 (Berlin 1889–1890).

2. Thomas Joyce, *South American Archaeology*, chap. 6, p. 129, Fig. 33b (London, 1912).

3. Rebeca Carrión Cachot, La Mujer y el Niño en el Antiguo Perú, *Inca*, Vol. 1, p. 347, Fig. 11 (1923).

4. Erland Nordenskiöld, *The Changes in the Material Culture of Two Indian Tribes under the Influence of New Surroundings*, p. 76 (Göteborg, 1920).

5. Everard F. Im Thurn, *Among the Indians of Guíana*, p. 193 (London, 1883).

6. A. Franssen Herderschee, *Verslagvan de Tapanahoni Expeditie Tijd*, pp. 941–942 (Kon. Ned. Aard. Gen, 1912).

7. Walter E. Roth, Additional Studies of the Arts, Crafts, and Customs of the Guiana Indians with Special Reference to Those of Southern British Guiana, *Bureau of American Ethnology, Bulletin* 91 (1929).

8. J. J. von Tschudi, *Untersuchungen über die Fauna Peruana* (St. Gallen, 1844–1846).

9. Alfred Nehring, *Ueber Rassebildung bei den Inca—hunden aus den gräbern von Ancon*, pp. 94–111 (Kosmos [Zietschr. ges. entw.—lehr], 1884); Alfred Nehring, Mammals, in Wilhelm Reiss and Alphons Stübel, *Peruvian Antiquities: The Necrópolis of Ancon in Perú*, Vol. 3, pt. 15 (London and Berlin, 1884); Alfred Nehring, *Ueber rassenbildung bei den Inca-hunden von dem todtenfelde bei Ancon in Peru*, pp. 5–13 (Sitzb. Ges. naturf, Freunde Berlin,

1885); Alfred Nehring, *Ueber altperuanische hundemumien und ueber rassebildung bei den sogenannten Inca-hunden Verh*, pp. 518–521 (Berlin, ges. anthrop., ethn. u. urgesch, 1885); Alfred Nehring, *Ueber eine neue sendung mumificirter Inca-hunde von Ancon in Perú Sitzb*, pp. 100–102 (Ges. naturf, freunde Berlin, 1886).

10. Glover M. Allen, Dogs of American Aborigines, *Bulletin of the Museum of Comparative Zoology at Harvard College*, pp. 472–476 (Cambridge, Mass., 1920).

11. Tschudi, *Untersuchungen über die Fauna Peruana*, p. 270, table, 24.

12. Ladislas Taczanowski, *Ornithologie*, Vol. 3, p. 221 (1886).

13. Taczanowski, *Ornithologie*, Vol. 3, p. 192.

14. Taczanowski, *Ornithologie*, Vol. 3, p. 193.

*Wira Kocha: Revista Peruana de Estudios Antropológicos* 1(1) (January 1931). Lima. Translated by Freda Wolf de Romero.

CHAPTER TWELVE

# The Ruins of Wari

**INTERESTED IN SEEING** the place of provenience of a certain type of fine ceramics that I knew only from drawings shown to me by the director of the Indigenous Section of the Ministry of Instruction, I decided to take advantage of the University's Independence Day holiday to take the journey which I had planned since the beginning of 1930 in order to complete the second volume of my work, *Antiguo Perú*. I had been unable to make this trip previously due to the political situation which, for almost a year, had paralyzed my research in that area.

Up to now, Peruvian archaeology is almost wholly Peruvian coastal archaeology because the material with which one has to work is almost entirely from that region. For this reason, practically all the theories which attempt to explain the origin and chronological succession of pre-Columbian cultures are based solely on studies of the materials found in archaeological deposits on the coast. It is currently believed that there is no archaeological evidence to be found in the highlands which withstood the rains and rigors of the climate except works of stone. Americanists of great renown such as Uhle, Lehmann, and Spinden have engaged in the search for the origin of our ancient cultures in Central America, because the most ancient and advanced Peruvian cultures, according to them, had no antecedents in Peru. Not one of these theories has taken into consideration highland cultures separated from the coast by the great barrier of the Western Cordillera because it was easier for them to imagine the communication of ancient peoples by way of the sea than thinking of the cultures which might have developed within the Andes.

From the beginning of my archaeological investigations in Peru, I have called attention to the necessity of studying the sierra and even the tropical forest as a priority for the solution of the problems related to the origin and history of Peruvian civilization. On the trip I made at the beginning of 1916 as a member of the Harvard Peruvian Expedition to the region lying between Paita and the Marañon, I substantiated that the Chimú culture of the North Coast had propagated as far as the tropical forest, and therefore its center of diffusion could just as well be found on the coast as in the highlands of the sierra or in the tropical forest.

In 1919, the exploration I carried out in the Department of Ancash allowed me to recognize that in that region there existed evidence of a very ancient culture of a lithic character, similar to that of San Augustín in Colombia, which I named Andean Archaic. Moreover, there was evidence of another culture already recorded on the coast and believed to come from Tiahuanaco, which turned out to be nothing but Northern Andean culture whose originating center of propagation was found in the inter-Andean valleys of the Marañon and the Callejón de Huaylas.

In 1925, I recorded with great surprise that most ancient tombs of Paracas contained objects closely linked to the Archaic culture of Chavín, which allowed us to suppose that in Chavín was to be found the center of diffusion of a vast culture which reached well into the South Coast—a diffusion which was also confirmed by the discovery of Chavín ceramics in Lambayeque.

At the end of 1926, I explored the district of Tupe, in the province of Yauyos, where they still speak Akaro, the mother tongue from which Keshwa and Aymara are derived. We encountered the remains of ceramics whose forms generally seem to have preceded Chincha ceramics.

A discovery in 1927, which took place on the Pacheco farm of Nazca and consisted of an enormous quantity of fragments of fine ceramics which had been deliberately broken and which by their technique, form, and ornamentation constitute the highest exponent of the art of pottery in Peru, confirmed the hypothesis that a certain type of pottery found on the coast had been transported from some of the inter-Andean and trans-Andean valleys of the interior of Peru.

The excavations which took place in that same year in Las Trancas further revealed that the ceramics formerly known as the local Nazca culture's own pottery contained different styles corresponding to a special class of graves which, based on their contents, I classified as Andean.

Archaic Megalithic culture, recognized by me in the Callejón de Huaylas and in Chavín, is none other than the same culture which appears as one of the oldest in America at San Augustín, Colombia. It is represented by a great abundance of evidence in the ruins of Wari and in the middens and cemeteries of Tanta Orko, situated in the drainage of the Huarpa, an affluent of the Marañon. The ruins of Wari are superior in certain aspects to the ruins of Tiahuanaco and generally similar to those of Chavín in their extent, in the enormous amount of architectural material contained, in the use of carved stone, in having underground structures, in the statues, and in having tunnels, caves, and galleries produced by the exploitation of clay and colored earths destined for ceramics and of stones for construction.

On Tanta Orko, which is a mesa or tableland adjoining the Horcasitas Hacienda, are found the remains of the ancient constructions of the Archaic period and middens of the same period. A transverse cut of one of these garbage mounds allowed me to study its important contents. They were composed of fragments of carved stones, some sculpted as if they were fragments of columns; of cornices; of statues or figures of pumas and serpents, and other decorative elements of temples or altars; of mortars, grinding stones, mace heads, rings, and many other broken objects; and of fragments of rough, primitive pottery such as utilitarian vessels, spoons, cups, pots, and three-footed cooking pots. They are all forms similar to that of the Archaic pottery of the Callejón de Huaylas.

In Wari and in the ruins I visited in the drainage basin of the Huarpa and of the Mantaro, I also found constructions corresponding to the Second Epoch, and garbage dumps containing fragments of Andean pottery, identical in material, technique, form, and ornamentation to the Andean ceramics of Pacheco, Las Trancas, and to the ceramics considered Tiawanako and Epigonal from other places on the Peruvian coast. One can rest well assured that the center or centers of manufacture of the fine Andean ceramics of the coast had been found, and one could be sure, moreover, that three-fourths of the so-called fine Nazca pottery which was believed to be from the coast is pottery made in the archaeological region of the Mantaro.

It is not yet possible to determine the exact dates when the Archaic and Andean cultures flourished. The chronological calculations are only approximate, and they are principally based on the study of the stratification of the middens. Nevertheless, one can rest assured that the Archaic Era undoubtedly goes back at least to several centuries before the Christian Era, and, given the enormous quantity and extension of the remains corresponding to the various cultures, I believe that we must extend the periods established for these cultures and, therefore, push back the date for the period of the appearance of man in Peru a very long way.

Besides the finds of archaeological jewels, as some of the fragments of ceramics indeed deserve to be called, a profusion of beads of turquoise, lapis lazuli, and a green stone similar in every respect to jadeite are widely disseminated in the garbage middens and over the whole extension of the ruins. They adorn the bodies from the graves along the littoral of the coast. In Wari and in nearby ruins, they are especially common, to the point that in almost every hut, one finds small collections of them, and in the possession of certain individuals, sculptured turquoise figures representing animals and humans, such as those in the hands of Dr. Demetrio García del Barco and in the Museum of Huanta. It is very possible that, in this region, there is a deposit of turquoise, because there is no other way to explain the abundance of fragments of this stone, a great many of which have been worked by man.

Published in *El Perú*, August 27, 1931. Lima.

# CHAPTER THIRTEEN

# Andean Civilization

## *Some Problems of Peruvian Archaeology*

**THE CORDILLERA OF THE ANDES** determines the predominant physical character of the geographical environment of Peru. It rises parallel to the littoral of the Pacific and divides, in the south, into two branches which unite in the junction of Vilcanota; in the center, into three branches which unite in the junction of Pasco; and, in the north, also in three (the western one of which, in its main section, divides in two) which unite in the junction of Loja. The first subdivision marks the boundaries of the highland or basin of Titicaca, and the second, those of the inter-Andean basins or valleys of the Urubamba, Apurimac, and Mantaro rivers, while the third bounds the inter-Andean basins or valleys of the Huallaga, the Marañon, and the Santa.

Small lateral ranges extend like buttresses from each side of the Andes, reaching on the east the vast plain of the Amazon forest and on the west the lowlands of the coast. The extension of the Cordillera determines the geographic aspect of the coast, plains, and deserts bounded by mountains. There are three mountainous regions: that of La Brea in the Department of Piura in the north, of the Department of Ancash and Lima in the center, and that of the province of Camaná in the south. There are also three plains: one which extends from the Valley of Tumbes to that of Chimú; another from the Valley of Wuarko to that of Acarí; and a third from the Valley of Ocoña to beyond Tacna.

For each of the many varieties of Andean topography, there is a corresponding climate. In general, the Andes divide the territory into three great regions; the trans-Andean, or that of the forest plains, with its tropical climate; the Andean, cold and temperate; and that of the littoral, mildly hot or subtropical. In the forest, rains are abundant and almost continuous; in the sierra, they are annual and less abundant; and, along the coast, scarce and sporadic.

The waters flowing down the western slope of the Cordillera reach the ocean by way of narrow ravines in the mountainous regions and more or less extensive valleys in the plains. Those of the eastern slopes, in similar manner, find their way to the tributaries of the Amazon.

The sierra region, due to the differences in altitude, also presents a diversity of climates which vary from the tropical of the deep inter-Andean valleys and ravines to the arctic of the Cordillera. The aborigines distinguished between these zones, giving a special name to each, calling the cold Cordilleras and high tablelands *suni* or *puna*, the temperate zones of the ravines and valleys *keshwa*, while hot zones, whether of the forest plains, the deep Andean ravines, or the low valleys of the coast, were called *yunka*.

When the Spaniards conquered Peru, they found the aborigines occupying the territory in its entirety: the *puna*, the sierra, the coast, and the forest region. With the exception of the forest tribes, they were densely populated nations, organized and controlled by a central government which had its seat at Cuzco.

The wealth or economic resources of this people—calculated at ten million inhabitants—lay, aside from the extraordinarily developed agriculture, in fishing on the coast and stock-raising in the sierra. Stock-raising and agriculture constituted the foundation of their civilization; the stock-raising was based on the llama and alpaca, obtained by domesticating the wild native animals of the highlands, and the agriculture was based on numerous grains and food roots, obtained by domesticating the wild native plants of the sierra and the forest regions.

The llama and the alpaca were utilized both by the inhabitants of the highlands and those of the plains and ravines, and similarly the territorial propagation of the edible fruits, grains, and roots had no other limitations than those imposed by the climate. Quinoa and various tubers, such as the potato, *oca*, *olluco*, and *mashwa*, were cultivated in the *keshwa* lands, artificially prepared and irrigated, as well as in the unimproved lands of the ravines contiguous to the *punas*, or on the hills of the coast, watered only by rain. The sweet potato, yuca, *yacón*, *achira*, peanut, squash, *arracacha*, pepper, lima bean, corn, cotton, *lagenas* [calabash], and coca were cultivated in all the *yunka* lands, trans-Andean, inter-Andean, cis-Andean, and coastal. Thus, the

Peruvians raised domesticated animals and cultivated domesticated plants throughout the land. These were such transcendent attainments that, whether acquired in their own territory or imported, they constituted the fundamental factors which determined the outstanding characteristics and the high grade of civilization reached by this people.

It is logical to think that agriculture and stock-raising assured the welfare and stimulated the growth of the population in proportion to the greater or lesser extension of the lands possessed and the facilities which the geographic environment offered for their benefit. Man found in the extensive pasturelands of the Andes the appropriate means for the development of stock-raising, and apart from his livestock, he had, in these high regions, the benefit of indigenous agricultural products of the temperate regions, and, even in certain places, of the products of tropical lands easily accessible by means of the natural trails of the ravines, by which the Indians descend even today, conducting their animals for commercial purposes. Also, in the trans-Andean valleys of almost tropical climate, man found the territory appropriate for the cultivation of edible plants, belonging to this environment and even to these places; and the Indians, in order to secure these products in exchange, descended from the highlands, carrying the meat, wool, and agricultural products of their region. On the coast the natural trails, marked by the transverse ravines which descend toward the Pacific, favored not only the commerce of the inhabitants of the highlands with those of the plains but also the formation within a single valley of intimately related communities, a more intimate cognation perhaps than that which could exist with the other inhabitants living near the coast, with whom but slight communication was had by way of the fishermen and from whom in most cases they were separated by coastal mountains and sandy desert plains.

The geographical environment of Peru leads one to think that the primitive population, on occupying the territory of Peru, whether it came by sea, by the high routes of the Cordillera, or ascended from the forest plains, spread itself over the entire territory and managed to utilize all its advantages, traversing it continuously in every direction. In their migrations, they undoubtedly utilized at first the natural trails, the ravines, and defiles, whether to ascend to the *punas* [high grasslands], to descend from these to the plains, or to cross the lofty Cordilleras. Later, impelled by necessity or genius, they utilized the trails which they constructed through the high tablelands and mountains, or through the sandy plains and mesas of the coastal region.

The investigator, in the presence of this historic-geographic panorama and the wealth of historical and archaeological testimony, feels impelled to learn whether the authors of the early civilization originally arrived in Peru, bringing with them an advanced culture; whether they arrived in a savage state, with scarcely the rudiments of an incipient culture; or whether, having reached this land, with a certain degree of culture, they were influenced by other more advanced cultures. In other words, the problem would consist in finding out, first, whether the Peruvian civilizations are the product of the modifications or degeneration of high immigrant cultures—in other words, whether they are exotic; or, on the other hand, whether they are the product of the development and differentiation of primitive cultures which arrived in Peru in an incipient state—that is to say, whether they are autochthonous.

Primarily, our efforts must be directed toward the recognition of those high cultures from which the existing cultures in Peru were derived. Second, they must be employed in knowing and defining the cultures in relation to their geographic environment, to discover their genesis and point out the evolutionary process of their development.

In the beginning of the archaeological investigations—based on the reports of the primitive writers and chroniclers of the Indians, and on the monumental megalithic sources found in the Andean region—it was supposed that, previous to the Inca Empire, there had existed another empire of equal or greater power, its greatest exponent being the ruins of Tiahuanaco. Later, thanks principally to the work of Max Uhle, it was established that the empire or civilization of Tiahuanaco, if indeed it had expanded throughout the sierra and the littoral before the Inca, was not the most ancient of Peru, because, preceding it, other cultures had flourished on the Peruvian coast, and even in the sierra. These, proceeding from other more advanced culture centers of the continent, were, in their turn, preceded by rudimentary cultures of fisherfolk whose remains were found in Arica, Ancón, and Supe. It is thus that the following cultures succeeded one another in chronological order:

1. That of the primitive fishermen of the coast.
2. Those called protoids: proto-Chimú, proto-Lima, proto-Nazca, and Chavín.
3. That of Tiahuanaco, and those derived from it, or Epigonals.
4. The local cultures of the coast: Chimú, Chancay, Ica or Chincha, and Atacameña.
5. The Inca.

All of which might be reduced to cultures of the littoral and Andean cultures, the latter derived from the former, and they in turn proceeding from other cultural centers of the continent.

It is venturesome to think that a primitive population of coast fishermen should have abandoned their habitual task of fishing for the cultivation of plants, native of the forest, or the sierra, especially when, together with the archaeological remains of these primitive people, are found agricultural products which lead one to suppose that if they were not tillers of the soil, at least these already existed in nearby places which can be no other than the contiguous valleys which communicated with those of the sierra. It is more reasonable to think that the savage of the forest, to whom is attributed the knowledge of certain primitive forms of agriculture, should have learned in the trans-Andean valleys the cultivation of certain plants such as the manioc, the sweet potato, corn, *lagena*, squash, lima bean, etc., and that he should have propagated these in the inter-Andean *yunka* lands: inter-Andean, cis-Andean, and the coastal valleys. And perhaps it is more logical to think that the Andean, still in a low stage of culture, or possessing knowledge of a rudimentary agriculture, may, in the course of the search for game and food for his flock, have multiplied throughout the Andean region, domesticating the indigenous animals and plants, and, after acquiring an appreciable degree of culture in that healthful and stimulating geographic environment, descended to and utilized the lowlands which, in general, are hot and unhealthful. In the forested lowlands flourished various endemic parasitic diseases, as *goiter* or *coto*, and leishmaniosis as well as such parasitic diseases of the digestive system as anquilostomasis, dysentery, and others. And in the lower Andean valleys and ravines of the coast are found such diseases as verrugas, the leishmaniosis, and malaria which can be conquered only when man acquires immunity, after a long adaptation to the environment; all of which presupposes the existence of a dense population in other parts. The mortal agents which besiege man are more numerous in the lowlands than in the highlands. To take advantage of the lowlands, perhaps it was necessary to acquire experience in the highlands. Furthermore, the hypothesis relative to the genesis of civilization in the highlands, and its later propagation in the lowlands, is strengthened if one takes into account that the *punas*, which are most excellent centers for stock-raising, form an almost unbroken stretch throughout the entire length of the Cordillera from Titicaca to Loja. The sierra constituted in ancient Peru one of the most important sources of economic wealth. The Indians lived in organized villages, on the summits of the hills contiguous to the *punas*, from which, as also from the *keshwa* ravines, they obtained their subsistence. It is for this reason that the shrines and *pakarinas* were always found on the summits of the hills, or at the foot of the Cordilleras, and all tradition unanimously agrees on these Cordilleras as the *locus geni* of the Indians.

The cultivated lowlands belonged to the families, or *ayllus*, but the highlands were communal. The Indian following his flocks could traverse the entire Andean region. The shepherd was, therefore, perhaps one of the first propagators of culture. Remains of corrals or enclosures of very ancient aspect are found everywhere and reveal a great development of stock-raising in those times. And in the contiguous lowlands the remains of terraced fields still exist in which, as at present in many places, were cultivated quinoa, *tarwi*, potatoes, and other products which required only the rainwater and the fertilizer from the stock.

The solution of these problems depends largely upon the study of the archaeological testimony. This is of three kinds: first, remains which still exist in all this territory and have not yet been properly studied; second, that which has been excavated by inexpert persons and is found scattered in museums and private collections; and third, that which has been excavated and studied scientifically. The first constitutes the most important source for future investigation; the second cannot be studied except in the light of knowledge contributed by the third.

During the past few years, thanks to the aid lent by the Peruvian government, a museum has been established in Lima, El Museo de Arqueología Peruana, which contains nearly all of the known private collections in the country, amounting to some tens of thousands of pieces. Archaeological explorations and excavations have also been undertaken with a view to studying, classifying, and exhibiting these collections, and satisfactory results have been obtained.

In this work of systematizing archaeological data, the investigations have been directed with a view to defining the characteristics of the known cultures, determining their area of propagation, and establishing their relation one to another—first, within the Peruvian area, in order to compare them later with the neighboring or distant cultures, and to establish the existing differences or links.

The study of the archaeological literature of Peru and the experience acquired in the museum, and in explorations, have afforded me the opportunity of verifying the existence of three great stages or epochs in the pre-Columbian history of Peru, as follows:

1. The Archaic Andean epoch or megalithic.

2. The epoch of the development and differentiation of the cultures of the coast.

3. The epoch of the great tribal confederation which culminated with the Inca Confederation of Tawantinsuyu.

These three great stages embrace a great variety of cultures and styles corresponding to the development and differentiation of only one civilization, nurtured in the Andes, the Andean civilization.

The first, to judge by the extensive distribution of the cultures which it includes and by the high degree of development reached, especially in the megalithic and textile arts, seems to have flourished for a greater number of centuries than the later epochs. In it two periods are evident: one represented by the Archaic culture of the Callejón de Huaylas and the other represented by Chavín and by Chongoyape and Paracas, which are Andean cultures propagated to the coast.

The second epoch corresponds to the second stage of the Andean culture which here acquires special characteristics which are uniform in their various manifestations. It descends to the plains through the cis-Andean ravines and coexists with and influences the Muchik and Nazca cultures derived from the Archaic. There is comprised then in this epoch the Andean culture, properly so-called, with Tiahuanaco as its highest exponent, and the great local cultures, Muchik in the north and Nazca in the south.

The third epoch—probably shorter and more recent than the former, to judge by the greater scarcity and freshness of its archaeological remains—corresponds to the stage of the development and organization of the tribal confederations which culminated in the Great Confederation of the Inca, or Tawantin Suyu. To this epoch belong the Chimú, Kuis Manko, Chek'e Manko, Chincha, Konchukos, Wankas, Rukanas, Chankas, Keshwas, Kollas, and Kollawas confederations, all of which were brought under the central government of Cuzco shortly before the Spanish Conquest.

I will point out, for the present, only the general characteristics of the cultures comprised in the first, because I consider them of importance for a better understanding of the intricate archaeological problems of Peru, and because I desire to call the attention of Americanists to certain facts which in my opinion have not been sufficiently considered.

On exploring, in 1919, the northern Andean region, I had an opportunity to verify the existence of two kinds of archaeological remains, corresponding to two distinct cultures. I noted that these cultures were related, but separated from each other by a considerable period of time. To the more ancient, I gave the name of Andean Archaic and to the one which followed it, that of Andean, properly so-called. The latter is the well-known culture of the little stone towers, *chaukallas* or *chullpas*, the architectural style of which was pointed out by Tschudi in 1844, insofar as the villages of the center of Peru are concerned. During my explorations, I found the remains of polychrome ceramics of the Tiahuanaco type in these structures, the area of propagation of which is very extensive, mixed at times with ceramics of the Inca type. In the same archaeological area I found ruins of villages, cemeteries, temples, stone sculptures, and ceramics of a special type which possessed a well-defined archaeological unity both in style and epoch. Because of its magnitude, its lack of contact with known recent cultures, and other diverse indications of its being deep-rooted in the territory, I was obliged to attribute a greater antiquity to this culture.

The Andean Archaic culture is defined:

1. By a special style and type of architecture in its structures, villages, tombs, and shrines or temples.

2. By a special predominant style in its stone sculptures and pottery, both as regards their ornamentation and their form.

## Villages

The villages of this epoch are similar to one another. They occupy lofty and strategic places and are defended by fortified walls and precipices. Villages of this type are numerous in the north Andean area, where they are found strung along the crests of the lateral or buttress ranges. Some of them, as, for example, Kiske in Nepeña and Calaveras in Casma, occupy almost the extreme end of the western spurs, and others, such as the five fortified villages of Pumpa, reach almost to the end of one of the eastern spurs. Many of them arouse admiration, not only because of their perpendicular and impregnable sites but also because of the enormous effort which their construction must have demanded.

It would be difficult to explain the existence of these villages erected in rough and inhospitable places near the Cordilleras—which must have sheltered a dense population to judge by the vast area they occupied—were it not for the contiguous terraced fields, which rise step

*13.1. Yayno, Pomabamba. Right:* Wairona, *or communal house; Left:* Pirwa, *or granary. Photo courtesy George Lau.*

by step from the bottoms of the ravines to the tops of the mountains, revealing an extraordinary mastery of nature by man.

The methodical study of these monuments will permit us in the future to learn something more about their antiquity, the life, customs, social organizations, and arts of the originators of the Archaic culture.

To give an approximate idea of the plan of these villages, of the predominating type of buildings, and of the systems of fortifications, I summarize the principal aspects of one of them, which is interesting for its simplicity and its good state of preservation.

In May 1919, I visited the ruins of Yayno. To reach them, starting from Pomabamba, one descends for a short stretch in the direction of the Yanamayo [River] as far as the Wilka Ragra estate, then turns to the west and ascends a very steep incline, broken here and there by level spaces or short terraces, until arriving at the summit where the ruins are found (fig. 13.1). Yayno lies three and a half leagues to the southwest of Pomabamba and 5,000 m above sea level. The hill gives the impression of a gigantic pyramid, formed by lofty terraces which rise step by step, and crowned by a towerlike building. The general view is enhanced by the large buildings of the lower part; the walls seemed covered with mosaic because of the contrast between the clear, brilliant, smooth faces of the large stones, arranged in horizontal rows, and the small opaque stones which pile up around and between them. On the north side, the hill rises in a sheer precipice in the upper part, while in the lower it forms a gradual incline. On the other sides the pronounced incline of the upper part diminishes gently and gradually until at the height of 500 m it reaches an ample mesa or tableland.

*13.2. Yayno. Gate opening on one of the terraces.*

*13.3. Yayno. Stairs and gate near top of hill.*

The terraces are high. In the lower part, principally toward the southwest side, they form extensive platforms on which are found some of the most important buildings. Farther up, they succeed one another on four levels which completely surround the hill. The terraces are fortified by walls perforated near their foundations with small openings, to allow the passage of the rainwater. The terraces rise irregularly because the salient portions or crests of the rocks have been utilized for defense. The lower portion of the village is also defended by a moat or trench, which is 3 or 4 m wide by 3 or 4 m deep, and surrounds the hill, excepting in the places fortified by projecting rocks.

The walls have doorways, the frames of which are formed by great stones (fig. 13.2) and are arranged in an almost vertical line on the south side. A long stone stairway which passes through these doorways serves as a means of ascent to the summit (fig. 13.3).

On the terraces are found the remains of small walls which may have been those of dwellings, the roofs of which were probably made of straw, for there are no stones here which could have served for this purpose.

The most important buildings of this village are:

1. The *Wairona*, or communal house, which occupies the lowest platform toward the southeast and is almost square, 80 m on a side. Its walls rise to a height of 8 m and within are found remains of small buildings.

2. The *Pirwa*, or granary. This is found a little to the west of the preceding and on a more elevated terrace. It is cylindrical, measuring 10 m in diameter, the walls rising to a height of 12 m. Contiguous to this building and toward the west lie the remains of other smaller cylindrical structures, which seem to have served as storehouses for food. There is no evidence of entrances to these buildings.

3. A building after the manner of Inti Watana, which crowns the hill. It is formed by three concentric circular walls, the intervening space divided into various compartments. The central wall bounds the space where the remains of other similar compartments are found (fig. 13.4).

In these ruins have been found stone objects such as hatchets and clubs, and also fragments of the ordinary ceramics of the Archaic type.

*13.4. Inti Watana, top of the hill, Yayno.*

## Tombs, Shrines, and Temples

Near the villages, or in distant high places, perhaps *pakarinas*, are found other interesting structures. They appear in diverse forms, and their function has not yet been determined. Some of these buildings seem to be sepulchers, others are storehouses or depositories for food, while still others have a manifest religious character.

All these structures can be reduced to the following types:

1. Holes, wells, and chambers, excavated in hard granite rock, provided with covers of hewn stone.
2. Holes or wells, excavated in loose earth, with the sides walled up with stone, and with covers of unhewn stone.
3. Subterranean chambers of stone constructed for the protection of a box of hewn stone provided with a cover.
4. More or less ample chambers containing niches or cells.
5. Multiple chambers intercommunicating by means of little windows or galleries, arranged on one level, or superimposed on two or more, forming small pyramids, provided with outside stairs.
6. Large terraced pyramids, with interior apartments and galleries with one or more buildings on the top, and with outside stairs.

1. In the year 1873, Antonio Raimondi had already called attention to the existence of these important structures and of many others in the Department of Ancash. Some of them greatly aroused his interest, and he described them minutely. Referring to the stone sepulchers which are found in the district of Sihuas in the province of Pomabamba, he says:

> On an elevated mesa between the Jocos estate and another called Quilca, are found some strange sepulchers of the ancient Peruvians. These sepulchers have been excavated in the very limestone rock which forms the foundation underlying a small hill. They take the form of small cylindrical wells of a meter and a half in diameter and a little less than a meter in depth. These wells are found in communication with four other cavities, arranged around the principal one in such manner as to form a cross. In each of these cavities many human bones are found. The cylindrical wells have a circular opening, covered by a stone, cut and hewn for the purpose. The other four cavities as we have said, communicate with

the central one but do not have an opening on the surface of the ground. The top of the central well is covered with earth and stone to hide the entrance.

Excavated rocks forming basins of greater or lesser depths are also found in other regions, especially in Tupe in the province of Yauyos, and in the higher parts of the Yana-Wanka estate, on the road from Cajamarca to Hualgayoc.

Some basins seem to have been utilized as mortars, others as depositories for food, and still others undoubtedly as sepulchers, because human bones have been found in them.

2. In the same area as the great subterranean chambers which are found principally in the Callejón de Huaylas, to which we will refer later, are found wells from a meter to a meter and a half in depth, and less than a meter in diameter. I had the opportunity of examining three of these wells which had recently been opened in the ruins of Kopa, situated a short distance from Carhuaz. In one of them, I found the remains of human bones almost pulverized, and examples of a very primitive ceramic art, which had been left by the explorers. These ceramic objects are found today in the museum of the University of San Marcos, and are of the well-known style of Callejón or of Recuay. The wells have stone and mud walls. Their form is approximately elliptical, and they are situated near a building of the Archaic type, which rises above the surface of the ground.

In other ruins of villages corresponding to this epoch, and even to the second epoch, I have seen wells similar to these which have given me the impression of *Pirwas*, or granaries, and not of sepulchers.

3. The construction of the third type offers special interest. I have not had an opportunity to study them, but in different parts of the Department of Ancash, I have seen stone boxes of various forms and dimensions showing diverse grades of ability in their hewing. Some are hewn from one solid block and some from two or more pieces.

In the state of La Merced (Aija) near the river of the same name, in Caraz, near Tumchu Kayko, in the hospital of Huaraz, and especially in Piscobamba, as well as in many other places, I have seen complete stone boxes, some provided with covers and others incomplete, consisting of stone frames, which seemed to be parts of a large box formed by placing these pieces one above the other. In all these places the natives still remember the discovery and the transportation of these stones from the nearby ruins. Raimondi calls them sepulchers and classifies them as truly monumental. He says, regarding one of them:

> At the west of the fortifications of Sipa (District of Pomabamba) in the highlands of the mineral estate of Pasacancha, some ridges or mounds are found whose surface, covered with a scant vegetation that would not lead one to suspect that it could hide such precious monuments. Some perpendicular stones, scattered here and there without any plan whatever, provoked the curiosity of the inhabitants of the place (in the year 1859) and having removed the earth they found at a depth of a little more than one foot, a great stone more than three and a half meters long by three meters wide and more than fifty centimeters thick with the upper surface slightly rounded. Continuing the excavation, to discover what might be below, it was found that the two edges of the stone rested upon two small walls, also constructed of stone, serving as a roof for another stone of cubic form, a meter and a half in dimension, which was completely buried, the upper surface being less than a meter below the roof stone. The cubic stone had a square cavity 120 cm in depth, and 80 cm square, and in the top, flush with the surface and resting on a supporting ledge, was fitted another stone which served as a cover. . . .
>
> In the quadrangular cavity, no human remains were found, but around the stone, at the corners were found other small stone-covered cavities containing some bones, together with finely wrought objects of gold and silver. . . . Other stone boxes of various and much simpler forms were found, among which one was in the shape of an egg divided into two parts, one of which contained the cavity in which to place the body, while the other part, resting on top, served merely as a cover. Several of these sepulchers have something of a stone wall around them and in this are two or three small canals superimposed on different levels, the purpose of which was undoubtedly that of collecting any water that filtered in, thus preventing its penetrating into the central part.

4. The fourth type of chamber is the commonest and most abundant, especially in the Callejón de Huaylas. The chambers are subterranean, and on the surface there is nothing to suggest their existence. The ground appears level, covered with crops, under which they lie. One sees piles of stones, both large and small, some of them long and prismatic, perpendicular in the manner of obelisks, and others

emerging from the surface; at other times mounds of greater or less height, and of pyramid form, appear on the surface, inside or outside the patios or plazas which are formed by lines of great perpendicular stone, similar to the enclosure of the Kalasasaya in Tiahuanaco.

These subterranean chambers consist principally of a more or less spacious rectangular habitation or hall, in whose walls are found niches of different sizes situated at various levels, with windows or small rectangular doorways which lead through galleries to the outside, or connect one chamber with another. The chambers lie on one, two, or more levels, in the last case rising from without, in the form of truncated, terraced pyramids, with stairs which lead to an upper platform, where the remains of the most important buildings are generally found.

The walls of these chambers are constructed of great blocks of stone, set vertically as foundations or columns, on which rests the stone forming the roof. As is common in this type of construction, the intervening spaces are filled in with small stones carefully piled up and arranged in such a way, with the plain surface toward the habitation, that the walls are solid and uniformly upright and smooth.

One of the best illustrations of this type of structure is that offered by the subterranean chambers of Katak, from which Don Agustín Icaza excavated the collection of ceramic objects of Recuay, which formed part of the Macedo Collection, at present found in the Museum für Völkerkunde of Berlin. In Katak, I have counted 148 of these subterranean chambers, of which No. 118 is one of the simplest and most typical (fig. 13.5). It is found near Katak Creek, which flows at the north. On the surface, the stone ground covered with vegetation presents a prominence of conical form about 2 m high, which has the appearance of a natural rise of ground (fig. 13.6). But upon raising one of the large flagstones, one enters a habitation lying from north to south, which has the form of a rectangle and measures 3.65 by 1.67 m.

The north wall is hidden by landslides. In the south walls, toward the southwest, is a small niche with a depth of 36 cm and width of 42 cm. The west wall has three compartments, or cells, each one of which has a height of 1.50 m. In the east wall is a cell 42 by 65 cm, and 45 cm deep, and also a rectangular window a meter from the ground level leading into a room. The roof is formed by three large stones, about 2 m long by 1 m wide. The floor of the chamber is of soft earth, and no remains of fire, bones, or ceramics are found there.

The object of these buildings has not yet been satisfactorily ascertained. The natives affirm that bodies and ceramics have been extracted from them. Nevertheless, I have not found in Katak or in

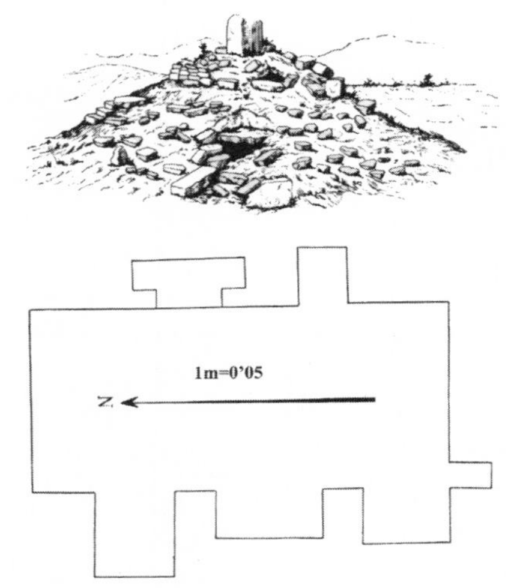


*13.5. Katak, Recuay. Subterranean Chamber No. 118.*

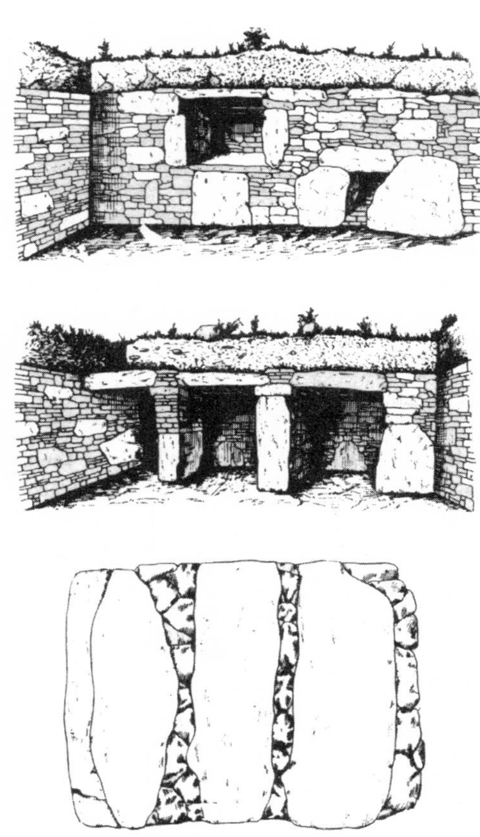

*13.6. Katak. East view, west view, and roof of Subterranean Chamber No. 118.*

the subterranean chambers of Gecosh, Castillopampa, or Wari Raxa any of these archaeological elements. Rodrigo Hernandez Príncipe, who in the second decade of the seventeenth century was in charge of the extirpation of the idolatry of the Indians in this region, refers to these subterranean chambers where he found stone idols and mummies which he extracted and destroyed. Nevertheless, one cannot base, on this report alone, the conclusion that all the subterranean chambers are sepulchers, for, apart from the fact that the human remains were scant in the few chambers in which they were found, one must take into account the custom of the Indians, preserved many years after the Conquest, of burying in the dwelling of their ancestors. Some of these chambers are so large that they give one the impression of dwellings or perhaps better, of depositories for food.

5. It is relatively easier to recognize the object or function of the buildings grouped in the fifth type, because within them, or nearby, are generally found idols, statues of human beings or animals, stelae, obelisks, and other stones carved with figures representing mythological beings. Because of their size, I consider them shrines or temples.

The shrines are small structures, some of which rise at the center of the area of the subterranean chambers, and others at the center or side of the enclosures of rectangular or circular form of the Kalasasaya type. Some, as, for instance, Illa Wain (House of Lighting), situated a short distance from the town of Aija, must have been a species of dolmen formed by great upright stones which sustained other transverse ones, to judge by their present arrangement. And in the same place, or near it, I found stone statues of warriors and women, which certainly formed part of these buildings. Near Huaraz are found two other magnificent models of this kind of shrine: Kilkay and Wilka Wain (fig. 13.7). Both are of the same style and differ only in size. The first consists of only one compartment, with niches in the walls; the second has two stories and is very interesting because of the strange distribution of the galleries inside, which lead to a large niche, near which a stone stairway rises to the second floor. It is believed that from these shrines and that of Pongor, which has nearly disappeared, come the majority of the stone statues which today adorn the cemetery and the hospital of Huaraz.

The temples are large, terraced, and truncated pyramids. The most notable are in the Callejón de Huaylas near its principal cities: Wari Raxa (fig. 13.8) to the east of Lakes Tapara and Matara at the extreme south of Callejón; Pomakayán in Huaraz; Wanasakay in Yungay; and

13.7. *Wilka Wain near Huaraz.*

13.8. *Ruins of Wari Raxa.*

Tumchu Kayko in Caras. The first has not been explored. It presents three terraces and five stairways and rises 4.5 m above the level of the ground. The second has been explored many times, and galleries made of hewn stone have been found within. From it comes the large granite plate and cup—magnificent works of art—which today are kept in the Museum of the University of San Marcos. The third (Wansakay) has been explored, and at present is used as a modern cemetery. The fourth (Tumchu Kayko) is only a pile of stones, but Raimondi reports that it was formed by great terraced walls.

6. These pyramid structures of the Archaic epoch have their highest representation in the temple of Chavín de Huantar, in the province of Huari, which is now the best-preserved example, since the temple of the Callejón de Huaylas is in ruins, due to the destruction caused by the eradicators of idolatry and by the treasure hunters, as well as to the exploitation of its building materials for use in modern constructions.

Chavín lies on the other side of the snow-covered Cordillera within a ravine where two small tributaries of the Marañon unite. It is 40 km to the east of Recuay and 28 km to the southeast of Huari, within the angle formed by the confluence of Mariash Huachecsa Creek, a mountain stream of the eastern Cordillera, with the Puccha Mosna, which comes down from the southern side. The narrow and abrupt ravine down which the Mariash flows widens to about half a kilometer before uniting with the Puccha and divides the Mariash into two sections: a level one, where the modern town of Chavín de Huantar is situated, and an undulating one to the south, where are found the ruins improperly called the Ruins of the Castle.

The land which forms the slope of the hill on the southern and southeastern sides presents the well-known aspect of the inter-Andean alluvial earth, in both the virgin lands and the cultivated fields, an aspect which is the same as that presented by the area of some 30,000 square meters occupied by the ruins. Thus, the archaeological field is found slightly broken by mounds, hillocks, and terraces covered with weeds, together with cultivated depressions or basins which do not, at first sight, suggest the existence of subterranean structures. And even the exposed section of the temple, which corresponds to one corner of one of the principal buildings, forms a platform or terraces partly stony and partly cultivated. Nevertheless, when one observes the field from the other bank of the river, the rectangular form and the symmetrical arrangement of some of the eminences and depressions attract his attention, and careful examination of these permits him to recognize the architectural plan of the temple.

This consists of two superimposed platforms. The first rises to a height of 6 m above the level of the river and is bounded on the north and the south sides by two rectangular buildings: that on the south lying from east to west, the other, from northeast to southwest. At a distance of 60 m behind this platform rises the second, about 2.5 m higher, the outline of which is not visible in every direction (fig. 13.9). On this, in its turn, rises a third, much more elevated platform, 6 m high in some places. This appears to be the principal edifice of the temple. Above it rises still another building which must have had various compartments; the walls, for the most part destroyed, are constructed of hewn stone (fig. 13.10). Also on the north side, and apparently on the outside of the platform, are two hillocks, a small one lying at the side of the principal building, to which it seems to me connected by means of a narrow terreplein; the other, which is larger, is in front of this and to the side of the rectangular edifice.

*13.9. Chavín. Ruins of the main temple.*

*13.10. Chavín. Ruins of the top floors; south side, below; north side, above.*

*13.11. Chavín. Stairway of the temple.*

On separating the brush to look for the entrance to the temple, I discovered on the facade of the principal building an admirably constructed stairway which certainly must have served to ascend to the upper edifice on the outside from the second platform (fig. 13.11). All of the temple must have risen above the plain at some distance from the hill, for a short time ago, on making a cut in the rear of this hill for the construction of a road, the southwest corner of the principal edifice was discovered, disclosing a cornice formed of carved stone with figures of jaguars and serpents, and a large human head of stone embedded in the wall.

One enters the principal edifice by means of two perforations which have perhaps been made by treasure hunters in the eastern facade. The interior (figs. 13.12–13.17) is a regular labyrinth of galleries or long passageways, which cross one another in different directions, though always at a right angle; they ascend and descend by means of stairs to other galleries, and are interrupted here and there by rectangular compartments from which, in their turn, other galleries lead in different directions. Due to the intricacy of the distribution of the galleries and to the difficulty of obtaining good light in the subterranean chambers, it has been impossible to explore the temple properly and much less to appreciate its proportions. The galleries are approximately from a meter to a meter and a half in width. It has not been possible to calculate their height, because all of them are at present filled in with earth and stones. Nevertheless, in the place where an excavation was made to discover the monolithic lansir which represents the supreme deity (fig. 13.14), to which, without doubt, this temple was dedicated, at a depth of 3 m the floor had not yet been reached. The walls of the galleries have large rectangular niches arranged horizontally and vertically like panels. The walls are traversed by a sort of almost quadrangular culvert, with an opening 60 to 70 square centimeters, the function of which is not known. Drawing near the entrance to one of these, which is reached after traversing various compartments and descending a few floors, one can clearly hear the sound of running water. The natives of Chavín believe that there are several of these streams which pass through canals constructed on different levels and that on the lowest levels the walls are found adorned with carved stone, while many, who perhaps exaggerate, affirm that the galleries continue under the river, communicating with other galleries which are supposed to lie beneath the ruins on the opposite bank.

The materials employed in the construction of Chavín, and, in general, the style of architecture, are similar to those of the Archaic structures of the Callejón. One notes in Chavín, however, a certain predilection toward the rectangular stones which have been cut for the purpose and toward the use of hewn, polished, and carved stones in the architectural adornments. The roofs are formed of large uniformly cut stones, and are arranged crossways with the walls, some placed end to end with others, like beams.

Up to the year 1919, the lithic art of Chavín was represented only by the Raimondi stone (see fig. 9.51), which was brought to Lima in 1874, and by two imperfect drawings of stone carvings made known

*13.12. Temple of Chavín. Details of the interior.*

*13.13. Temple of Chavín. Details of the interior.*

13.14. *Temple of Chavín. Details of the interior.*

13.15. *Temple of Chavín. Details of the interior.*

13.16. *Temple of Chavín. Details of the interior.*

13.17. *Temple of Chavín. Details of the interior.*

by Weiner. In that year, I found sculptures in Chavín as important as the Raimondi stone, which were used by the natives in construction and as objects for domestic use. I have made replicas of some of them and have had others brought to Lima, but the majority of those discovered still remain in Chavín. Two sculptured human heads adorn the stone bridge which is found on the Mariash; one tile, covered with mythological figures, forms part of the altar of a Catholic chapel adjoining the bridge; fragments of tiles with sculptured figures representing felines and conventionalized condors form part of the foundation of the house; other sculptured heads are used in the corrals as stakes, to which domestic animals are tied; while tiles, with various sculptured figures, have been broken in order to fit into the lintels and thresholds of the public and private buildings of the town of Chavín. One obelisk covered with figures in relief, which was found with a piece of the upper part missing, served as a decoration for the entrance of the church. Happily, this obelisk was completed, thanks to my discovery of the missing part, and it is now in the University Museum (fig. 9.16). In front of the principal edifice of Chavín, I also found a large stone; on turning it over, suspecting that it may be the cover to a subterranean entrance, I was surprised to find that it was carved with figures in relief which represented condors.

The number of discoveries of works of art of this kind is sure to increase greatly when the ruins are methodically explored. To judge by the lithic fragments already found, by the excellence of their work of art, by the complexity of their representation, and the richness of mythological religious symbols, it may be supposed that the temple of Chavín must have been adorned with stelae, obelisks, and statues both within and without, which made of it one of the most notable monuments of American aboriginal art.

7. There exists also a kind of structure to which attention has not yet been sufficiently directed. Apart from the numerous corrals which are found nearly everywhere in the *punas*, as signs of the development of stock-raising, there are other corrals, patios, or enclosed plazas of different sizes and of rectangular or circular form, situated near the shrines or at the foot of snow-covered hills which have been taken to be *pakarinas*, or sacred places. The construction of these corrals must have demanded the joint efforts of an organized people, for they are formed of great stones, planted vertically and arranged in rows in the same style as the enclosure of Kalasasaya in Tiahuanaco. These corrals were sacred places where the Indians congregated for the celebration of ceremonies destined to conserve the flocks and make them multiply. Thus affirms Hernandez Príncipe, the zealous extirpator of idolatry, who gives not only information regarding the function of these corrals but also says that other small corrals which are found were used to care for the animals specially selected for their extraordinary beauty or monstrosity, which were to serve as sacrifice animals, and were called *Wari Wilka*.

Another of the manifestations of the Archaic culture is the considerable development attained in the art of monolithic sculpture, which is intimately related to the architecture. Sculptures are found which serve as adornment for the villages; others form parts of the shrines; and still others, notable for their artistic refinement and complex idealization of shape, form parts of the temples which were dedicated to the worship of the supreme divinity symbolized by the jaguar.

In the villages, the lintels of the principal entrances and those of the arches which lead into the different wards or districts into which they are divided are ornamented with symbolic figures in low relief, which clearly reveal the fact that they have been placed there to defend the villages from human enemies and malevolent genii.

The presence of human figures, guarded over by jaguars or condors, and equipped with sacred or magic attributes such as serpents, *mak'anas*, and trophy heads or, in other cases, figures representing the heads of human beings or felines, adorned with serpentine appendages, also guarded by jaguars, could have no other significance.

Thus, one notes a close relationship between the statuary sculpture and the structures called shrines, for the lack of an appropriate name. These consist, as has already been stated, of small pyramids, subterranean chambers, enclosed patios, and other special depositories. The pyramids are adorned with stone statues, representing warriors and women; the subterranean chambers served for the preservation of the mummified bodies of the immediate ancestors; the patios were devoted to the care of llamas and other animals destined for sacrifice; and the buildings especially to the storing of food offerings and the various objects of idol worship, such as gallstones; small idols, or *konopas*; and probably also ceremonial pottery vessels.

The statues (figs. 13.18–13.22) are numerous and are found scattered in nearly every part of the sierra of the Department of Ancash. They represent the entire body of men and women. Their size varies: there are small ones of 40 cm and large ones up to 1.30 m in height; the maximum circumference varies between 1 and 1.60 m. Nearly all of them have been carved in granite. The personage is usually represented in a sitting position; only rarely, standing. The extremities are flexed; the knees at the height of the abdomen or chest, and the lower legs either straight or crossed. In the former case, the toes are pointed inward so that they nearly touch, and in exceptional instances they are in reverse position, that is, the heels are turned in and the toes out. In the latter case, the feet are placed at the sides or turned toward the back, and this circumstance permits the representation of the genitals above or below the crossing of the legs.

13.18. *Aija, Huaraz. Statues.*

13.19. *Aija, Huaraz. Statues.*

13.20. *Aija, Huaraz. Statues.*

13.21. *Aija, Huaraz. Statues.*

13.22. *Aija, Huaraz. Statues.*

The statues assume a diversity of forms prismatic, quadrangular, elliptic, egg-shaped or oblong, or even sometimes approximate a truncated cone. The narrow part corresponds to the head and includes a half or a third of the statue. The face is elliptical or egg-shaped, with the major axis vertical; the narrow part corresponds to the cranium, which at times is high and cylindrical, as if to represent its artificial deformation. The nose is high and carved, with smooth facets; the eye is represented by a ring which surrounds a central disk corresponding to the pupil; the mouth is indicated by an indentation, or carefully carved; while the ear is represented by a semilunar eminence, adorned with ear caps or hidden beneath the head cover.

The apparel differs according to the sex, there being certain uniform features characteristic of the clothing of men and others characteristic of that of the women. The best-adorned men use a cap of feline fur, with a posterior flap, or *talaria*; a collar, or tippet, which protects the throat and chest; a kind of shirt or tunic; and trunks, or *wara*. The women wear a kerchief, or *Ñañaka*, fastened to the head by means of a headband, or *wincha*. Their apparel is much better represented. It generally consists of a tunic adorned with mythological figures in rows, fastened about the waist, in certain cases, by means of an ornamented belt; a *llikla*, or small mantle on the back, equally ornamented; and a plaque in front which looks like a bag decorated with two circles and a long strip hanging from it.

Also certain personages, men or women, wear other ornamental accessories. For example, on their knitted hoods, circular or semilunar, the men display plaques or disks; the women also adorn themselves with rectangular or quadrangular plaques on the headband or the belt, and with earrings of various forms. But the most characteristic features of these representations are the almost universal use, on the part of the men, of two human heads hung from the neck, one hanging down the back and the other on the chest; the wearing of a feline fur cap showing the head and especially the claws of the animal, or adorned with small human heads; and the use of a club and a shield. The women's dress may be characterized by the *llikla* and ceremonial plaque which are displayed in front.

The unity of style in these sculptures is manifested in the almost universal employment of the same decorative motives consisting of human or feline heads provided with serpentine appendages; the employment of felines and birds represented almost realistically or conventionalized, effecting diverse forms, which if we did not know their origin, might be taken for worms, fish, or toads; and the use of a bicephalous serpentine monster derived from the jaguar, which generally adorns the shields of the men. In addition to the statues of warriors and women are also found human and feline heads of different sizes, adorning the shrine, being embedded in the walls. There are very small heads of the size of one's fist and large ones nearly a meter high. Some are crudely sculptured, and others are notable for the perfection of their carving. Nearly all of the heads are of men and women who wear a headdress similar to that of the personages represented in the full-body statues. Finally, there exists a close relationship between the sculptures representing mythological personages and the large temples.

The monolithic sculpture of the Archaic epoch has its finest representation in the art of Chavín. The fundamental features which define and distinguish it are: first, representation of an animal divinity, the origin and inexhaustible source of their artistic conceptions; second, the mastery over stone which is shown not only by its manipulation in enormous blocks and the construction of their temples but also in the perpetuation of the figures of their gods; and third, the sculpture for assuring the fidelity and beauty of their conceptions.

The sculptural art of Chavín is represented by tablets or stelae, obelisks, statues, and various smaller objects such as stone plates, cups, and vases. The figures appear engraved by means of incisions or furrows, standing out in plain relief, carved in high or low relief, or laboriously hewn out in bust form. The commonest are the tablets with figures engraved and in plain relief.

The study and classification of the different figures represented permits one to recognize certain principles which help in an understanding of Chavín art, as follows:

1. Only one archetype motive, represented by an idealized feline, serves as a basis for all the representations.

2. The feline motive becomes simplified, forming simpler ornamental motives. Thus, the feline is reduced to a head and an appendage, which takes the form of a serpent; or perchance it is reduced to the representation of one of its morphological characteristics, such as the claws, spots, jaws, or nose, these being the ones which abound most in the ornamentations, especially those of the smaller stone objects which have been found not only in the area of Chavín but in more distant places.

3. The feline motive multiplies in harmonious combinations and originates the most complex representations.

4. The process of multiplication or repetition of the motive itself follows the tendency to create and define new forms among which the condor and the fish figure principally, in which the feline seems to incarnate itself. The jaguar-divinity is an idealized form of the common jaguar. It is currently found in profile and in its form as a quadruped, but idealized by the addition of serpents which seem to emanate from its body; it bears on its back fruits or food roots, such as manioc, peppers, lima beans, or beans. At other times it is found in the ventral position, giving the impression of a great worm, of a fish, or of other monstrous forms, originated perhaps by the necessity of the artist to adapt the figure of the divinity to the not always regular or proportionate form of the stone. In other cases, it clearly takes the form of a condor with extended wings, but even in its most insignificant details it is formed with elements derived from the head of the jaguar. And finally, the divinity is anthropomorphized in a

vertical position, with human attributes, with fine apparel and bearing arms and scepters in its hands. This is the most notable form and is illustrated in the Raimondi stone (see fig. 9.51), in the short thick monolithic lance (fig. 13.14), in ceramic objects, or stamped on objects of gold.

Apart from the many representations based on the jaguar, there are other works of sculpture in bust form, consisting of feline and human heads, idealized by the use of serpents or motives derived from the jaguar, which served to adorn the temples.

It is not yet possible to determine the area of propagation of the Archaic culture represented by its two most notable manifestations: its architecture and its sculpture. A stela of the characteristic style of Chavín was found in Yauya, twenty leagues to the north of that place. Smaller stone objects with ornamentations of the same style have been found in much more distant places, as in Pomabamba, Pallasca, and in the littoral. Stone statues of the same Archaic type as those found in the Department of Ancash have been found in the ruins of Huari, situated between the provinces of Cangallo and Huanta of the Department of Ayacucho, and Luis E. Valcárcel and José Frisancho have recently described the ruins of Pukara in the province of Lampa, Department of Puno, which belong equally to the same type as the ruins classified in the Department of Ancash as Archaic.

In Pukara, there is a corral or enclosure like that of Kalasasaya, constructed with large upright stones, which served to enclose the stock destined for sacrifice, or as a place for the great heathen ceremonies which are characteristic of this epoch. There are also stone statues representing men and women, one of which, 1.57 m high, represents a man clothed after the manner of the personages represented in the statues of Aija, that is, with a headdress made of jaguar skin and a tippet, and armed with a knife and a human head. There is also a large stela of rectangular form, which is 3.7 m high, 1.26 m wide, 0.246 m thick, which in ventral position represents the same monster as that recognized in some of the broken stelae of Chavín, ornamented in front and behind with serpentine motives and jaguar heads and with vermiform body, which reminds one of the decorations of the stone of Yauya. This serpentine representation of the feline appears to better advantage in another stone discovered at the same place, 1.66 m long and 0.47 m in its greatest width, in which the monster appears in the act of dragging himself along as if to grasp a disk or ring which he has before him.

Perhaps it would not be too venturesome to affirm that the area of the Archaic Andean culture, revealed by its architecture and sculpture, extended on the south to Tiahuanaco and on the north to San Augustin in Colombia, for some of the structures and sculptures of these places present certain analogies to the monuments which have served to characterize this culture, and to define the first stage of the Andean civilization.

In ceramics we have another valuable trait of Andean Archaic art. Though not as important as the architecture and the sculpture when we consider the local modifications ceramics pass through, making difficult the recognition of its genetic relationships, the fragile character of the material which makes it less durable than stone and the facility with which it can be carried from its place of origin render it difficult to know the real area of propagation. Its importance is great, however, as a historical document because in it have been registered, and with certain fidelity, if we consider the plasticity of the material, certain aspects of the life, customs, uses, and even religious conceptions of the people of the Archaic epoch at times by means of the form and at others through the carving and painting.

In the Archaic, as in the later stages, are found different styles of pottery within the same cultural horizon. There are local variations which correspond to divisions or differentiations of the same culture and even variations depending on the purposes which determined its manufacture.

Up to the present, four ceramic types are recognized in the Archaic culture; the center for two of these seems to be found in the Callejón de Huaylas; the center for another has not yet been determined, but corresponds to the style belonging to Chavín, and its area of propagation must be very extensive in the sierra as well as on the coast, to judge by the fragments which have been found; and the last, the center of which is also unknown, although abundant remains of it were discovered a short time ago along the littoral, between Paracas, near the Valley of Pisco, and the mouth of the Ica River.

I will treat the ceramics of the Archaic culture of Paracas on some other occasion [see chapter 10, this volume].

The two types of pottery of the Callejón de Huaylas are very similar and differ only in certain characteristics. The more primitive technique, the predominance of the utilitarian forms, the lack of ornamentation, and the incipient form of the first type contrast with the more advanced technique, the better material, and the variety of form and ornamentation which the second type affords.

I had an opportunity to examine, in the ruins of Kopa, near Carhuaz, three tombs which had recently been opened by treasure hunters, in which nearly 200 pieces of pottery had been found, part of which were transported to Carhuaz and the rest abandoned in the tombs, some as too ordinary and the rest because it was broken.

The tombs were cists situated near a small stone edifice similar to those shrinelike structures which rise at the center of the area where subterranean chambers are found. They were not very deep, less than 1.50 m, and the diameter of the opening, 1 m, the sides being walled up with dry stone. I did not find any skeletal remains in them, and, rather than tombs, they gave me the impression of being depositories or granaries called *kolkas* such as are common in other ruins. Later in 1912, Thomas Dextre presented the University Museum with a collection of ceramics from the same ruins of Kopa, nearly half of which belonged to this type. Dextre assures us that he extracted them from a cist similar to those which I found, which always contain bodies.

Attention is directed, in the first place, to the reduced size of the objects of art of this pottery, to the simplicity of its forms, and to the rusticity of its technique. The material is the ordinary unrefined clay, not well baked. The clay is in its natural color, brick red or black. The walls are thick and rough; the polishing is also imperfect. All of the vessels seem to be modeled by hand, and there are some figures roughly outlined, but within the simplicity of forms are a great many which are mere imitation of fruits or vegetables, the shells of which are utilized as containers. Thus, all of the forms of this interesting pottery can be reduced to four principal types, each one of which comprises several varieties of vessels derived from a single form of fruit or vegetable. Three of these groups have been derived from three morphological types of the calabash, or *lagena*, and one from a tuberous root, the *arracacha*.

In the Indian language the three morphological types of containers coming from the *lagena* are known as *kushuna*, *puru* or *purucha*, and *puto*.

The *kushuna* is the spherical form of the *lagena*, with a tubular projection similar to a halt or handle, and in the body of the handle a square or circular opening has been made in order to use it as a vessel. The globular part is the container proper, and the tubular or horn-shaped part is the handle. Generally, a perforation is also made on a level with the hilum or insertion of the peduncle, to allow the liquid contents to flow out as from a teakettle, or *packcha* (fig. 13.23 [964, 308, and 18/30]). These vessels pass through modifications in the form of both the body and the handle, depending principally upon the

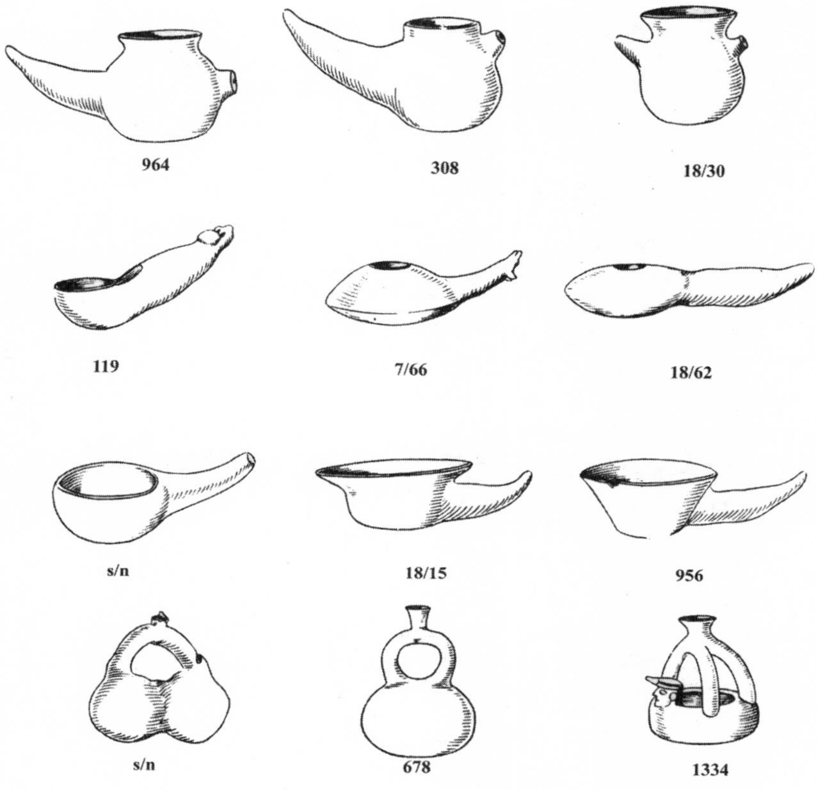


13.23. Kushuna *form of pottery.*

treatment given the mouths of the vessel. This may be a simple perforation, more or less open, or protected by lips expanded outward, thus producing different forms (fig. 13.23 [119, 18/62, 7/66, s/n, 18/15, 956]) which are utilized, some as ladles or spoons, others as plates and cups with a handle, and others as toasters for corn.

When the lengthened tubular portion of the *lagena* is very curved, it is difficult to use the vessel as a container if an opening is made in the globular or tubular portion, but this difficulty is overcome with advantage by using the tube as a handle and attaching a branch conveying the tube to the middle part of the arch. This is the way the globular decanters with arched tubular handles must have originated; a form which, like many others, is common in this pottery as in the Muchika (fig. 13.23 [s/n and 678]).

The *puru* or *purucha* is the pear-shaped fruit of the *lagena* in which an opening is made in the top of the cone or at one side of it. The cut may take in only the upper surface, or it be made lower down near the

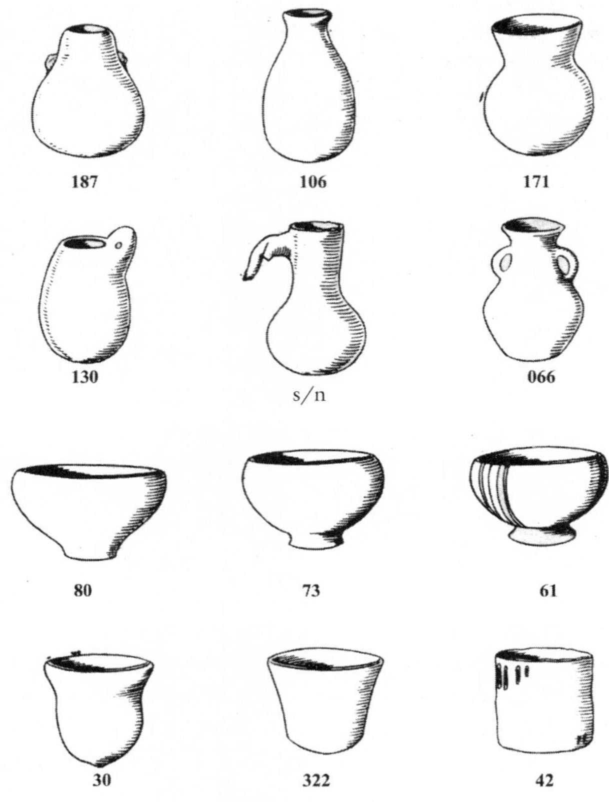


*13.24.* Puru *or* purucha *form of pottery.*

body of the fruit, leading by imitation to [pottery] vessels formed by an enlarged container and a slim and more or less elongated portion, or narrow neck. From this fundamental form come different types of decanters, all of them intimately related, derived through modifications of the body and of the neck.

Very often, this form is utilized by inverting it and using the slim narrow portion as a base or pedestal for the vessel and making an ample opening in the body of the container. It is probable that many cups with cylindrical or bell-shaped supports have this origin, for one is struck by the similarity between these vessels and those of the *lagena*, not only in their shape but also in the decorations engraved with fire which imitate the ornamentation of the *lagenas*. There is also found among the primitive forms of this pottery one which imitates the upper, reduced portion of the *lagena*, which, inverted, is used as a drinking vessel. From this prototype are derived a variety of cups and cylindrical drinking vessels (fig. 13.24).

*Puto* is the spherical or globular form of the *lagena* in which a circular opening is made at one of the poles. The cut may slice off a disk or a bowl-shaped section, or may pass straight through the fruit at the middle, cutting it into two equal pieces. The resulting parts are covers for the kettles and mates of greater or less depth. These forms are well illustrated and with considerable realism in the Archaic pottery, and the decorations of many pieces seem to imitate, as has already been said, the ornamentation of the *lagenas* (fig. 13.25).

The vessels of tripod form which appear with some frequency in this pottery seem to imitate the tuberous root of the *arracacha*. In the sierra, the butt-end of the *arracacha* is at present utilized as a container. Some specimens of this pottery imitate the *arracacha* with marked realism as is also found in the Muchika pottery.

The interest aroused by the study of the morphology of this pottery of the first group because of its derivation from certain vegetable forms is augmented when one verifies in it the efforts of an incipient form and ornamentation.

The pottery of the second type is known as Recuay pottery because the first specimens carried to the Museum für Völkerkunde in Berlin in the Macedo Collection were extracted from the subterranean chambers of Katak near Recuay by Don Agustín Icaza. In 1919, during my journeys in the Department of Ancash, I had the opportunity to acquire from private individuals nearly 600 specimens from various estates and towns of the Callejón, as well as in the provinces of Huari and Pomabamba, which are found today in the University Museum. I was not fortunate enough to find a grave intact, and I found only fragments of this kind of ceramics in some of the subterranean chambers.

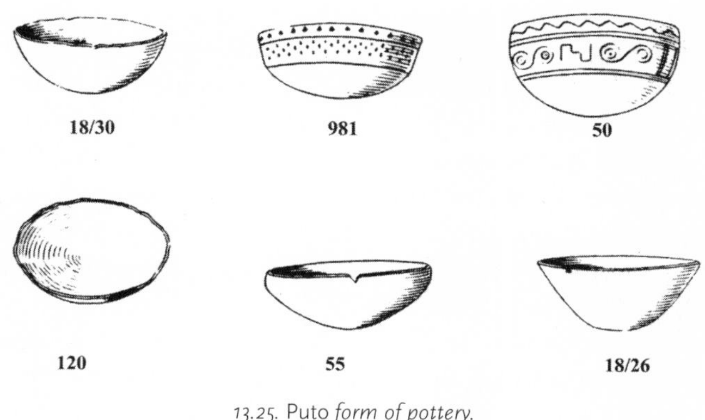


13.25. Puto *form of pottery.*

It still remains to be determined whether the pottery of primitive technique found in Kopa is more ancient than or contemporaneous with that of Recuay.

The ceramics of Recuay are varied in their general characteristics. In the majority of the specimens the clay is fine and white like kaolin. It is found also in red, gray, and black. Every piece of pottery seems made by hand; even in those of the best form one does not discover the use of a mold. The walls are strong and relatively thick. In the ornamentation, the color of the vessel itself is used as background, if the vessel is white. When it is red, gray, or black a wash of white color is applied, and the decoration is made in dark brown bands or panels which serve as background for the white figures drawn in, or the white figures painted red. The average height of the vessels is 25 to 30 cm and the maximum circumference 50 cm. There are some very small vessels, although a few, like those of the first type, and some exceptionally large which are 50 cm high.

The fundamental morphological types are identical with those described in the preceding type, derived like them from diverse forms of the *lagena*. The figuration consists of a determined number of individual and scenographic representations. Among the former we find, apart from the vegetable representations derived from the *lagena*, the zoomorphic representations among which predominate the condor, heron, owl, jaguar, and armadillo, all of which are found superimposed on the vessels as ornaments. The anthropomorphic forms are men and women who imitate the forms corresponding to those of the statues, that is, men armed with a club, shield, and trophy head, or guarded by jaguars, and women arrayed like those of the statues, in the attitude of offering drinks or food. Among the scenographic decorations there are: first, a priest with elegant apparel who leads a llama to the sound of the *antara*; second, a chief or priest surrounded by women who do him homage; third, reproductions of shrines on terraces, whose walls are decorated with symbolic figures and with sculptured human heads which seem to be embedded in them, and whose upper edifices are guarded by human figures which clearly reproduce the stone statues. The relation of these scenographic ceramic forms to the sculptural forms is made still more evident when one discovers in the ceramics, in the pictographs and forms, the same symbolic figures which adorn the lintels of the doorways of the villages.

Lastly, among the most important forms in these ceramics is found a mythological being or priest who wears rich apparel and is armed with a knife in one hand and a human head in the other.

The ornamentation is based on the almost exclusive treatment of the jaguar, the condor, and the serpent, which are arranged in panels. The jaguar rarely appears realistically; the conventionalized zoomorphic figures have probably been derived from those which decorate the textiles. The jaguar appears in the attitude of jumping or running, adorned with a long cephalous appendage and with various rings and crosses which appear to be stars. The geometric ornamental motifs consist of crossed parallel lines, rings, hooks, volutes, feline claws, and serpents' heads intertwined after the manner of their arrangement in the textiles.

The third type of Archaic ceramics is represented by the black pottery of the Chavín style. In this, as in the Archaic of the Callejón, there are two classes: one of primitive technique and incipient ornamentation and the other of an advanced technique with ornamentations similar to if not identical with those of the stones of Chavín.

In the subterranean chambers of the north Andean [area] and in Chavín, sherds of black, coarse ceramics are found, mixed with fragments of the Callejón style. I laid no importance to this fact in 1919 because I thought that such pieces represented only the propagation in the sierra of the black ceramics of Chimú, a propagation which I had been able to follow in 1916 from Paita to the basin of the Marañon. However, I had occasion later on to see some pieces of black pottery from the provinces of Cajatambo, Canta, and Huarochirí. Also at the end of 1926 I extracted from a cave near Tupe, in the province of Yauyos, where the natives still conserve, in all their purity, many of their ancient customs as also the Ak'aro or Kauke language, which seems to be the primitive Andean tongue, some fragments and complete pieces of black pottery, some of them similar in style to the Archaic of the Callejón and others to that of the Chavín type and perhaps closer still to a certain type of black pottery of Paracas. These facts show that the area of propagation of the black ceramics of the sierra is probably as extensive as on the coast and corresponds to a period earlier than that of the well-known Chimú pottery and even earlier than the black pottery of Muchik. In my journey to the Marañon I saw in a collection of antiquities formed in Morropón by a Señor Elías and composed almost in its entirety of black pottery of the Chimú style, a decanter of rare form which is found today in the Museo de Arqueología Peruana. The container is similar to a fruit or perhaps a tuberous root, the mouth is flaring and thick-lipped, the ornamentation is based on feline heads of the Chavín style made by means of incisions.

At the end of 1919, I observed that among the objects coming from the Valley of Chicama, of the well-known Muchika style, there were some specimens of black pottery with a neck similar to the decanter mentioned and with ornamentations also of Chavín style. Since then I have noted that among the collections of Muchik ceramics there were always pieces of the Chavín style and even stone objects of the same style. This led me to recognize also the Chavín style in many specimens of the Muchik type of pottery in the genesis and evolution of that pottery.

This influence of the Chavín art on that of Muchik and the presence of black pottery of a different style from that of the Muchik and Chimú made me suspect the existence of a new style of pottery which from its ornamentation could not be considered other than Chavín pottery.

The recent discovery of a Chavín tomb in Chongoyape in the Department of Lambayeque by the brothers Alexander and Antonio Galloso has confirmed my opinion. On making an excavation in the waterworks tank of Chongoyape for the purpose of enlarging it, they found, at a depth of 3 m and in ground that gave no signs of having been formerly disturbed, three reclining bodies with remains of fire on each side. The bones were very fragile and broken in pieces, but with them they found breast-pins, earrings, rings, and other pieces of gold jewelry, some with figures in répoussé of the typical style of Chavín and two specimens of black pottery of the same type. They also obtained from some boys a collection of gold objects which had been laid bare by the caving-in of an ancient irrigation ditch on the Almendral estate. The collection contained bracelets, anklets, and pendants, all of them with répoussé figures of jaguars in the Chavín style. This important discovery proved that the Chavín culture as revealed by its ceramics has an area of propagation that extends to the littoral. In my opinion the ceramics found in fragments in the shell heaps at Ancón and Supe by Uhle in 1904 and 1905, and considered by him as the most ancient remains of the Peruvian coast, belong to this type.

The Archaic ceramics of Chavín may be characterized as follows: the predominant color is jet black; the clay is fine, well baked, and polished; the common form is globular, with the tubular neck straight or curved, thick, and provided with a salient lip; the ornamentation is based on the representation of the head of the feline or the condor; and, as in the stones of Chavín, the figures are engraved in plain or high relief. The background of the ornamentation is fluted, dotted, or netted.

*Proceedings of the Twenty-third International Congress of Americanists*, pp. 259–290 (New York, 1930).

CHAPTER FOURTEEN

# The Empire of the Incas

**AT THE BEGINNING** of the sixteenth century, the Tawantin Suyo, or Empire of the Incas, was the most important nation of South America, not only because of its notable civilization but because of its vast territorial dominion. It embraced the greater part of the mountain system of the Andes, from 2° north of the Equator to 35 1/2° south, and from the Pacific Ocean to the margin of the jungle-covered Amazon basin.

The information in the documentary sources concerning the geographic area of the empire is contradictory; however, the majority of writers name the Ancasmayo River—a small tributary of the Patía—as the northern boundary, and the Maule River as the southern boundary. Both of these limits, as well as the eastern, must have been unstable because of the territorial conflicts between the Incas and the various marginal groups.

If one takes into account the mountainous character of this territory, the similarity of its physical and biological conditions, and the ethnic and cultural affinities of the peoples who inhabited it, the Tawantin Suyo may be considered a well-defined ethnographic area limited by natural frontiers. The northern boundary of the area seems to have been at the northern limits of the equatorial Andes, in Colombian territory at 2° 5', and was marked by the divide between the basin of the north-running Cauca and the basin of the south-running Almaguer. The southern limit of the area falls between 37° and 38° south latitude, more particularly between the Andes of the Cordillera Real and those of Patagonia.

The Andes, the trade winds, and the Humboldt and Niño ocean currents are the principal factors which define the physiography of this territory and determine the peculiarities of its four great natural regions—the region of the coastal plains; the cis-Andean region, or the western slopes and watershed of the Andes; the inter-Andean region, or the longitudinal valleys and high plateaus; and the trans-Andean region, or the eastern slopes and watershed of the Andes. These regions offer varieties and extremes of altitudes, climate, fauna, and flora.

The empire was a confederation of nations of different cultures and languages, some of which had attained political power and territorial control before the Incas. Four great divisions, or Suyos, controlled by the central government at Cuzco, made up the empire, which was called in the Keshua language Tawantin Suyo. Those divisions were, namely: Konti Suyo, Kolla Suyo, Chinchay Suyo, and Anti Suyo. These names correspond to the territories situated in the four cardinal directions from Cuzco. They originally were applied to the districts adjacent to Cuzco, which were inhabited by groups having the totemic names: Konti (condor), Kolla (llama), Chinchay (puma), and Anti (jaguar). Subsequently, as the empire increased in territory, these designations became generalized and finally were assigned to the four great divisions of the country. Thus, in the sixteenth century, the Inca metropolis in reality occupied the center of Tawantin Suyo.

The Konti Suyo, or the region of the *kuntur* (condor), must have been limited at one time to the area lying west of Cuzco, at the head of the Ocoña River, where, even today, the name Condesuyo, given to one of the Arequipa provinces, survives, and from where it was extended with the Inca conquest throughout the coastal region.

The Kolla Suyo, or the region of the llama, must have been limited at one time to the area lying south of Cuzco, at the head of the Majes River, inhabited by the old group, the Kollawa, and from where it subsequently was extended southward along the cis-Andean region to the plateau of Titicaca, thence along the eastern borders of the empire. The Majes River is of special importance in the ethnography of this region, since it marks the boundary between the Konti Suyo and Kolla Suyo, which originally were inhabited by two different groups. These were the Kontisuyos, who had artificially flattened heads—termed in Indian language *palta* (avocado)—and who probably spoke the Pukina language, and the Kollawas or Kollasuyos, who had elongated heads—termed in Indian language *saytu*—and who spoke the Aymara language.

The Chinchay Suyo, or region of the puma, must have been limited at one time to the area lying north of Cuzco only to the Urubamba and Apurimac area and including the neighboring regions of the coast, where one of the provinces of the Department of Ica has the name Chincha. From there it subsequently was extended to the mountains and high basins of Mantaro, Huallaga, and Marañon, which were inhabited by groups speaking the Keshua language.

The Anti Suyo, or the region of the jaguar, must have been limited at one time to the area lying east of Cuzco as far as the valley of Paucartambo, from where it subsequently was extended through the trans-Andean valleys, which the Spaniards called "hot lands of the Anti." It was noted for the cultivation of coca.

Among the more important groups whose records have been preserved through tradition, one can mention the following in the coastal region of Konti Suyo: the Esmeralda, Caranque, Huancavilca, Tumpis, Tallán, Eten, Chimú, Muchika, Chincha, Pukina, and Chango; in the cis-Andean and inter-Andean regions on the Kolla Suyo are the Pasto, Cara (Quito), Latacunga, Puruhua, Cañari, Palta, Huancapampa, Chachapoya, Cajamarca, Huamachuco, Huacrachuco, Conchuco, Pinco, Huayla, Huanuco, Anchiwaila, Yauyo, Chucurpo, Rucana, Wanka, Pokra, Sora, Chanka, Kechua, Inca, Kana, Kollana, and Kolla; and in the trans-Andean region, or Anti Suyo, are the Panatahuas, Pallanse (Amuesha), Tuki, Cholón, Jivito, Omahuaca, and Diaguita.

These groups spoke various languages, the more important of which were: Aymara, language of the highland and of the Kolla Suyo; Keshua, language of the inter-Andean region; and Muchik and Pukina (related to the Amazonian linguistic stocks—Carib and Arawak), spoken on the coast.

The Inca physical stock is that American or Indian breed which was found by the European, distributed in the southern continent. Certain regional and ethnic variants still survive almost pure. In the mountains, there exists a type of Indian, of mesocephalic head, medium height, ample chest, aquiline profile, long and curved nose, high forehead, and of small eyes and mouth, whose facial characteristics are similar to those which appear in the portraits on ancient Andean pottery. On the coast there still exists a brachycephalic type of Indian, of small stature; ample chest; broad face; slightly slanting and protruding eyes; short, wide, and aquiline nose; small mouth and thick lips; and slightly wavy hair. This type is frequently found in the indigenous population of Catacaos, Colán, Eten, Huacho, Chincha, and Moquegua, and its facial aspects are similar to those which appear in the well-known "head portraits" of the sculptural pottery of north Peru.

An actual count of the population of the Inca Empire at the time of the Spanish Conquest does not exist. Certain testimonies, however, lead to the supposition that it must have been no less than ten million. According to the census taken in 1580, during the rule of Felipe II, Peru had eight million inhabitants, in spite of the various factors resulting from the Conquest which would have tended to bring a decrease in population—for example: the introduction of new diseases and epidemics, the displacement of communities from their original locations, and the enforced work in the mines and in the unhealthful valleys east of the Andes. Furthermore, other evidence aids in estimating the population—the numerous ruins of the cities and villages of the last period which are scattered all over the territory; the evidence of an extensive cultivation of the soil; and the cemeteries, rubbish heaps, and other remains of human industry which can be attributed to the Inca nation. All these indicate a dense population. Lastly, the *kipu*, the device of the Incas for keeping the census and other statistical accounts, provides also new and valuable data in this connection. In the *kipus*, found in Inca cemeteries of the coast, are registered, by means of cords and knots, large numbers which evidently pertain to population. The grouping of the numbers, and the way the groups are totaled, indicate a classification according to sex and age. The *kipu* constitutes the best register of the population. It also provides an exhibit of the system of social and political organization of the Incas. Data from the *kipu* coincide in the main with historical records.

Very little is known concerning the character and level of civilization reached by the Incas. The history of this legendary people was first given in the accounts of the conquerors, and was interpreted by historians who used these accounts as source material. Archaeological investigation and critical research in history have subsequently brought forth a new interpretation of the past, based on historical documents and the scientific study of archaeological monuments and Indian traditions. From the sources of these studies two attitudes which correspond to two tendencies can be distinguished—one speculative and the other scientific. In the first way of thinking, two extreme opposing opinions are maintained. One extreme evaluates the events in accordance with the traditions given by those who were sympathetic to the Indian—the best representative of this extreme was Garcilaso. The other extreme gives its evaluation in accordance with the hostile opinions of the conquerors—the best representative of this was Bandelier. In the second way of thinking, the course of events is set down only in the light of archaeological investigation and in accordance with critical historical research.

Garcilaso maintains that Peruvian civilization started with the coming of the Incas, that the monuments spread over the whole territory are exponents of Inca art, and that civilization did not exist in Peru before the Incas. The empire was, according to Garcilaso, a vast political organization of nations united by means of social aggregation, so well regulated that the dynastic ruler governed it with benevolence, in spite of the great territorial dominion and the dense population. Bandelier supported the contrary view that the empire was simply a confederation of barbaric, autonomous, and independent tribes, each of which had its own chief, language, and culture, and, therefore, that a homogeneous nationality did not exist. Moreover, according to Bandelier, the power of the Incas was solely the result of the ambition of a single tribe which came out of the Urubamba Valley and which, by the beginning of the sixteenth century, had grown in military power until it had subjugated the neighboring tribes and had imposed upon them a system of forced tribute. Neither of these two interpretations of Inca history, so opposed to each other despite the fact that they are drawn from the same documentary source, has a solid foundation. They are based upon unsubstantiated tradition which is always vague and fragmentary, and which was imperfectly obtained by the conquerors because of their ignorance of native psychology. The prejudice of the conqueror against the conquered, originating in a difference of race and civilization, would further contribute to the imperfection of the traditions recorded during the Conquest.

In some cases the chroniclers and historians were Spaniards or mestizos, who were foreigners to the mind and sentiments of the Indians, whom they judged by European criteria. In other cases they were Indians, converts of Catholicism, who subordinated historical accuracy to the religious desires of the conquerors.

Historical investigation concerning the Incas, in order to be well rounded, must be prosecuted in the light of archaeological data as well as those derived from the comparative study of documentary sources. In effect, all information, written or traditional, is much more valuable when confirmed and supported by archaeological testimony. The historical material is more creditable when it was written during the actual time of the Conquest, or when those who transmitted it were eyewitnesses of the fall of the empire. Lastly, since the character and function of the various elements which became integrated in the Inca culture were not sufficiently defined, it was not possible to draw accurate comparisons with similar elements of foreign cultures. This the chroniclers attempted, but with results of consequently questionable accuracy.

It is an evident fact that in the sixteenth century there existed, on the western margin of South America, an empire made up of a group of nations subject to the government of the Incas of Cuzco. In a short time—perhaps no more than one century—a powerful nation, whose native origin is still unknown, acquired political and territorial dominion over many other groups of equal or superior culture. This took place by means of alliances and wars of conquest.

Throughout the archaeological area of Tawantin Suyo are found evidences of Inca culture, almost always superposed upon preceding aboriginal cultures. The testimonies which illustrate the conflict between the two are obvious, even to the casual observer. Wherever Inca structures are found along with structures corresponding to the earlier periods, evidences of an intentional destruction of the latter and the appropriation of their materials of construction into new buildings appear. The later buildings have the appearance of having been erected by means of large groups of workers, to judge from the magnitude of the structures. The size of the buildings seems to indicate that they were used as headquarters and depositories of provisions in the maintenance of a numerous army.

At the famous archaeological centers, Huánuco Viejo, Wilkas Waman, Huaytará, and those of the Urubamba Valley, are evidences of an invading people who violently occupied the places and destroyed the buildings—these by their magnificence and extraordinary architecture should correspond to an era of splendor in aboriginal art. In effect, pyramid temples and buildings which appear to be palaces, constructed of cut and shaped stone, exponents of an epoch of highest lithic art, are found in ruins. Built over them and using the materials of construction of the earlier ruins are buildings of more recent aspect. Many archaeological centers of the coast show a similar course of events. Here structures pertaining to the Inca complex, which have unmistakable characteristics, are superposed upon the ruins of pre-Inca buildings. The former are recognized by the use of rectangular adobe bricks, by a characteristic type of polychrome frescos which adorn the walls, and by the remains of Inca pottery which are found in the vicinity. At Tambo Huarapo, in the Nepeña Valley; at Paramonga, in the Pativilca Valley; at Pachakamac, in the Lurín Valley; at a small building to the southeast of Waka La Centinela, in the Chincha Valley; and at the ruins of Paredones, Tambo de Poroma, and other sites in the Nazca Valley, Inca architectural remains, tombs, and rubbish heaps occupy always the upper strata. The enforced implantation of this Inca culture is clearly to be noted. The pottery found at communities conquered by the Incas, and even that belonging to adjacent coeval sites, shows marks of a strong assimilation of true Inca style.

In the Chimú and Chincha regions, Inca forms appear pure, and hybrids resulting from a fusion of both styles are rare. Fine textiles of tapestry, or *kumpi*; the sling, or *waraka*; the bag, or *chuspa*; the belt, or *chumpi*; the turban, or *llauto*; the balance, or *wipe*; the *kipu*; small idols of copper, silver, and turquoise, are elements inevitably encountered in sites dominated by the Inca complex, but they are exotic in the remains of the other and earlier cultures.

All these facts show that the diffusion of the Inca culture was recent and rapid. This is in agreement with the generalized tradition concerning the origin and organization of the Tawantin Suyo, which places the expansion of the Incas beyond the Urubamba and Apurimac valleys during the time of Pachacutec, who was entitled "Reformer of the World" and who ruled near the middle of the fifteenth century.

Furthermore, if the Incas were the indigenes of Cuzco—which is the general belief—in the subsoil of this city would be found evidences of their evolutionary history. For example: in the strata at Cuzco would be the type of pottery from which the excellent Cuzco wares originated. If the megalithic structures of Cuzco were the works of the Incas, there is yet no explanation why they are broken down and are replaced by somewhat inferior buildings associated with Inca pottery. Moreover, this is in accord with the sequence at other megalithic ruins throughout the country. The facts are so evident, inasmuch as they concern the double architectural aspect, that one feels obliged to postulate that a megalithic culture—distinct and more advanced—preceded the Inca, and that the Incas, if not its destroyers, were at least the ones who appropriated its abandoned structures and materials.

The Inca culture left its typical pottery scattered over the megalithic monuments, but there is nothing that would indicate a contemporary association between megalithic and Inca cultures. The lithic objects and monuments, found today in Cuzco and other Inca centers, probably are not of Inca origin, but are survivals of the preceding advanced megalithic culture. On the contrary, Inca pottery is always present at those places where the evidence of the recent prehistoric conquests appear. The manufacture of Inca pottery was at its height at the time of the Spanish Conquest, and it lasted even into the colonial period.

It is difficult to determine the elements which can be considered true items of Inca culture. This is due in part to our own lack of knowledge concerning the center of origin of Inca culture. There, presumably, one could obtain a complete picture of the complex which would facilitate its identification elsewhere. From this might come at least a partial explanation of its rapid spread and prevalence over nations which possessed a grade of culture equal to and even superior to it, and from which it received much benefit but to which it had little to offer in return.

When the empire reached its maximum territorial extent during the rule of Huayna Capac, the subjugated or confederated nations had scarcely felt the impact of conflict with a conquering people. This impact, in certain cases, such as with nations peripherally situated, was felt only through the system of imposed tribute. On the other hand, the Inca centers in the Cuzco region were materially improved by the revenue derived from the tribute paid by the subjugated nations.

The expansion of the Incas was preferably of political and religious character. They imposed a wise system of government based upon cooperative public work, oriented by the policy of forming a homogeneous nationality from the many heterogeneous groups. They introduced the Sun cult, although without detriment to the cults of the local gods. This explains the reason for the existence of some of their most important institutions, among which are: the *Amautas*, representing a kind of university; the *Kipukamayoks*, or professional accountants of the state, who kept the statistics and records of the census, tribute, etc.; the colonization policy, which transplanted Inca-sympathetic population to newly acquired areas in exchange for an equivalent number of the new population which was transplanted to the older parts of the empire; and the great program of public works, which included the system of highways throughout the empire, large irrigation projects, etc.

When the Spaniards began their conquests, the Tawantin Suyo was found to be in an era of great prosperity. Agriculture had reached an extraordinary development. The crafts, especially those of pottery making, metallurgy, and textile works, had been, for the most part, industrialized in order to satisfy the demands of an enormous population. Great use was made of the mold in pottery manufacture, and of the stamp in ornamentation of textiles. Alloying and gilding were extensively employed in the fabrication of the ceremonial objects and jewelry. All this contributed to the economic well-being and the wealth of the empire, which so excited and dazzled the Castilians.

In going over the country, the Spaniards found everywhere cultivated lands, cities, inns filled with clothing and foods, and temples and palaces decorated with rich objects of gold and silver. Relations between the towns in the more distant regions of the country were maintained by the development of highways as routes of communication and commerce. Colonies of highland people were found established on the coast for the purpose of trade in the precious products of these lands—such as tropical shells, feathers, fine wood, etc.—which were used in making ceremonial and religious objects. At that time the rule of the Great Chimú prevailed. The Chimú state was undoubtedly the most important of the nations subjugated by the Incas. The documentary sources concerning the Atahualpa ransom mention the fact that the most valuable and artistic pieces of gold and silver work came from the Chimú province.

In the enormous mass of heterogeneous cultural elements which were left by the various provinces of the Tawantin Suyo, it is hard to determine those which pertain to the Inca proper. However, some are identifiable because of their constant presence at known Inca sites. Moreover, that they are of Inca origin, and would seem to be indices of Inca influence, is borne out equally by historical and archaeological data. In light of existing evidence, the following can be considered the characteristic elements of the Inca complex: the *tampu*, or inn, residence of the Inca sovereign, or garrison of the army; the *urpu*, or aryballos type of vessel, which constitutes the best example of Inca pottery; the *kumpi*, or fine tapestry, a celebrated piece of royal apparel; the *kero*, a cylindrical vase of wood, engraved or richly decorated with scenes of the epoch; the *wipe*, or balance scale; the *pakcha*, a ceremonial object for agricultural, religious ritual; the *wauke*, a small statue of stone or metal which represents a person's spirit or personifies his ancestors; the *ullti*, or small stone figures of the llama, having a ceremonial significance; the *kipu*, a bundle of cords used to record numbers or statistics by means of a system of knots and conventional colors based upon the decimal count; the cult of the Sun; and a typical social organization.

Complete agreement exists between the picture of Inca cities, inns, and temples furnished by the descriptions of the chroniclers and that based on archaeological remains. The material used in construction, in general, is that found at hand in each region: stone, gravel, straw, and clay. The most salient characteristic of the architecture is its magnitude and simple execution, built apparently in a hasty manner by employing many laborers disciplined in cooperative work. This stands in contrast with the construction of former epochs, which used tediously cut and shaped stones. It reveals an extraordinary expenditure of energy, and displays an artistic sense that could exist only with architects of great experience in the building crafts.

In each Inca establishment, the following principal structures are recognized: the Temple of the Sun; the great plaza surrounded by spacious rooms; granaries and depositories of foods and clothing, called *pirwa* and *colka*; cemeteries called *Agraraja* or *Ayawasi*; the great terrace of amusement, or *Kusipata*; the royal residence, or *pukamarka*; the house of the *mamakonas* called *Aklla-wasi*; and many small structures. This same type of Inca residence is found all along the great routes or royal highways, whether at Koillur, Cajamarca, Tarma Tambo (near the modern city of Tarma), or Pikillakta, which is one of the most typical of Inca cities.

Inca pottery has unmistakable typical characteristics. Its forms are limited, and apparently reproduce vessels carved from wood. The faceted and angular aspect which it displays reveals its derivation from a primitive art in wood. In Inca tombs of the coast are encountered vases of clay, of cylindrical form, ornamented with geometric figures in relief, so well made with respect to the imitation of their primitive models that, at first sight, they give the impression of the wooden vessels called *keros*, which are still manufactured in some towns in the valleys of Markapata and Kuchoa in the trans-Andean province of Paucartambo. The plates, cups, pitchers, kettles, and spoons, all of clay, and even the small sculptures of stone which represent small llamas or alpacas, are all identical with their wooden counterparts. Furthermore, their ornamentation has a hybrid character. On one hand are seen zoomorphic motifs taken from the jungle, such as the armadillo—which is one of the most conspicuous—parrots, and monkeys; and on the other hand, phytomorphic motifs taken from the Andean flora. Furthermore, some of the vessels imitate certain items of aboriginal apparel such as the bags, or *chuspas* (in which the Indians generally carry coca), and an *ishkupuru*, or lime burner, with their respective ornamentations. The decoration is in colors of vegetable origin. The fabrication of wooden vessels probably existed during the development of the Incaic pottery. It coexisted, together with pottery, during the empire. Woodwork maintained itself through the colonial period, and even down into the period of the Republic. In different places of the sierra and trans-Andean valleys, pottery and wooden vessels similar to those of the Inca are still made. Certain communities, or *ayllus*, of the Departments of Huancavelica, Ayacucho, and Cuzco, still use these wooden vases, or *keros*—some ornamented with pure Inca scenes, such as those of war between the Inca and the woodland tribes, and some ornamented with scenes corresponding to later epochs showing European influence.

Parallel with the ceramics is the development of the textile craft.

The use of cotton, wool, and other textile materials of lesser importance was very widespread from times prior to the Inca. It would be quite out of the question to attribute to the Inca not only the introduction of the textile craft but also the various technological processes employed, for all these appear in a superior quality in the antecedent cultures. Brocades, embroideries, gauze, and tapestries in all periods, and their original invention, must be traced to Archaic Andean cultures. However, in the chronicles left by the Spaniards (many of great descriptive value because of their clearness and richness of detail concerning the habits and customs of the Incas) it is found that a type of apparel more or less homogeneous in form and style was characteristic of the Inca complex. This clothing, found in tombs, is identical to that which appears in the paintings of native scenes even in post-Columbian times. The Inca peoples dressed in polychrome tunics—some simple and with very little ornamentation, others very fine and beautifully ornamented, depending upon the social position of the one who wore it. The ornamental motifs are typically Inca and of symbolical character, perhaps emblematic, since they appear in many varied items of Inca art. The Inca sovereigns and their *koyas* (wives) dressed in apparel corresponding to their rank. Those of highest rank wore a tunic of fine tapestry, or *kumpi*, decorated with symbolic motifs distributed harmoniously over the fabric; a kind of cape, or collar, of feathers; a belt, or *chumpi*; a bag, or *wallka*; sandals of llama skin; and jewels and insignia-accessories whose names have been preserved by the chroniclers of the Indies. The head of the sovereign adorned with the *llauto*, the royal bonnet, and the *maskaipacha* [royal tassel on forehead] are characteristic of Inca culture.

Among the various Inca elements, none compares with the *kipu* and the accounting system used by the Incas. At all Inca establishments, such as *tambos*, the residences of the rulers and of the agents in charge of tolls and tribute, the depositories for the surplus, the House of the Virgins, Temple of the Sun, and such purely Inca buildings, the *kipu* always appears in association with the pottery and other items of the Inca complex. In the Department of Ica, the remains of the recent Chincha culture constitute the upper archaeological stratum. In this level are always found the *kipu* and Inca pottery, which indicates that the Chincha and Inca cultures were coeval. The *kipu* is the objective manifestation of a well-defined system. It was an ingenious means of controlling, with exactitude, the number of inhabitants of a given region. It also was used in carrying statistics of production. The *kipu* is a fine example of a simple mechanism created as an aid in regulating the economics of a complex empire built up of many nations, the tribute from which must take into account many varied products. Schools must have existed where the key to the use of the *kipu* was taught. Since its use depended upon the knowledge of the distribution of the cords in groups, the use of principal and secondary cords according to thickness and length, the use of different kinds of knots, and the conventional significance of the various colors, to become a *kipu-kamayok*, or accountant, would require considerable training in the technique and system of the *kipu*. The *kipu* is encountered repeatedly all over Peru. In it can always be seen a uniform and constant system. The use of the *kipu* was imposed upon all the agents of the government and upon the *kurakas* (hereditary chieftains) of all provinces, and even upon the official at the head of the *ayllu*.

Also characteristic of the Inca complex are the *huaukes* (small statues of clay, stone, or metal), which generally represent human figures in vertical position. They have been found at Inca sites, and represent personages dressed in Inca style. These objects are very numerous. The Museum of the University of Cuzco possesses a large collection which came from the ruins of Pikillacta. The Museum of Peruvian Archaeology at Lima has several examples that came from Chulpaca, the cemetery of Chincha, and the Valley of Ica. The Field Museum of Chicago also has certain examples, in the Emilio Montes Collection, which came from Andahuaylas. The Inca character of these statuettes is obvious, not only from their derivation but from the type of clothing portrayed on them. In the apparel represented on these statuettes can be detected the different items of dress and ornamentation pertaining to the Inca style. The semicircular padded cap which protects the head shows three parts: two narrow ones which cover the ears, and a wide one which hangs over the back. This cap is either of a solid color or is adorned with wide vertical or horizontal bands. In certain cases, folds imitative of a turban can be seen. When too bulky it is protected by means of a band which goes around the head several times, and fastens under the mantle by means of a clamp. The crown of the cap has, as an ornament, a transverse crest or, better, a tassel. Lastly, it appears decorated with rectangular plates, probably metallic. Another type of headgear portrayed is the well-known *llauto*, which is coiled around the head, sometimes as if it were simply a cord and at other times as a wide band in the fashion of a turban. A thick cord gives the effect of a crown. The tunic is generally decorated with vertical bands of geometrical or checkered designs or even spots which imitate the jaguar skin. The cape is also represented with circular and rectangular decorations which might be intended to portray metallic plates. The *wauke*, then, is a typical element of Inca culture.

The *pakcha* is a utensil of ceremonial character, a receptacle of sacred drinks probably of a special quality, judging from the small capacity of the vessel. It is provided with a channel or tube for the purpose of carrying off the overflow. Some are of wood and others of terra cotta. In symbolism, an *aryballos* (typical Inca vessel mentioned above) is commonly represented as the receptacle, and a small *taklla* (Inca foot-plow) or an ear of corn is pictured as representing the overflow tube. The ceremonial character of the object is thus attested. It must have been employed in some agricultural ceremony, such as that of the *mama-pacha* (mother earth), each year, inaugurating the first agricultural activities at the plowing of the soil. In ancient times, during this ceremony, *chicha* (maize beer) was offered to *mama-pacha*; today *aguardiente* replaces *chicha*. Since the *pakchas* of wood are similar to the *keros*, and since those of pottery are associated with the *aryballos*, the *pakcha* as a culture trait would seem to pertain to the Inca complex.

With respect to the social organization and government of Tawantin Suyo, attention will first be directed to the highlands. In the sierra of Peru, the Indians and mestizos, especially those of the proletarian class, live in *estancias*, or communities established by the Spaniards, which comprise several small social groups. These groups are composed of various families, and are a survival of a very archaic unit—the *ayllu*, which was a kind of sib. The *ayllu* represented a group of individuals whose social bond was blood relationship or tradition of a common ancestry, either real or virtual. The home of the *ayllu* was a parcel of land where it had resided for generations. There were kept its sacred objects. Attached to this land were the enemies of the past, memories of common prosperity, or suffering.

The study of the cultural remains and refuse, heaps left by an *ayllu*, at the site of its occupation, yields interesting information. Take, for example, the site of the ancient *ayllu* called Nimak, now incorporated in the community of San Mateo de Hucanhor and situated in the heights of Okatara in the Rimac drainage. The place today is almost abandoned. It is a sheep ranch with very little land under cultivation, and occupies a ridge of the Cordillera with an area approximately 12 km long by 3 or 4 km wide. The area gradually rises from the level of Tambo de Viso to the snow line. It has a varied terrain with diverse climates and naturally divides itself into zones of pasturelands and cultivated lands. The agricultural products range from quinoa to potatoes and maize, according to the altitude. Upon one of the crests of this ride, where the cliff drops vertically to the edge of the river, is situated the principal settlement of the *ayllu*. Still to be seen here are the family dwellings; the tombs of the principal personages; the burial caves where the bodies of the common people were deposited; the plaza or meeting place of the *ayllu*, with its stone seats; community structures; a small fortress or acropolis at the highest point of the rocky cliff; and around it watchtowers, walls, and the ditches of fortification, etc. Toward the higher levels, almost at the foot of the Cordillera, is an abandoned reservoir from which acequias (irrigation ditches) conducted water across the ridge to supply the village and the cultivated fields. At lower levels are the grazing lands where remains of corrals are still well preserved.

The traditional names applied to the various kinds of lands—uncultivated, or grazing—in ancient times, for assignment to the families, are still reserved among the Indians. Certain *ayllus* maintain fiestas which are nothing less than reminiscences of ancient ceremonies. The common people today make use of such terms as *ayllu-waris* (autochthonous *ayllu*) and *ayllu-llakwas* (foreign *ayllu*). The term "*marka*" is applied to the country of the autochthones and "*llakta*" to the land of the foreigners. The fiestas, social activities, cleaning of the acequias and reservoirs, construction of buildings, and all activities of common interest to the *ayllu* fall under the control of the *ayllu* organization inherited from ancient times. When activities are involved that affect a whole community or a whole province, and social orders greater than the *ayllu*, then there appears a tradition of a system of regulation based upon a political hierarchy with such divisions as that of 100 households (called *pachakas*), and that of 1,000 households (called *warankas*). The functions and attributes of these which appear today are confused with the social and political organization imposed first by the viceroyalty, and then the Republic.

A fortunate circumstance permits an approximate reconstruction of the aboriginal social organization of Callejón de Huaylas, one of the most important archaeological centers of the sierra of Peru. Here are to be found abundant archaeological evidences showing the various developments and stages of its culture history. Concerning Callejón de Huaylas, there is also a quantity of important documentary historical material coming from the extirpators of idolatry in the sixteenth century. In the light of these data, of course supplemented by modern ethnologic studies, a clear concept can be obtained not only of the social and religious organization of the primitive inhabitants but also of the influence exercised over them by the Incas. It is possible to reconstruct the system and structure of Peruvian society. Upon this base, the following can be considered as sufficiently founded to be called historic fact:

1. The Europeans found the Indians adhering to kinship groups or *ayllus*, which were distributed all over the territory and which recognized a communal inheritance from remote antiquity of a definite parcel of land. There were two kinds of *ayllus*: *wari*, or autochthonous, and *llakta*, or foreign.

2. These *ayllus* were made up of a group of families, or *Churí*, bonded in the memory of a common ancestor, real or virtual.

3. The *ayllu* was regulated by a council of the elder individuals of the families. This council elected a chief called either *sinchi*, *ilakatas*, or *kamayok*, who directed the common activities of the group.

4. A group of *ayllus*, united by a traditional bond of kinship or of mutual services, constituted the *Kurí*. The chief of the *Kurí* was the *kuraka*.

5. An organized group of *Kurís* formed the *Waman*, or province; and groups of *Wamans*—small nations which had different names—formed the *Suyu*.

The *Churi*, or family, maintained a cult of the remains of its forebears. The ancestral mummies pertaining to this cult were kept in caves or special buildings situated on or near the settlement. To them, offerings were deposited, which consisted of such items as: *sañu-mama*, or the fine clay used in pottery-making; *illas*, or bezoar stones; and *konopas* (amulets or effigies) in the shape of the llama, etc. The *ayllu* had special buildings, altars, and sacred enclosures or sanctuaries, where sacrifices, etc., were performed. In the sanctuaries, *chicha* was poured as an offering to the gods. There the sacrificed llamas were skinned, grease was burned, and various other ceremonies were held. The *Kuri* and *Waman* each also had buildings corresponding to its category, and had, as well, shrines where stone images of its gods were preserved. The extirpators found these idols, objects, and items, which the archaeologist's shovel turns up today.

The question of the social and political conditions of coastal nations during the Inca domination offers greater difficulties than that of the sierra. Documentary history is almost entirely lacking, while the native villages have been displaced since the Conquest. Scarcely in a single place do direct descendants of the prehistoric inhabitants remain.

Little or nothing which has not been determined from archaeological remains is known of the governmental and social organization. However, ruins of large and small communities are scattered throughout the whole area—on the very shores of the Pacific, in the desert (at times, even beyond the limits of cultivated lands), and along the ridges reaching down to the ocean from the Cordillera.

When the ruins of these villages and cities are studied, it is noted that they all present the same plan and belong to the same structural type. This is as true of those in the desert as of those in the valleys or on the coast—whether they be constructed of handmade adobe bricks, of hand-cut stones, or simply of cane. They all follow the same system, and seem to have been built under the impulse of social need. The materials used in construction were those at hand in the locality. In general, one or two cities were situated at the widest part of the mouth of each valley, with a multitude of villages scattered over the adjacent hills and plain.

There is a marked difference in the structural plan of city and village. The latter is the residence of the rural population, and the former that of the superior class—officials, priests, and artisans.

In each village, the dwellings are grouped into barrios, or wards. Beneath the floors of the dwellings, the sepulchers usually are found. In many cases, the ground level of the villages has gradually risen with the accumulation of rubbish and of debris from abandoned dwellings. This debris of rubbish forms thick layers upon which new dwellings are built. In each village are special buildings for the residence of the chief, for the depository of foodstuffs, etc. The fact that the villages are divided into barrios suggests a complex social organization.

The physical plan of the cities comprises pyramidal structures, acropolis, forts, citadels, etc.—the whole contained within a fortification wall. Within each citadel are groups of buildings arranged always in rows. Some of these are dwellings and some workshops. Others, cell-like, are perhaps prisons, habitations for priests, artisans, or persons whose work demanded special quarters. At various cities—Chan Chan, for example—special buildings are found within certain citadels which, because of their complex structure and highly decorated walls, might have been sanctuaries, or places of sacrifice, or residences of the dignitaries of a cult. Likewise, in other citadels, smelting ovens with quantities of slag and ash are found. Along with these are the usual living-quarters, workshops, and the like, grouped in the standard manner. All of this leads one to presume that the citadels were the sites of institutions dedicated to specialized industrial or professional work.

By such system of organized craft and industry, through an efficient division of labor, the degree of progress attained in such crafts as metallurgy, textile, ceramics, etc. was made possible. Moreover, there certainly existed craftsmen's guilds, since *ayllus* were dedicated to particular crafts. In certain places, village sites are found almost buried under enormous quantities of pottery fragments. In addition to the great accumulation of pottery sherds at these sites, various items used in the ceramic craft have also been found—for example, mills for grinding the clay, pits from which clay was taken, ovens, etc. This might suggest a specialization of activity for the village. Such villages were probably the home of a potter's guild.

In origin, all this is reminiscent of times long before the Inca conquest, and reveals a very ancient organization of society upon a basis of specialization of religion, arts, and crafts. The degree of development of commerce also is indicated by finds showing that products from the intra-Andean and jungle regions were traded to the coast. Likewise, coastal products have been found in the lowest stratum at Chavín, which is in the Marañon basin. The routes of communication, so highly developed in Inca times and which divided the territory in many places in both transverse as well as longitudinal directions, must also then have had their origins long before the Inca. Nevertheless, all was the heritage of the Inca.

The traces left by the Inca are perfectly clear—from reports of eyewitnesses to the fall of the empire, from archaeological evidence, and from tradition of the living Indians. The Inca institutions left unmistakable traces in public buildings. At Inca sites it is always possible to identify the house of the chief official, the Temple of the Sun, the house of the *mamaconas*, etc. Living tradition preserves the names of the institutions as well as officials of administration. In short, the great accomplishment of the Inca was the welding of the multitude of small differentiated groups into a great confederated nation of uniform government, race, language, religion, and culture. The Empire of the Inca, Tawantin Suyo, was great, then, not only because of its ten million inhabitants, or because of its vast territorial extent—including, as it did, almost one-fourth of South America—but also because of its admirable political organization, its economic sufficiency, its unity of language and religion, and above all because of the horizon it had attained in the arts and crafts and in commerce and industry. Peru was conquered by the Spaniard not because it had a barbarian people but because it *was* a progressive and civilized nation.

From *So Live the Works of Men*, Seventieth Anniversary Volume Honoring Edgar Lee Hewitt, pp. 349–366 (Albuquerque: University of New Mexico, 1939). The manuscript of this article was prepared by Tello in Spanish. The English translation was made by Reginald G. Fisher, and approved by Tello. A Spanish version of this article appeared in Letras 3(6) (1937): 5–37. Lima. This version has been used to correct errors in the place and personal names.

# An Annotated Bibliography of Julio C. Tello

RICHARD E. DAGGETT AND RICHARD L. BURGER

**THE YEAR FOLLOWING HIS DEATH,** three bibliographies were published for Julio C. Tello. Two are directly attributable to Julio Espejo Núñez (1948a, b), while a third may be indirectly attributed to him (Lothrop 1948, 54, n.7). Though representing a single source, these three bibliographies reflect numerous inconsistencies, and they each contain errors of commission and omission. The present work strives to correct these problems. In addition, the three original bibliographies were found to have included anonymous articles, which, for the most part, were either reports based upon interviews with Tello or were reports on public presentations made by Tello. Though not commonly included in bibliographies, these sources have been retained in the present work because they represent a unique resource representing Tello's views on diverse matters. In this regard, other such articles, culled by the principal author from the Lima daily *El Comercio*, have been included as well. An attempt has been made to note the existence of republications of particular works and to note any inconsistencies that may exist between these republications and the originals. Secondary publications by Tello are fully cited following the original, while such publications by others are fully cited at the end of this work.

Finally, included at the end of this bibliography are works published subsequent to 1947. These publications, the earliest undertaken by Toribio Mejía Xesspe (1956–1979) and more recently by Ruth Shady Solís and Pedro Novoa Bellota (1999–2002) and most recently by Virgilio Freddy Cabanillas Delgadillo (2004), Harold Hernández Lefrane (2005), and Rafael Vega-Centeno Sara-Lafosse (2005), are based on the Tello Archive at the Universidad Nacional Mayor de San Marcos in Lima. The authors of this bibliography applaud the efforts extended in this most important undertaking. We would also like to take this opportunity to thank the following for their assistance in reconstructing the Tello bibliography: Víctor Falcon, Daniel H. Sandweiss, María de Carmen Sandweiss, the staff of the Biblioteca Nacional de Lima, and the staff of the Interlibrary Loan Office of the University of Massachusetts at Amherst.

1906

La craniectomía en el Perú pre-histórico: Conferencia dada anoche en la Sociedad Geográfica. *El Comercio*, May 5, p. 2. Lima. An anonymous report on a talk given by Tello.

En la Sociedad Geográfica: La conferencia de anoche. *La Prensa*, May 5, pp. 1–2. Lima. An anonymous report on a talk given by Tello.

1908–1909

La antiguedad de la sífilis en el Perú. *Revista Universitaria* year 3, vol. 2, no. 26, pp. 373–408 (December 1908); year 4, vol. 3, no. 28, pp. 154–202 (May 1909); year 4, vol. 1 (new series), pp. 385–408 (July 1909); year 4, vol. 2 (new series), pp. 438–473 (August 1909). Lima. Reprinted in 1909 by Sanmarti y Cia., Lima with minor changes. Another, quite likely, earlier version, which included an introduction by Tello, was presented on December 29, 1908, at the Scientific Congress (First Pan American) held at Santiago, Chile, from December 25, 1908, to January 5, 1909. Tello's paper was published by the Congress in Santiago in 1909 in *Trabajos de la Sección Ciencias Médicase Higiene*, ed. German Greve, Vol. 1, pp. 441–496.

1909

With Ricardo Palma, the son, as principal author. *Algunas Consideraciones sobre la Monografía "La Uta en el Perú," por el Dr. Manuel O. Tamayo, Delegado de la Sociedad Geográfica de Lima y de la Universidad de Arequipa, ante el IV Congreso Científico Latino Americano de Santiago de Chile*. Lima: Impresa San Pedro. Dated February 8, 1909.

1912

Prehistoric Trephining among the Yauyos of Peru. *Proceedings of the XVIII International Congress of Americanists*, pp. 75–83. London. This meeting was held in London from May 27 to June 1, 1912. Tello presented his paper on May 28.

1913

La ciencia antropológica en el Perú: Importante informe del Doctor Julio C. Tello, Comunicado al Ministerio de Fomento sobre una excursión al valle de Huacho bajo la dirección del Dr. Ales Hrdlicka. *La Prensa*, March 23, pp. 1–2. Lima. Tello's official report is dated March 19, 1913, and is preceded by an unsigned introduction.

*Presente y Futuro del Museo Nacional*. Lima: Sanmarti y Cia. This was the publication of Tello's official report dated July 14, 1913. It was republished by Toribio Mejía Xesspe (Tello and Mejía X. 1967:85–95) sans the original illustration.

La Universidad Mayor de San Marcos y la Universidad de Harvard. *Revista del Centro Universitaria*. Lima. Dated September 14, 1913. Unconfirmed. Reprinted by Tello in 1928 on pp. 1–11 in *Reforma Universitaria: Ensayos y discursos*, published in Lima by Sanmarti y Cia.

Algunas conexiones gramaticales de las lenguas Campa, Ipurina, Moxa, Baure, Amuesha, Goajira, del grupo o familia Arawak o Maipuro. *Revista Universitaria* 1:506–532. Lima. Republished separately in 1913 by Impresa del Centro Editorial in Lima under the title *Arawak: Fragmento de linguística indígena sudamericana*.

1914

Patología y prácticas quirúrgicas entre los antiguos peruanos. Congreso Médico Americano. November. Unconfirmed.

Las supuestas maravillas del Valle del Rimac. *La Crónica*, December 19, pp. 12–13. Lima. Letter to the editor dated December 1914.

Las antiguas riquezas del Valle de Lima (Para el Doctor Urteaga). *La Crónica*, December 30, pp. 5–7. Lima. Letter to the editor dated December 29, 1914.

1915

El curioso final de una polémica arqueológica. *La Crónica*, January 15, p. 13. Lima. Letter to the editor dated January 1915.

El uso de las cabezas humanas artificialmente momificadas. *El Comercio*, August 29. Lima. Unconfirmed.

El diagnóstico diferencial entre las aberturas craneales por trepanación y las practicadas en las cabezas trofeo. Conferencia en la "Sociedad Médica Unión Fernandina." October. Lima. Unconfirmed.

1916

Title unknown. *El Progreso*, October. Chiclayo. The only source for this publication (Gutiérrez de Q. 1922:138) reports this to be based on an interview with Tello subsequent to the Harvard expedition of 1918. In fact, this expedition took place in 1916 (Anonymous 1916).

1917

Los antiguos cementerios del Valle de Nasca. *Proceedings of the Second Pan-American Scientific Congress*, section 1, vol. 1, pp. 283–291. Washington, D.C. This conference was held in Washington, D.C., from December 27, 1915, to January 8, 1916. Tello presented his paper on January 3, 1916.

With Luis Alberto Arguedas, E. Samanez, Santiago D. Parodi, and M. E. Ascurra. Estudios de legislación procesal: Médicos forenses para el servicio judicial de la República. *La Revista del Foro*, year 4, no. 8, pp. 209–211. Lima. Dated August 4, 1917.

### 1918

El uso de las cabezas humanas artificialmente momificadas y su representación en el antiguo arte peruano. *Revista Universitaria*, year 13, vol. 1, part 2, pp. 478–533. Lima. Republished in 1918 by Lima's Casa Editora Ernesto R. Villarán.

Arqueología y primitiva religión del Perú: Resumen de la comunicación preliminar que presenta el Dr. Julio C. Tello a la Sociedad Americana de Antropología de los Estados Unidos sobre el resultado de sus investigaciones en el Perú, durante los dos últimos años. *La Prensa*, July 11. Lima. Unconfirmed.

Untitled letter to the editor. *El Tiempo*, October 5. Lima. Republished by Emilio Gutiérrez de Quintanilla (1922:106).

### 1919

Con el Dr. Julio C. Tello. *El Departamento*, March 24, p. 1. Huaraz anonymous article based on an interview with Tello.

La necesidad de reconstruír la historia de la civilización y de la cultura patria remontándose hasta su origen: Conferencia sustentada en el Teatro Rivera de Huaraz. *El Departamento*, April 1. Huaraz. Unconfirmed. Toribio Mejía Xesspe (1947), who was with Tello at the time, was the first to provide the title for this public talk, and appears to be the only source regarding the specifics of the talk.

Folk-lore indiano: Leyenda de la génesis de los Amueshas. *Revista de Psiquiatría y Disciplinas Conexas* 1(2): 51–55. Lima. Dated September 1, 1918.

### 1920

Prólogo. In *Los Incas del Perú*, by Sir Clements R. Markham, translated into Spanish by Manuel Beltroy, pp. xiii–xix. Lima: Sanmarti y Cia. Tello's contribution is dated July 1920.

### 1921

Sobre un proyecto del Museo Incaico is reported (J. Espejo 1948a:15, 1948b:63; Lothrop 1948:54) to have been written by Tello and published in Lima's *El Comercio* on p. 4 of the November 26 edition, when, in fact, it was written by Pedro F. Ulloa (1921).

La renuncia del Director del Museo Nacional de Arqueología: Un interesante reportaje al Dr. Julio C. Tello. *El Tiempo*, March 11, p. 1, Lima. An anonymous article that includes information derived from an interview with Tello.

1922

La investigación científica. Sanmarti y Cia. Lima. Tello's paper, presented at the July 30, 1922, session of the Asociación Peruano para el Progreso de la Ciéncia. Republished (and distributed in July 1924) in Archivos de la Asociación Peruano para el Progreso de la Ciencia 2:155–167. Lima: Imp. Americana. Republished by Tello in 1928 on pp. 65–79 of *Reforma Universitaria: Ensayos y discursos*, which was published in Lima by Sanmarti y Cia. Republished (Macera 1977). Republished by Toribio Mejía Xesspe (Tello 1967:37–42) in a reordered format and sans footnotes.

Estudios antropológicos en el Departamento de Ancash. *Archivos de la Asociación Peruana para el Progreso de la Ciencia* 1:131–137. Lima. Paper presented at the June 13, 1921, session.

La raza peruana y la civilización. *La Prensa*, July 28, supplement, p. 63. Lima. Unconfirmed. *Introducción a la Historia Antigua del Perú*. Lima: Editorial Euforión. Republished in 1922 by Sanmarti y Cia., Lima. An edited version was published by Toribio Mejía Xesspe (Tello 1967:197–212) sans accompanying drawings and diagrams. The original was translated into English and published in 1922 under the title "Prehistoric Peru," in *Inter-America* 5(4): 238–250. There are some differences in the pictures used to illustrate the Spanish and English editions published in 1921 and 1922, respectively. This English version was republished in Lima's *West Coast Leader* on May 10, 1922, pp. 14–16, and May 17, 1922, pp. 14–16, 20, sans all illustrations but one.

1923

Wira Kocha. *Inca* 1(1): 93–320 (January–March); *Inca* 1(2): 583–606 (April–June). Lima. The last line indicates that the work was to have been continued. This is also indicated in the republication by Sanmarti y Cia of Lima dated November 9, 1949. The work does give every appearance of being incomplete, and there is no evidence that it ever was completed.

Observaciones del editor al discurso del Profesor Seler. *Inca* 1(2): 375–382 (April–June). Lima. Published by Tello as editor.

Ortografía fonética de las lenguas indígenas: Sistema de sonidos de la Keshwa. *Inca* 1(2): 550–556 (April–June). Lima. Published by Tello as editor.

With Próspero Miranda. Wallallo: Ceremonias gentílicas realizadas en la región cisandina del Perú Central. (Distrito arqueológico de Casta). *Inca* 1(2): 475–549 (April–June). Lima. Dated June 1923.

1924

Sobre la autenticidad de unos huacos: El Doctor Julio C. Tello, conocido arqueólogo, cree en la legitimidad de las piezas. *El Comercio*, June 13, p. 2. Lima. An anonymous publication of an interview with Tello.

Inauguración del Museo Arqueológico Nacional. *El Comercio*, December 14, pp. 1–2. Lima. Anonymous publication that includes the transcript of a speech made by Tello the previous day. Republished by Toribio Mejía Xesspe (Tello and Mejía X. 1967:130–134). Reprinted with added footnotes and subtitles by Tello in 1928 as "El Museo de Arqueología Peruana: Sus fines y propósitos" on pp. 83–91 of *Reforma Universitaria: Ensayos y discursos*, which was published in Lima by Sanmarti y Cia. This latter version, sans footnotes, was republished by Toribio Mejía Xesspe (Tello 1967:105–110).

1925

Los estudios históricos en la Universidad Mayor de San Marcos: Trabajos arqueológicos en la Provincia de Cañete. Importantes descubrimientos en la Waka Malena. *El Comercio*, October 11, p. 12. Lima. Republished in 1926, sans the accompanying five photos, in *Revista Universitaria* 20(3): 589–597. Lima.

1926

Interesantes descubrimientos arqueológicos en Cerro Colorado (Paracas). *El Comercio*, February 6, p. 3. Lima. Though unsigned, this appears to be a report written by Tello.

Dr. W. M. McGovern and Pre-Inca Peru: Letter of the Director of the Museum of Peruvian Archaeology, Lima. Peru. *Cradle of the South* 2(24): 440–441 (June). London. Letter dated April 5, 1926.

En la Península de Paracas se han hallado yacimientos arqueológicos de tres culturas precolombinas diferentes. *La Prensa*, June 7–8. Lima. Dated May 29, 1926, this article was republished, sans the original drawings, under the title "Los descubrimientos del Museo de Arqueología Peruana en la Península de Paracas," in the *Proceedings of the XXII International Congress of Americanists*, vol. 1, pp. 679–690. This meeting was held in Rome, September 23–30, 1926, and the proceedings were published in 1928. Using the title employed in the Congress of Americanists, the article was republished by Ravines (1970:439–450), sans the original drawings.

1927

Primer Congreso Nacional de Medicina: La visita a los museos de Arqueología Nacional y de Historia Natural de la Universidad Mayor de San Marcos. *El*

*Comercio*, December 24, pp. 14–15. Lima. Anonymous article that includes the transcript of a speech made by Tello.

Bibliografía antropológica del Perú. *Boletín Bibliográfico* 3(3): 31–36. Lima.

1928

Review of *Coricancha: El Templo del Sol en el Cuzco y las Imágenes de su Altar Mayor*, by R. Lehmann-Nitsche, Imprenta y Casa Editora "Coni," Buenos Aires, Argentina, 1928. *Boletín Bibliográfico* 3(4): 208–209. Lima.

La reforma de la Universidad Mayor de San Marcos: De la universidad profesional a la universidad científica. *Mercurio Peruano*, year 11, vol. 17, no. 116 (February), pp. 128–138. Lima. A slightly edited version was printed by Tello in 1928 on pp. 137–152 of *Reforma Universitaria: Ensayos y discursos*, which was published in Lima by Sanmarti y Cia. Republished by Toribio Mejía Xesspe (Tello 1967:27–36).

La verdad de lo ocurrido en el Museo de Arqueología Peruana: Una carta del Director Dr. Julio C. Tello. *El Tiempo*, May 14, p. 2. Lima. Letter to the editor dated May 13, 1928.

Campo neutral: Las acusaciones de Don Víctor Larco Herrera a Don Julio C. Tello. *La Prensa*, May 18, p. 9. Lima. Letter to the editor written on May 18, 1928.

La solemne inauguración del Congreso de Americanistas: Discurso del delegado del Perú, Doctor Julio Tello, Director del Museo Nacional de Arqueología de Lima. *El Comercio*, September 18, pp. 5–6. Lima. This anonymous report contains a partial reprint of the talk Tello presented at this meeting, which was entitled "Andean Civilization: Some Problems of Peruvian Archaeology."

*Reforma Universitaria: Ensayos y discursos.* Lima: Sanmarti y Cia.

1929

Memoria de Director del Museo de Arqueología. *Revista Universitaria*, year 23, vols. 1–2, pp. 319–322. Lima. Tello's report is dated March 15, 1929.

La indumentaria de los Inkas. *Letras* 1(2): 413–419. Lima. This article was to have been continued, but there is no evidence that it ever was. Though reported to have been reprinted in *El Comercio* on January 29–31, 1936 (Lothrop 1948:55), it was not published at this time, or any other time, in this Lima daily.

En el Museo de Arqueología Peruana: Se inauguró ayer una exposición especial.

*El Comercio*, October 17, p. 2. Lima. This anonymous report includes the transcript of a speech given by Tello. This speech was reprinted by Toribio Mejía Xesspe (Tello and Mejía X. 1967:169–170).

*Antiguo Perú: Primera época*. Comisión Organizadora del Segundo Congreso Sudamericano de Turismo. Lima: Empresa Editoral Excelsior, Lima.

1930

Memoria del Director del Museo de Arqueología. *Revista Universitaria*, year 24, vol. 2, pp. 357–360. Lima.

Andean Civilization: Some Problems of Peruvian Archaeology. *Proceedings of the XXIII International Congress of Americanists*, pp. 259–290. New York. This meeting was held September 17–22, 1928. Tello presented his paper on September 17.

With Herbert U. Williams. An Ancient Syphilitic Skull from Paracas in Peru. *Annals of Medical History* 2(5): 515–529.

Las colecciones del Museo de Arqueología Peruana. *El Comercio*, September 6, p. 2. Lima. This official memorandum written by Tello is dated September 5, 1930.

Intereses generales: Una carta del Director del Museo de Arqueología Peruana. *El Comercio*, September 16, p. 15. Lima. Letter to the editor dated September 13, 1930.

1931

Las ruinas de Wari son, por su extensión, el enorme material arquitectónico, la piedra tallada, los edificios subterraneos, estatuas, etc., superiores en ciertos aspectos, a las de Tiawanaku y semejantes a las de Chavín–nos dice el Doctor Julio C. Tello a su regreso de la última expedición. *El Perú*, August 27, pp. 1–2. Lima. Republished by Ravines (1970:519–525) as "Las ruinas de Huari," substituting four new photographs for the ones originally published.

Nota editorial. *Wira-Kocha* 1(1): 1–3 (January–March). Lima. Unsigned but attributed to Tello as the editor.

Sistema fonético de las lenguas indígenas del Perú. *Wira-Kocha* 1(1): 4–8 (January–March). Lima. Unsigned but attributed to Tello as the editor.

Un modelo de escenografía plástica en el arte antiguo peruano. *Wira-Kocha* 1(1): 86–112 (January–March). Lima. An edited version, sans the original drawings, was published by Toribio Mejía Xesspe (Tello 1967:182–187) under the title "Consideraciones generales sobre la escenografía plástica en el arte del antiguo Perú."

1932

Tello is reported (J. Espejo 1948a:16, 1948b:64; Lothrop 1948:55) to have published an article entitled "Instituto de Antropologia" in vol. 1, part 2, of *Wira-Kocha*. Though this may have been the plan, this issue, for reasons unknown, was never published (T. Espejo 1948:23).

La defensa de nuestros tesoros arqueológicos. *El Comercio*, May 26, p. 3. Lima. Letter to the editor dated May 23, 1932. Unconfirmed is the report (J. Espejo 1948a:16) that it was republished in Piura's *La Industria* on June 3, 1932.

1933

Importante descubrimiento arqueológico en el Valle de Nepeña: El señor Julio C. Tello anuncia el hallazgo de un notable monumento antiguo. *El Comercio*, September 10, p. 20. Lima. This anonymous article includes an official report by Tello dated August 21, 1933. Republished, sans the original two site photographs, by Daggett (1987:133–134).

Nuevo descubrimiento arqueológico en el norte peruano viene a enriquecer el acervo de nuestra cultura: Este hallazgo va a constituír un extraordinario acontecimiento en la arqueología nacional. *La Crónica*, September 11, p. 12. Lima. This anonymous article includes an official report by Tello dated August 21, 1933.

Continúan efectuando excavaciones de índole arqueológica en Nepeña: El Doctor Julio C. Tello, declara que se trata de un sensacional y valioso hallazgo de carácter científico. *El Comercio*, September 24, p. 15. Lima. Republished by Daggett (1987:134–136).

Se descubrió la estatua del Gran Demonio de Chavín, en barro y piedra pintada, al hacerse los trabajos del templo Punkurí: totalmente cubierto de figuras en relieve esta el paramento del edificio interior. Primeras informaciones enviadas por el Dr. Tello a Lima. *La Crónica*, September 29, p. 9. Lima. Dated September 28, 1933.

Nuevas excavaciones arqueológicas serán practicadas en la próxima quincena en el Palacio de "Cerro Blanco," en Nepeña: El Dr. Tello explica a un representante de la Cadelp los recientes hallazgos. *El Comercio*, October 3, p. 13. Lima. This anonymous article includes the text of a report made by Tello. Republished by Daggett (1987:138–140).

Una civilización superior a todas las civilizaciones precolombinas cree encontrar el Doctor Tello en el Valle de Nepeña: Regresará proximamente para continuar los trabajos que ha iniciado y cuya importancia es excepcional. *La Crónica*, October 5, pp. 1 and 7. Lima. Anonymous report based, in part, on an interview with Tello.

Las ruinas del Valle de Nepeña: Lo que refieren los doctores Tello, Valcárcel y Antúnez de Mayolo. *El Comercio*, October 5, p. 7. Lima. Anonymous report based, in part, on an interview with Tello. Republished sans the photo of Tello, by Daggett (1987:140–144).

Es muy lamentada en la Provincia de Santa la paralización de los trabajos arqueológicos en el Valle de Nepeña: A su paso por Chimbote, el Dr. Julio Tello hizo importantes declaraciones. *El Comercio*, October 5, p. 11. Lima. Anonymous report based upon comments made by Tello.

Las ruinas del Valle de Nepeña. *El Comercio*, October 6, p. 4. Lima. Dated October 5, 1933. Republished, sans two site drawings, by Daggett (1987:144–148).

Las ruinas del Valle de Nepeña II: Los testimonios de la más vieja y más adelantada civilización del Perú, recientemente descubierta. *El Comercio*, October 9, p. 7. Lima. Dated October 7, 1933. Republished, sans four photographs and three drawings, by Daggett (1987:148–152).

Las ruinas del Valle de Nepeña III: De la necesidad de preservar y estudiar los tesoros arqueológicos descubiertos en el Valle de Nepeña. *El Comercio*, October 14, p. 7. Lima. Dated October 11, 1933. Republished, sans four drawings, by Daggett (1987:152–155).

Agasajo al Doctor Julio C. Tello. *El Comercio*, October 27, p. 5. Lima. This anonymous report includes the transcript of a speech given by Tello. An edited version of Tello's speech was printed by Toribio Mejía Xesspe (Tello 1967:49–56).

1934

El oro en el antiguo Perú. *El Comercio*, January 1, p. 9. Lima. Dated January 1, 1934. This article was reproduced, with minor editing, by Toribio Mejía Xesspe (Tello 1967:128–136).

Las excavaciones arqueológicas en el Departamento del Cuzco. *El Liberal*, March 4–5. Lima. Dated March 3, 1934. This article was republished in Lima's *El Comercio* on March 12 (p. 10) and on March 13 (pp. 2–3), 1934. More recently, it was reprinted, with criticisms edited out, by Toribio Mejía Xesspe (Tello 1967:187–197) under the title "La defensa del patrimonio arqueológico."

Origen, desarrollo y correlación de las antiguas culturas peruanas. *Revista de la Universidad Católica del Perú* 2(10): 151–168. Lima.

Las inter-relaciones de diversas culturas del Perú. Summary prepared by Mrs. B. W. Aitken. *Proceedings of the First International Congress of Anthropological and Ethnological Sciences*, pp. 239–240. London. This meeting was held in London July 30–August 4, 1934. Tello's paper was presented for him on August 1.

1935

La Notal Social: Conferencia. *La Crónica*, May 30, p. 4. Lima. Though cited (J. Espejo 1948a:17, 1948b:64; Lothrop 1948:55) as an article by Tello entitled "Las civilizaciones pre-Inkas, su antiguedad y sucesión cronológica," it is a brief, anonymous report regarding a talk so titled that Tello gave at the British embassy in Lima. This is reported (Mejía X. 1948:29) to have occurred on May 29, 1935.

Conferencia del Dr. Julio C. Tello en la Legación Británica. *El Universal*, June 13, p. 3. Lima. Anonymous report on a talk given the previous evening by Tello.

Interesante informe presentó el Dr. Julio C. Tello en la sesión que celebró el Patronato de Arqueología Nacional. *El Universal*, August 19, p. 3. Lima. Anonymous report on a talk given by Tello.

Sobre la desaparición de objetos arqueológicos. *El Comercio*, September 1. p. 16. Lima. Letter to the editor dated August 13, 1935.

Prólogo. In *Las Culturas Pre-hispánicas del Departamento de Lima*, by Pedro Eduardo Villar Córdova. Lima: Talleres Gráficos de la Escuela de la Guardia Civil y Policia. The brief statement by Tello is dated September 12, 1935. The book was authorized by the Municipality of Lima and published in homage to the fourth centennial of the founding of Lima, the ancient City of the Kings.

¿Barbarie o civilización? *El Comercio*, October 19. Lima. Unconfirmed.

1936

Tello is reported (J. Espejo 1948a:18, 1948b:65; Lothrop 1948:55) to have published an article in January 1936 in Gaceta Municipal of Magdalena Vieja (Lima) entitled "Monumentos arqueológicos de Magdalena Vieja y la necesidad de conservarlos." No such article could be located; however, a report dated January 24, 1936 (Trudela 1936) was so published and may be the article in question.

Prólogo. In *Del Ayllu al Cooperativismo Socialista*, by Hilderbrando Castro Pozo, pp. ix–xiii. Biblioteca de la "Revista de Economía y Finanzas," vol. 2. Lima. Tello's contribution is signed and dated June 1936.

Old Civilization in Peru Region Described Here: Archaeologist Tello of Lima Tells of Discoveries in South America. *Post-Bulletin*, September 25, p. 4. Rochester, Minn. Anonymous report on a talk given by Tello the previous evening. Translated into Spanish and republished in Lima's *El Comercio* on

October 22, 1936, on p. 4 under the title "Una conferencia del Doctor J. C. Tello en la ciudad de Rochester, Minn. EE.UU."

Conferencias: "Dioses y demonios del antiguo Perú," por el Dr. Julio C. Tello, en la Academia Nacional de Ciencias "Antonio Alzate." *El Universal*, November 8, p. 5. Mexico City. Anonymous report on a talk given by Tello. Reprinted in Lima's *La Prensa* on November 22, 1936, on p. 3 under the title "Relaciones culturales e intelectuales entre México y el Perú: Labor cultural realizada en México por Dr. Julio C. Tello."

1937

Son de imponderable valor arqueológico los hallazgos en la huaca de "Batan Grande." *El Comercio*, January 18, p. 13. Lima. Anonymous report based on comments made by Tello.

Los trabajos arqueológicos en el Departamento de Lambayeque. *El Comercio*, January 29, p. 5; January 30, p. 10; January 31, p. 2. Lima. Dated January 22, 1937.

La búsqueda de tesoros ocultos en las huacas del Departamento de Lambayeque. *El Comercio*, March 11, p. 15. Lima. Dated March 10, 1937.

El oro de Batan Grande: Algunas apuntes de la reciente conferencia del Doctor Julio Tello. *El Comercio*, April 18, section 2, pp. 3, 6. Lima. Anonymous report based on a press conference given by Tello.

Nota editorial. *Ayllu* 1(1): 1–3 (June). Lima.

El Strombus en el Arte Chavín. Editorial Antena, Lima. Dated June 15, 1937. Republished in Lima's *Turismo* in August 1938. Although reported (J. Espejo 1948a:18, 1948b:65; Lothrop 1948:55) to have been reprinted in the Lima daily *El Comercio* on April 18, 1938, this was not the case. Nor, apparently, was it printed in this daily on any other date.

La civilización de los Inkas. *Letras* 3(6): 5–37. Lima. Reported (Schwab 1938:75) to have been one of a series of lectures given by Tello at Lima's British embassy. This lecture is reported (Mejía X. 1948:29) to have taken place on May 15, 1935. Republished by Toribio Mejía Xesspe (Tello 1967:87–105). Republished in 1939 as "The Empire of the Inkas" on pp. 349–366 of *So Live the Works of Men: Seventieth Anniversary Volume Honoring Edgar Lee Hewett*, edited by Donald D. Brand and Fred E. Harvey, University of New Mexico Press, Albuquerque. The translation into English, with Tello's approval, was by Reginald D. Fisher.

Se realizó importante descubrimiento arqueológico en el Valle de Sechín: Numerosas piedras labradas han sido descubiertas allí. *El Comercio*, August 8, p. 13. Lima. Anonymous report based, in part, on an interview with Tello.

Han descubierto en Casma las ruinas milenarias de un templo: Los restos del templo incaico del Cerro Sechín. *Universal*, September 28, p. 4. Lima. Anonymous report based on information derived from Tello.

Conferencia del Doctor Julio C. Tello en Casma. *El Comercio*, September 26, p. 11. Lima. Anonymous report providing some details about talk given by Tello the evening of September 24, 1937.

Importante hallazgo arqueológico en La Huaca, Cerro Sechín, de Casma: Son desenterrados muchos monolitos de gran valor para la prehistoria nacional. *El Comercio*, September 28, p. 5. Lima. Anonymous report based on information derived from Tello.

Se comprueba la existencía de un acueducto megalítico en la Quebrada de Cumbe-Mayo. *El Comercio*, October 15, p. 13. Lima. Anonymous report based on information derived from Tello.

La expedición arqueológica de Sechín. *El Comercio*, October 25, p. 4. Lima. Tello telegram from Cajamarca dated October 20, 1937.

Objeto y propósito de la expedición arqueológica al Marañón. *El Comercio*, October 31, section 2, p. 1. Lima. Republished in 1937, changing only the accompanying photograph, in *Boletín de la Sociedad Geográfica de Lima* 55:123–131.

Expedición arqueológica. *El Comercio*, November 9, p. 2. Lima. Tello telegram from Celendín dated November 1, 1937.

Interesantes declaraciones del Dr. Tello respecto a sus últimos descubrimientos arqueológicos. *El Comercio*, November 22, p. 13. Lima. Anonymous report based on comments made by Tello.

Expedición arqueológica al Marañón. *El Comercio*, December 17, p. 4. Lima. Tello telegram from Tayabamba dated December 14, 1937.

1938

Preliminary Report. *Annual Report of the Institute of Andean Research*. Cambridge, Mass.

Los resultados de la expedición arqueológica al Marañón de 1937. *El Comercio*, January 9, section 2, pp. 3–4. Lima.

Las excavaciones que se efectúan en Pachacamac: Interesante opinión del Dr. Julio C. Tello. *El Comercio*, September 13, p. 11. Lima. Anonymous report based on an interview with Tello.

La gran muralla del norte del Perú: "Es un camino de penetración de la costa a la sierra, de carácter comercial y principalmente religioso," dice, entre otras cosas, el Doctor Julio C. Tello. *El Comercio*, October 11, p. 2. Lima. Dated October 10, 1938.

Una notable insignia de oro del antiguo Perú. *Turismo* 133 (November). Lima.

Arte antiguo peruano: Album fotográfico de las principales especies arqueológicas de cerámica existentes en los museos de Lima. Primera parte: Tecnología y morfología. *Inca* 2. Lima. Entire issue. Republished, in part and sans photos, by Toribio Mejía Xesspe (Tello 1967:111–127) and by Ravines (1978:415–432). The latter reproduces much of what was printed in the former as well as other parts of the original.

1939

El condor en el arte antiguo peruano. *Turismo* (May). Lima. Dated May 22, 1939.

El XXVII Congreso de Americanistas reunido en Ciudad de México: Breve entrevista con el Doctor Julio C. Tello, uno de los delegados del Perú. *El Comercio*, August 27, p. 2. Lima. Anonymous report containing an interview with Tello.

Algunos monumentos arqueológicos existentes entre Lima y Paramonga. *El Comercio*, September 26, p. 3. Lima.

With Toribio Mejía Xesspe. *Las Primeras Edades del Perú por Guaman Poma: Ensayo de interpretación*. Publicación del Museo de Antropología, Vol. 1, No. 1. Empresa Gráfica T. Scheuch. Lima. The authors discuss one chapter, titled above, in the 1613 book, entitled "El Primer Nueva Crónicay Buen Gobierno," by Felipe Guamán Pomade Ayalla.

With Luís E. Valcárcel and Pedro Villar Córdova. Asociación Peruana de Arqueología; Introducción. Lima. Tello is reported (J. Espejo 1948a:19, 1948b:66; Lothrop 1948:56) to have published in *Chaski* 1(1): 84–85 (January–February 1940) an article titled "El lugar que ocupa la ciencia arqueológica en el campo del conocimiento humano." No article per se exists. However, in the report of the January 2, 1940, session of the Asociación Peruana de Arqueología, which is published on the cited pages, mention is made of the fact that Tello spoke on this very matter.

1940

Prólogo. *Chaski* 1(1): 1 (January–February). Lima.

Vaso de piedra de Nasca: Primeros indicios de una cultura megalítica semejante a la de Chavín en la región central del Perú. *Chaski* 1(1): 27–48

(January–February) Lima. Republished in 1940 in Lima by Compañia de Impresiones.

El descubrimiento de esculturas monolíticas en la Waka Cerro Sechín, Valle de Casma. *La Prensa*, January 7, section 2, p. 1. Lima.

El Doctor Julio C. Tello nos habla de los descubrimientos realizados en las ruinas de Pachacámac: Como se llegó a descubrir la ciudad de piedra oculta bajo el desmonte y los templos de adobe. *El Comercio*, July 18, pp. 3–4. Lima. Anonymous publication of a Tello interview.

Los recientes descubrimientos arqueológicos en las ruinas de Pachacamac. *Turismo* (July). Lima. Anonymous report on Tello's work at Pachacamac.

Pachacamac. *El Comercio*, August 4, p. 13. Lima. Incorrectly reported (Lothrop 1948:56) to have been republished in 1940 in *Chaski* 1(2): 1–4.

Pachacamac. *Chaski* 1(2): 1–4 (September). Lima.

Novedades arqueológicas: Un ejemplar de cerámica de Cajabamba. *Chaski* 1(2): 77 (September). Lima. Republished by Silva S. et al. (1985:128).

Review of *Verruga Peruana*, by Raul Rebagliáti, Imprenta Torres Aguirre, Lima, 1940. *Chaski* 1(2): 87–88 (September). Lima.

Importantes nuevos hallazgos arqueológicos en las ruinas del Castillo de Chavín. *El Comercio*, December 14, p. 17. Lima. Anonymous report based on information derived from Tello.

De vuelta de las milenarias ruinas de Chavín, el Dr. Tello nos habla de esa fascinante cultura: Un hermoso templo sepultado bajo las ruinas. *El Universal*, December 19, p. 4. Lima. Anonymous report based on an interview with Tello.

1941

Tello is reported (J. Espejo 1948a:19, 1948b:66; Lothrop 1948:56) to have published in *El Comercio* of Lima sometime in 1941 an article titled "El valor nacionalista de la arqueología." No such article has been found.

La ciudad inkaica de Cajamarca. *Chaski* 1(3): 3–7. Lima. Republished by Silva S. et al. (1985:105–108), substituting a drawing for the photograph in the original.

El Museo de Antropología e Instituto de Investigaciones Antropológicas. *Chaski* 1(3): 72–78. Lima.

Los nuevos descubrimientos en la zona arqueológica de Chavín: Las excavaciones practicadas han dejado al descubierto los restos de un templo de piedra. Entrevista con el Doctor Julio C. Tello. *El Comercio*, January 18, p. 19. Lima. Anonymous report based on an interview with Tello.

La creación de parques históricos nacionales: Conversando con el Doctor Julio C. Tello. *El Comercio*, January 29, pp. 3, 5. Lima. Anonymous report based on an interview with Tello.

Interesante hallazgo arqueológico en una zona entre Arequipa y Tingo: En el lugar de nominado "Las Tres Cruces" se descubre una necrópolis antiquísimo. Objetos de cerámica y restos de huesos humanos. Declaraciones del Doctor Julio C. Tello. *El Comercio*, March 30, p. 3. Lima. Anonymous report based on information derived from Tello.

Donación al Director del Museo de Antropología. *El Comercio*, August 22, p. 4. Lima. Letter to the editor dated August 21, 1941.

Hacia el Perú en pos del oro de los Incas. *Boletín de la Comisión Nacional Peruana de Cooperación Intelectual*, first trimester, pp. 57–61. Lima. Republished in 1943 in Mexico as "To Peru in Quest of Inca Gold," in *América Indígena* 3(2): 115–126.

1942

Sobre la necesidad de fundar un Instituto Interamericano de Arqueología Andina. *Proceedings of the VIII Pan American Scientific Congress*, vol. 2, pp. 335–337. Washington, D.C. This meeting was held in Washington, D.C., May 10–18, 1940.

La "Civilización Wari" (Conferencia). Municipalidad de Ayacucho. *Huamanga* 8(48): 62–71 (June–July). Ayacucho. Cited by Santisteban T. (1956:55), this article remains unconfirmed.

Sobre el descubrimiento de la cultura Chavín del Perú. *Proceedings of the XXVII International Congress of Americanists*, vol. 1, pp. 231–252. Mexico City. This meeting was held in Mexico City, August 5–15, 1939. In 1943, what may have been an updated version of this paper was published in *Letras* (pp. 326–373). Footnotes were added, and there are some differences in the accompanying photos and illustrations. This *Letras* version excludes some lines from the original text and includes new text; it was republished separately in 1943 by Librería é Imprenta Gil S.A. The same year, another version was published in English in *American Antiquity* (9:135–160). This version is dated August 1942 and differs from both the original and the *Letras* versions in text and accompanying photos and illustrations. Finally, Ravines (1970:69–110) essentially republished the *Letras* version. However, the accompanying illustrations and photos were selected from those published in the original *Letras* and *American Antiquity* versions.

Origen y desarrollo de las civilizaciones prehistóricas andinas. *Proceedings of the XXVII International Congress of Americanists*, vol. 1, part 2, pp. 589–720. Lima. This meeting was held in Lima September 10–16, 1939. Tello presented his paper on September 16. Republished separately in 1942 in Lima by Librería Gil S.A. Edited versions of pp. 589–616 and 710–714 of the original were republished by Toribio Mejía Xesspe (Tello 1967:1–28).

Aporte de los Estados Unidos a la arqueología peruana. *Peruanidad* 2(6): 483–485 (April–May). Lima. Unconfirmed is the report (J. Espejo 1948a:20, 1948b:66; Lothrop 1948:56) that this article was republished in *El Callao* on December 25, 1944.

1943

Memoria del Doctor Julio C. Tello sobre los trabajos arqueológicos efectuados en las ruinas de Pachacamac durante los años de 1940 y 1941. Memoria de la Junta Departamental Pro-Desocupados de Lima 1939, 1940, and 1941. Lima. This official report, dated December 31, 1941, was republished by Aguilar et al. (1953).

1944

Tello is reported (J. Espejo 1948a:20, 1948b:66; Lothrop 1948:56) to have published in 1944 an article entitled "América puede llegar a ser un país de Indios." This article, based on an interview with Tello, was actually published by Luís Spota (1944).

La falsificación como síntoma de una cultura descendente. *La Prensa*, February 28, p. 5. Lima. Letter to the editor dated February 25, 1944.

1945

Colocación de la primera piedra del Museo Nacional de Antropología: También fueron inauguradas las salas recientemente instaladas y obras de mejoramiento local. *El Comercio*, July 27, p. 9. Lima. Anonymous report based, in part, on Tello's activities.

La primera piedra del edificio del Museo Nacional de Antropología y Arqueología. *La Crónica*, July 27. Lima. Anonymous report based, in part, on Tello's activities.

El país de los Inkas. In *Perú en Cifras: 1944–1945*, edited by Dario Dainte Marie S., pp. 592–613. Lima: Empresa Gráfica Scheuch S.A. A shortened, edited version was published by Toribio Mejía Xesspe (Tello 1967:213–235).

1946

Los tesoros arqueológicos de Ancón. *El Comercio*, March 17, p. 3. Lima.

1947

El hallazgo en el Perú de una ciudad muy antigua construidas bajo formas relativamente modernas: Declaraciones del Dr. Julio C Tello sobre el descubrimiento de una "antigua ciudad planificada" en el Valle del Virú por una expedición arqueológica de los Estados Unidos. *La Prensa*, February 16. Lima. This anonymous report contains information derived from Tello, which was originally presented in another uncited article.

## PUBLICATIONS BASED ON THE TELLO ARCHIVE

Tello, Julio C.

1956 *Arqueología del Valle de Casma. Culturas: Chavín, Santa o Huaylas Yunga y Sub-Chimú.* Publicación antropológica del archivo "Julio C. Tello" de la Universidad Nacional Mayor de San Marcos, Vol. 1. Lima. Edited by Toribio Mejía Xesspe.

1959 *Paracas: Primera parte.* Lima: Empresa Gráfica T. Scheuch S. A. Edited by Toribio Mejía Xesspe.

1960 *Chavín: Cultura Matriz de la Civilización Andina. Primera parte.* Publicación antropológica del archivo "Julio C. Tello" de la Universidad Nacional Mayor de San Marcos, Vol. 2. Lima. Edited by Toribio Mejía Xesspe.

1967 *Páginas Escogidas.* Selection and prologue by Toribio Mejía Xesspe. Lima: Universidad Nacional Mayor de San Marcos.

1999 *Arqueología del Valle de Lima.* Cuadernos de Investigación del Archivo Tello No. 1. Museo de Arqueología y Antropología, Universidad Nacional Mayor de San Marcos. Lima. Edited by Ruth Shady Solís and Pedro Novoa Bellota.

2000 *Arqueología del Valle de Asia: Huaca Malena.* Cuadernos de Investigación del Archivo Tello No. 2. Museo de Arqueología y Antropología, Universidad Nacional Mayor de San Marcos. Lima. Edited by Ruth Shady Solís and Pedro Novoa Bellota.

2002 *Arqueología de la Cuenca del Rio Grande de Nasca.* Cuadernos de Investigación del Archivo Tello No. 3. Museo de Arqueología y Antropología, Universidad Nacional Mayor de San Marcos. Lima. Edited by Ruth Shady Solís and Pedro Novoa Bellota.

2004 *Arqueología de Cajamarca: Expedición al Marañon-1937.* Julio César Tello, Obras Completas, Vol. 1. Fondo Editorial Universidad Nacional Mayor de San Marcos. Lima. Edited by Virgilio Freddy Cabanillas Delgadillo.

2005 *Paracas primera parte. Julio César Tello, Obras Completas*, Vol. 2. Fondo Editorial Universidad Nacional Mayor de San Marcos. Lima. Edited by Virgilio Freddy Cabanillas Delgadillo.

2005 *Arqueología del valle de Nepeña. Excavaciones en Cerro Blanco y Punkurí.* Cuadernos de Investigación del Archivo Tello No. 4. Museo de Arqueología, Universidad Nacional Mayor de San Marcos. Lima. Edited by Rafael Vega-Centeno Sara-Lafosse.

Tello, Julio C., and Toribio Mejía Xesspe
1967 Historia de los Museos Nacionales del Perú, 1822–1946. *Arqueológicas* 10. Lima. Entire volume.

1979 *Paracas II Parte: Cavernas y Necropolis.* Publicación antropológica del archivo "Julio C. Tello," Universidad Nacional Mayor de San Marcos y de Institute of Andean Research de Nueva York. Lima.

## OTHER SOURCES CITED

Aguilar, Rafael, Carlos Barandiarán, Pedro Dulanto, José Antonio Encinas, Eduardo Fontcuberta, Luís Enrique Galván, Romulo Jordán Cánepa, Domingo López de la Torre, Pío Max Medina, and Francisco Tamayo (Senators).
1953 *Los Monumentos Arqueológicos del Perú.* Publicación de la Comisión de Investigación del Estado de los Monumentos Arqueológicos. Lima: Imprenta "El Condor."

Anonymous
1916 Found Ancient Cities. *New York Times*, October 31.

Daggett, Richard E.
1987 Reconstructing the Evidence for Cerro Blanco and Punkuri. Appendix. *Andean Past* 1:133–163.

Espejo Núñez, Julio
1948a Bibliografía sintética del Dr. Julio C. Tello. *Boletín Bibliográfico* 18(1–2): 13–20. Lima.

1948b Bibliografía del Dr. Julio C. Tello: Índice cronológico. *Revista del Museo Nacional de Antropología y Arqueología* 2(1): 62–66. Lima.

Espejo Núñez, Teófilo
1948 3 revistas de antropología peruana: Inca, Wira-Kocha y Chaski. *Boletín Bibliográfico* 18(1–2): 21–38. Lima.

Gutiérrez de Quintanilla, Emilio
1922 El Manco Capac de la Arqueología Peruana Julio C. Tello (Señor de Huarochirí) contra Emilio Gutiérrez de Quintanilla Autor de este Folleto. Lima.

Lothrop, Samuel K.
1948 Julio C. Tello, 1880–1947. *American Antiquity* 14:50–56.

Macera, Pablo, ed.
1977 *La Investigación Científica*, by Julio C. Tello, with an introduction by Jaime Maista G. Seminario de Historia Rural Andina. Lima: Universidad Nacional Mayor de San Marcos.

Mejía Xesspe, Toribio
1947 Algunas descubrimientos arqueológicas del sabio peruano doctor Julio C. Tello en el país de los inkas. *El Comercio*, July 28, p. 14. Lima.
1948 Apuntes biográficos sobre el Dr. Julio C. Tello. *Revista del Museo Nacional de Antropología y Arqueología* 2(1): 35–49; 2(2):? Lima.

Ravines, Rogger, ed.
1970 *100 Años de Arqueología en el Perú*. Lima: Instituto de Estudios Peruanos.

1978 *Tecnología Andina*. Lima: Instituto de Estudios Peruanos e Instituto de Investigación Tecnología Industrial e de Normas Técnicas.

Schwab, Federico
1938 Bibliografía de antropología peruana 1936–37. *Boletín Bibliográfico* 8(1): 48–85. Lima.

Silva Santisteban, Fernando, Waldemar Espinoza Soriano, and Rogger Ravines, eds.
1985 *Historia de Cajamarca. 1: Arqueología*. Cajamarca: Instituto Nacional de Cultura e Cooporación de Desarrollo.

Spota, Luís
1944 América puede llegar a ser un país de indios: No habrá mexicanos, peruanos o chilenos, sino todos indígenas, augura Julio Tello. *Excelsior*, January 28. Mexico.

Trudela C., B.
1936 Documentos del Concejo. El problema urbano de las huacas y ruinas incaicas. *Gaceta Municipal*, pp. 236–237 (February). Lima.

Ulloa, Pedro F.
1921 Sobre un proyecto del Museo Incaico. *El Comercio*, November 26, p. 4. Lima.

# Index